UNDERSTANDING THE BOOK OF DANIEL FOR THIS GENERATION

COMPRENSIÓN EL LIBRO DE DANIEL PARA ESTA GENERACIÓN

UNDERSTANDING THE BOOK OF DANIEL FOR THIS GENERATION

COMPRENSIÓN EL LIBRO DE DANIEL PARA ESTA GENERACIÓN

Revealing the important Biblical concepts from the book of Daniel

Revelando los conceptos bíblicos importantes del libro de Daniel

BIBLE PROPHECY: ITS ALL ABOUT WORSHIP

PROFECÍA BÍBLICA: TODO SE TRATA DE ADORACIÓN

Earl B. Schrock

To order additional copies of this book, contact:
Xlibris
844-714-8691
www.Xlibris.com
Orders@Xlibris.com
838246

CONTENTS

Please take the time to pray
for God's guidance as you seek His truth as revealed in the
Holy Bible.

"In the third year of the reign of Jehoiakim king of Judah came Nebuchadnezzar king of Babylon unto Jerusalem, and besieged it. And the Lord gave Jehoiakim king of Judah into his hand, with part of the vessels of the house of God: which he carried into the land of Shinar to the house of his god; and he brought the vessels into the treasure house of his god." Daniel 1:1,2

Special recognition is given to the website https://
www.biblestudytools.com/ Bible Study Tools for the
access they provide to the Reina-Valera 1960 Bible.

Se otorga un reconocimiento especial al sitio web https://
www.biblestudytools.com/ Herramientas de Estudio bíblico
por el acceso que brindan a la Biblia Reina-Valera 1960

Books written by Earl B. Schrock are:

The Three Secrets of Success and Happiness
Los Tres Secretos del Éxito y Felicidad
Hodgepodge: Thoughts and Tales from Davidson County, North Carolina
The Kingdom of Heaven and the Kingdom of God
The 3 Visible Advents of Jesus
Las 3 venidas de Jesús
Understanding the book of Daniel for this Generation
Entendiendo el libro de Daniel para esta generación
COMING SOON:
Understanding the book of Revelation for this Generation
Entendiendo el libro de Apocalipsis para esta Generación

Prophecy Presentation YouTube videos by Earl Schrock:

1. Chapter by chapter discussion on the book of **Daniel**
2. **The Book of Revelation Explained** (abridged)

Contact Information
Earl B. Schrock, P.O. Box 2302, Thomasville, NC 27361
ProphecyPresentation@gmail.com

Suggested on line Bible Study site
http://studies.itiswritten.com/discover/
Earl Benjamin Schrock is a 1969 graduate
of Pioneer Valley Academy
and a 1979 Theology Major graduate of
Southern Missionary College (SAU)

Since prophecy interpretation is an art and not a science the author retains the right to change or amend any and all ideas of his interpretations as directed by the Holy Spirit of God.

Special mention and gratitude to http://referencebible.org/
for their Biblos.com Bible search and information website
in assisting me greatly with searching the Scriptures.

Reading this little book through one time will not cement the information you need to understand and to teach the material being discussed. Please take your time absorbing the content of this little book, taking notes, and return to read it as often as you can, to understand and teach the prophetic concepts revealed within as they apply to this generation.

INTRODUCTION

BIBLE PROPHECY: IT'S ALL ABOUT WORSHIP

Our heavenly Father is not surprised by the thousands of different religious organizations around the world today. In the book of Daniel God reveals an image whose feet is made of iron fragments and ceramic clay. Each of the thousands of different religious organizations are represented by a single chunk of iron imbedded in the feet's hardened clay. These organizations are unyielding as iron and refuse to be altered or improved.

Where did all the worldwide confusion come from in religion today?

We have one Book, the 66 book Holy Bible, which says one thing to one people, yet we have thousands of different belief systems. Why?

The book of Daniel helps reveal the answer to that question.

Attempting to understand and interpret Bible prophecy has been the goal of every generation since the prophecies were first written, read, and made public. Each succeeding generation interpreted Bible prophecy with the knowledge and mindset they possessed. Each generation, from the time the book of Daniel became available to the public, attempted to make each prophecy personal, applying it to themselves for the day in which they lived and experienced, believing it applied to them "living in the last days".

We all believe what we have been taught from those living in the generation before us. Many people today are satisfied with the past interpretations and understandings of Bible prophecy which they learned from others and have no interest in seeking a possible better conclusion or prophetic interpretation. But what about this generation? Should we be content abiding beneath the understanding of the people which lived generations before us? Unless a person sets aside preconceived ideas of Bible prophecy, then what they have been taught, by those who were taught by others, will continue to believe and teach the same truth and errors to future generations. We need to study the Bible for ourselves to be sure what we believe is the truth as per the Bible, as it applies to our generation. The timely day in which we live does not allow us to just accept the opinion of others.

> "**Who** shall ascend into the hill of the LORD? or **who** shall stand in his holy place? He that hath clean hands, and a pure heart; who hath not lifted up his soul unto vanity, nor sworn deceitfully. He shall receive the blessing from the LORD, and righteousness from the God of his salvation. **This is the generation** of them that seek him, that seek thy face, O Jacob. Selah." Psalm 24:3-6

Each of us are the product of our environment. We only know what we have been taught or gleaned for ourselves from others and from the influences around us. We are influenced by the leaders in our lives, like parents, teachers, pastors, and other people. We are influenced by the books we read, the television and movies we watch, the internet, the radio we listen to, as well as magazines, video games, etc. We are influenced by our friends and sometimes by our enemies, whether by direct or indirect communication or casual conversation. But to properly study and understand the Bible, we must set aside all we know and understand, to approach the Bible with an open mind. We must understand the Bible is the only source of truth we can rely on. Sola Scriptura: The Bible only. We must be able to defend the Bible by the Bible and no other extra-biblical material.

We must interpret the Bible for ourselves as we are led by the indwelling Holy Spirit which will lead us into all truth:

> "Howbeit when he, the Spirit of truth, is come, he will guide you into all truth: for he shall not speak of himself; but whatsoever he shall hear, *that* shall he speak: and he will shew you things to come." John 16:13

To be a vessel of God an open mind and receptive heart is necessary as we are molded like clay in His hands through His Word. Being hard headed promotes hard heartedness.

> "But now, O LORD, thou *art* our father; we *are* the clay, and thou our potter; and we all *are* the work of thy hand." Isaiah 64:8.

Sometimes we must challenge ourselves and our Bible understanding. We can challenge our own ideas of Bible prophecy interpretation by considering an optional view. Once an optional view of Bible prophecy interpretation has been considered then each person has the choice to continue with their original interpretation or amend their way of understanding Bible prophecy in light of the current time in which they live.

Please do not close this little book at any point because it does not flow with your own preconceived ideas. Test your concepts with this little book and with the Word of God. Let it be said of you what was said concerning the Berean's in Paul's day in Acts 17:11:

> "These were more noble than those in Thessalonica, in that they received the word with all readiness of mind, and searched the scriptures daily, whether those things were so."

All scripture in this little pamphlet is quoted from the King James Version of the Bible because the author believes it's the most accurate translation when it comes to Bible prophecy, with the least amount of human preconceived ideas mixed in. Every Bible chapter of the book of Daniel is located at the end of each chapter of this little book for your convenience. It's advised and prudent to also read Daniel from the Bible of your choice for each chapter being represented as you read through this little book.

This is not a verse by verse explanation of the book of Daniel. The idea in this writing is to glean from each chapter the main lesson or lessons needed to understand each chapter and in turn the entire book and that of the book of Revelation as well. It's impossible to rightly understand the book of Revelation without first understanding Daniel.

Bible prophecy is all about WORSHIP.

The book of Daniel is not so much about ruling kings and rising and falling empires as it is about WORSHIP. Each generation which have read and studied the books of Daniel and Revelation have been blessed in one way or another as they applied the life lessons gleaned from their study and made practical application with them. But in reality, the books of Daniel and Revelation are actually more important and more applicable to the last generation of this worlds history than to any other generation since the days of Daniel. It's with the last generation that both the books of Daniel and Revelation will have their complete and final fulfillment.

The lesson to be learned from the entire book of Daniel is to recognize how the solid-as-gold worship to and for God, in the days of Daniel, became diluted and polluted with the teachings of paganism, down through time to our day, via the empires which ruled over God's people. Just as King Nebuchadnezzar mixed the "vessels of God" with his own pagan worship in "the treasure house of his god", so has worship to the true God deteriorated from the solid worship it was in Daniel's day to what it is in the world today, not just in Christianity, but in all the current religions around the globe. The pagan influence, whether a little or a lot, takes the WORSHIP away from the true Creator God and directs it to Satan, the one who wants to be worshiped as God:

> "How art thou fallen from heaven, O Lucifer, son of the morning! *how* art thou cut down to the ground, which didst weaken the nations! For thou hast said in thine heart, I will ascend into heaven, I will exalt my throne above the stars of God: I will sit also upon the mount of the congregation, in the sides of the north: I will ascend above the heights of the clouds; I will be like the most High." Isaiah 14:12-14.

The great controversy on this planet from week one, when God created this world and all that it contains, was to answer the question of who deserves the right of mankind's worship and praise. God clearly claims the right to be worshipped as our Creator, Redeemer, and Sustainer. Yet Satan says God is unfair and if people were to worship him instead of the Creator he would make a better leader with a better life for all those which follow him (Isaiah 14:12-14). Of course history, since the fall of Adam and Eve, has proven over and over again that Satan is a liar and a murderer (John 8:44), and that our Creator God is worthy (Revelation 4:11) of all the worship we can muster.

In His Holy Bible God clearly reveals His character and the worship which He requires from the people which accept Him as Lord and Master of their lives. Satan's goal is to steal that worship from God and have it directed toward himself by infiltrating the true Bible worship of God and mixing it with false information and pagan practices. God's last day servants want to know Him and will search the scriptures daily to meet that goal and to learn the proper way of worshipping the Creator as He has revealed. Be blessed.

See the **YouTube** video **INTRODUCTION TO DANIEL** by Earl Schrock.

DANIEL CHAPTER ONE

Our lifestyle should remind us of our Creator God from the places we go, the things we do, the words we use, and the food we eat.

> "Whether therefore ye eat, or drink, or whatsoever ye do, do all to the glory of God." 1 Corinthians 10:31.

The **key text** in the book of Daniel, that offers a clue to what the entire book is about, is found in Daniel 1:2:

> "And the Lord gave Jehoiakim king of Judah into his hand, with part of the vessels of the house of God: which he carried into the land of Shinar to the house of his god; and he brought the vessels into the treasure house of his god."

Just as King Nebuchadnezzar mixed the sacred articles from Jerusalem with the profane pagan Babylonian vessels in the temple of his god, chapter one further reveals he attempted to dilute the trust and love to the Creator God of the Hebrew captives, by mixing truth with error. There are three main areas the king attacked in his attempt to distract Daniel, Hananiah, Mishael, and Azariah from being true to their Designer God.

1. He changed their names from those that pointed to the Creator God to names which stressed his pagan gods.
2. He changed their diet from that which reminded them of the Sovereign God to the diet that praised his pagan gods.
3. He promoted a pagan education which stressed his language, his concepts, and his ideas to make them worthy to serve in his government.

This was a deliberate plan of the king because in Daniel 1:3,4 the Bible reads:

> "And the king spake unto Ashpenaz the master of his eunuchs, that he should bring *certain* of the children of Israel, and of the king's seed, and of the princes; Children in whom *was* no blemish, but well favoured, and skilful in all wisdom, and cunning in knowledge, and understanding science, and such as *had* ability in them to stand in the king's palace, and whom they might teach the learning and the tongue of the Chaldeans."

NAME CHANGE

King Nebuchadnezzar took away their Godly names and gave them pagan names related to the gods he served.

> "Now among these were of the children of Judah, Daniel, Hananiah, Mishael, and Azariah: Unto whom the prince of the eunuchs gave names: for he gave unto Daniel *the name* of Belteshazzar; and to Hananiah, of Shadrach; and to Mishael, of Meshach; and to Azariah, of Abednego." Daniel 1:7

Daniel means "God is my Judge".

Belteshazzar means "Bel's treasurer".

Hananiah means "whom Jehovah favored".

Shadrach means "messenger of the sun".

Mishael means "comparable to God".

Mishach means "of the god Shach".

Azariah means "whom Jehovah helps".

Obednego means "worshiper of Nego".

DIET

Nebuchadnezzar also is guilty of attempting to change them by introducing his diet into their lives as opposed to the kosher diet established by God (Leviticus 11) who separates the clean from the unclean, even in the food they ate. Yet Daniel 1:8 says:

> "But Daniel purposed in his heart that he would not defile himself with the portion of the king's meat, nor with the wine which he drank: therefore he requested of the prince of the eunuchs that he might not defile himself."

Eating food, as directed by God, is not only a heath issue it is an obedience issue. Are we going to obey God or are we going to disobey Him? The few things mentioned in the Bible as being unclean for human consumption is far outnumbered by all the wonderful food items God says we can eat. Other than areas of famine, people, the world over, have available food to eat without eating any unclean food. It's a choice. Obey or disobey?

Food has been a worship issue since the Garden of Eden. God told Adam and Eve not to eat the fruit of "the tree of the knowledge of Good and Evil" or they would die (Genesis

2:15-17). But Satan called God a liar and told Eve (Genesis 3:4) God had misled her:

> "And the serpent said unto the woman,
> Ye shall not surely die."

Eve believed him and the Bible says in Genesis 3:6:

> "And when the woman saw that the tree *was* good for food, and that it *was* pleasant to the eyes, and a tree to be desired to make *one* wise, she took of the fruit thereof, and did eat, and gave also unto her husband with her; and he did eat."

Satan's lie is still alive and well today and many of God's family are still believing him. They are convinced that eating unclean food will not lead to death as God warned Adam and Eve. But the Bible is clear. Obey God and live, disobey God and die. It's called sin.

There was nothing inherently wrong or bad with the fruit Adam and Eve were forbidden to eat. The delicious looking fruit was not poisonous or else they would have died immediately after eating it, not nine hundred years later. But it was a test of faith, a test of obedience. The test is the same today for us as it was for them. God's will or our will?

Disobeying God, even in the things we cannot explain, directs our worship to Satan. It's sad to say that today, not only in Christianity, but the world over, God is being ignored as humans consume unclean foods of every sort. And the argument that people give, even those who know what God has demanded, is that God changed His mind.

God is omniscient, He never changes. His plans are established on a timely basis:

"For I *am* the LORD, I change not." Malachi 3:6

"Jesus Christ the same yesterday, and today, and forever." Hebrews 13:8.

Nowhere in scripture, when correctly understood, does God go back on His values or ours about what is clean and unclean when it comes to food. The reasons people disobey God are the same reasons Eve clung to when she disobeyed God: PRIDE:

"For all that *is* in the world, the lust of the flesh, and the lust of the eyes, and the pride of life, is not of the Father, but is of the world." 1 John 2:16

Some well-meaning folks misread the Bible, or accept other's groundless reasoning, in order to satisfy their particular lifestyle. Wouldn't it be better for the servants of the living God to spend their time in the Bible to correctly understand it rather than to use valuable time attempting to distort the scriptures to satisfy their own lust and pride? Remember the saying: "If God says it, I believe it, and that settles it for me."

EDUCATION

Not only did Nebuchadnezzar attempt to distract the Hebrews attention from their God with name changes, and by tempting them with unclean and forbidden foods, he also sponsored a three year Babylonian University scholarship for each one of them. Fortunately, for the devoted four Hebrew champions, a Babylonian education did not let them be drawn away from their cherished Creator. A good education, then and now, is something to be valued and cherished. With a good education you control the world around you, but with a bad education the world around you controls you. But sometimes a good public education can be a snare for God's children.

Historically, for many, the better educated a person becomes, according to the world's standards, the further from God they develop. For some people the more they know the less useful they become in the service of the King. That is why in all things we must keep our eyes focused on God, even during our education exercises. Spend time with God every single day to stay focused on Him, even with an overly busy work/ school schedule.

In all three of these areas Daniel and his three companions set an example for us:

> "But Daniel purposed in his heart that he would not defile himself with the portion of the king's meat, nor with the wine which he drank: therefore he requested of the prince of the eunuchs that he might not defile himself." Daniel 1:8

We must live a determined life to daily turn ourselves over to God in surrendering our will, in order to live the lifestyle in our conversation, our diet, our education choices, and all other parts of our existence to live totally for God. This must be a daily decision from the time we wake up to the time we go to sleep because the devil will do all he can to distract us from serving God. Notice what it says in 1 Peter 5:5-11:

> "Yea, all *of you* be subject one to another, and be clothed with humility: for God resisteth the proud, and giveth grace to the humble. Humble yourselves therefore under the mighty hand of

> God, that he may exalt you in due time: Casting all your care upon him; for he careth for you. Be sober, be vigilant; because your adversary the devil, as a roaring lion, walketh about, seeking whom he may devour: Whom resist stedfast in the faith, knowing that the same afflictions are accomplished in your brethren that are in the world. But the God of all grace, who hath called us unto his eternal glory by Christ Jesus, after that ye have suffered a while, make you perfect, stablish, strengthen, settle *you*. To him *be* glory and dominion for ever and ever. Amen"

The changes King Nebuchadnezzar brought into the lives of Daniel and his three companions are warnings to all of God's children to be on the alert for those things in our lives which can separate us from God. But that is not all we find in Daniel chapter one.

Understanding the Book of Daniel opens the door for us to understand the Book of Revelation. There is a connection between these two books we need to be aware of.

Notice the Revelation connection in Daniel 1:12-16 as you watch for how many times the words "ten days" are used in the following text:

> "Prove thy servants, I beseech thee, **ten days**; and let them give us pulse to eat, and water to drink. Then let our countenances be looked upon before thee, and the countenance of the children that eat of the portion of the king's meat: and as thou seest, deal with thy servants. So he consented to them in this matter, and proved them **ten days**. And at the end of **ten days** their

7

countenances appeared fairer and fatter in flesh than all the children which did eat the portion of the king's meat. Thus Melzar took away the portion of their meat, and the wine that they should drink; and gave them pulse."

When God repeats himself in the Bible it's time for us to perk up and pay special attention because normally He's trying to tell us something important. Joseph, in the book of Genesis, brings this to our attention when speaking to Pharaoh, King of Egypt, concerning his two dreams (Genesis 41:1-7). Joseph said to Pharaoh:

"And for that the dream was doubled unto Pharaoh twice; *it is* because the thing *is* established by God, and God will shortly bring it to pass." Genesis 41:32

Remember, if you're not familiar with the book of Daniel, you'll not be able to adequately understand the book of Revelation. As a matter of fact, the book of Revelation supports what I'm saying by dropping clues throughout itself which encourages us to look at, be familiar with, and know the book of Daniel.

Three times we are told in Daniel 1:12-16 that the children of Israel, the prisoners of King Nebuchadnezzar, were given a test that lasted "**ten days**". Why is that important?

It's important because we must each come to the point in our Christian experience, in our search for truth, in our desire to understand and know the Bible, that we MUST LET THE BIBLE INTERPRET ITSELF. Any time we go to the history books or the newspaper or the latest social media, or some other outside literary influence, to discover Bible truth, we will eventually be disappointed. The Bible and the Bible only can interpret itself. Notice the following:

> "We have also a more sure word of prophecy; whereunto ye do well that ye take heed, as unto a light that shineth in a dark place, until the day dawn, and the day star arise in your hearts: Knowing this first, that no prophecy of the scripture is of any private interpretation. For the prophecy came not in old time by the will of man: but holy men of God spake *as they were* moved by the Holy Ghost." 2 Peter 1:19-21

So what is so important about God repeating Himself three times in Daniel 1:12-16? Notice Revelation 2:10:

> "Do not fear what you are about to suffer. Behold, the devil is about to cast *some* of you into prison, so that you might be tested; and you shall have tribulation **ten days**. Be faithful unto death, and I will give to you the crown of life."

This **"in prison ten days"** statement in Revelation 2:10 is a direct reference to the book of Daniel. WHY? For a number of reasons: (1) To correctly understand the book Revelation you must know and understand the book of Daniel. (2) Matthew 24 and Revelation 13 lets us know that there's a time coming when God's people will be persecuted, even put in prison, as Daniel was, and some killed. To stand firm for God in times of extreme difficulty, we must stand firm for Him today in easier times. We must be like Daniel, who "purposed in his heart" that he would be true to God, for whatever He requires, no matter what. (3) Today God still has a particular diet for His children as a test of faith similar to that in the Garden of Eden and in Babylon.

We must be obedient to God today, even in our food choices, if we're going to be faithful to Him in difficult times.

Read the Holy Spirit's message to the church of Smyrna in Revelation 2:8-11. A last day group or assembly of God's servants need this message. Is that a message for you to pay closer attention to obeying the Word of God concerning eating meat and clean foods?

The clean and unclean diet of Leviticus eleven has not changed, neither has God (Malachi 3:6, Hebrews 13:8). God still requires us to obey Him concerning what we eat. It's not the fact that unclean food is harmful to us, it's just a simple test of faith. Obey or not obey? That is the question. Try it! Test it! Go "a full three weeks" (Daniel 10:2,3), 21 days, without eating any unclean food and see what happens. Daniel proved to be **ten times** (Daniel 1:20) better off than those who disobeyed, you can be that way also, especially with a clear conscience from obedience to the clear Word of God.

The book of Daniel, like all Bible prophecy, is all about WORSHIP. Daniel reveals the debilitation of pure religion by the introduction of pagan influences from his day to our day. Daniel chapter one reveals the ways in which the Babylonian Empire, under King Nebuchadnezzar, took steps to enter the minds and corrupt the bodies of God's people.

This chapter also reveals the determined mindset God's people must have to be able to ward off the influences that we face daily which are designed to pull us away from our Creator God. The fulfillment of the book of Daniel will be accomplished "in the appointed time of the end" (Daniel 8:19) as all twelve chapters continually remind us. That is the reason the final generation will actually be the only generation which will fully understand the book of Daniel and see its prophecies revealed in person for themselves.

Outline of Daniel chapter one:

Verses 1,2: King Nebuchadnezzar began the weakening and diluting of God's true worship by mixing truth with error when he placed the "items of God" from His holy temple with the pagan items in the temple of his pagan gods.

Verses 3-18: Daniel and his three companions are determined to be true to the Most High God in every way possible in their very thoughts, words, and actions.

See the **YouTube** video **DANIEL CHAPTER ONE** by Earl Schrock.

DANIEL CHAPTER ONE (KJV)

1In the third year of the reign of Jehoiakim king of Judah came Nebuchadnezzar king of Babylon unto Jerusalem, and besieged it. **2**And the Lord gave Jehoiakim king of Judah into his hand, with part of the vessels of the house of God: which he carried into the land of Shinar to the house of his god; and he brought the vessels into the treasure house of his god.

3And the king spake unto Ashpenaz the master of his eunuchs, that he should bring *certain* of the children of Israel, and of the king's seed, and of the princes; **4**Children in whom *was* no blemish, but well favoured, and skilful in all wisdom, and cunning in knowledge, and understanding science, and such as *had* ability in them to stand in the king's palace, and whom they might teach the learning and the tongue of the Chaldeans.

5And the king appointed them a daily provision of the king's meat, and of the wine which he drank: so nourishing them three years, that at the end thereof they might stand before the king. **6**Now among these were of the children of Judah, Daniel, Hananiah, Mishael, and Azariah: **7**Unto whom the prince of the eunuchs gave names: for he gave unto Daniel *the name* of Belteshazzar; and to Hananiah, of Shadrach; and to Mishael, of Meshach; and to Azariah, of Abednego.

8But Daniel purposed in his heart that he would not defile himself with the portion of the king's meat, nor with the wine which he drank: therefore he requested of the prince of the eunuchs that he might not defile himself. **9**Now God had brought Daniel into favour and tender love with the prince of the eunuchs. **10**And the prince of the eunuchs said unto Daniel, I fear my lord the king, who hath appointed your meat and your drink: for why should he see your faces worse liking than the children which *are* of your sort? then shall ye make *me* endanger my head to the king. **11**Then said Daniel to Melzar, whom the prince of the eunuchs had set over Daniel, Hananiah, Mishael, and Azariah, **12**Prove thy servants, I beseech thee, ten days; and let them give us pulse to eat, and water to drink. **13**Then let our countenances be looked upon before thee, and the countenance of the children that eat of the portion of the king's meat: and as thou seest, deal with thy servants.

14So he consented to them in this matter, and proved them ten days. **15**And at the end of ten days their countenances appeared fairer and fatter in flesh than all the children which did eat the portion of the king's meat. **16**Thus Melzar took away the portion of their meat, and the wine that they should drink; and gave them pulse. **17**As for these four children, God gave them knowledge and skill in all learning and wisdom: and Daniel had understanding in all visions and dreams.**18**Now at the end of the days that the king had said he should bring them in, then the prince of the eunuchs brought them in before Nebuchadnezzar. **19**And the king communed with them; and among them all was found none like Daniel, Hananiah, Mishael, and Azariah: therefore stood they before the king. **20**And in all matters of wisdom *and* understanding, that the king inquired of them, he found them ten times better than all the magicians *and* astrologers that *were* in all his realm. **21**And Daniel continued *even* unto the first year of king Cyrus.

DANIEL CHAPTER TWO

"For no one can lay any foundation other than the one already laid, which is Jesus Christ. If anyone builds on this foundation using gold, silver, costly stones, wood, hay or straw, their work will be shown for what it is, because the Day will bring it to light. It will be revealed with fire, and the fire will test the quality of each person's work." 1 Corinthians 3:11-13.

Daniel chapter one reveals the worship of the true God was diluted with pagan ideas and influences under King Nebuchadnezzar. Daniel chapter two reveals the amalgamation of pagan ideas into the true worship of God did not end when the Babylonian Empire fell. Daniel two reveals the source of the pagan practices and ideas that have trickled down to our day which has polluted true worship worldwide under the empires which ruled over the people of God since the days of Daniel.

In this chapter King Nebuchadnezzar has an interesting dream. The next day he knows the dream is important but he can't remember it. Since his pagan counselors, the wise guys, who are supposed to be able to reveal secrets and mysteries, were not able to tell the king his dream, he declares a death decree for all the counselors, which included Daniel and his three companions.

Daniel respectfully and tactfully asked the king for more time and King Nebuchadnezzar granted his request. With his three friends, Daniel conducted a prayer meeting asking God to reveal the dream so they could satisfy the king's request and save their lives. During the night God showed Daniel the dream and the next day Daniel told the dream to the king giving God all the glory.

In the dream King Nebuchadnezzar sees a statue. It has a head of gold, chest and arms of silver, belly and thighs of brass, legs of iron, with its feet and ten toes a mixture of iron and clay. As the king is beholding the image a small stone is cut out of a mountain without hands and crashes into the statue's feet causing it to crumble into a pile of dust which the wind blows away. After the dust clears the stone becomes a great mountain and fills the entire earth.

Daniel then reveals the meaning of the dream. He explains to the king that the head of gold represents the king and the Babylonian empire which rules over men and beasts. He continues by revealing to the king that the chest and arms of silver, the belly and thighs of brass, the legs of iron, the feet of iron and clay, and the toes of iron and clay represent other empires or kingdoms which would follow his and would also rule over all the earth. Thus the statue in his dream represented seven total kingdoms, Babylon and five others which will arise after his, as well as the kingdom represented by the destructive stone. Daniel tells us the stone which destroys the statue is a kingdom which will annihilate the statue, become huge, envelope the entire earth, and will last forever. From this dream of King Nebuchadnezzar seven kingdoms are represented in total.

In the next chapters of Daniel God reveals the identity of the other three kingdoms which "rule over all the earth" after the Babylonian empire. In Daniel 2:37 and 38 Daniel tells the

king that the head of gold represents him or in other words the kingdom of Babylon. Daniel 5:30,31 and Daniel 8:20 reveals that the chest and arms of silver represent the kingdom of the Medes and Persians. Daniel 8:21 reveals the belly and thighs of brass represent the kingdom of Greece under Alexander the Great. The fourth kingdom is described in Daniel two and seven but it is not explicitly named. History reveals that the empire that overcame the Grecian Empire was the Roman Empire, which was the ruling kingdom when Christ was born. It's assumed the Roman Empire is represented by the legs of Iron.

The feet and the toes also represent two separate kingdoms. Notice Daniel 2:41-43:

> "And whereas thou sawest the feet and toes, part of potters' clay, and part of iron, the kingdom shall be divided; but there shall be in it of the strength of the iron, forasmuch as thou sawest the iron mixed with miry clay.
>
> And *as* the toes of the feet *were* part of iron, and part of clay, *so* the kingdom shall be partly strong, and partly broken. And whereas thou sawest iron mixed with miry clay, they shall mingle themselves with the seed of men: but they shall not cleave one to another, even as iron is not mixed with clay."

KING NEBUCHADNEZZAR'S DREAM IMAGE OF DANIEL TWO

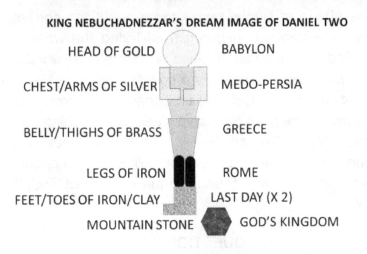

HEAD OF GOLD — BABYLON

CHEST/ARMS OF SILVER — MEDO-PERSIA

BELLY/THIGHS OF BRASS — GREECE

LEGS OF IRON — ROME

FEET/TOES OF IRON/CLAY — LAST DAY (X 2)

MOUNTAIN STONE — GOD'S KINGDOM

It's believed by many, that right now, God's people are living in the time of the "iron mixed with miry clay" or the time of the feet. There are differing opinions on this, since the Bible is not perfectly clear to distinguish it. Some teach we are living in the time of the feet and some believe we are living in the time of the toes. For this author, I believe we are living in the time where the feet join the toes, or in other words, where the distal foot meets the proximal toes. Revelation reveals this when it says:

> "They are also seven kings. Five have fallen, one is, the other has not yet come; but when he does come, he must remain for only a little while." Revelation 17:10

> ""The ten horns you saw are ten kings who have not yet received a kingdom, but who for one hour will receive authority as kings along with the beast." Revelation 17:12

I believe the "ten toes" and the "ten horns" represent the same end time kingdom which has a short lifespan. But keep in mind; the statue of Daniel two is more about the corrupting influence of pagan worship, which infiltrated the worship of the true God, than the identification of nations. The worship of God was "pure" as gold when the king attacked Jerusalem and the Jerusalem temple. But over time that worship was diluted and polluted by the pagan worship ideas and teachings of the Babylonian, Medo-Persian, Greek, and Roman empires. The iron in the legs and feet represent the culmination of paganism from all those kingdoms influencing the worship of God, then and now.

QUESTION:

Why does it say in Daniel 2:38 and 39 these four kingdoms, represented by the four different metals, "will rule over all the earth"? In consideration of these four kingdoms, none of them ever ruled over "all the earth". The two empires that actually can be said to have ruled over most of this world is that of England and Spain, but they are not mentioned in the dream of King Nebuchadnezzar. So the question has to be asked,

"What does it mean to rule **over all the earth**?"

We must remember the book of Daniel is more than just a world history lesson. It also reveals that our God is omniscient because He knows everything, He knows the end from the beginning (Isaiah 46:9,10). He knows what kingdoms will rise and fall and most of all, in accordance with the intent of the book of Daniel, He also knows which empires would have the greatest influence for introducing pagan ideas and practices into His pure-as-gold worship which He established through the Hebrew nation of Israel. Notice that in these kingdoms the only people mentioned of being ruled over is God's people.

ANSWER:

Though these kingdoms never ruled over every section of this planet, all these kingdoms did rule over Mesopotamia and the surrounding territories (Psalm 80:8-11) where God's people lived at that time. With that in mind we must conclude that, in most cases, in Bible prophecy, when the Bible talks about the "earth" it's referring to God's people, His kingdom, and not this entire planet. In Deuteronomy Moses is addressing the children of Israel, God's people, and giving them advice as how to stay close to God. Notice Deuteronomy 32:1-4:

> "Give ear, O ye heavens, and I will speak; and hear, O **earth**, the words of my mouth. My doctrine shall drop as the rain, my speech shall distil as the dew, as the small rain upon the tender herb, and as the showers upon the grass: Because I will publish the name of the LORD: ascribe ye greatness unto our God. *He is* the Rock, his work *is* perfect: for all his ways *are* judgment: God of truth and without iniquity, just and right *is* he."

Please note: In reading and studying the Bible a number of things must be considered in order to come up with the proper understanding of what's being read. We must consider context, content, and history. We must know: who is talking, who is being addressed, what is the occasion, what is the message at that time, and how does that message relate to us in our day. The same applies whenever we read about the "**earth**" in the Bible. We need to determine, during our reading, is it referring to this planet or is it referring to God's people, His kingdom?

Notice the following text found in Isaiah 66:1,2:

19

> Thus saith the LORD, The heaven *is* my throne, and the <u>earth</u> *is* my footstool: where *is* the house that ye build unto me? and where *is* the place of my rest? For all those *things* hath mine hand made, and all those *things* have been, saith the LORD: but to this *man* will I look, *even to him that is* poor and of a contrite spirit, and trembleth at my word."

Heaven is where God dwells. Where God dwells that is heaven. The **earth** under his feet is what God rules over and controls. Those people who gladly and voluntarily allow God to live in their hearts and take up residence in their lives, is where God dwells, that is heaven.

Those people that must be controlled and constantly restrained from following their own ways, that is the **earth people**. Sad to say, most of us fall into the "earth people" category. But the difference between the "earth people" and the "sea people" is that the "earth people" are activiely seeking the Lord as is revealed in Psalm 24. Also notice verse six: "This is the generation of them that seek him, that seek thy face."

Understand that the Hebrew word for "earth" is Strong's number 772: "ara" (pronounce ar-ah') which can also be translated as "land" or "ground". And in the Greek the word for "earth" is Strong's number 1093: "gé" (pronounce "ghay") and can also be translated as land, soil, region, and country. In your Bible research and study when you find the word "earth" or "land" consider the context and the content and ask yourself which word is most appropriate, "earth" or "land" and if the word "earth" or "land" is referring to God's people, His kingdom, His "earth people", or not.

Why would God call His kingdom people "earth" in order to distinguish them from people who are not in His kingdom? Consider the following:

> "And the LORD God formed man *of* the dust of the ground, and breathed into his nostrils the breath of life; and man became a living soul." Genesis 2:7

> "In the sweat of thy face shalt thou eat bread, till thou return unto the ground; for out of it wast thou taken: for dust thou *art*, and unto dust shalt thou return." Genesis 3:19

There is a distinguishing mark between those who believe in God and those who don't. Those which believe in God know that He exists (Hebrews 11:6) and that He is the Creator of all things (Ephesians 3:9). Those that deny God do not believe in Him and do not believe He is the Creator of all things. The difference between the two is that one group, believing God created man from the earth, is in the "city" or "kingdom" of God and the other group is outside the "city" or "kingdom" of God. One group dwells in the spiritual city of Jerusalem the other in the spiritual city of Babylon.

> "Blessed *are* they that do his commandments, that they may have right to the tree of life, and may enter in through the gates into the city. For without *are* dogs, and sorcerers, and whoremongers, and murderers, and idolaters, and whosoever loveth and maketh a lie." Revelation 22:14,15.

> "This know also, that in the last days perilous times shall come. For men shall be lovers of their own selves, covetous, boasters, proud,

blasphemers, disobedient to parents, unthankful, unholy, Without natural affection, trucebreakers, false accusers, incontinent, fierce, despisers of those that are good, Traitors, heady, highminded, lovers of pleasures more than lovers of God; Having a form of godliness, but denying the power thereof: from such turn away. For of this sort are they which creep into houses, and lead captive silly women laden with sins, led away with divers lusts, Ever learning, and never able to come to the knowledge of the truth. Now as Jannes and Jambres withstood Moses, so do these also resist the truth: men of corrupt minds, reprobate concerning the faith. But they shall proceed no further: for their folly shall be manifest unto all *men*, as theirs also was."

2 Timothy 3:1-9.

"Earth" people, those living in the kingdom of God, right here and right now, know they were Created from the soil just as God says. Those living outside the kingdom of God do not believe they were created from the soil. **

God's kingdom people live the life He ordains. Throughout the Bible God tells us our disobedient actions can pollute the earth (Isaiah 24:4-6), His people. The lifestyle and life choices of God's people reflect their faith, trust, and belief in Him. The desire of the kingdom people is to be like Jesus, completely surrendering their will to God in obedience to His will. Notice Revelation 11:18:

"And the nations were angry, and thy wrath is come, and the time of the dead, that they should be judged, and that thou shouldest give reward unto thy servants the prophets, and to the saints, and them that fear thy name, small and great; and shouldest destroy them which destroy the **earth**."

God has a love and desire for His people, the earth, and His end time anger will be against those which desire to destroy His people. Those which persecute His people, even killing them, will in the end be judged, destroyed, and annihilated. Notice Malachi 4:1-3:

"For, behold, the day cometh, that shall burn as an oven; and all the proud, yea, and all that do wickedly, shall be stubble: and the day that cometh shall burn them up, saith the LORD of hosts, that it shall leave them neither root nor branch. But unto you that fear my name shall the Sun of righteousness arise with healing in his wings; and ye shall go forth, and grow up as calves of the stall. And ye shall tread down the wicked; for they shall be ashes under the soles of your feet in the day that I shall do *this*, saith the LORD of hosts."

Are there other examples in the Bible where the word "earth" is clearly referring to the people making up the current kingdom of God on this planet?

Notice the following:

"And, behold, the LORD stood above it, and said, I *am* the LORD God of Abraham thy father, and the God of Isaac: the land whereon thou liest, to thee will I give it, and to thy seed; And thy seed shall be as the dust of the **earth**, and thou shalt spread abroad to the west, and to the east, and to the north, and to the south: and in thee and in thy seed shall all the families of the **earth** be blessed. And, behold, I *am* with thee, and will keep thee in all *places* whither thou goest, and will bring thee again into this land; for I will not leave thee, until I have done *that* which I have spoken to thee of." Genesis 28:13-15

"Again I say unto you, That if two of you shall agree on **earth** as touching any thing that they shall ask, it shall be done for them of my Father which is in heaven. For where two or three are gathered together in my name, there am I in the midst of them."

Matthew 18:19,20.

"But the meek shall inherit the **earth**; and shall delight themselves in the abundance of peace." Psalm 37:11.

"Blessed *are* the meek: for they shall inherit the **earth**." Matthew 5:5.

"They were told not to harm the grass of the **earth** or any plant or tree, but only those **people** who did not have the seal of God on their foreheads." Revelation 9:4

"And I saw another angel fly in the midst of heaven, having the everlasting gospel to preach unto them that dwell on the **earth**, and to every nation, and kindred, and tongue, and people, Saying with a loud voice, Fear God, and give glory to him; for the hour of his judgment is

come: and worship him that made **heaven**, and
earth, and the **sea**, and the fountains of waters."
Revelation 14:6,7

We should not be amazed to learn that the word "earth" refers
to the people of God. The word "sea" or "water" also refers to
people:

> "And he saith unto me, The **waters** which thou
> sawest, where the whore sitteth, are **peoples**,
> and multitudes, and nations, and tongues."
> Revelation 17:15.

Notice the following verse which utilizes "heaven", "earth", and
"sea" as being the people of God which inhabit His kingdom
right here and right now:

> "Therefore rejoice, *ye* **heavens**, and ye that dwell
> in them. Woe to the inhabiters of the **earth** and
> of the **sea**! for the devil is come down unto you,
> having great wrath, because he knoweth that he
> hath but a short time." Revelation 12:12.

** Learn more about the kingdom of God by reading the eBook,
"The Kingdom of Heaven and the Kingdom of God" by Earl B.
Schrock, found at Xlibris,com, Amazon, Barnes and Noble, etc.

CONCLUSION: The dream of King Nebuchadnezzar is not
just about empires rising and falling or about kings coming and
going, or even about the omniscience of God. The dream of
Daniel chapter two is about the pagan influence that came out
of these nations, which ruled over God's people. These empires
introduced pagan ideas into the pure worship of God that He
had established over time during the history of mankind.

Contemplate the metals in the statue in consideration of the purity in the worship to God. At first, during Daniel's day, the worship of God was pure because the previous pagan interferences of Egypt were sternly dealt with and deleted before King Nebuchadnezzar. The people had the Word of God to guide them in their worship. But as each succeeding heathen kingdom added its pagan influence into the mix, the pure worship of God deteriorated thus the metals become harder and less flexible, and of less value. And finally, in the last days, the feet and toes represent the myriad of worship groups which occupy this planet, each unwilling to concede to the other in the manner of how to rightly and correctly worship God the way He demands. But the story does not stop there.

In the last days, the days of the feet and toes, God will have a people which will become so familiar with Him and His worship that they will set aside all the pagan influences that debilitated the worship of God through the centuries and will not only worship Him "in spirit and in truth" (John 4:23) but will teach others the same.

> "For finding fault with them, he saith, Behold, the days come, saith the Lord, when I will make a new covenant with the house of Israel and with the house of Judah: Not according to the covenant that I made with their fathers in the day when I took them by the hand to lead them out of the land of Egypt; because they continued not in my covenant, and I regarded them not, saith the Lord. For this is the covenant that I will make with the house of Israel after those days, saith the Lord; I will put my laws into their mind, and write them in their hearts: and I will be to them a God, and they shall be to me a people: And they shall

not teach every man his neighbour, and every man his brother, saying, Know the Lord: for all shall know me, from the least to the greatest. For I will be merciful to their unrighteousness, and their sins and their iniquities will I remember no more. In that he saith, A new covenant, he hath made the first old. Now that which decayeth and waxeth old is ready to vanish away." Hebrews 8:8-13

DISCOVERING THE TRUTH ABOUT THE STONE THAT STRIKES THE STATUE:

There tends to be a difference of opinion concerning what the stone that strikes the statue in King Nebuchadnezzar's dream represents. As in all cases of consideration with Biblical things the best place to turn to discover this secret is to the Bible itself. Tradition or previous concepts and ideas of others, or even what the pastor or Bible instructor says must be set aside until all the information from the Bible is discovered and made plain. The Bible and the Bible only must interpret itself.

Some consider the image to be the history of sin or of mankind. Thus they assume the stone is the second coming of Jesus at the end of time which wipes out the history of sinful mankind. But verses 35 and 45 in Daniel two reveal that the statue is in its complete form from head to foot when the stone hits it. The head did not disappear when King Nebuchadnezzar died or the Medo-Persians took over the kingdom. The statue does not represent sin history and the stone is not the second coming of Jesus.

We must remember: Bible prophecy is all about WORSHIP. So we have to ask ourselves, "What does the stone in King Nebuchadnezzar's dream have to do with worship?"

NOTICE ALL THE DANIEL TWO TEXTS CONCERNING THE DESTRUCTIVE STONE:

33His legs of iron, his feet part of iron and part of clay. **34**Thou sawest till that a stone was cut out without hands, which smote the image upon his feet *that were* of iron and clay, and brake them to pieces. **35**Then was the iron, the clay, the brass, the silver, and the gold, broken to pieces together, and became like the chaff of the summer threshingfloors; and the wind carried them away, that no place was found for them: and the stone that smote the image became a great mountain, and filled the whole earth.

42And *as* the toes of the feet *were* part of iron, and part of clay, *so* the kingdom shall be partly strong, and partly broken. **43**And whereas thou sawest iron mixed with miry clay, they shall mingle themselves with the seed of men: but they shall not cleave one to another, even as iron is not mixed with clay.

44And in the days of these kings shall the God of heaven set up a kingdom, which shall never be destroyed: and the kingdom shall not be left to other people, *but* it shall break in pieces and consume all these kingdoms, and it shall stand for ever. **45**Forasmuch as thou sawest that the stone was cut out of the mountain without hands, and that it brake in pieces the iron, the brass, the clay, the silver, and the gold; the great God hath made known to the king what shall come to pass hereafter: and the dream *is* certain, and the interpretation thereof sure.

INFORMATION GLEANED FROM THE ABOVE TEXTS:

1. The stone strikes the toes sometime after the kingdom of the feet (Verse 33).
2. The stone is cut out without hands (Verse 34)

3. It hit the feet and toes which are made of iron and clay (Verse 34).
4. When it strikes, the different metals pulverize together, at the same time (Vs 35).
5. The metals of iron, clay, brass, silver, and gold become like wheat chaff (Vs 35).
6. The wind blows the metallic dust away (Verse 35).
7. Once destroyed, the metallic dust cannot be found (Verse 35).
8. The stone becomes a great mountain (Verse 35).
9. It completely fills the whole earth (Verse 35).
10. The ten toes represent a kingdom (Verse 42).
11. The feet and the toes are two separate kingdoms (Verses 41, 42).
12. The iron and clay in the feet represent divided people groups (Verse 43).
13. The crowds represented in the feet and toes will never agree (Verse 43).
14. The toe kingdom will remain divided till the statue is demolished (Verse 44).
15. God's kingdom is made up of people (Verse 44).
16. It hits the image specifically during the time of the toe kingdom (verse 42-44).
17. During the time of the "toe kingdom" God sets up His kingdom (Verse 44).
18. God's kingdom will never be destroyed (Verse 44).
19. God's kingdom will never change ownership (Verse 44).
20. God's kingdom will destroy and consume all the previous kingdoms (Verse 44).
21. God's kingdom will last forever (Verse 44).
22. The stone is cut out of a mountain (Verse 45).
23. It is cut out of the mountain with no hands (Verse 45).
24. God's kingdom pulverizes the metallic image from feet to head (Verse 45).

25. The stone that destroys the image is way distant future from the king (Verse 45).
26. Daniel tells the king the dream will happen just as was revealed (Verse 45).

What does it mean that the stone is "cut out of a mountain" (verse 45)? This question will be further answered during the discussion on Daniel chapter nine.

What does it mean "without hands" (verse 34)? God has developed a people that make up His kingdom by His own methods and not by man's. He has developed His kingdom people to be a temple or a sanctuary to house His Spirit. Something developed by God, in His way, is built without hands.

> "What? know ye not that your body is the temple of the Holy Ghost *which is* in you, which ye have of God, and ye are not your own?" 1 Corinthians 6:19.

What does it mean the stone became a great mountain (verse 35)? The kingdom of heaven has been growing since the days of Jesus. The spiritual Mt. Zion has developed into a huge mountain as of today. See Psalm 74:1,2; Psalm 125:1,2; Acts 17:24; Exodus 25:8; 1 Cor. 3:16; Luke 17:21; Micah 4:1-5; and Isaiah 2:1-5.

We, His kingdom people, are Mt. Zion, His people, His mountain. Ephesians 2:11-22:

> "Wherefore remember, that ye *being* in time past Gentiles in the flesh, who are called Uncircumcision by that which is called the Circumcision in the flesh made by hands; That at that time ye were without Christ, being aliens from the commonwealth of Israel, and strangers

30

from the covenants of promise, having no hope, and without God in the world: But now in Christ Jesus ye who sometimes were far off are made nigh by the blood of Christ. For he is our peace, who hath made both one, and hath broken down the middle wall of partition *between us*; Having abolished in his flesh the enmity, *even* the law of commandments *contained* in ordinances; for to make in himself of twain one new man, *so* making peace; And that he might reconcile both unto God in one body by the cross, having slain the enmity thereby: And came and preached peace to you which were afar off, and to them that were nigh. For through him we both have access by one Spirit unto the Father. Now therefore ye are no more strangers and foreigners, but fellow citizens with the saints, and of the household of God; And are built upon the foundation of the apostles and prophets, Jesus Christ himself being the chief corner *stone*; In whom all the building fitly framed together groweth unto an holy temple in the Lord: In whom ye also are builded together for an habitation of God through the Spirit."

What does it mean that it "filled the whole earth" (verse 35)? The "earth" in Bible prophecy represents the "earthly kingdom of God". It is composed of the "great" and "small" (Revelation 20:12) which are people familiar with Jesus from all nations around this globe.

WHAT DOES IT MEAN: "MINGLE THEMSELVES WITH THE **SEED** OF MEN" in verse 43? WHAT IS THE DEFINITION OF THE "SEED OF MEN"? Notice the following:

Jesus is the "seed" of Abraham, who was a man (Galatians 3:15).

Abraham's seed is to be as the dust, stars and sand (Genesis 13:16, 22:17, 32:12).

The Word of God, the Bible, is the "seed" (Luke 8:11).

Good seed represents the righteous; bad seed represents the lost (Matt. 13:24-30, 38).

Seed is used to determine the value of land (Leviticus 27:16).

Seed is used to sustain life (Genesis 47:23).

Seed represents righteousness (Hosea 10:12).

Seed can refer to descendants (Greek word Sperma: Strong's 4690) (Acts 7:5).

Seed represents "offspring" or descendants (Hebrew zera: Strong's 2234) (Dan. 2:43).

It is assumed by many that this phrase "mingle with the seed of men" means intermarrying to bring about solidarity between kingdoms. But is that what it really means?

Who are the "they" and "themselves" in verse 43 when it says,

> "And whereas thou sawest iron mixed with miry
> clay, **they** shall mingle themselves with the seed
> of men: but **they** shall not cleave one to another,
> even as iron is not mixed with clay."?

The "they" and "themselves" mean people, God's people, living in His kingdom, right here and right now, not empires or kingdoms. The people of God today, in different denominations or worship groups, the world over are very adamant to change. It's like "once a Baptist always a Baptist" no matter what anyone or anything says. Most people will argue their way of thinking and worshipping to the death, because that is the way they were raised to worship. Thus the iron fragmented worship communities refuse to unite.

CONCLUSION OF THE STONE:

From the above we know that the stone represents the "kingdom of God" which He developed or formed without human hands, when Jesus died on the cross, after drinking the "fruit of the vine", the vinegar (Read the chapter "The Vinegar at the Cross of Calvary" on page 199). At Jesus' death, the Chief Cornerstone (Ephesians 2:19-22), the kingdom of heaven, or of God, was made up of a few people, but over the last 2000 years the kingdom of Christ has come to include every part of this planet. I believe the mountain the stone was cut out of was Mt. Zion, the kingdom God developed over the previous 4000 years from the days of Adam to that of Christ. Jesus said, "Salvation is of the Jews" (John 4:22) because He came out of the family tree that is outlined in Matthew chapter one and Luke chapter two which goes from God the Father, to Jesus the Son.

From the days of Daniel in the kingdom of Babylon to the days of Jesus, the kingdom of God had become polluted with the paganism from Babylon, Medo-Persia, Greece, and Rome. Those pagan teachings are still embedded in worship around the world today. But the development of the kingdom of Christ, "stone cut out without hands", from the days of Jesus to our day has slowly come to recognize the pagan teachings and now in the last days there are a people which serve God "in spirit and in truth" as they dedicate themselves to be led by the Holy

Spirit through the Word of God, the 66 book Holy Bible. These servants of God, from every walk of life and every religious community, are called His elect and they are willing to "follow the Lamb whithersoever he goeth" (Revelation 14:4) to perform His will, not their own. They want to serve God totally, according to His Word, and not according to the traditions of men. These are the "heaven" people. There are others which refuse to completely obey God in His Word, the "earth" and "sea" people: All three of these groups occupy the Kingdom of God. **

> "This people draweth nigh unto me with their mouth, and honoureth me with *their* lips; but their heart is far from me. But in vain they do worship me, teaching *for* doctrines the commandments of men." Matthew 15:8,9.

When considering Daniel chapter seven, which addresses these four kingdoms as creatures such as a lion, bear, leopard, and ten horned beast; and taking into account Revelation 13:1,2; the pagan ideas of the past still linger today in worship to the true God. But a day is soon coming when all those pagan teachings will be made plain and God's true people will "come out of her my people" (Revelation 18:4).

The image of Daniel chapter two will be destroyed when the people of God, His last day kingdom, realize the difference between "the traditions of men and the commandments of God" (Mark 7:8) and they will worship Him free of the pagan attachments that have been accumulated and fastened to the true worship of God since the days of Daniel.

> "Thus have ye made the commandment of God of none effect by your tradition. *Ye* hypocrites, well did Esaias prophesy of you, saying, This people draweth nigh unto me with their mouth,

and honoureth me with *their* lips; but their heart is far from me. But in vain they do worship me, teaching *for* doctrines the commandments of men." Matthew 15:6-9.

See the **YouTube** videos **Daniel Chapter Two** and **The Stone of Daniel Chapter Two** by Earl Schrock.

**Learn more about the kingdom of God in the eBook, "The Kingdom of Heaven and the Kingdom of God" by Earl B. Schrock; at Xlibris,com, Amazon, Barnes and Noble, etc.

DANIEL CHAPTER TWO (KJV)

1And in the second year of the reign of Nebuchadnezzar Nebuchadnezzar dreamed dreams, wherewith his spirit was troubled, and his sleep brake from him. **2**Then the king commanded to call the magicians, and the astrologers, and the sorcerers, and the Chaldeans, for to shew the king his dreams. So they came and stood before the king. **3**And the king said unto them, I have dreamed a dream, and my spirit was troubled to know the dream.

4Then spake the Chaldeans to the king in Syriack, O king, live for ever: tell thy servants the dream, and we will shew the interpretation. **5**The king answered and said to the Chaldeans, The thing is gone from me: if ye will not make known unto me the dream, with the interpretation thereof, ye shall be cut in pieces, and your houses shall be made a dunghill. **6**But if ye shew the dream, and the interpretation thereof, ye shall receive of me gifts and rewards and great honour: therefore shew me the dream, and the interpretation thereof.

7They answered again and said, Let the king tell his servants the dream, and we will shew the interpretation of it. **8**The king answered and said, I know of certainty that ye would gain the time, because ye see the thing is gone from me. **9**But if ye will not make known unto me the dream, *there is but* one decree for you: for ye have prepared lying and corrupt words to speak before me, till the time be changed: therefore tell me the dream, and I shall know that ye can shew me the interpretation thereof. **10**The Chaldeans answered before the king, and said, There is not a man upon the earth that can shew the king's matter: therefore *there is* no king, lord, nor ruler, *that* asked such things at any magician, or astrologer, or Chaldean. **11**And *it is* a rare thing that the king requireth, and there is none other that can shew it before the king, except the gods, whose dwelling is not with flesh.

12For this cause the king was angry and very furious, and commanded to destroy all the wise *men* of Babylon. **13**And the decree went forth that the wise *men* should be slain; and they sought Daniel and his fellows to be slain. **14**Then Daniel answered with counsel and wisdom to Arioch the captain of the king's guard, which was gone forth to slay the wise *men* of Babylon: **15**He answered and said to Arioch the king's captain, Why *is* the decree *so* hasty from the king? Then Arioch made the thing known to Daniel. **16**Then Daniel went in, and desired of the king that he would give him time, and that he would shew the king the interpretation.

17Then Daniel went to his house, and made the thing known to Hananiah, Mishael, and Azariah, his companions: **18**That they would desire mercies of the God of heaven concerning this secret; that Daniel and his fellows should not perish with the rest of the wise *men* of Babylon. **19**Then was the secret revealed unto Daniel in a night vision. Then Daniel blessed the God of heaven. **20**Daniel answered and said, Blessed be the name of God for ever and ever: for wisdom and might are his:

21And he changeth the times and the seasons: he removeth kings, and setteth up kings: he giveth wisdom unto the wise, and knowledge to them that know understanding:

22He revealeth the deep and secret things: he knoweth what *is* in the darkness, and the light dwelleth with him. **23**I thank thee, and praise thee, O thou God of my fathers, who hast given me wisdom and might, and hast made known unto me now what we desired of thee: for thou hast *now* made known unto us the king's matter. **24**Therefore Daniel went in unto Arioch, whom the king had ordained to destroy the wise *men* of Babylon: he went and said thus unto him; Destroy not the wise *men* of Babylon: bring me in before the king, and I will shew unto the king the interpretation.

25Then Arioch brought in Daniel before the king in haste, and said thus unto him, I have found a man of the captives of Judah, that will make known unto the king the interpretation. **26**The king answered and said to Daniel, whose name *was* Belteshazzar, Art thou able to make known unto me the dream which I have seen, and the interpretation thereof? **27**Daniel answered in the presence of the king, and said, The secret which the king hath demanded cannot the wise *men*, the astrologers, the magicians, the soothsayers, shew unto the king; **28**But there is a God in heaven that revealeth secrets, and maketh known to the king Nebuchadnezzar what shall be in the latter days. Thy dream, and the visions of thy head upon thy bed, are these;

29As for thee, O king, thy thoughts came *into thy mind* upon thy bed, what should come to pass hereafter: and he that revealeth secrets maketh known to thee what shall come to pass. **30**But as for me, this secret is not revealed to me for *any* wisdom that I have more than any living, but for *their* sakes that shall make known the interpretation to the king, and that thou mightest know the thoughts of thy heart.

31Thou, O king, sawest, and behold a great image. This great image, whose brightness *was* excellent, stood before thee; and the form thereof *was* terrible. **32**This image's head *was* of fine gold, his breast and his arms of silver, his belly and his thighs of brass, **33**His legs of iron, his feet part of iron and part of clay. **34**Thou sawest till that a stone was cut out without hands, which smote the image upon his feet *that were* of iron and clay, and brake them to pieces. **35**Then was the iron, the clay, the brass, the silver, and the gold, broken to pieces together, and became like the chaff of the summer threshingfloors; and the wind carried them away, that no place was found for them: and the stone that smote the image became a great mountain, and filled the whole earth.

36This *is* the dream; and we will tell the interpretation thereof before the king. **37**Thou, O king, *art* a king of kings: for the God of heaven hath given thee a kingdom, power, and strength, and glory. **38**And wheresoever the children of men dwell, the beasts of the field and the fowls of the heaven hath he given into thine hand, and hath made thee ruler over them all. Thou *art* this head of gold.

39And after thee shall arise another kingdom inferior to thee, and another third kingdom of brass, which shall bear rule over all the earth.

40And the fourth kingdom shall be strong as iron: forasmuch as iron breaketh in pieces and subdueth all *things*: and as iron that breaketh all these, shall it break in pieces and bruise. **41**And whereas thou sawest the feet and toes, part of potters' clay, and part of iron, the kingdom shall be divided; but there shall be in it of the strength of the iron, forasmuch as thou sawest the iron mixed with miry clay. **42**And *as* the toes of the feet *were* part of iron, and part of clay, *so* the kingdom shall be partly strong, and partly broken. **43**And whereas thou sawest iron mixed with miry clay, they shall mingle themselves with the seed of men: but they shall not cleave one to another, even as iron is not mixed with clay.

44And in the days of these kings shall the God of heaven set up a kingdom, which shall never be destroyed: and the kingdom shall not be left to other people, *but* it shall break in pieces and consume all these kingdoms, and it shall stand for ever. **45**Forasmuch as thou sawest that the stone was cut out of the mountain without hands, and that it brake in pieces the iron, the brass, the clay, the silver, and the gold; the great God hath made known to the king what shall come to pass hereafter: and the dream *is* certain, and the interpretation thereof sure

46Then the king Nebuchadnezzar fell upon his face, and worshipped Daniel, and commanded that they should offer an oblation and sweet odours unto him. **47**The king answered unto Daniel, and said, Of a truth *it is*, that your God *is* a God of gods, and a Lord of kings, and a revealer of secrets, seeing thou couldest reveal this secret. **48**Then the king made Daniel a great man, and gave him many great gifts, and made him ruler over the whole province of Babylon, and chief of the governors over all the wise *men* of Babylon. **49**Then Daniel requested of the king, and he set Shadrach, Meshach, and Abednego, over the affairs of the province of Babylon: but Daniel *sat* in the gate of the king.

DANIEL CHAPTER THREE

"Finally, brethren, whatsoever things are true, whatsoever things *are* honest, whatsoever things *are* just, whatsoever things *are* pure, whatsoever things *are* lovely, whatsoever things *are* of good report; if *there be* any virtue, and if *there be* any praise, think on these things." Philippians 4:8

King Nebuchadnezzar took captive Daniel and his three companions in the year 605 BCE. After the full three years attending the Babylonian university, as established by the king (Daniel 1:3-5), the four friends graduated with honors (Daniel 1:17-20). In about 602 BC the king had his multi-metal dream as recorded in Daniel chapter two. Daniel revealed to the king that Babylon was the head of gold and that another three empires would arise after his.

Apparently not happy with being just the head of gold in his dream, King Nebuchadnezzar commissioned the building of a sculpture, similar to his dream image, but this time the entire statue would be gold, signifying his empire would last forever.

The statue was to be huge so it could be seen for miles around. It would be 60 cubits high and 6 cubits wide (100 feet tall and 10 feet wide). The image was prepared under the king's specifications and in the year 600 BCE the image was revealed on the plain of Dura, in the province of Babylon (Daniel 3:1).

The unveiling took place with a tremendous amount of fanfare including lots of music (verse 5) and celebrations. A huge crowd of people were there which included all the officials making up the king's cabinet (verse 2) and government.

But there was more taking place in all this than meets the eye.

Chief over King Nebuchadnezzar's kingdom was Daniel because of his honesty and integrity. The other government officials did not like having Daniel and his three honest companions watching over them and their every business arrangement (Daniel 2:48,49). I think the jealous counselors not only encouraged the king to build the image, but also established the penalty for anyone not willing to worship it. The wise guys could not find anything wrong with Daniel and his three friends when it came to business or their service to the king, but they also realized these four men would never, never, never bow down to the king's statue. The penalty for not worshiping the king's image was immediate death by being thrown into one of the surrounding smelting furnaces (verses 4-6).

I don't think the king was wise to their treachery until the day of the revealing and the festivities when the wise guys approached him and told him some of the people in the crowd refuse to bow down and worship his image. As soon as they told him it was Shadrach, Meshach, and Abednego, he recognized their deceitfulness and he immediately was angry at himself and at them (verses 12,13). The trap had been set, he had been hoodwinked, and now there was no way out for him to save the three young men. The king had agreed to all the arrangements taking place and now all eyes of his entire government were focused on him. He only had one choice and one chance to save his three trusted leaders.

King Nebuchadnezzar called the young men to himself, in full view of all the officials in his government, and gave them one more opportunity to worship the image or be thrown into the fiery burning furnace (verses 14,15). Daniel was not there at this celebration to calm the king or defend his three comrades. I can only imagine the wise guys had arranged for him to be far away from the area when they set their plan in action. If he had been there, things would probably have been quite different. But for now, his three companion's lives were at stake and they were on their own.

Maybe Daniel would have been more tactful in answering the king than were his three companions but they revealed no tact in their response to the already frustrated king.

> "Shadrach, Meshach, and Abednego, answered and said to the king, O Nebuchadnezzar, we *are* not careful to answer thee in this matter. If it be *so*, our God whom we serve is able to deliver us from the burning fiery furnace, and he will deliver *us* out of thine hand, O king. But if not, be it known unto thee, O king, that we will not serve thy gods, nor worship the golden image which thou hast set up." Daniel 3:16-18.

At this arrogant response, the king was not only angry at himself for not seeing through the wise guy's trick, he now really was extremely angry (verse 19) at his three top supervisors for answering him so ruthlessly in front of the entire Babylonian world. In his angry haste he had the furnace heated way beyond its legal limit. This may also have been a move of mercy on the part of the king to make the deaths of his beloved servants instantaneous. When the strong soldiers tossed the three men into the mouth of the furnace it was so hot the soldiers died from being too close to the heat (verse 22).

But the king soon forgot his rage when he noticed that someone had joined Shadrach, Meshach, and Abednego in the raging flames. Now he counted four figures in the furnace walking around unharmed and the one was "like the son of God" (verse 25). As soon as possible the king got as near as he could to the furnace and called the young men to come out to him. When they walked out of the death trap, not a hair on their heads was singed and there was no smoke smell on their clothes, to the astonished surprise of all the men present, including the sneaky wise guys and the attending "satraps, administrators, governors, and the king's counselors" (verse 27).

After seeing this, which apparently took his mind off his frustration and anger, the king gave praise to the God of Shadrach, Meshach, and Abednego (verse 28) but he did not forget the deceit of his officials so he said in verse 29:

> "Therefore I make a decree, that every people, nation, and language, which speak anything amiss against the God of Shadrach, Meshach, and Abednego, shall be cut in pieces, and their houses shall be made a dunghill: because there is no other God that can deliver after this sort."

Apparently this gigantic trick, which almost worked, stuck in the mind of the wise guys, or that of their companions, for in the future (Daniel 6) they will try it again. Why not, they got by with it the first time unscathed, why not try it again under different leadership? The problem is, the outcome next time goes very different than expected.

CONCLUSION:

The story of "the burning fiery furnace" (verse 23) is much more than just an interesting Bible story of three brave men dedicated to God. It's a life lesson for the generation living in the last days of this worlds history. There is a future time of tribulation coming which Jesus warned us about in Matthew 24:21-25:

> "For then shall be great tribulation, such as was not since the beginning of the world to this time, no, nor ever shall be. And except those days should be shortened, there should no flesh be saved: but for the elect's sake those days shall be shortened. Then if any man shall say unto you, Lo, here *is* Christ, or there; believe *it* not. For there shall arise false Christs, and false prophets, and shall shew great signs and wonders; insomuch that, if *it were* possible, they shall deceive the very elect. Behold, I have told you before."

This information being understood today is not by accident. God said He would reveal His secrets to His servants before the promised event, at the right time and right place:

> "Surely the Lord GOD will do nothing, but he revealeth his secret unto his servants the prophets" Amos 3:7.

Revelation thirteen continues with this warning mentioning in greater detail what those days of tribulation will involve for all mankind. Notice Revelation 13:11-18:

> "And I beheld another beast coming up out of the **earth**; and he had two horns like a lamb,

and he spake as a dragon. And he exerciseth all the power of the first beast before him, and causeth the **earth** and them which dwell therein to worship the first beast, whose deadly wound was healed. And he doeth great wonders, so that he maketh fire come down from heaven on the **earth** in the sight of men. And deceiveth them that dwell on the **earth** by *the means of* those miracles which he had power to do in the sight of the beast; saying to them that dwell on the **earth**, that they should make an image to the beast, which had the wound by a sword, and did live. And he had power to give life unto the image of the beast, that the image of the beast should both speak, and cause that as many as would not worship the image of the beast should be killed.

And he causeth all, both small and great, rich and poor, free and bond, to receive a mark in their right hand, or in their foreheads: And that no man might buy or sell, save he that had the mark, or the name of the beast, or the number of his name. Here is wisdom. Let him that hath understanding count the number of the beast: for it is the number of a man; and his number *is* Six hundred threescore *and* six."

The beast of Revelation thirteen desires worship for itself. Because of that, FORCED WORSHIP will be instituted, under the guise of accomplishing something else. For that reason, Revelation 13:18 refers us back to Daniel chapter three. Notice what it says:

"Here is wisdom. Let him that hath understanding count the number of the beast: for it is the number of a man; and his number *is* Six hundred threescore *and* six."

I believe that number, 666, refers us back to Daniel chapter three because "the number of a man" in this verse, has to be concerning a man in the Bible, not outside the Bible. King Nebuchadnezzar set up the image and forced everyone to worship that image or be killed. Notice the image was set up in 600 BCE, and it was 60 cubits high, and 6 cubits wide: thus six hundred and sixty-six (666).

Ezra 2:13 supports this premise of King Nebuchadnezzar being the man in the Bible whose number is 666. One of King Nebuchadnezzar's Hebrew captives, in 605 BCE, was a man named Adonikam which had 666 descendants return to Jerusalem from Babylon "in the first year of Cyrus, king of Persia" (Ezra 1:1). Of the three places in the Bible including 1 Kings 10:14 which can be related to the number 666, Daniel 3:1 and Ezra 2:13, point to King Nebuchadnezzar who mixed false worship with true worship and which forced false worship on all the people, at the threat of death, like what Jesus predicted would happen in the coming tribulation period on the last generation.

It's very important that we realize some of us may be put into the same situation as Shadrach, Meshach, and Abednego. We may be positioned to be threatened by force to turn away from our Creator to worship the created. Remember: Bible prophecy is all about WORSHIP.

To be prepared and able to stand strong for God, each one of us must live every single moment, every single day, being faithful to God in everything. That way when the temptation comes to obey or disobey God, the choice will not be difficult for those who live their lives now being completely obedient to God and to His will.

QUESTION: How do we know God's will for us?

ANSWER: We devote precious time in DAILY prayer with reading and studying of the Word of God, the 66 book Bible. It's a matter of life or death.

See **YouTube** for the video on **DANIEL CHAPTER THREE** by Earl Schrock.

DANIEL CHAPTER THREE (KJV)

1Nebuchadnezzar the king made an image of gold, whose height *was* threescore cubits, *and* the breadth thereof six cubits: he set it up in the plain of Dura, in the province of Babylon. **2**Then Nebuchadnezzar the king sent to gather together the princes, the governors, and the captains, the judges, the treasurers, the counsellers, the sheriffs, and all the rulers of the provinces, to come to the dedication of the image which Nebuchadnezzar the king had set up.

3Then the princes, the governors, and captains, the judges, the treasurers, the counsellers, the sheriffs, and all the rulers of the provinces, were gathered together unto the dedication of the image that Nebuchadnezzar the king had set up; and they stood before the image that Nebuchadnezzar had set up. **4**Then an herald cried aloud, To you it is commanded, O people, nations, and languages, **5***That* at what time ye hear the sound of the cornet, flute, harp, sackbut, psaltery, dulcimer, and all kinds of musick, ye fall down and worship the golden image that Nebuchadnezzar the king hath set up: **6**And whoso falleth not down and worshippeth shall the same hour be cast into the midst of a burning fiery furnace. 7Therefore at that time, when all the people heard the sound of the cornet, flute, harp, sackbut, psaltery, and all kinds of musick, all the people, the nations, and the languages, fell down *and* worshipped the golden image that Nebuchadnezzar the king had set up.

8Wherefore at that time certain Chaldeans came near, and accused the Jews. 9They spake and said to the king Nebuchadnezzar, O king, live for ever. 10Thou, O king, hast made a decree, that every man that shall hear the sound of the cornet, flute, harp, sackbut, psaltery, and dulcimer, and all kinds of musick, shall fall down and worship the golden image: 11And whoso falleth not down and worshippeth, *that* he should be cast into the midst of a burning fiery furnace. 12There are certain Jews whom thou hast set over the affairs of the province of Babylon, Shadrach, Meshach, and Abednego; these men, O king, have not regarded thee: they serve not thy gods, nor worship the golden image which thou hast set up.

13Then Nebuchadnezzar in *his* rage and fury commanded to bring Shadrach, Meshach, and Abednego. Then they brought these men before the king. 14Nebuchadnezzar spake and said unto them, *Is it* true, O Shadrach, Meshach, and Abednego, do not ye serve my gods, nor worship the golden image which I have set up? 15Now if ye be ready that at what time ye hear the sound of the cornet, flute, harp, sackbut, psaltery, and dulcimer, and all kinds of musick, ye fall down and worship the image which I have made; *well*: but if ye worship not, ye shall be cast the same hour into the midst of a burning fiery furnace; and who *is* that God that shall deliver you out of my hands?

16Shadrach, Meshach, and Abednego, answered and said to the king, O Nebuchadnezzar, we *are* not careful to answer thee in this matter. 17If it be *so*, our God whom we serve is able to deliver us from the burning fiery furnace, and he will deliver *us* out of thine hand, O king. 18But if not, be it known unto thee, O king, that we will not serve thy gods, nor worship the golden image which thou hast set up.

19Then was Nebuchadnezzar full of fury, and the form of his visage was changed against Shadrach, Meshach, and Abednego: *therefore* he spake, and commanded that they should heat the furnace one seven times more than it was wont to be heated. 20And he commanded the most mighty men that *were* in his army to bind Shadrach, Meshach, and Abednego, *and* to cast *them* into the burning fiery furnace. 21Then these men were bound in their coats, their hosen, and their hats, and their *other* garments, and were cast into the midst of the burning fiery furnace. 22Therefore because the king's commandment was urgent, and the furnace exceeding hot, the flame of the fire slew those men that took up Shadrach, Meshach, and Abednego. 23And these three men, Shadrach, Meshach, and Abednego, fell down bound into the midst of the burning fiery furnace.

24Then Nebuchadnezzar the king was astonied, and rose up in haste, *and* spake, and said unto his counsellers, Did not we cast three men bound into the midst of the fire? They answered and said unto the king, True, O king. 25He answered and said, Lo, I see four men loose, walking in the midst of the fire, and they have no hurt; and the form of the fourth is like the Son of God. 26Then Nebuchadnezzar came near to the mouth of the burning fiery furnace, *and* spake, and said, Shadrach, Meshach, and Abednego, ye servants of the most high God, come forth, and come *hither.* Then Shadrach, Meshach, and Abednego, came forth of the midst of the fire. 27And the princes, governors, and captains, and the king's counsellers, being gathered together, saw these men, upon whose bodies the fire had no power, nor was an hair of their head singed, neither were their coats changed, nor the smell of fire had passed on them.

28*Then* Nebuchadnezzar spake, and said, Blessed *be* the God of Shadrach, Meshach, and Abednego, who hath sent his angel, and delivered his servants that trusted in him, and have changed the king's word, and yielded their bodies, that they might not serve nor worship any god, except their own God. **29**Therefore I make a decree, That every people, nation, and language, which speak anything amiss against the God of Shadrach, Meshach, and Abednego, shall be cut in pieces, and their houses shall be made a dunghill: because there is no other God that can deliver after this sort. **30**Then the king promoted Shadrach, Meshach, and Abednego, in the province of Babylon.

DANIEL CHAPTER FOUR

"Pride *goeth* before destruction, and an haughty spirit before a fall." Proverbs 16:18

Important things to realize while considering Daniel chapter four:

1. In Daniel chapter 2 the king did not remember the dream.
2. In Daniel 4 he remembers the dream but does not understand what it means.
3. Chapter four is addressed to the people that "dwell in all the earth" (vs 1), not this planet because the king was not ruler of this planet, but he was ruler over God's kingdom, His people, the earth.
4. In Daniel 4:2,3 the king praises the Most High God, Daniel's God, and then he commences to explain why he is praising the Heavenly Father.
5. In Daniel four dream the king sees a tree "in the middle of the earth" (verse 10).
6. The tree reaches to heaven and could be seen from the ends of the earth (11).
7. All the creatures in the "earth" were sustained by the tree (verse 12).
8. In Verses 13-18 the king describes a heavenly being he calls "the watcher" descend from heaven and order the tree be cut down and dismantled.

9. The stump will have "its roots in the earth" to be left in place with a band of iron and a band of brass wrapped around it to sustain it and keep it alive.

10. In verses 15 and 16 the stump is given human characteristics saying, "*let* **his** portion *be* with the beasts in the grass of the earth: Let **his** heart be changed from man's, and let a beast's heart be given unto **him**; and let seven times pass over **him**."

11. Verse 16 mentions a time period of "seven times" to pass.

12. In verse 17 the "watcher" tells the reason for the future actions to be done, "to the intent that the living may know that the Most High ruleth in the kingdom of men, and giveth it to whomsoever he will, and setteth up over it the basest of men."

13. In verses 19-27 Daniel explains the dream.

14. The tree represents King Nebuchadnezzar.

15. It's a warning to him to adjust his way of thinking and treating other people.

16. If he refuses to accept the warning, the Most High God will drive him from men and he will live like an animal until seven times passes over him (verse 23).

17. In verses 28-33 we are told that the king did not change his ways and that he bragged that all the success he had in life was because of his own actions. At that moment a voice reminds him of the dream and he is given the mindset of a wild beast. He lives like an animal, eating grass and living in the wild, till the seven times pass.

18. In verses 34-37 the king explains that his reasoning powers returned to him at the end of the seven times (seven years) and that he was restored to his royal position.

19. The king praises the God of heaven and says that the "inhabitants of the earth" are nothing and that God

controls the affairs of the people in the earth (verse 35) and God is above being questioned concerning the things He does.

The seven times are actually seven years. A single time is how long it takes for our planet to circle the sun. Besides revealing the power and glory of God, and the humbling effect He has on the people that praise Him, this vision of Daniel four is important to reveal in Bible prophecy that:

1. Trees and plants can represent a person or people. Revelation 9:4 says:
    "And it was commanded them that they should not hurt the **grass** of the earth, neither any **green thing**, neither any **tree**; but only those men which have not the seal of God in their foreheads."

2. God is the Lord of the "earth people" which is His people, making up His kingdom, right here and right now.
3. A single "time" is one complete year.

CONCLUSION: Pride is a downfall of humanity (Proverbs 11:2; 16:18). Often people put their own wants, needs, and desires ahead of others and ahead of God. But we need to remember all we own, manage, watch over, and care for, comes from God. We are His ambassadors and His stewards. When we develop the prideful attitude that we have become what we are because of our own efforts, God will and can step in and break our prideful defiance. Keeping our eyes on Jesus, on a daily basis, in His Word will help us remain humble and effective witnesses for our Heavenly Father.

See the **YouTube** video for **DANIEL CHAPTER FOUR** by Earl Schrock.

DANIEL CHAPTER FOUR (KJV)

1Nebuchadnezzar the king, unto all people, nations, and languages, that dwell in all the earth; Peace be multiplied unto you. 2I thought it good to shew the signs and wonders that the high God hath wrought toward me.

3How great *are* his signs! and how mighty *are* his wonders! his kingdom *is* an everlasting kingdom, and his dominion *is* from generation to generation

4I Nebuchadnezzar was at rest in mine house, and flourishing in my palace: 5I saw a dream which made me afraid, and the thoughts upon my bed and the visions of my head troubled me. 6Therefore made I a decree to bring in all the wise *men* of Babylon before me, that they might make known unto me the interpretation of the dream. 7Then came in the magicians, the astrologers, the Chaldeans, and the soothsayers: and I told the dream before them; but they did not make known unto me the interpretation thereof.

8But at the last Daniel came in before me, whose name *was* Belteshazzar, according to the name of my god, and in whom *is* the spirit of the holy gods: and before him I told the dream, *saying*, 9O Belteshazzar, master of the magicians, because I know that the spirit of the holy gods *is* in thee, and no secret troubleth thee, tell me the visions of my dream that I have seen, and the interpretation thereof.

10Thus *were* the visions of mine head in my bed; I saw, and behold a tree in the midst of the earth, and the height thereof *was* great.

11The tree grew, and was strong, and the height thereof reached unto heaven, and the sight thereof to the end of all the earth:

12The leaves thereof *were* fair, and the fruit thereof much, and in it *was* meat for all: the beasts of the field had shadow under it, and the fowls of the heaven dwelt in the boughs thereof, and all flesh was fed of it.

13I saw in the visions of my head upon my bed, and, behold, a watcher and an holy one came down from heaven; **14**He cried aloud, and said thus, Hew down the tree, and cut off his branches, shake off his leaves, and scatter his fruit: let the beasts get away from under it, and the fowls from his branches:

15Nevertheless leave the stump of his roots in the earth, even with a band of iron and brass, in the tender grass of the field; and let it be wet with the dew of heaven, and *let* his portion *be* with the beasts in the grass of the earth:

16Let his heart be changed from man's, and let a beast's heart be given unto him; and let seven times pass over him.

17This matter *is* by the decree of the watchers, and the demand by the word of the holy ones: to the intent that the living may know that the most High ruleth in the kingdom of men, and giveth it to whomsoever he will, and setteth up over it the basest of men.

18This dream I king Nebuchadnezzar have seen. Now thou, O Belteshazzar, declare the interpretation thereof, forasmuch as all the wise *men* of my kingdom are not able to make known unto me the interpretation: but thou *art* able; for the spirit of the holy gods *is* in thee.

19Then Daniel, whose name *was* Belteshazzar, was astonied for one hour, and his thoughts troubled him. The king spake, and said, Belteshazzar, let not the dream, or the interpretation thereof, trouble thee. Belteshazzar answered and said, My lord, the dream *be* to them that hate thee, and the interpretation thereof to thine enemies. **20**The tree that thou sawest, which grew, and was strong, whose height reached unto the heaven, and the sight thereof to all the earth; **21**Whose leaves *were* fair, and the fruit thereof much, and in it *was* meat for all; under which the beasts of the field dwelt, and upon whose branches the fowls of the heaven had their habitation:

22It *is* thou, O king, that art grown and become strong: for thy greatness is grown, and reacheth unto heaven, and thy dominion to the end of the earth. **23**And whereas the king saw a watcher and an holy one coming down from heaven, and saying, Hew the tree down, and destroy it; yet leave the stump of the roots thereof in the earth, even with a band of iron and brass, in the tender grass of the field; and let it be wet with the dew of heaven, and *let* his portion *be* with the beasts of the field, till seven times pass over him;

24This *is* the interpretation, O king, and this *is* the decree of the most High, which is come upon my lord the king: **25**That they shall drive thee from men, and thy dwelling shall be with the beasts of the field, and they shall make thee to eat grass as oxen, and they shall wet thee with the dew of heaven, and seven times shall pass over thee, till thou know that the most High ruleth in the kingdom of men, and giveth it to whomsoever he will. **26**And whereas they commanded to leave the stump of the tree roots; thy kingdom shall be sure unto thee, after that thou shalt have known that the heavens do rule.

27Wherefore, O king, let my counsel be acceptable unto thee, and break off thy sins by righteousness, and thine iniquities by shewing mercy to the poor; if it may be a lengthening of thy tranquillity.

28All this came upon the king Nebuchadnezzar. **29**At the end of twelve months he walked in the palace of the kingdom of

Babylon. **30**The king spake, and said, Is not this great Babylon, that I have built for the house of the kingdom by the might of my power, and for the honour of my majesty? **31**While the word *was* in the king's mouth, there fell a voice from heaven, *saying,* O king Nebuchadnezzar, to thee it is spoken; The kingdom is departed from thee. **32**And they shall drive thee from men, and thy dwelling *shall be* with the beasts of the field: they shall make thee to eat grass as oxen, and seven times shall pass over thee, until thou know that the most High ruleth in the kingdom of men, and giveth it to whomsoever he will.

33The same hour was the thing fulfilled upon Nebuchadnezzar: and he was driven from men, and did eat grass as oxen, and his body was wet with the dew of heaven, till his hairs were grown like eagles' *feathers*, and his nails like birds' *claws*

34And at the end of the days I Nebuchadnezzar lifted up mine eyes unto heaven, and mine understanding returned unto me, and I blessed the most High, and I praised and honoured him that liveth for ever, whose dominion *is* an everlasting dominion, and his kingdom *is* from generation to generation:

35And all the inhabitants of the earth *are* reputed as nothing: and he doeth according to his will in the army of heaven, and *among* the inhabitants of the earth: and none can stay his hand, or say unto him, What doest thou?

36At the same time my reason returned unto me; and for the glory of my kingdom, mine honour and brightness returned unto me; and my counsellers and my lords sought unto me; and I was established in my kingdom, and excellent majesty was added unto me. **37**Now I Nebuchadnezzar praise and extol and honour the King of heaven, all whose works *are* truth, and his ways judgment: and those that walk in pride he is able to abase.

DANIEL CHAPTER FIVE

"And that ye may put difference between holy and unholy, and between unclean and clean." Leviticus 10:10

King Belshazzar is the grandson of King Nebuchadnezzar. His father is Nabonidus, the son of King Nebuchadnezzar. By this time King Nebuchadnezzar is dead and the Babylonian kingdom is in the hands of both King Nabonidus and his son, Belshazzar.

Outside the fortress of Babylon is the Army of the Medes. Since the inhabitants of Babylon considered themselves safe from the enemy army, King Belshazzar sponsors a party. This chapter of Daniel demonstrates what the book of Daniel is all about. It's all about worship and mixing of paganism with the pure worship of the Most High God. The weakening influence in the unification of the sacred with the secular in worship has lasted all these years and is very much alive and evident in the worship of God even today. Mixing the sacred with the profane began in the empire of Babylon and continued under the rule of all the kingdoms which came up after the Babylonian Empire.

King Belshazzar, who was raised at the knee of Daniel, decides to bring in the gold and silver vessels from the "treasure house of his gods". These sacred vessels are those his grandfather had taken from Jerusalem and "placed in the temple of his gods" (Daniel 1:2) Belshazzar arrogantly prompted his quests to drink wine from them. King Nebuchadnezzar had humbled himself before God and accepted His sovereignty, the same cannot be said of his grandson. Apparently he had no respect for sacred things. While the wives, concubines, and guests of the king were drinking wine from the sacred vessels they "praised the gods of gold, and of silver, of brass, of iron, of wood, and of stone" (verse 4), the same idolatry pointed out by the same metals in Daniel chapter two.

Suddenly a bloodless hand appears and begins writing words on the distant plastered wall bringing the fiesta to a screeching halt. The king is very much afraid and immediately demands the presence of all the wise guys and counselors of the kingdom with the promise that:

> "The person who can read and explain the words shew me the interpretation thereof, shall be clothed with scarlet, and *have* a chain of gold about his neck, and shall be the third ruler in the kingdom" (verse 7).

To the king's chagrin none of the wise guys or magicians could explain the writing.

The proud arrogant king became a weak, frail, crying mass with his knees knocking against each other in fear (verse 6). His mother, the queen, heard the uproar and came to her son's aid. She calmed her son and suggested he call for Daniel who historically solved problems like this in the past.

By the time Daniel arrived the frightened king had regained some of his composure and again showed his arrogance by asking Daniel if he was the one he had heard about that could solve the mystery and if he did solve the puzzle he would be greatly rewarded. Needless to say Daniel, in his aged wisdom, boldly put the king in his place by reminding him that he knew who Daniel was and that he also was well aware of the stories that surrounded him and King Nebuchadnezzar. Daniel refused the gifts but said he would tell the king why the hand appeared, what was written, and the meaning of the words.

In Daniel 5:25-28 Daniel said

> "And this *is* the writing that was written, MENE, MENE, TEKEL, UPHARSIN. This *is* the interpretation of the thing: MENE; God hath numbered thy kingdom, and finished it. TEKEL; Thou art weighed in the balances, and art found wanting. PERES; Thy kingdom is divided, and given to the Medes and Persians."

That night the Median Army rerouted the Euphrates River, which ran through the city, and entered the city in the shallow water. The flood gates had been carelessly left open allowing the army to enter the city and take control of it, killing King Belshazzar in the process.

Pride and arrogance has little place in the kingdom of God. A humble and meek obedient spirit, which recognizes and praises the Creator of the universe, is preferred. A portion of Daniel two was fulfilled that evening. The demonstration of gold being followed by silver in the king's dream of Daniel chapter two became a reality. The secular influence of the Babylonians upon the pure gold worship which God had demanded was planted and now the pagan influence of the Medo-Persian empire would take its toll as well, further diluting and polluting true worship. Those pagan influences would spread and grow for centuries.

Though King Belshazzar, and many other people who ruled over God's kingdom, did not accept the Most High God, apparently there were some which did. Five hundred years after Daniel, the Magi come from the east seeking the King which was born in Bethlehem. Were these descendants of the Jewish captives from Nebuchadnezzar's day or were they descendants of the following ruling empires? We don't know. But God has always had His remnant people which sought Him. Are you to be found in that remnant today?

QUESTION: Are you interested in seeking the King?

Give yourself to Him today. Listen to His voice as He daily speaks to you in His Word.

See the **YouTube** for video on **DANIEL CHAPTER FIVE** by Earl Schrock.

DANIEL CHAPTER FIVE (KJV)

1Belshazzar the king made a great feast to a thousand of his lords, and drank wine before the thousand. 2Belshazzar, whiles he tasted the wine, commanded to bring the golden and silver vessels which his father Nebuchadnezzar had taken out of the temple which *was* in Jerusalem; that the king, and his princes, his wives, and his concubines, might drink therein. 3Then they brought the golden vessels that were taken out of the temple of the house of God which *was* at Jerusalem; and the king, and his princes, his wives, and his concubines, drank in them. 4They drank wine, and praised the gods of gold, and of silver, of brass, of iron, of wood, and of stone.

5In the same hour came forth fingers of a man's hand, and wrote over against the candlestick upon the plaister of the wall of the king's palace: and the king saw the part of the hand that wrote. 6Then the king's countenance was changed, and his thoughts troubled him, so that the joints of his loins were loosed, and his knees smote one against another. 7The king cried aloud to bring in the astrologers, the Chaldeans, and the soothsayers. *And* the king spake, and said to the wise *men* of Babylon, Whosoever shall read this writing, and shew me the interpretation thereof, shall be clothed with scarlet, and *have* a chain of gold about his neck, and shall be the third ruler in the kingdom. 8Then came in all the king's wise *men*: but they could not read the writing, nor make known to the king the interpretation thereof. 9Then was king Belshazzar greatly troubled, and his countenance was changed in him, and his lords were astonied.

10*Now* the queen, by reason of the words of the king and his lords, came into the banquet house: *and* the queen spake and said, O king, live for ever: let not thy thoughts trouble thee, nor let thy countenance be changed: 11There is a man in thy kingdom, in whom *is* the spirit of the holy gods; and in the days of thy father light and understanding and wisdom, like the wisdom of the gods, was found in him; whom the king Nebuchadnezzar thy father, the king, *I say*, thy father, made master of the magicians, astrologers, Chaldeans, *and* soothsayers; 12Forasmuch as an excellent spirit, and knowledge, and understanding, interpreting of dreams, and shewing of hard sentences, and dissolving of doubts, were found in the same Daniel, whom the king named Belteshazzar: now let Daniel be called, and he will shew the interpretation.

13Then was Daniel brought in before the king. *And* the king spake and said unto Daniel, *Art* thou that Daniel, which *art* of the children of the captivity of Judah, whom the king my father brought out of Jewry? 14I have even heard of thee, that the spirit of the gods *is* in thee, and *that* light and understanding and excellent wisdom is found in thee. 15And now the wise *men*, the astrologers, have been brought in before me, that they should read this writing, and make known unto me the interpretation thereof: but they could not shew the interpretation of the thing: 16And I have heard of thee, that thou canst make interpretations, and dissolve doubts: now if thou canst read the writing, and make known to me the interpretation thereof, thou shalt be clothed with scarlet, and *have* a chain of gold about thy neck, and shalt be the third ruler in the kingdom.

17Then Daniel answered and said before the king, Let thy gifts be to thyself, and give thy rewards to another; yet I will read the writing unto the king, and make known to him the interpretation. 18O thou king, the most high God gave Nebuchadnezzar thy father a kingdom, and majesty, and glory, and honour: 19And for the majesty that he gave him, all people, nations, and languages, trembled and feared before him: whom he would he slew; and whom he would he kept alive; and whom he would he set up; and whom he would he put down. 20But when his heart was lifted up, and his mind hardened in pride, he was deposed from his kingly throne, and they took his glory from him: 21And he was driven from the sons of men; and his heart was made like the beasts, and his dwelling *was* with the wild asses: they fed him with grass like oxen, and his body was wet with the dew of heaven; till he knew that the most high God ruled in the kingdom of men, and *that* he appointeth over it whomsoever he will. 22And thou his son, O Belshazzar, hast not humbled thine heart, though thou knewest all this; 23But hast lifted up thyself against the Lord of heaven; and they have brought the vessels of his house before thee, and thou, and thy lords, thy wives, and thy concubines, have drunk wine in them; and thou hast praised the gods of silver, and gold, of brass, iron, wood, and stone, which see not, nor hear, nor know: and the God in whose hand thy breath *is*, and whose *are* all thy ways, hast thou not

63

glorified: 24Then was the part of the hand sent from him; and this writing was written.

25And this *is* the writing that was written, MENE, MENE, TEKEL, UPHARSIN. 26This *is* the interpretation of the thing: MENE; God hath numbered thy kingdom, and finished it. 27TEKEL; Thou art weighed in the balances, and art found wanting. 28PERES; Thy kingdom is divided, and given to the Medes and Persians.

29Then commanded Belshazzar, and they clothed Daniel with scarlet, and *put* a chain of gold about his neck, and made a proclamation concerning him, that he should be the third ruler in the kingdom.

30In that night was Belshazzar the king of the Chaldeans slain. 31And Darius the Median took the kingdom, *being* about threescore and two years old.

DANIEL CHAPTER SIX

"He that dwelleth in the secret place of the most High shall abide under the shadow of the Almighty. I will say of the LORD, *He is* my refuge and my fortress: my God; in him will I trust." Psalm 91:1,2

Under the leadership of Darius, the first Median king to rule over God's people after the fall of Babylon, the wise guys, soothsayers, magicians, counselors, and government princes faced the same threatening problem they had experienced before. The threat to them was the prophet Daniel as their immediate supervisor. Under his watchful care, while being the chief counselor for King Nebuchadnezzar, they were unable to get away with any shenanigans that could cause the king to lose a portion of his assets.

Darius was aware of the unfaithfulness of the wise guys and the integrity of Daniel. He wanted to protect his assets from being distributed without his knowledge. His plan was a simple one. He would set three presidents over the affairs of the kingdom and Daniel would be the first. Everyone would again have to answer to Daniel for their expenditures. This did not go well with the rest of the king's cabinet.

I believe the crooked counselors reflected back on the "fiery furnace fiasco" of Daniel chapter three and the wise guys planned to let history repeat itself. This time they tricked the king into signing into a law stating that no person could call on any god, for the next thirty days, except to the king himself (verse 7). His pride was used against him and he agreed with the idea, being told that ALL the counselors had agreed on this. He was not told that Daniel had not been a party to this plan.

The penalty for anyone praying to any other god, other than the king, would be getting tossed into the Lion's den. We are not informed why the king had a den of lions but apparently they served some purpose. The wise guys knew Daniel would not comply with this arrangement and I assume they allowed the ferocious beasts to go without food for a period of time in preparation for the quick, certain, yet humane death of Daniel.

Even though Daniel was informed of the plan, after the petition had been signed, it did not prevent him from communicating with the Most High God, as he did three times a day, on a daily basis. The wise guys planned on this and they set up witnesses to be able to testify before the king against Daniel.

When the king was boldly approached concerning Daniel praying to another god, other than the king, he realized immediately he had been tricked and bamboozled. All the crooked wise guys were pleased to keep informing the king that a law signed by the king could not be retracted. Though the king tried every way possible to get Daniel released, it was to no avail.

When Daniel was thrown into the den of lions the king was there and he said to Daniel,

"Thy God whom thou servest continually, he will deliver thee" (verse 16).

After sealing the entrance covering with his signet ring the king spent the rest of the sleepless night worrying about Daniel.

Though the Bible does not say, I believe the king probably prayed to Daniel's God asking for His protection upon His special servant.

The next morning the king rushed to the den and having the stone removed the king asked:

> "Daniel, O Daniel, servant of the living God, is thy God, whom thou servest continually, able to deliver thee from the lions?" (verse 20).

Then Daniel answered the king with one of the first memory verses that my beautiful two-year-old daughter, Wendi, memorized,

"My God hath sent his angel, and hath shut the lions' mouths" (verse 22).

The king was pleased to hear Daniel's voice and he had him immediately withdrawn from the lion's den.

Apparently the trick the wise guys pulled on King Nebuchadnezzar, in Daniel chapter three, was so well planned and orchestrated, the king could not retaliate against them, even though at the time I'm pretty sure the king realized he had been hoodwinked. His initial anger against them proved that. But apparently when the three Hebrews answered him so crudely, the anger toward the counselors was a springboard that heightened the kings anger against Shadrach, Meshach, and Abednego for their insolence. In chapter three, in the days of King Nebuchadnezzar, the shrewd wise-guys had gotten away with almost murdering Shadrach, Meshach, and Abednego.

But that was not going to be the case with King Darius.

As soon as Daniel was free, the king set into motion his own plan. He gathered all the clever counselors together that had tricked him, along with their families. Without fanfare or delay he had all of them thrown into the den of starving beasts. Verse 24 says,

> "And the lions had the mastery of them, and brake all their bones in pieces or ever they came at the bottom of the den."

Then the king sent out a decree. Verses 26 and 27 says,

> "I make a decree, That in every dominion of my kingdom men tremble and fear before the God of Daniel: for he *is* the living God, and stedfast for ever, and his kingdom *that* which shall not be destroyed, and his dominion *shall be even* unto the end. He delivereth and rescueth, and he worketh signs and wonders in heaven and in earth, who hath delivered Daniel from the power of the lions."

Like King Nebuchadnezzar, King Darius recognized the power of Daniel's God and shared his conviction with all the people in his kingdom. And again, just like with King Nebuchadnezzar, King Darius issued orders of forced worship to the God of heaven (Daniel 3:29). God does not promote forced worship. He wants His people to worship Him voluntarily out of respect and admiration for who He is and what He has done. To understand more of what God has done for us and our dutiful response to Him read Ephesians chapters two and three.

CONCLUSION: What are the lessons to be learned from Daniel chapter six?

(1) God draws a clear line of distinction between the sacred and the profane. It's our responsibility to study and know His Word to realize what those are.

(2) We, God's kingdom, have a responsibility to all we interact with to demonstrate pure integrity. There is no place for dishonesty in His kingdom (Rev. 22:15) even in the smallest of things.

> "He that is faithful in that which is least is faithful also in much: and he that is unjust in the least is unjust also in much." Luke 16:10.

(3) Other people are watching God's children and noticing them. None of us live in a bubble. Our witness to others can draw them to the Savior or away. Our choice 24/7.

(4) In times of stress and calamity, we must maintain our faith in God. It's possible that we may lose our lives in our effort to be faithful, but we must remain strong and know that if that happens we are in good company when we consider the faithful in the Bible which gave all for Christ.

(5) A time of trouble and tribulation is coming. We must live our lives being completely faithful to God now. We cannot wait till the time of trouble comes to develop the type of faith needed to suffer in the name of God. We must live totally dependent on God today.

See **YouTube** for the video on **DANIEL CHAPTER SIX** by Earl Schrock.

DANIEL CHAPTER SIX (KJV)

₁It pleased Darius to set over the kingdom an hundred and twenty princes, which should be over the whole kingdom; ₂And over these three presidents; of whom Daniel *was* first: that the princes might give accounts unto them, and the king should have no damage. ₃Then this Daniel was preferred above the presidents and princes, because an excellent spirit *was* in him; and the king thought to set him over the whole realm. ₄Then the presidents and princes sought to find occasion against Daniel concerning the kingdom; but they could find none occasion nor fault; forasmuch as he *was* faithful, neither was there any error or fault found in him. ₅Then said these men, We shall not find any occasion against this Daniel, except we find *it* against him concerning the law of his God.

₆Then these presidents and princes assembled together to the king, and said thus unto him, King Darius, live for ever. ₇All the presidents of the kingdom, the governors, and the princes, the counsellers, and the captains, have consulted together to establish a royal statute, and to make a firm decree, that whosoever shall ask a petition of any God or man for thirty days, save of thee, O king, he shall be cast into the den of lions. ₈Now, O king, establish the decree, and sign the writing, that it be not changed, according to the law of the Medes and Persians, which altereth not. ₉Wherefore king Darius signed the writing and the decree.

₁₀Now when Daniel knew that the writing was signed, he went into his house; and his windows being open in his chamber toward Jerusalem, he kneeled upon his knees three times a day, and prayed, and gave thanks before his God, as he did aforetime. ₁₁Then these men assembled, and found Daniel praying and making supplication before his God. ₁₂Then they came near, and spake before the king concerning the king's decree; Hast thou not signed a decree, that every man that shall ask *a petition* of any God or man within thirty days, save of thee, O king, shall be cast into the den of lions? The king answered and said, The thing *is* true, according to the law of the Medes and Persians, which altereth not. 13Then answered they and said before the king, That Daniel, which *is* of the children of the captivity of Judah, regardeth not thee, O king, nor the decree that thou hast signed, but maketh his petition three times a day.

14Then the king, when he heard *these* words, was sore displeased with himself, and set *his* heart on Daniel to deliver him: and he laboured till the going down of the sun to deliver him. 15Then these men assembled unto the king, and said unto the king, Know, O king, that the law of the Medes and Persians *is*, That no decree nor statute which the king establisheth may be changed.

16Then the king commanded, and they brought Daniel, and cast *him* into the den of lions. *Now* the king spake and said unto Daniel, Thy God whom thou servest continually, he will deliver thee. 17And a stone was brought, and laid upon the mouth of the den; and the king sealed it with his own signet, and with the signet of his lords; that the purpose might not be changed concerning Daniel. 18Then the king went to his palace, and passed the night fasting: neither were instruments of musick brought before him: and his sleep went from him.

19Then the king arose very early in the morning, and went in haste unto the den of lions. 20And when he came to the den, he cried with a lamentable voice unto Daniel: *and* the king spake and said to Daniel, O Daniel, servant of the living God, is thy God, whom thou servest continually, able to deliver thee from the lions? 21Then said Daniel unto the king, O king, live for ever. 22My God hath sent his angel, and hath shut the lions' mouths, that they have not hurt me: forasmuch as before him innocency was found in me; and also before thee, O king, have I done no hurt. 23Then was the king exceeding glad for him, and commanded that they should take Daniel up out of the den. So Daniel was taken up out of the den, and no manner of hurt was found upon him, because he believed in his God.

24And the king commanded, and they brought those men which had accused Daniel, and they cast *them* into the den of lions, them, their children, and their wives; and the lions had the mastery of them, and brake all their bones in pieces or ever they came at the bottom of the den.

25Then king Darius wrote unto all people, nations, and languages, that dwell in all the earth; Peace be multiplied unto you.

26I make a decree, That in every dominion of my kingdom men tremble and fear before the God of Daniel: for he *is* the living God, and stedfast for ever, and his kingdom *that* which shall not be destroyed, and his dominion *shall be even* unto the end.

27He delivereth and rescueth, and he worketh signs and wonders in heaven and in earth, who hath delivered Daniel from the power of the lions.

28So this Daniel prospered in the reign of Darius, and in the reign of Cyrus the Persian.

DANIEL CHAPTER SEVEN

"Do ye not know that the saints shall judge the world? and if the world shall be judged by you, are ye unworthy to judge the smallest matters? Know ye not that we shall judge angels? how much more things that pertain to this life?" 1 Corinthians 6:2,3

Daniel has a dream. In the dream he sees a large sea being tossed back and forth by the four winds of heaven. As he watches the churning sea four different beasts come up out of the sea, one after the other.

In verses 1 through 8 Daniel sees:

1. A **lion** with two wings of an eagle attached to its back come up out of the sea. As he watches the lion its two wings are torn off, it stands up on its hind legs, and it is given the heart of a man.
2. After the lion Daniel sees a **bear** come up out of the sea. One side of the bear is higher than the other and it has three rib bones in its mouth between its teeth. The bear is told to "Arise, devour much flesh." (The explanation of the tree ribs are revealed in the Old Testament book of Esther.)
3. After the bear, Daniel sees a **leopard** come up out of the sea. The Leopard has four wings and four heads. It is given dominion.

4. The fourth **beast** coming up out of the sea was different than the rest. It was *"dreadful and terrible, and strong exceedingly; and it had great iron teeth: it devoured and brake in pieces, and stamped the residue with the feet of it: and it was diverse from all the beasts that were before it; and it had ten horns."* As Daniel was looking at the ten horns, a little horn grew up amongst them. As the little horn grew, three of the ten horns were uprooted. Daniel notices the little horn has the eyes of a man and a mouth speaking bold things.

In verses 9 through 14 Daniel sees the judgement scene, revealed in Revelation 20, which takes place during the future 1000 years, after the second coming of Jesus **. He watches till the four beasts are destroyed and God's eternal sinless kingdom is forever established.

** Read the eBook or hard copy book "The 3 Visible Advents of Jesus" by Earl B. Schrock from Xlibris.com, Amazon, Barnes and Nobles, etc.

In verses 15 through 18 it's revealed to Daniel that the four beasts he saw coming up out of the sea are actually four kingdoms. These four kingdoms will rule over God's people but in the end they will lose their dominion and His people will be eternally victorious.

It's very interesting to notice in verse seventeen Daniel is told the four beasts come up out of "the earth". What does it mean when at first they come up out of "the sea" (verse three) and then later they come up out of "the earth" (verse seventeen)?

In verses 23 through 27 Daniel's attention is drawn to the fourth beast which has ten horns, iron teeth, and brass toe nails which defeats and violently pounces on "the earth". He notices a little horn which (1) uproots three of the ten horns, (2) speaks great words "against the Most High", (3) persecutes "the saints of the Most High", (4) attempts "to change times and laws", and (5) rules over God's people, His saints, for "a time and times and the dividing of time." In the judgment the little horn's (6) power is taken away and (7) it is destroyed forever. (8) After which God's saints will inherit the kingdom and reign with God in peace forever and ever.

In verse 28 Daniel confesses that even though he was worried about what he saw, he went about his business, keeping these things in his heart.

INTERPRETATION:

The four beasts, or four kingdoms, Daniel saw correspond with the four kingdoms of Daniel chapter two. The four kingdoms which ruled over the "earth" or God's people are Babylon, Medo-Persia, Greece, and assumedly, Rome.

Babylon is represented by the gold head of the statue and the winged lion.

Medo-Persia is represented by the silver upper torso of the image as well as the bear.

Greece is represented by the belly and thigh of brass and the four winged leopard.

Rome is represented by the legs of iron and the dreadful beast with ten horns.

Though there have been many convincing suggestions as to the identity of "the little horn", this author believes it is an enemy of God which is yet to appear during the future coming seven-year tribulation for reasons to be itemized in our discussion on the coming chapters of Daniel 8 through 12 including discussing the "times, time, and dividing of time".

QUESTION: Why is the four empires, which dominated over God's people from the days of King Nebuchadnezzar to the times of the Roman emperors, represented by the metals of Daniel two and the beasts of Daniel seven?

ANSWER: Remember Bible prophecy is ALL ABOUT WORSHIP. Daniel two reveals the empirical sources of the debilitating pagan influences which diluted and polluted the way God desires to be worshipped. Daniel seven helps us to further identify those ruling empires but also provides additional vital information which is necessary to understand and interpret the book of Revelation.

Notice Revelation 13:1,2 John says:

> "And I stood upon the sand of the sea, and saw a beast rise up out of the sea, having seven heads and ten horns, and upon his horns ten crowns, and upon his heads the name of blasphemy. And the beast which I saw was like unto a leopard, and his feet were as the feet of a bear, and his mouth as the mouth of a lion: and the dragon gave him his power, and his seat, and great authority."

In Revelation, while standing on the sand of the beach, the earth, the Apostle John sees one beast rise up out of the sea. This single beast is composed of different parts from the four beasts Daniel saw in chapter seven. It has **seven heads**, **ten horns**, body of a **leopard**, the feet of a **bear**, the mouth of a **lion**, and it gets its authority from the **dragon**.

QUESTION: Who is the dragon this creature gets its authority, power, and life from?

ANSWER: The dragon that gives the beast life and power is Satan, the devil. Revelation 12:9 says:

> "And the great dragon was cast out, that old serpent, called the Devil, and Satan, which deceiveth the whole world."

Notice the artist's concept of this seven headed beast which John sees in Revelation thirteen:

Revelation 13 combination beast from Daniel seven

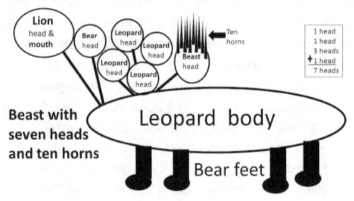

The seven heads of this one beast is made up of the seven heads from the four beasts of Daniel chapter seven. Count them: **Lion**: one head; **Bear**: one head; **Leopard**: four heads; and monster **beast**: one head.

Lion: one = 1
Bear: one = 1
Leopard: four = 4
Beast: one = 1
Total: 7 heads on one beast representing pagan worship mixed with sacred.

QUESTION: Why does the one single beast show up in the book of Revelation made up of different parts of the four beasts of Daniel chapter seven?

ANSWER: The image in Daniel chapter two reveals the historical process by which the pagan religious practices became imbedded in the worship of today. The four kingdoms of Babylon, Medo-Persia, Greece, and Rome each played a role in promoting the pagan religious mindsets that occupy todays religious mindsets. As the metals became less valuable, they also became more durable, until the pagan practices are so impregnated in the religions of the world that the pagan practices are unrecognizable. Some worshippers are determined to defend these pagan practices thinking they are living and worshipping the way God desires, to the point of ignoring and disobeying the written Word of God. They prefer to close their eyes, ears, and minds to defend their own worship.

The combination beast represents all the pagan practices that have infiltrated God's true worship since the days of Daniel. That beast is alive and well in our day and will soon play a major role in the "appointed time of the end".

QUESTION: Why do the four beasts of Daniel chapter seven come out of "the sea" in verse 3, and out of "the earth" in verse 17?

ANSWER: The four beasts coming out of the "sea" refer us back to the days of Daniel as the pagan practices were introduced into the true worship of God from each of the four different kingdoms beginning with Babylon in the days of King Nebuchadnezzar. The four beasts coming out of the "earth" refers us forward to the time of the end when the pagan practices are a normal part of end time worship as practiced worldwide by the people of God. In the future the misguided people of God will bring about forced worship to meet the demands being placed on mankind the world over, during the awful "time of the end'.

Notice the single combination beast of Revelation 13:1,2 comes up out of the sea.

QUESTION: What does water or "sea" represent in the Bible?

ANSWER: Notice Revelation 17:15 says:

> "And he saith unto me, The waters which thou sawest, where the whore sitteth, are peoples, and multitudes, and nations, and tongues."

The "sea" represents people of all nations and tongues. But not just any people. These are people which believe in God, yet refuse to follow Him as He dictates in the Bible just as the "sea" represented the rebellious Israelites in the days of Daniel (Daniel 7:2,3).

Remember, in Bible prophecy:

The "heaven" represents the people of God which serve Him with all their heart, mind, and soul. The "heaven people" serve God 100%.

The "earth" represents people of all nations and tongues which are familiar with the commandments of God, yet refuse to follow Him completely, doing ALL He requires. The "earth people" serve God partially, picking and choosing what they will and will not do.

The "sea people" believe in God yet they refuse to obey Him.

Notice Revelation 21:1 which says "and there was no more sea". This phrase has nothing to do with literal water, it is talking figuratively. Bodies of water have a relaxing calming effect on people. Surely there will be amazing and literal bodies of water in the new earth. But figuratively, there is no "sea" in the new earth because there is no rebellion in the coming glorious, eternal, sinless kingdom. All people will know God and will voluntarily worship Him as He demands. Notice Jeremiah 31:31-34:

> "Behold, the days come, saith the LORD, that I will make a new covenant with the house of Israel, and with the house of Judah: Not according to the covenant that I made with their fathers in the day *that* I took them by the hand to bring them out of the land of Egypt; which my covenant they brake, although I was an husband unto them, saith the LORD: But this *shall be* the covenant that I will make with the house of Israel; After those days, saith the LORD, I will put my law in their inward parts, and write it in their hearts; and will be their God, and they shall be my people. And they shall teach no more every man his neighbour, and every man his brother, saying, Know the LORD: for they shall all know me, from the least of them unto the greatest of them, saith the LORD: for I will forgive their iniquity, and I will remember their sin no more."

Notice also Revelation 12:12 which refers to people of heaven, earth, and sea:

> "Therefore rejoice, *ye* **heavens**, and ye that dwell in them. Woe to the inhabiters of the **earth** and of the **sea**! for the devil is come down unto you, having great wrath, because he knoweth that he hath but a short time."

In the future, just before and during the seven-year tribulation, God will have a people which will worship and honor Him as the Bible says, giving themselves 100% to Him, obeying Him in all He requires. These are called "heaven" people. There is a future time coming when God will block Satan from being able to enter these people's minds and lives because they will be surrounded by the protection of God. They will have "the seal of God" (Revelation 7:3; 9:4). But the "earth" and the "sea" people will not have that protection. When the devil realizes he has lost his influence over the "heaven people" he will turn his diabolical hate toward the "earth" and the "sea" people. Read carefully:

> "Therefore rejoice, *ye* heavens, and ye that dwell in them. **Woe** to the inhabiters of the earth and of the sea! for the devil is come down unto you, having great **wrath**, because he knoweth that he hath but a short time" Revelation 12:12.

QUESTION: How does one prepare themselves to be in the last day group of people called "heaven", those sealed with the "seal of God" (Revelation 7:3; 9:4)?

ANSWER: By surrendering our all to God today, seeking Him with all our hearts, minds, and souls (Jeremiah 29:13; Matthew 22:37), with the desire to give ourselves totally to Him in all we think, say, and do, we prepare ourselves to be in the group of people called "heaven". In the book of Revelation, the "heaven people" make up the group of people known as the "144,000" of Revelation 7:1-8 and 14:1-5. Those who wait to surrender their all to God, till when the time of trouble comes, will be those which will have the most difficult experiences during the coming seven-year great tribulation (Matthew 24:21) since their surrendering is because of duress, not because they voluntarily gave their all to Jesus before the time of trouble began.

Now consider the metals of Daniel two in comparison to Revelation 9:20, 21:

> "And the rest of the men which were not killed by these plagues yet repented not of the works of their hands, that they should not worship devils, and idols of **gold**, and **silver**, and **brass**, and **stone**, and of wood: which neither can see, nor hear, nor walk: Neither repented they of their murders, nor of their sorceries, nor of their fornication, nor of their thefts."

To understand the Book of Revelation in the New Testament a person must first understand the interpretation of the book of Daniel in the Old Testament. All of the book of Revelation will be fulfilled during the soon coming seven-year tribulation and not before.

The intent of the entire book of Revelation is to provide God's last day generation with the information they need just prior to and during, the coming seven-year tribulation, to explain the events taking place around them and to prepare others for that which is coming. People familiar with their Bibles and with the messages of Daniel and Revelation will worship God the way He dictates. They will know their God and what He wants. Up to this point in human history all the prophecies fulfilled in the Bible have been recognized in hindsight. But the book of Revelation prepares God's people for what is coming in the future if they are able to interpret it correctly.

Remember: Bible prophecy: ITS ALL ABOUT WORSHIP.

See the **YouTube** video on **DANIEL CHAPTER SEVEN** by Earl Schrock.

DANIEL CHAPTER SEVEN (KJV)

1In the first year of Belshazzar king of Babylon Daniel had a dream and visions of his head upon his bed: then he wrote the dream, *and* told the sum of the matters. 2Daniel spake and said, I saw in my vision by night, and, behold, the four winds of the heaven strove upon the great sea. 3And four great beasts came up from the sea, diverse one from another. 4The first *was* like a lion, and had eagle's wings: I beheld till the wings thereof were plucked, and it was lifted up from the earth, and made stand upon the feet as a man, and a man's heart was given to it. 5And behold another beast, a second, like to a bear, and it raised up itself on one side, and *it had* three ribs in the mouth of it between the teeth of it: and they said thus unto it, Arise, devour much flesh. 6After this I beheld, and lo another, like a leopard, which had upon the back of it four wings of a fowl; the beast had also four heads; and dominion was given to it. 7After this I saw in the night visions, and behold a fourth beast, dreadful and terrible, and strong exceedingly; and it had great iron teeth: it devoured and brake in pieces, and stamped the residue with the feet of it: and it *was* diverse from all the beasts that *were* before it; and it had ten horns. 8I considered the horns, and, behold, there came up among them another little horn, before whom there were three of the first horns plucked up by the roots: and, behold, in this horn *were* eyes like the eyes of man, and a mouth speaking great things.

9I beheld till the thrones were cast down, and the Ancient of days did sit, whose garment *was* white as snow, and the hair of his head like the pure wool: his throne *was like* the fiery flame, *and* his wheels *as* burning fire. 10A fiery stream issued and came forth from before him: thousand thousands ministered unto him, and ten thousand times ten thousand stood before him: the judgment was set, and the books were opened.

11I beheld then because of the voice of the great words which the horn spake: I beheld *even* till the beast was slain, and his body destroyed, and given to the burning flame. 12As concerning the rest of the beasts, they had their dominion taken away: yet their lives were prolonged for a season and time. 13I saw in the night visions, and, behold, *one* like the Son of man came with the clouds of heaven, and came to the Ancient of days, and they brought him near before him.14And there was given him dominion, and glory, and a kingdom, that all people, nations, and languages, should serve him: his dominion *is* an everlasting dominion, which shall not pass away, and his kingdom *that* which shall not be destroyed.

15I Daniel was grieved in my spirit in the midst of *my* body, and the visions of my head troubled me. 16I came near unto one of them that stood by, and asked him the truth of all this. So he told me, and made me know the interpretation of the things. 17These great beasts, which are four, *are* four kings, *which* shall arise out of the earth. 18But the saints of the most High shall take the kingdom, and possess the kingdom for ever, even for ever and ever.

19Then I would know the truth of the fourth beast, which was diverse from all the others, exceeding dreadful, whose teeth *were of* iron, and his nails *of* brass; *which* devoured, brake in pieces, and stamped the residue with his feet; 20And of the ten horns that *were* in his head, and *of* the other which came up, and before whom three fell; even *of* that horn that had eyes, and a mouth that spake very great things, whose look *was* more stout than his fellows. 21I beheld, and the same horn made war with the saints, and prevailed against them; 22Until the Ancient of days came, and judgment was given to the saints of the most High; and the time came that the saints possessed the kingdom.

23Thus he said, The fourth beast shall be the fourth kingdom upon earth, which shall be diverse from all kingdoms, and shall devour the whole earth, and shall tread it down, and break it in pieces. 24And the ten horns out of this kingdom *are* ten kings *that* shall arise: and another shall rise after them; and he shall be diverse from the first, and he shall subdue three kings. 25And he shall speak *great* words against the most High, and shall wear out the saints of the most High, and think to change times and laws: and they shall be given into his hand until a time and times and the dividing of time. 26But the judgment shall sit, and they shall take away his dominion, to consume and to destroy *it* unto the end. 27And the kingdom and dominion, and the greatness of the kingdom under the whole heaven, shall be given to the people of the saints of the most High, whose kingdom *is* an everlasting kingdom, and all dominions shall serve and obey him.

28Hitherto *is* the end of the matter. As for me Daniel, my cogitations much troubled me, and my countenance changed in me: but I kept the matter in my heart.

DANIEL CHAPTER EIGHT

"When ye therefore shall see the abomination of desolation, spoken of by Daniel the prophet, stand in the holy place, (whoso readeth, let him understand:) Then let them which be in Judaea flee into the mountains." Matthew 24:15,16

The first vision Daniel had, in chapter seven, was in the first year of King Belshazzar. Now the vision for chapter eight is during the king's third year, co-reigning with his father, Nabonidus. In this dream, from Daniel's vantage point, he sees himself in the Shushan palace by the river of Ulai. He sees a ram with two horns, one higher than the other, pushing its way from the east going toward the west, the north, and the south. This ram was running free and was unchallenged, doing whatever it wanted. Notice this ram is moving in all the directions of the compass at once. This should be a clue to us that it is the pagan influence of this animal spreading in all directions and not the animal itself.

Then out of the west comes a male goat which had one huge horn between its eyes. The male goat was furious and he was moving east so fast that his feet did not touch the ground. He approached the ram in such fury that he broke off its two horns, leaving it powerless, and the goat trampled the ram under its feet. Afterwards the goat became so powerful no one could challenge it. Then once the goat got very powerful its single large horn was broken off and four smaller horns grew in its place and the pagan influence of the goat also grew toward the four directions of the compass.

Then from the north a little horn began to grow and it grew to the south, to the east, and to the west. It also grew in all the directions of the compass like the Medo-Persian Empire and the Grecian Empire. It grew very great even to the heavens and it cast some of the host and the stars out of heaven and threw them to the earth and trampled on them. It magnified itself to the prince of the host of heaven and by it the CONTINUAL (daily) was taken away and the holy was cast down. An army of people supported it taking away the CONTINUAL and truth was cast to the ground and it prospered and grew.

(In many Bibles the word "daily" is used instead of the word "perpetual" or "continual")

According to the King James Version of the Bible, verses 13 and 14 say,

> "Then I heard one saint speaking, and another saint said unto that certain *saint* which spake, How long *shall be* the vision *concerning* the daily *sacrifice*, and the transgression of desolation, to give both the sanctuary and the host to be trodden under foot? And he said unto me, Unto two thousand and three hundred days; then shall the sanctuary be cleansed."

In reality, from the original Hebrew, verses 13 and 14 should actually be translated differently. The following is in my own words, since a correct translation is unavailable.

> "Then I heard a holy one speaking to the other holy one which was speaking and he asked,

'How long will be the vision of the continual (perpetual) and the transgression of desolation for the holy and the host to be trampled? And he said to me, unto two thousand and three hundred evenings and mornings then shall the holy be made righteous (justified or vindicated)."

SPECIAL NOTE: In the book of Daniel, the Hebrew word tamid (taw-meed'), Strong's 8548, was incorrectly translated to the word "daily" and then the word "sacrifice" was added because the translators mistakenly reasoned the word "perpetual" or "continual" referred to the perpetual daily sacrifices God established in the book of Moses. They did not understand how the "perpetual" or "continual" could be "taken away". They did not know what was being referred to by the word "tamid". They assumed the word "tamid" of Daniel 8:13 referred to the perpetual evening and morning sacrifice of Exodus 29:38-42, since a "continual" sacrifice could literally be stopped or abandoned. But their assumption has created tremendous misunderstanding for centuries. This little book will reveal what the message of Daniel 8:13; and Daniel 12:11 actually represents, concerning the "perpetual" or "continual" being taken away.

UNDERSTANDING DANIEL 8:14

"Then I heard a holy one speaking to the other holy one which was speaking and he asked, 'How long will be the vision of the perpetual (or continual) and the transgression of desolation for the holy and the host to be trampled? And he said to me, unto two thousand and three hundred evenings and mornings then shall the holy be made righteous (justified or vindicated)." Daniel 8:13,14 in my words.

In Daniel 8:14 the 2,300 days (evenings and mornings) are literal 24 hour days since they are called the 2,300 "evenings and mornings" just as the days of creation week were one evening and one morning each (Genesis one). Also the 2,300 days will be a reality during the time of God's wrath, at the time of the end, when sin has reached its fullest. The 2,300 days also were "shut up" (Daniel 8:26) or sealed or locked so their mystery would not be understood until God was ready to reveal what they truly are, just before the time they would be applied during the seven-year tribulation of 2,520 days.

QUESTION: What was to happen during the 2,300 days, which is a little over 6 years?

ANSWER: During the literal 2,300 days (1) the CONTINUAL will be done away, (2) the "transgression of desolation" will be set up, (3) the "holy" will be disrespected, (4) the "host" or holy people will be trampled underfoot or persecuted, (5) at the end of the 2,300 days the "holy" people, the folks faithful to God, will be vindicated and shown that they made the right choice to be obedient to God in the face of persecution and death.

When the vision was over, Daniel tried to understand the meaning of the vision but could not. Then he heard a man's voice say, "*Gabriel, make this man understand the vision.*" Gabriel approached Daniel and said, "*Understand O son of man this vision refers to **the time of the end**.*" Daniel 8:16,17.

Daniel felt very weak, afraid, and alone. The messenger touched him, strengthening Daniel, then Gabriel continued talking. He said in verse 19:

89

"Behold, I will make thee know what shall be in the last **end** of the indignation: for at the time appointed the **end** *shall be.*"

Gabriel told Daniel that he would explain the vision but that Daniel needed to understand that this vision applies to the very last days of this earth's history, during the time of God's wrath, at the appointed time of the end, way after his life was over.

Gabriel continued by explaining that the Ram represents the kingdom of the Medes and the Persians, while the goat represents the kingdom of Greece. He said the large horn is its first king, which is Alexander the Great, and after his death his kingdom would be divided into four kingdoms. History reveals that that is exactly what happened as Daniel's vision foretold.

It needs to be recognized that a horn represents power. The bigger the horn, or the more horns a creature has, the stronger it is. The one huge goat horn was more powerful than the two smaller horns on the ram. When the ram's horns were broken off it had no strength (Daniel 8:6-8). Plus, it took four new horns to grow in order to match the power of the one large horn which represented Alexander the Great. The more horns, the more power. In Daniel 7 the monster beast has ten horns. Then one Little Horn comes up making it have 11 individual horns. But 3 of the ten horns give their power over to the Little Horn making it four allied horns against 7 individual horns making the Little Horn Power the strongest.

Verses 23 to 25 are dedicated to explaining more about the Little Horn Power. Gabriel says that during the last days, when sin has reached it fullness, a fierced face king which understands dark sentences will arise. He will be powerful but not in his own power. He will prosper and practice and will destroy the mighty and holy people and magnify himself to the Prince of princes. He will then be broken, but not by a human hand.

"And through his policy also he shall cause craft to prosper in his hand; and he shall magnify *himself* in his heart, and by peace shall destroy many: he shall also stand up against the Prince of princes; but he shall be broken without hand." Daniel 8:25.

Who is the Prince of princes?

"The God of our fathers raised up Jesus, whom ye slew and hanged on a tree. Him hath God exalted with his right hand *to be* a Prince and a Saviour, for to give repentance to Israel, and forgiveness of sins." Acts 5:30,31.

Jesus is the Prince of princes. The future coming end time Little Horn Power will challenge Jesus, but he will be partially successful in his attempt, but he will be broken in the end.

In verse 26 Gabriel says,

"And the vision of the evening and the morning which was told *is* true: wherefore shut thou up the vision; for it *shall be* for many days."

Gabriel, thus God, assures Daniel that "the 2,300 evening and morning" prophecy will take place just as he was told, but that he was to "shut up" the vision because it would take place way in the future. The meaning of the vision would be "shut up" or sealed, so it would remain a mystery until the very time of the end when it would be a reality. Many are the current interpretations of verse fourteen but it is not to be correctly identified until the end time. Daniel fell ill after the vision and he could find no one who could explain it.

CONCLUSION: Daniel chapter eight gives more information which helps us further understand the dream of King Nebuchadnezzar in Daniel chapter two and the vision of Daniel in chapter seven. **Medo-Persia** is represented by (1) the shoulders of silver, (2) the lopsided bear, and (3) the ram. The empire of **Greece** is represented by (1) the belly of brass, (2) the four headed leopard, and (3) the furious goat.

We also have more information concerning the Little Horn of Daniel seven and eight. It will come up at the end of time, during the appointed time of the end, during the time of God's wrath. It will be instrumental is doing away with the CONTINUAL or perpetual (the daily) and will bring about "the abomination of desolation". It will be powerful and popular and will be instrumental in the persecution against God's people, even to the point of challenging the Prince of princes, which is Jesus Himself.

In Isaiah 9:6 Jesus is called the Prince of peace. Acts 5:31 says Jesus is our Prince and our Savior. Revelation 1:5 says Jesus is the Prince of the kings of the earth.

All the things mentioned above will take place during the 2,300 literal days which takes up a huge portion of the 2,520 days, or seven-year, tribulation. Daniel chapter eight must be considered as a whole. Daniel 8:14 does not and cannot stand alone. That time period cannot be put just anywhere a person chooses. God has a specific time for it to begin and we will discover that beginning point when we study Daniel chapter twelve.

See the **YouTube** video on **DANIEL CHAPTER EIGHT** by Earl Schrock.

DANIEL CHAPTER EIGHT (KJV)

1In the third year of the reign of king Belshazzar a vision appeared unto me, *even unto* me Daniel, after that which appeared unto me at the first. 2And I saw in a vision; and it came to pass, when I saw, that I *was* at Shushan *in* the palace, which *is* in the province of Elam; and I saw in a vision, and I was by the river of Ulai. 3Then I lifted up mine eyes, and saw, and, behold, there stood before the river a ram which had *two* horns: and the *two* horns *were* high; but one *was* higher than the other, and the higher came up last. 4I saw the ram pushing westward, and northward, and southward; so that no beasts might stand before him, neither *was there any* that could deliver out of his hand; but he did according to his will, and became great.

5And as I was considering, behold, an he goat came from the west on the face of the whole earth, and touched not the ground: and the goat *had* a notable horn between his eyes. 6And he came to the ram that had *two* horns, which I had seen standing before the river, and ran unto him in the fury of his power. 7And I saw him come close unto the ram, and he was moved with choler against him, and smote the ram, and brake his two horns: and there was no power in the ram to stand before him, but he cast him down to the ground, and stamped upon him: and there was none that could deliver the ram out of his hand. 8Therefore the he goat waxed very great: and when he was strong, the great horn was broken; and for it came up four notable ones toward the four winds of heaven.

9And out of one of them came forth a little horn, which waxed exceeding great, toward the south, and toward the east, and toward the pleasant *land.* 10And it waxed great, *even* to the host of heaven; and it cast down *some* of the host and of the stars to the ground, and stamped upon them. 11Yea, he magnified *himself* even to the prince of the host, and by him the daily *sacrifice* was taken away, and the place of his sanctuary was cast down. 12And an host was given *him* against the daily *sacrifice* by reason of transgression, and it cast down the truth to the ground; and it practised, and prospered. 13Then I heard one saint speaking, and another saint said unto that certain *saint* which spake, How long *shall be* the vision *concerning* the daily *sacrifice*, and the transgression of desolation, to give both the sanctuary and the host to be trodden under foot? 14And he said unto me, Unto two thousand and three hundred days; then shall the sanctuary be cleansed.

15And it came to pass, when I, *even* I Daniel, had seen the vision, and sought for the meaning, then, behold, there stood before me as the appearance of a man. 16And I heard a man's voice between *the banks of* Ulai, which called, and said, Gabriel, make this *man* to understand the vision. 17So he came near where I stood: and when he came, I was afraid, and fell upon my face: but he said unto me, Understand, O son of man: for at the time of the end *shall be* the vision. 18Now as he was speaking with me, I was in a deep sleep on my face toward the ground: but he touched me, and set me upright. 19And he said, Behold, I will make thee know what shall be in the last end of the indignation: for at the time appointed the end *shall be*. 20The ram which thou sawest having *two* horns *are* the kings of Media and Persia. 21And the rough goat *is* the king of Grecia: and the great horn that *is* between his eyes *is* the first king. 22Now that being broken, whereas four stood up for it, four kingdoms shall stand up out of the nation, but not in his power.23And in the latter time of their kingdom, when the transgressors are come to the full, a king of fierce countenance, and understanding dark sentences, shall stand up. 24And his power shall be mighty, but not by his own power: and he shall destroy wonderfully, and shall prosper, and practise, and shall destroy the mighty and the holy people. 25And through his policy also he shall cause craft to prosper in his hand; and he shall magnify *himself* in his heart, and by peace shall destroy many: he shall also stand up against the Prince of princes; but he shall be broken without hand.

26And the vision of the evening and the morning which was told *is* true: wherefore shut thou up the vision; for it *shall be* for many days. 27And I Daniel fainted, and was sick *certain* days; afterward I rose up, and did the king's business; and I was astonished at the vision, but none understood *it*.

DANIEL CHAPTER NINE

"Sing unto the LORD, all the **earth**; shew forth from day to day his salvation. Declare his glory among the heathen; his marvellous works among all nations. Fear before him, all the **earth**: the world also shall be stable, that it be not moved. Let the heavens be glad, and let the **earth** rejoice: and let *men* say among the nations, The LORD reigneth. Let the sea roar, and the fulness thereof: let the fields rejoice, and all that *is* therein. Then shall the trees of the wood sing out at the presence of the LORD, because he cometh to judge the **earth**." 1 Chronicles 16:23,24; 30-33

The "realm of the Chaldeans" and the "earth" are referring to the same people or territory.

"In the first year of Darius the son of Ahasuerus, of the seed of the Medes, which was made king over the realm of the Chaldeans." Daniel 9:1

EARTH!! What does the word "EARTH" apply to in Bible prophecy? Daniel 2:39 says:

"And after thee shall arise another kingdom inferior to thee, and another third kingdom of brass, which shall bear rule over all the earth."

And Daniel 4:22:

"It *is* thou, O king, that art grown and become strong: for thy greatness is grown, and reacheth unto heaven, and thy dominion to the end of the earth."

Daniel told King Nebuchadnezzar that he would rule over all the earth and so would the kingdoms that followed him. But history reveals that none of these kings ever ruled over all the earth when referring of this globe; our planet. King Nebuchadnezzar, ruler of Babylon, nor the other kings of the three following empires of Daniel chapter two, were as large in geographical ownership as some of other the nations of the world, not mentioned in the book of Daniel. So what or who does the word "earth" apply to?

Daniel 9:2 provides us with the answer. It says:

"In the first year of Darius the son of Ahasuerus, of the seed of the Medes, which was made king over the realm of the Chaldeans."

The "earth" in the book of Daniel, in most cases, refers to the "realm of the Chaldeans".

What or who was Nebuchadnezzar, the Chaldean, in charge over? Notice Daniel 4:35:

"All the **peoples of the earth** are regarded as nothing. He does as he pleases with the powers of heaven and **the peoples of the earth**. No one can hold back his hand or say to him: "What have you done?"

Who are the "peoples of the earth"? Notice Psalm 98:4-6:

> "Make a joyful noise unto the LORD, **all the earth**: make a loud noise, and rejoice, and sing praise. Sing unto the LORD with the harp; with the harp, and the voice of a psalm. With trumpets and sound of cornet make a joyful noise before the LORD, the King."

The "peoples of the earth" or the "**earth people**" are all the people who make up the "invisible church" from around the globe; the kingdom of God. Anyone and everyone which believes in the Creator God falls into the category of the "earth people".

DANIEL 9:2-6

In 605 BCE King Nebuchadnezzar attacked the tribe of Judah and he carried off many people to Babylon. After they arrived in Babylon God sent them messages by way of (via) letters from the prophet Jeremiah.

When Daniel was in his eighties he was reading the letters sent to Babylon by the prophet Jeremiah. While he was reading the letters he made an important timely discovery. In Jeremiah 29:1-9 God tells the captured people of Israel to settle in where they have been taken. They are to build houses, plant gardens, and enlarge their families because they are going to be there for a long time. Then in verse ten God says:

> "For thus saith the LORD, That after seventy years be accomplished at Babylon I will visit you, and perform my good word toward you, in causing you to return to this place."

This discovery must have filled Daniel's heart with joy. Even though he had been taken away from home at an early age, the desire to return, for himself and his fellow country men and women was a wonderful dream of hope they all shared. Now Daniel realized the seventy years, as spoken of by Jeremiah, was almost complete.

QUESTION: Why seventy (70) years for the children of Israel to be captives in Babylon?

Notice 2 Chronicle 36:20,21:

> "And them that had escaped from the sword carried he away to Babylon; where they were servants to him and his sons until the reign of the kingdom of Persia: To fulfil the word of the LORD by the mouth of Jeremiah, until the land had enjoyed her sabbaths: *for* as long as she lay desolate she kept sabbath, to fulfil threescore and ten years."

We are told the reason God sent the tribe of Judah into captivity for seventy years was because the children of Israel had not kept the Sabbath Years, for the land, holy as God had told them to.

QUESTION: What is a Sabbath year? Notice Leviticus 25:3,4:

> "Six years thou shalt sow thy field, and six years thou shalt prune thy vineyard, and gather in the fruit thereof; But in the seventh year shall be a sabbath of rest unto the land, a sabbath for the LORD: thou shalt neither sow thy field, nor prune thy vineyard."

In Leviticus 25 God specifically told the children of Israel that once they had entered the promised land they were to work the ground for six years but on the seventh year they were to let the ground rest. Verses 1-7 speaks very clearly that they were not to plow, or plant, or harvest as they had done during the six previous years of farming. They were to let the land alone to have its Sabbath rest. God promised them He would take care of them during that time, if only they would trust Him. This they failed to do. Apparently the children of Israel had failed to give the land the Sabbath year rest God demanded. So the children of Judah were sent into captivity for 70 years, one year for each Sabbath year not honored.

LET'S DO SOME MATH!

QUESTION: If the children of Israel had neglected to keep or honor 70 of the seventh years as a Sabbath of rest, how many years in total had they disobeyed God?

70 Sabbath years times 7 years = 490 years. AS: 70 Sabbath
$$\begin{array}{r} \text{years} \\ \times\ 7\ \text{years} \\ \hline 490\ \text{years} \end{array}$$

The children of Israel had disobeyed God and failed to trust Him for 490 years of defiance.

Daniel 9:7-14

In Daniel 9:7-14 Daniel prays a prayer of contrition. In this beautiful prayer, Daniel asks for God's forgiveness and confesses for all the people in disregarding God's commands. Daniel mentions the sins the children of Israel committed against God by not obeying the law of Moses.

What is the specific part of the law of Moses the children of Israel disobeyed?

And what is the punishment for that disobedience?

Notice Leviticus 26:14-16: God said:

> "But if ye will not hearken unto me, and will not do all these commandments; And if ye shall despise my statutes, or if your soul abhor my judgments, so that ye will not do all my commandments, *but* that ye break my covenant: I also will do this unto you."

Then Leviticus 26:32-35:

> "And I will bring the land into desolation: and your enemies which dwell therein shall be astonished at it. And I will scatter you among the heathen, and will draw out a sword after you: and your land shall be desolate, and your cities waste. Then shall the land enjoy her sabbaths, as long as it lieth desolate, and ye *be* in your enemies' land; *even* then shall the land rest, and enjoy her sabbaths. As long as it lieth desolate it shall rest; because it did not rest in your sabbaths, when ye dwelt upon it."

Daniel was very familiar with the law of Moses and for this he earnestly prayed that God would forgive the past sins of his people for disobeying Him in not keeping the law of Moses in regards to the seventh Sabbath yearly rest He demanded.

Daniel 9:15-19

In Daniel 9:15-19 Daniel humbly pleads for God to remember the people, His people, His holy city, His Jerusalem, His mountain, and remember they have suffered these past seventy years as no other peoples have and that they have paid the penalty for their sins as He established. Daniel pleads earnestly for God's mercy. Verse 19 reads:

> "O Lord, hear; O Lord, forgive; O Lord, hearken and do; defer not, for thine own sake, O my God: for thy city and thy people are called by thy name."

Daniel 9:20-23

During this prayer Daniel uses a number of terms to describe God's people, **"the peoples of the earth"**. He names God's people as: the men of Judah, the people of Jerusalem, all Israel, your people, your city Jerusalem, your holy mountain, your desolate sanctuary, the city that bears your name, your city, your people, my people Israel, and His holy mountain. Even though some of these terms can be applied to physical geographical locations; they are also applied to the people of God, His kingdom, not only in Daniel's day, but in our day as well.

Recall the vision of King Nebuchadnezzar in Daniel chapter two. In the vision the king sees a stone that is cut out of the mountain. What is the mountain the kingdom stone is cut out of that destroys the pagan image? That mountain was none other than Mt. Zion, the mountain of God, the Israelites in the days of Jesus. Jesus is from the Israelite people which God established and developed beginning with one man, Abraham (Genesis 12). Jesus is the Rock, the chief corner stone (1 Peter 2:4-9), that was cut out of that mountain, Mt. Zion, and from Him the kingdom of God grew starting as a small stone, hanging on a cruel cross, to the point of enveloping this entire planet, creating the kingdom of God that is alive and well today. Mt. Zion, the mountain that filled the entire earth, since the days of Jesus, is not only a place in the Palestinian region, it is also a people; an earth people, the people of God which are spread around this globe in every continent, nation, tongue, and people which accept Jesus Christ as their personal Saviour: the kingdom of God.

(Learn more about the kingdom of God in an eBook titled: "The Kingdom of Heaven and the Kingdom of God" by Earl Schrock from Xlibris.com, Amazon, Barnes and Nobles, etc.)

God's promise to Abraham has been fulfilled. God told Abraham, Isaac, and Jacob they would be the fathers of **many nations**, not just the nation of Israel. People of very nation around the world, which accept and follower Jesus Christ, are Mt. Zion, His kingdom.

Notice Galatians 3:26-29:

> "For ye are all the children of God by faith in Christ Jesus. For as many of you as have been baptized into Christ have put on Christ. There is neither Jew nor Greek, there is neither bond nor free, there is neither male nor female: for ye are all one in Christ Jesus. And if ye *be* Christ's, then are ye Abraham's seed, and heirs according to the promise."

Daniel's desire is for God to forgive His people, His holy mountain, and let them return to their country. As he is praying the angel Gabriel appears to him. Verses 22 and 23 read:

"And he informed *me*, and talked with me, and said, O Daniel, I am now come forth to give thee skill and understanding. At the beginning of thy supplications the commandment came forth, and I am come to shew *thee*; for thou *art* greatly beloved: therefore understand the matter, and consider the vision."

Then the angel Gabriel fills Daniel's heart with hope. Daniel's original prayer plea was for his people to be forgiven and allowed to go back home. Gabriel tells Daniel his people will be able to go back home in 70 weeks of time. Notice the following:

Daniel 9:24

"Seventy weeks are determined upon thy people and upon thy holy city, to finish the transgression, and to make an end of sins, and to make reconciliation for iniquity, and to bring in everlasting righteousness, and to seal up the vision and prophecy, and to anoint the most Holy."

From Daniel's perspective he may have thought God was going to release the children of Israel in 490 days (70 literal weeks is 490 literal days) which is about a year and a half from the time of the prayer of Daniel nine. That would have filled his heart with hope. When Cyrus, King of Persia, gave the freedom decree in 538 BCE, (Ezra 1:1-4) Daniel might have figured the 70 years were completed. The first year of Darius, King of the Medes (Daniel 9:1) and the first year of Cyrus, King of the Persians (Ezra 1:1) is the same, 538 or 539 BCE. And at that time some of the people did return to the promised land.

Daniel 9:24-27

""Seventy weeks are determined upon thy people and upon thy holy city, to finish the transgression, and to make an end of sins, and to make reconciliation for iniquity, and to bring in everlasting righteousness, and to seal up the vision and prophecy, and to anoint the most Holy. Know therefore and understand, *that* from the going forth of the commandment to restore and to build Jerusalem unto the Messiah the Prince *shall be* seven weeks, and threescore and two weeks: the street shall be built again, and the wall, even in troublous times. And after threescore and two weeks shall Messiah be cut off, but not for himself: and the people of the prince that shall come shall destroy the city and the sanctuary; and the end thereof *shall be* with a flood, and unto the end of the war desolations are determined. And he shall confirm the covenant with many for one week: and in the midst of the week he shall cause the sacrifice and the oblation to cease, and for the overspreading of abominations he shall make *it* desolate, even until the consummation, and that determined shall be poured upon the desolate."

So what did the angel Gabriel mean with the entire Daniel nine vision he gave to Daniel?

What is the 70 weeks all about in reference to the entire prophecy?

As in all things, hindsight is 20/20. We always understand more as we look back as opposed to when we look forward, especially when it comes to Bible prophecy. God has His particular appointed time for all things to take place and they will always be spot on. We cannot fulfil scripture by assigning time periods to random events they were not meant, planned, or timed for. But we humans, in an attempt to solve all the mysteries of the Bible, applying them to our own time period of life, often make that mistake.

For example, Paul misunderstood when the world would end. He thought it would be in his day. In 1 Corinthians 7:1-9 and 25-31 he encourages people not to marry, to be like him, since the time is short. But he adds, it's not a sin to marry if they wanted to. God did not correct him with this misunderstanding that the end of the age was during his lifetime.

John, the disciple of Jesus, misunderstood when the world would end; he thought it would end in his day also. He said in 1 John 2:18:

> "Little children, it is the last time: and as ye have heard that antichrist shall come, even now are there many antichrists; whereby we know that it is the last time."

We should not feel bad if we have done the same. Mankind has been guilty of guessing or trying to put a time or event on the prophecies of God in relation to the day in which they live since the prophecies were made public. Many have tried mathematical equations, scientific data, and even historical events to explain Bible prophecy and most of them have been inaccurate in revealing the correct interpretation of Bible prophecy or the timing for the end of the world. The ONLY way to interpret Bible prophecy and to get the correct understanding of it is from the Bible and the Bible only. History books, internet, and local and world news will always fail in revealing Biblical truth, especially prophecy.

QUESTION: What does the seventy-week prophecy of Daniel 9:24-27 point to?

One key to understanding this prophecy is to apply the "day for a year" interpretation as God did with the children of Israel. God told the Israelites, fresh out of the land of Egypt, to go into Canaan, and He would be with them and fight for them. They refused to trust Him. After forty days of spying out the land, ten of the twelve spies doubted and they caused the entire community to doubt God (Numbers 13). Because of this doubt, for every day they were in the land as spies, God made them serve one year in the wilderness: a day for a year as per Numbers 14:34:

> "After the number of the days in which ye searched the land, *even* forty days, each day for a year, shall ye bear your iniquities, *even* forty years, and ye shall know my breach of promise."

The day for a year principle is used in considering the time prophecy of Daniel 9:24-27. If we take 70 X 7 we get 490. When using the day for a year principle, that comes out to 490 years. From the time the prophecy began until it was completed would be four hundred and ninety years of history.

Four hundred and ninety years. Does the number 490 sound familiar? When we say "four hundred and ninety years" that should take our attention back to our previous discussion of Daniel nine verses two thru six. Remember the discussion about the Sabbath year? The reason the children of Israel were in Babylonian captivity for 70 years is because they had refused to recognize 70 of God's Sabbath years. Since there are 7 years in each week of years, then 7 X 70 = 490 literal years. The children of Israel had disobeyed God for 490 years, and now, according to the prophecy of Daniel nine, He is giving them another 490 years of grace, the same amount of time the Israelites disobeyed God with the seventh year annual Sabbath for the land to rest in the days before Daniel, to turn from their evil ways.

All Bible time prophecies have two points of interest. There is the beginning point of time and the ending point of time. When either of these two points of time are known, then the other can be realized. When we consider the past fulfilled Bible time prophecies we are able to see their beginning and ending points in hindsight. The same is with the 70-week prophecy of Daniel nine.

Let's think rationally for a moment concerning the 70-week prophecy of Daniel chapter nine. Looking at it on the back side, from Daniel's perspective, when did the prophecy begin? He may have thought the prophecy began within two years of the Medo-Persian empire taking over Babylon. But time revealed that that was not the case. Apparently nobody discovered the real meaning of the 70-week prophecy until our day. Thus the 70-week prophecy is really only understood in hindsight, 20/20.

So the 70-week prophecy of Daniel chapter nine was lost to history from Daniel's day to ours. The only people, before the Bible was made public, who would have tripped over it would have been those people which had access to the temple scrolls. And even then, what kind of sense could they have made of it. No, this prophecy was only to be recognized as satisfied on the front end of history, long after it had been fulfilled. Surely, if any person, during those five centuries, before Christ, would have had an interest in this prophecy, it would have lost its importance during the generations that followed them.

Let's do the same as previously advised. Let's use hindsight to determine the fulfilling of the seventy-week time prophecy of Daniel chapter nine. There are clues that are presented that only we, in our day, can clearly and positively identify in this prophecy. First, let's reread the prophecy before we list the clues: Daniel 9:24-27:

"Seventy weeks are determined upon thy people and upon thy holy city, to finish the transgression, and to make an end of sins, and to make reconciliation for iniquity, and to bring in everlasting righteousness, and to seal up the vision and prophecy, and to anoint the most Holy. Know therefore and understand, *that* from the going forth of the commandment to restore and to build Jerusalem unto the Messiah the Prince *shall be* seven weeks, and threescore and two weeks: the street shall be built again, and the wall, even in troublous times. And after threescore and two weeks shall Messiah be cut off, but not for himself: and the people of the prince that shall come shall destroy the city and the sanctuary; and the end thereof *shall be* with a flood, and unto the end of the war desolations are determined. And he shall confirm the covenant with many for one week: and in the midst of the week he shall cause the sacrifice and the oblation to cease, and for the overspreading of abominations he shall make *it* desolate, even until the consummation, and that determined shall be poured upon the desolate."

Clues to solving the beginning of the seventy-week prophecy, we:

1. Need a time when a decree went out to rebuild and restore Jerusalem (verse 25).
2. Need a time when the "most holy" is anointed (verse 24).

3. Need a time for the arrival of the Messiah, the Prince (verse 25).
4. Need a time when the Messiah is "cut off" or killed (verse 26).

Let's begin with number two and three above? When was the "most holy" anointed or when did the Messiah, the Prince, arrive? According to Mark 1:9-11 Jesus was anointed by the Father and the Holy Spirit on the day of His baptism.

> "And it came to pass in those days, that Jesus came from Nazareth of Galilee, and was baptized of John in Jordan. And straightway coming up out of the water, he saw the heavens opened, and the Spirit like a dove descending upon him: And there came a voice from heaven, *saying*, Thou art my beloved Son, in whom I am well pleased."

Historically Jesus was baptized by John in 27 AD. So we have the answer to numbers 2 and 3 above. After His baptism, Jesus taught for 3 ½ years then died bringing us to 31 ADE. So now we have the answer to number 4. So what do we do with these numbers?

Notice the prophecy. It said in Daniel 9 verses 25 and 26:

> "Know therefore and understand, *that* from the going forth of the commandment to restore and to build Jerusalem unto the Messiah the Prince *shall be* seven weeks, and threescore and two weeks: the street shall be built again, and the wall, even in troublous times. And after threescore and two weeks shall Messiah be cut off, but not for himself."

A single score of weeks is 20 weeks. Threescore weeks is 60 weeks. Seven weeks plus sixty weeks plus 2 weeks is 69 weeks. Sixty-nine weeks' times 7 days per week equals 483 days or 483 days of years, or 483 years. So something had to happen 483 years before the Messiah was baptized to begin the prophecy on the front side of Daniel's vision. Let's do the math: 27 ADE

       -483 years

       457 BCE

So what happened in 457 BCE. For this answer let's consider another clue in the prophecy itself: Notice verse 25 again:

> "Know therefore and understand, *that* from the going forth of the commandment to restore and to build Jerusalem unto the Messiah the Prince *shall be* seven weeks, and threescore and two weeks: the street shall be built again, and the wall, even in troublous times."

Where in the Bible does it talk about a commandment to restore and rebuild Jerusalem? Notice in the book of Ezra there are three different decrees given in scripture for the children of Israel to return to Jerusalem from Babylon.

1. 537 or 538 BCE by King Cyrus found in Ezra 1:2-4.
2. 519 BCE by Darius I Hystaspes (Not Darius the Mede) Ezra 6:1-12.
3. 457 BCE by Artaxerxes I in Ezra 7:11-26.

All three of these kings are mentioned in Ezra 6:14:

> "And the elders of the Jews builded, and they prospered through the prophesying of Haggai the prophet and Zechariah the son of Iddo.

And they builded, and finished *it*, according to the commandment of the God of Israel, and according to the commandment of Cyrus, and Darius, and Artaxerxes king of Persia."

We have two ways to pinpoint when the 70-week prophecy began. (1) Notice from our math, considering the baptism of Jesus and subtracting 483 years, we came to 457 BCE for Daniel's 70-week prophecy to begin. (2) Also in the Bible and historical records, we realize that Artaxerxes issued a decree for the children of Israel to return to rebuild Jerusalem in 457 BCE. But is there another way to determine if the date of 457 BCE is accurate? Yes, there is!

Notice how the first 69 weeks are divided into two different time sections in verse 25.

"*shall be* seven weeks, and threescore and two weeks"

Why did God divide the seventy weeks into 7 weeks, 62 weeks, and finally 1 week in verse 27?

It's because our God is sssooo smart. The reason God started this time prophecy with a seven-week time period is because He wanted to give an extra clue that only someone familiar with His Sabbath years of rest could truly understand.

Earlier we discussed the Sabbath year of rest God established in Leviticus 25:1-7. But that is not all God established in Leviticus 25. He also established the Jubilee Calendar revealing the timing for the very important year of Jubilee for His people.

It works like this: Every seventh year is a Sabbath year of rest for the land, and thus for the people also. Then God said after seven Sabbath years, 7 years' times 7 Sabbath years, the land,

and the people, are to have a special rest during the following year of Jubilee. The year of Jubilee would be the next year after the seventh Sabbath year which is the 49th year. So the fiftieth year would be a year of Jubilee. Realize that the 50th year of Jubilee from the previous Jubilee Calendar cycle would also be the first year of the next Jubilee calendar or Jubilee cycle. It would look like this on a calendar:

Seven Sabbath **years in a row**

1	2	3	4	5	6	7
1	2	3	4	5	6	7
	2	3	4	5	6	7
	2	3	4	5	6	7
1	2	3	4	5	6	7
1	2	3	4	5	6	7
1	2	3	4	5	6	7

Year of Jubilee

Sabbath Number 49

The 50th year is the next 1st year ...the year of Jubilee!!!!

QUESTION: Why is it important to understand the layout of the Jubilee Calendar?

ANSWER: It's important to understand how the year of Jubilee is calculated because of the huge important clue God gave when the 70-week prophecy of Daniel nine was to begin. The reason God divided the sixty-nine weeks into seven weeks and sixty-two weeks, to lead up to the time the Messiah was baptized or anointed, was because He wanted His earth people to understand that the decree to begin the 70-week prophecy must be decreed on a Jubilee year. Of the three different decrees or commands to "restore and rebuild Jerusalem" in the book of Ezra, the only one that is given on a Jubilee year is the date of 457 BCE. (By the way, the next Jubilee year for us is the year 2043).

So: in a nutshell. The seventy-week prophecy began on a Jubilee year in 457 BCE. The Messiah was baptized sixty-nine weeks of years later in 27 BCE. But the prophecy does not stop there. It also says in verses 26 and 27:

> "Messiah be cut off, but not for himself... And he shall confirm the covenant with many for one week: and in the midst of the week he shall cause the sacrifice and the oblation to cease."

Jesus was baptized 27 AD, the beginning of the 70th week. He died 3 ½ years later in the middle of the seventieth week at 31 ADE. Three and a half years later, in 34 ADE Steven was stoned (Acts 6,7) as a martyr, killed by the Jewish religious leaders, because he believed in Jesus as the Messiah. Thus the 70-week prophecy was completed in 34 ADE. 457 BCE to 34 ADE entails the entire seventy-week prophecy.

What does it mean when verse 27 says?

> "and in the midst of the week he shall cause the sacrifice and the oblation to cease."

When Jesus died in the middle of the 70th week, He fulfilled the requirements of the ceremonial law and the ceremonial Sabbaths found in Leviticus 23 for a blood sacrifice. Jesus is the "lamb of God that takes away the sins of the world" (John 1:29). The ceremonial Sabbaths of Leviticus 23 could fall on any day of the week, including the 7th.

Hebrews 9:22 says:

"And almost all things are by the law purged with blood; and without shedding of blood is no remission."

The blood of Jesus dying on the cross is where type met antitype. All the Old Testament ceremonies and feast Sabbaths pointing to the Messiah, which demanded a blood sacrifice, were fulfilled in Christ Jesus. He said in Matthew 5:17:

"Think not that I am come to destroy the law, or the prophets: I am not come to destroy, but to fulfil."

Notice what Paul says about the ceremonial law in Colossians 2:6-17:

"As ye have therefore received Christ Jesus the Lord, so walk ye in him: Rooted and built up in him, and stablished in the faith, as ye have been taught, abounding therein with thanksgiving. Beware lest any man spoil you through philosophy and vain deceit, after the tradition of men, after the rudiments of the world, and not after Christ. For in him dwelleth all the fulness of the Godhead bodily. And ye are complete in him, which is the head of all principality and power: In whom also ye are circumcised with the circumcision made without hands, in putting off the body of the sins of the flesh by the circumcision of Christ: Buried with him in baptism, wherein also ye are risen with him through the faith of the operation of God, who hath raised him from the dead. And you, being dead in your sins and the uncircumcision of your flesh, hath he quickened together with him, having forgiven you all trespasses; Blotting out the handwriting of ordinances that was against us, which was contrary to us, and took it out of the way, nailing it to his cross; *And* having spoiled principalities and powers, he made a shew of them openly, triumphing over them in it. Let no man therefore judge you in meat, or in drink, or in respect of an holyday, or of the new moon, or of the sabbath *days*: Which are a shadow of things to come; but the body *is* of Christ."

I must advise you at this point. Do not confuse the seventh day Sabbath of the week with the ceremonial Sabbaths of Leviticus 23. The seventh-day Sabbath is woven into the fabric of the Ten Commandments, which are an expression of the character of God, which He established at creation, for all peoples, everywhere, for all time. The fourth commandment can never be done away with or pulled out of the Decalogue nor can its timing be changed. The seventh-day Sabbath, from sunset Friday to sunset Saturday, stands forever, perpetually or continually, and will be honored throughout all eternity even after this world is destroyed and made new:

"For as the new heavens and the new earth, which I will make, shall remain before me, saith the LORD, so shall your seed and your name remain. And it shall come to pass, *that* from one new moon to another, and from one sabbath to another, shall all flesh come to worship before me, saith the LORD." Isaiah 66:22,23.

The seventh-day Sabbath is honored by "the peoples of the earth", His kingdom, for the same reason the other nine commandments are honored, respected, and kept. The people which accept Jesus Christ as their Creator, Redeemer, and Sustainer keep the Ten Commandments because they love the Lord. Notice what Jesus says in John 14:15 and in Luke 6:46:

"If ye love me, keep my commandments."

"And why call ye me, Lord, Lord, and do not the things which I say?"

The people of God, which obey Him and keep His Ten Commandments, do it not to be saved, because no person is saved by obeying the law (Galatians 3:11,12), but they keep the Ten Commandments because they are saved and they want to obey God in all things.

> "But that no man is justified by the law in the sight of God, *it is* evident: for, The just shall live by faith. And the law is not of faith: but, The man that doeth them shall live in them."

Some people claim keeping the seventh-day Sabbath is legalism. If honoring the fourth commandment is legalism, what is it called honoring the other nine commandments?

Also... Though the ceremonial Sabbaths were fulfilled during and after the death and resurrection of Jesus, it is not wrong to recognize them. As Paul says, it's not for us to judge a person if they still wish to celebrate them or not. I believe all God's dedicated Bible students should intimately realize the beauty and intent of each of the ceremonial Sabbaths and what they represented. Some are under the impression they still have a future context toward the end of this world. How about you?

BUT THERE IS MORE...

What was the intent, or the reason, for the seventy-week prophecy?

What did God want His people, the children of Israel, to do before the end of the seventy- week prophecy of 490 years? Notice verse 24:

> "Seventy weeks are determined upon thy people and upon thy holy city, to finish the transgression, and to make an end of sins, and to make reconciliation for iniquity, and to bring in everlasting righteousness, and to seal up the vision and prophecy, and to anoint the most Holy."

What are the seven things God wanted His people to accomplish?

The seventy-week, 490-year prophecy, was for the people of God, the Israelites, to do seven things:

1. Finish transgression
2. Make an end of sins
3. Make reconciliation for iniquity
4. Bring in everlasting righteousness.
5. Seal up the vision
6. Seal up the prophecy
7. Anoint the most Holy.

What does those seven things above mean? Let's rewrite them to bring out their meaning:

1. Recognize their error and rebellion against God and repent.

2. Stop sinning and planning sin against God.
3. Payback or return whatever they can to reconcile for their disobedience.
4. Start living a life of righteousness or right doing.
5. Understand Daniel's vision.
6. Recognize the importance of and the aspects of prophecy.
7. Welcome the Messiah when He comes the first time, as a baby.

BUT THERE IS EVEN MORE...

The prophecy of Daniel 9:24-27 does not end with the stoning of Stephen. Notice all of verses 26 and 27:

> "And after threescore and two weeks shall Messiah be cut off, but not for himself: and the people of the prince that shall come shall destroy the city and the sanctuary; and the end thereof *shall be* with a flood, and unto the end of the war desolations are determined. And he shall confirm the covenant with many for one week: and in the midst of the week he shall cause the sacrifice and the oblation to cease, and for the overspreading of abominations he shall make *it* desolate, even until the consummation, and that determined shall be poured upon the desolate."

To grasp more information from this important vision let's break it down further:

1. After 69 weeks the Messiah would die (be cut off) for all mankind.
2. The people of the prince would come.
3. They would destroy the city and the sanctuary.

4. The end would come like a destructive flood.
5. Toward the end of time desolations and wars would be determined.
6. The covenant would be confirmed with many for one week.
7. In the middle of that week sacrifice and oblations would cease.
8. There would be an abomination of desolation set up.
9. The abomination of desolation would last till the end of the ages.
10. That abomination would precede the pouring out of God's wrath on mankind.

Notice the chronology of events which takes place for us to grasp and understand.

1. After 69 weeks the Messiah would die for all mankind: 31 ADE
2. The people of the prince would come.   70 ADE
3. They would destroy the city and the sanctuary.   70 ADE
4. The end would come like a destructive flood.   Now and in the future.
5. Toward the end desolations and wars are determined.   Now and in the future.
6. The covenant would be confirmed for one week.   Our future
7. Middle of the week sacrifice and oblations would cease.   Our future.
8. There would be an abomination of desolation.   Our future.
9. The abomination of desolation would last till the end.   Our future.

10. the wrath of God would be poured out
mankind (Rev. 16).   Our future.

Further explanation of the above noting the perfect chronology of events:

1. The Messiah died for all mankind in 31 AD as prophesied. Afterwards:
2. In 70 ADE the Roman Army, in this case the prince, attacked Jerusalem and broke down all its walls.
3. The Roman Army also tore down the temple in Jerusalem "leaving not one stone upon another" as Jesus predicted in Matthew 24:2.
4. We are now living in the times of number 4.
5. We are now living in the times of number 5.
6. There is coming a one week, or seven years, tribulation Jesus predicted in Mathew 24:21 during which the covenant is to be confirmed.
7. In the middle of the coming seven-year tribulation, 1260 days after it begins, church services and Bible teaching will be discontinued worldwide.
8. 1290 days after the seven-year tribulation begins a false day of worship will be set up or established as is predicted in Daniel 12:11.
9. The abomination of desolation will stand until the time of the end is completed.
10. God's wrath will be poured out on those people supporting the abomination of desolation, which refuse to obey Him, as revealed in Revelation 16.

BUT THERE IS EVEN MUCH MORE...

From the time Daniel had the vision of Daniel nine, until the decree of King Artaxerxes in 457 BCE to "rebuild and restore

Jerusalem", about 80 years had already passed. Daniel, and all the people of his day, were long dead. Then add to it the actual 490 years of the prophecy, that totals 537 years since the prophecy had been put in writing on the books. During that time discovering the interpretation of the prophecy had most likely long been given up. No one was aware of the prophecy nor the requirements God had established for His people when the prophecy was alive and being fulfilled. No one could have known or would have known to expect the Messiah in 27 ADE from this prophecy.

Why did God give the 70-week vision to Daniel?

Our Heavenly Father understood that His vision and the interpretation of the vision would not be understood or known until after the prophecy was fulfilled. He also realized the 66 book Holy Bible, the Word of God, containing Daniel nine, would not be printed for all the world to see until around 1800 ADE when the American Bible Society was established. God gave the seventy-week prophecy to Daniel, not for the children of Israel to understand it, but for us, God's last day generation, to understand it.

The Israelites could not have understood this prophecy or figured it out. They had no concept of BCE and ADE. So... How does that prophecy impact us? Let's do some math.

In Bible prophecy there are 24 hours in a day, 30 days per month, and 360 days per year as was developed by God and recognized by the Babylonians and adapted by the world. So please follow carefully:

70 weeks X 7 days per week, equals 490 weeks of years.

490 years X 360 days per year, equals 176,400 literal days.

176,400 literal days divided by 70, equals 2,520 literal days.

2,520 literal days divided by 360 days per year, equals 7 years.

7 years in Daniel 9:27 is one prophetic week, as supported by Daniel 9:24,27.

Daniel 9:27 says:

> "And he shall confirm the covenant with many for one week: and in the midst of the week he shall cause the sacrifice and the oblation to cease."

At times the Bible uses dual application in Bible prophecy meaning a single prophecy can be applied in two or more different places, situations, or time periods. This is the case with the above text.

This prophecy of the "one week" found in Daniel 9:27:

(1) Applied to the 70th week between 27 ADE and 34 ADE as we discussed above.
(2) It told the exact day Jesus would die in 31 AD, which was on Wednesday, and
(3) It applies to the time of the end, our near future.
(4) Twice this prophecy reveals a coming 7-year tribulation.

God has established a one week or 7-year period time of tribulation to take place before He comes back the second time. Notice the following from Matthew 24:

"Then shall they deliver you up to be afflicted, and shall kill you: and ye shall be hated of all nations for my name's sake. And then shall many be offended, and shall betray one another, and shall hate one another. And many false prophets shall rise, and shall deceive many. And because iniquity shall abound, the love of many shall wax cold. But he that shall endure unto the end, the same shall be saved." Verses 9-13.

"For then shall be great tribulation, such as was not since the beginning of the world to this time, no, nor ever shall be." Verse 21.

"But of that day and hour knoweth no *man*, no, not the angels of heaven, but my Father only. But as the days of Noe *were*, so shall also the coming of the Son of man be. For as in the days that were before the flood they were eating and drinking, marrying and giving in marriage, until the day that Noe entered into the ark, And knew not until the flood came, and took them all away; so shall also the coming of the Son of man be." Verses 36-39.

What did Jesus mean when He said?

"But as the days of Noe *were*, so shall also the coming of the Son of man be"

The answer to that question can be discovered as we carefully look at what else Jesus said before we go to Genesis chapter seven to understand more about "the days of Noah." Consider the text again, but this time with certain words highlighted.

"But of that **day** and hour knoweth no *man*, no, not the angels of heaven, but my Father only. But as the **days** of Noe *were*, so shall also the coming of the Son of man be. For as in the **days** that were **before the flood** they were eating and drinking, marrying and giving in marriage, until the **day** that **Noe entered into the ark**, And knew not **until the flood** *came*, and took them all away; so shall also the coming of the Son of man be." Verses 36-39.

Notice Jesus stresses the days of Noah **from** the time he entered the Ark **until** the time the flood waters actually began.

Notice how many times the word **day** or **days** is used in the verse from Matthew 24. Jesus is repeating himself for a specific purpose.

What does it mean when God repeats Himself in the Bible?

Joseph told the Pharaoh that when God repeats himself that means to pay close attention and the prophecy is sure to take place, just as he said it would. Notice Genesis 41:32:

"And for that the dream was doubled unto Pharaoh twice; *it is* because the thing *is* established by God, and God will shortly bring it to pass."

Also look carefully at what Jesus is saying in the above text. He is talking about the time difference from when Noah **entered** the Ark **until** the flood waters came. How do we discover how many **days** there were from the time Noah **entered** the Ark **until** the rain began that brought on the flood? Notice the following, in my words, from Genesis 7:1,4,5,10.

"Go into the ark, you and your whole family.... **Seven days** from now I will send rain on the earth for forty days and forty nights, and I will wipe from the face of the earth every living creature I have made.... And Noah did all that the LORD commanded him... And after the **seven days** the floodwaters came on the earth."

Just like Noah and his family were safe in the Ark for **seven days** before the destruction of all mankind, God has planned a seven-year tribulation with His last day people safely in His care during that time. In thinking about the one week of Daniel 9:27 we must remember that one prophetic day in Bible prophecy equals one literal year. Jesus is telling us in Matthew 24 that there will be a coming time of tribulation that will last for **seven years** before He comes back for His second advent. **

Just like Jesus fed the Israelites manna in the wilderness (Exodus 16:35) and led Elijah to the bubbling brook, feeding Him by way of the Ravens (1 kings 17:1-6), He will watch over His elect servants during this time meeting their needs as well. A seven-year period of time for God's wrath (Daniel 11:36; Romans 1:18; Revelation 15:17) against sin and disobedience should not surprise us. God has often put times in groups of seven years.

The Bible lists numerous times God used a seven-year time period:

1. Seven years of plenty in the days of Joseph: Genesis 41.
2. Seven years of famine in the days of Joseph: Genesis 41.
3. Seven years of insanity with King Nebuchadnezzar: Daniel 4.
4. Jacob served for seven years for each of his two wives: Genesis 29.

5. There was a seven year famine in the days of Elisha: 2 Kings 8:1.

6. The widow woman returned to her home after seven years: 2 Kings 8:1-6.

7. Joash was seven years old when he became king: 2 Kings 11:21.

8. Solomon took seven years to build the temple of God: 1 Kings 6:38.

9. A Hebrew could be a slave to a Hebrew for seven years only: Jeremiah 34:14.

10. The Israelites were to burn their enemies weapons for seven years: Ezekiel 39:9.

11. Anna the prophetess was married for seven years: Luke 2:36.

12. Jesus has promised a seven-year tribulation before He comes the second time.

The 70-week prophecy reveals two times that there will be a seven-year or 2,520 days' tribulation before the second coming of Jesus. What is that time period for? The seven-year tribulation has the exact same goals for us as listed for Israel during their 490 years.

** Read the eBook or hard copy book "The 3 Visible Advents of Jesus" by Earl B. Schrock from Xlibris.com, Amazon, Barnes and Nobles, etc.

The seventy-week, 490-year prophecy, was for the people of God, the Israelites to do seven (7) things. Those same goals are established for God's last day servants as well:

Before and during the seven-year tribulation, God wants his "earth people" to:

1. Finish transgression
2. Make an end of sins
3. Make reconciliation for iniquity
4. Bring in everlasting righteousness.
5. Seal up the vision
6. Seal up the prophecy
7. Anoint the most Holy.

What does those seven things above mean in our vernacular? Let's rewrite them to bring out their meaning:

1. Recognize our errors and our rebellion against God and repent.
2. Stop sinning and disobeying God.
3. Payback or return whatever we can to reconcile for our disobedience.
4. Start living a life of righteousness or right doing.
5. Complete and understand Daniel's vision.
6. Recognize the importance and the aspects of Bible prophecy.
7. Welcome the Messiah when He comes the second time as Redeemer.

The seventy-week prophecy was not understood or calculated by the Israelites, even though God did fulfill that prophecy just as He said He would and right on time. But that time prophecy is more important for us than it was applicable to them. It's more important to us because it helps us understand how wonderful and on time God is, plus since we know about it, we can understand it, and we can apply it to our situation right here and right now. The choice of serving God, as He dictates, or of disobeying Him and doing our own thing, is ours to make. As Joshua said:

"Choose you this day whom ye will serve;... but as for me and my house, we will serve the LORD." Joshua 24:15

Now is the time for all God's children, His modern day "mountain", His servants, His elect to make a determined decision to give their all to Him in every thought, word, and action.

Those which do not adjust their lifestyles now, voluntarily, to be obedient servants of God, will be forced to do so under duress, during the future 2,520 day or seven-year tribulation.

If you haven't already, will you today, right now, turn your life over to Jesus and live the life God the Father has laid out for you, through the power of the indwelling Holy Spirit?

See the **YouTube** video on **DANIEL CHAPTER NINE** by Earl Schrock.

DANIEL CHAPTER NINE (KJV)

1In the first year of Darius the son of Ahasuerus, of the seed of the Medes, which was made king over the realm of the Chaldeans; 2In the first year of his reign I Daniel understood by books the number of the years, whereof the word of the LORD came to Jeremiah the prophet, that he would accomplish seventy years in the desolations of Jerusalem. 3And I set my face unto the Lord God, to seek by prayer and supplications, with fasting, and sackcloth, and ashes: 4And I prayed unto the LORD my God, and made my confession, and said, O Lord, the great and dreadful God, keeping the covenant and mercy to them that love him, and to them that keep his commandments; 5We have sinned, and have committed iniquity, and have done wickedly, and have rebelled, even by departing from thy precepts and from thy judgments: 6Neither have we hearkened unto thy servants the prophets, which spake in thy name to our kings, our princes, and our fathers, and to all the people of the land.

7O Lord, righteousness *belongeth* unto thee, but unto us confusion of faces, as at this day; to the men of Judah, and to the inhabitants of Jerusalem, and unto all Israel, *that are* near, and *that are* far off, through all the countries whither thou hast driven them, because of their trespass that they have trespassed against thee. 8O Lord, to us *belongeth* confusion of face, to our kings, to our princes, and to our fathers, because we have sinned against thee. 9To the Lord our God *belong* mercies and forgivenesses, though we have rebelled against him; 10Neither have we obeyed the voice of the LORD our God, to walk in his laws, which he set before us by his servants the prophets. 11Yea, all Israel have transgressed thy law, even by departing, that they might not obey thy voice; therefore the curse is poured upon us, and the oath that *is* written in the law of Moses the servant of God, because we have sinned against him. 12And he hath confirmed his words, which he spake against us, and against our judges that judged us, by bringing upon us a great evil: for under the whole heaven hath not been done as hath been done upon Jerusalem. 13As *it is* written in the law of Moses, all this evil is come upon us: yet made we not our prayer before the LORD our God, that we might turn from our iniquities, and understand thy truth. 14Therefore hath the LORD watched upon the evil, and brought it upon us: for the LORD our God *is* righteous in all his works which he doeth: for we obeyed not his voice.

15And now, O Lord our God, that hast brought thy people forth out of the land of Egypt with a mighty hand, and hast gotten thee renown, as at this day; we have sinned, we have done wickedly. 16O Lord, according to all thy righteousness, I beseech thee, let thine anger and thy fury be turned away from thy city Jerusalem, thy holy mountain: because for our sins, and for the iniquities of our fathers, Jerusalem and thy people *are become* a reproach to all *that are* about us. 17Now therefore, O our God, hear the prayer of thy servant, and his supplications, and cause thy face to shine upon thy sanctuary that is desolate, for the Lord's sake. 18O my God, incline thine ear, and hear; open thine eyes, and behold our desolations, and the city which is called by thy name: for we do not present our supplications before thee for our righteousnesses, but for thy great mercies. 19O Lord, hear; O Lord, forgive; O Lord, hearken and do; defer not, for thine own sake, O my God: for thy city and thy people are called by thy name.

20And whiles I *was* speaking, and praying, and confessing my sin and the sin of my people Israel, and presenting my supplication before the LORD my God for the holy mountain of my God; 21Yea, whiles I *was* speaking in prayer, even the man Gabriel, whom I had seen in the vision at the beginning, being caused to fly swiftly, touched me about the time of the evening oblation. 22And he informed *me*, and talked with me, and said, O Daniel, I am now come forth to give thee skill and understanding. 23At the beginning of thy supplications the commandment came forth, and I am come to shew *thee*; for thou *art* greatly beloved: therefore understand the matter, and consider the vision.

24Seventy weeks are determined upon thy people and upon thy holy city, to finish the transgression, and to make an end of sins, and to make reconciliation for iniquity, and to bring in everlasting righteousness, and to seal up the vision and prophecy, and to anoint the most Holy. 25Know therefore and understand, *that* from the going forth of the commandment to restore and to build Jerusalem unto the Messiah the Prince *shall be* seven weeks, and threescore and two weeks: the street shall be built again, and the wall, even in troublous times. 26And after threescore and two weeks shall Messiah be cut off, but not for himself: and the people of the prince that shall come shall destroy the city and the sanctuary; and the end thereof *shall be* with a flood, and unto the end of the war desolations are determined. 27And he shall confirm the covenant with many for one week: and in the midst of the week he shall cause the sacrifice and the oblation to cease, and for the overspreading of abominations he shall make *it* desolate, even until the consummation, and that determined shall be poured upon the desolate.

DANIEL CHAPTER TEN

"This know also, that in the last days perilous times shall come. For men shall be lovers of their own selves, covetous, boasters, proud, blasphemers, disobedient to parents, unthankful, unholy, Without natural affection, trucebreakers, false accusers, incontinent, fierce, despisers of those that are good, Traitors, heady, highminded, lovers of pleasures more than lovers of God; Having a form of godliness, but denying the power thereof: from such turn away. For of this sort are they which creep into houses, and lead captive silly women laden with sins, led away with divers lusts, Ever learning, and never able to come to the knowledge of the truth. Now as Jannes and Jambres withstood Moses, so do these also resist the truth: men of corrupt minds, reprobate concerning the faith. But they shall proceed no further: for their folly shall be manifest unto all *men*, as theirs also was." 2 Timothy 3:1-9.

The last three chapters of Daniel are united as one letter, adding information to Daniel nine. They are like three different puzzle pieces that make one complete puzzle when combined. Chapter ten is the introduction to chapters eleven and twelve. From this introduction of these three chapters it's very important to understand the timing for the vision to be fulfilled. Notice the following emphasis in Daniel ten from the following verses:

1. Verse one: "the thing *was* true, but **the time appointed *was* long**"

2. Verse fourteen: **"Now I am come to make thee** understand what shall befall thy people **in the latter days**: for yet **the vision *is* for *many* days**."

The entire book of Daniel was written with the intent of informing the last generation living "in the latter days" at "the appointed time". Notice other references to the last generation from the previous chapters we have discussed:

1. Daniel 2:28: "But there is a God in heaven that revealeth secrets, and maketh known to the king Nebuchadnezzar what shall be **in the latter days**."

2. Daniel 2:29: "what should come to pass **hereafter**."

3. Daniel 2:45: "the great God hath made known to the king **what shall come to pass hereafter**: and the dream *is* certain, and the interpretation thereof sure."

4. Daniel 8:17: "Understand, O son of man: for **at the time of the end *shall be* the vision**."

5. Daniel 8:19: "I will make thee know what shall be **in the last end of the indignation**: for at **the time appointed the end *shall be*.**"

6. Daniel 8:23: "And in **the latter time of their kingdom**, when **the transgressors are come to the full**, a king of fierce countenance, and understanding dark sentences, shall stand up.

7. Daniel 8:26: "wherefore shut thou up the vision; **for it *shall be* for many days**."

8. Daniel 9:26,27: "and **the end thereof *shall be*** with a flood, and **unto the end** of the war desolations are determined. And he shall confirm **the covenant with many for one week**: and in the midst of **the week** he shall cause the sacrifice and the oblation to cease, and

for the **overspreading of abominations** <u>he shall</u> make *it* desolate, even **until the consummation**, and that determined shall be **poured upon the desolate**."

Through the centuries many have attempted to solve the mysteries and unravel the secrets of the book of Daniel through historical events, current news, and political actions, but all were prone to fail. The truth of understanding and interpreting the entire book of Daniel is reserved for the generation which will experience what Daniel is being shown; the generation just preceding the seven-year tribulation. The unsealing of Daniel has been in progression for centuries, yet there are more mysteries being revealed to each successive generation, including this one. We cannot be content with past conclusions.

See the **YouTube** video **DANIEL CHAPTER TEN** by Earl Schrock.

DANIEL CHAPTER TEN (KJV)

1In the third year of Cyrus king of Persia a thing was revealed unto Daniel, whose name was called Belteshazzar; and the thing *was* true, but the time appointed *was* long: and he understood the thing, and had understanding of the vision.

2In those days I Daniel was mourning three full weeks. 3I ate no pleasant bread, neither came flesh nor wine in my mouth, neither did I anoint myself at all, till three whole weeks were fulfilled. 4And in the four and twentieth day of the first month, as I was by the side of the great river, which *is* Hiddekel; 5Then I lifted up mine eyes, and looked, and behold a certain man clothed in linen, whose loins *were* girded with fine gold of Uphaz: 6His body also *was* like the beryl, and his face as the appearance of lightning, and his eyes as lamps of fire, and his arms and his feet like in colour to polished brass, and the voice of his words like the voice of a multitude. 7And I Daniel alone saw the vision: for the men that were with me saw not the vision; but a great quaking fell upon them, so that they fled to hide themselves. 8Therefore I was left alone, and saw this great vision, and there remained no strength in me: for my comeliness was turned in me into corruption, and I retained no strength. 9Yet heard I the voice of his words: and when I heard the voice of his words, then was I in a deep sleep on my face, and my face toward the ground.

10And, behold, an hand touched me, which set me upon my knees and *upon* the palms of my hands. 11And he said unto me, O Daniel, a man greatly beloved, understand the words that I speak unto thee, and stand upright: for unto thee am I now sent. And when he had spoken this word unto me, I stood trembling. 12Then said he unto me, Fear not, Daniel: for from the first day that thou didst set thine heart to understand, and to chasten thyself before thy God, thy words were heard, and I am come for thy words. 13But the prince of the kingdom of Persia withstood me one and twenty days: but, lo, Michael, one of the chief princes, came to help me; and I remained there with the kings of Persia. 14Now I am come to make thee understand what shall befall thy people in the latter days: for yet the vision *is* for *many* days.

15And when he had spoken such words unto me, I set my face toward the ground, and I became dumb. 16And, behold, *one* like the similitude of the sons of men touched my lips: then I opened my mouth, and spake, and said unto him that stood before me, O my lord, by the vision my sorrows are turned upon me, and I have retained no strength. 17For how can the servant of this my lord talk with this my lord? for as for me, straightway there remained no strength in me, neither is there breath left in me.

18Then there came again and touched me *one* like the appearance of a man, and he strengthened me, 19And said, O man greatly beloved, fear not: peace *be* unto thee, be strong, yea, be strong. And when he had spoken unto me, I was strengthened, and said, Let my lord speak; for thou hast strengthened me. 20Then said he, Knowest thou wherefore I come unto thee? and now will I return to fight with the prince of Persia: and when I am gone forth, lo, the prince of Grecia shall come. 21But I will shew thee that which is noted in the scripture of truth: and *there is* none that holdeth with me in these things, but Michael your prince.

DANIEL CHAPTER ELEVEN

"And God spake all these words, saying, I *am* the
LORD thy God, which have brought thee out of
the land of Egypt, out of the house of bondage.
Thou shalt have no other gods before me."
Exodus 20:1-3

The first four verses of this chapter clearly correspond with
what we have learned from the previous ten chapters:

1. God's people, "the earth", will be ruled over by many
   nations because of disobedience.
2. Those ruling nations are Babylon, Medo-Persia, and
   Greece; plus, one more.
3. The Grecian kingdom will be ruled by Alexander the
   Great and after his death it will be divided into four
   different kingdoms whose pagan influence will spread
   to the four points of the compass to comprise the entire
   planet.

After verse four, the rest of Daniel chapter eleven becomes
difficult to understand or interpret. The information in Daniel
11 from verse five onward, is vague and scattered. Because
of its vagueness many have successfully tagged their own
interpretation to the chapter fooling many who accepted their
explanation without question because it was the only viable
solution or interpretation available or that was offered.

We must understand that the Bible must interpret itself. History books, news sources, and the internet are not the basis to discover Bible prophecy interpretation. Though not explained in this chapter, on this page, we will better understand chapter eleven after we consider the secrets realized in Daniel chapter twelve.

But don't be discouraged. A huge portion of Daniel chapter eleven will be revealed by the time we end our Bible discussion on the book of Daniel.

BREAKING DOWN THE VERSES IN DANIEL CHAPTER ELEVEN:

Concerning Daniel chapter eleven we mentioned above that verses 1-4 provides information concerning the past Medo-Persian and the Grecian empires. And we previously discussed the coming Little Horn Power in chapters seven and eight which Daniel eleven in verses 21-45 mentions again.

The current mystery to be better understood in Daniel eleven is between verses 5-20.

Verses 5-15 deals with the unnamed King of the South and the King of the North.

Then in verse 16 a different protagonist is introduced. He is the center of attention from verses 16 through19, which mentions "he shall stumble and fall, and not be found".

Verse 20 introduces yet another protagonist that arises but does not last long because "within few days he shall be destroyed, neither in anger, nor in battle."

The verse by verse outline of Daniel chapter eleven is as follows:

Verses 1-4: The Medo-Persian and Grecian Empires.

Verses 5-15: The King of the South and the King of the North.

Verses 16-19: A protagonist which will "stumble and fall, and not be found".

Verse 20: Another short-lived different protagonist which "shall be destroyed."

Verses 21-45: Information related to the future coming Little Horn Power.

At this time my **guess** as to the identity of the Kings of the North and South are:

> King of the North: the spiritually minded people from around the globe.
>
> King of the South: the politically minded non-religious people of the world.

I **guess** at the above description of these two kings because a world-wide problem(s) or catastrophe is in our future. Those problems could be related to the global climate crises currently taking place as our atmosphere, bodies of water, and land masses increase in temperature. This climate change is bringing about many world-wide problems of drought, famine, earthquakes, volcanic eruptions, huge devastating storms, large destructive forest fires, sickness and health concerns as well as medical pandemics, the world over.

Though deadly climate change is an option to the future global problem facing all mankind there may be any number of unforeseen events which could threaten the human existence and bring about uniting the world on a common problem to a point where the religious world and the non-religious world could be at odds one with the other on coming up with a viable solution to prevent the extinction of mankind.

Eventually the world will unite on attempting to recognize and solve the problems that are adversely affecting every man, woman, and child on this planet. The politically minded will seek an answer via science or some other way. The religious spiritually minded will seek an answer via the intervention of the power of God. Each of these groups will make laws to force a change in the manner people live in an attempt to try to improve the living conditions of the entire world. My **guess** is flexible as world events happen and change.

At one point the politically minded will be setting the bar for God's children and when that fails the spiritually minded will include their own rules and regulations, even to the point of going against the written Word and will of God in forcing worship. People will be forced to go against their own conscience to obey the majority rule. Consequences will be established to force people to fall in line with the will of the majority. Those faithful to the will of God will be caught in the middle of these two factions. The stories of Daniel chapter three and six are object lessons for us and will be repeated. We must then remain faithful.

See the **YouTube** video **DANIEL CHAPTER ELEVEN** by Earl Schrock.

DANIEL CHAPTER ELEVEN (KJV)

1Also I in the first year of Darius the Mede, *even* I, stood to confirm and to strengthen him. 2And now will I shew thee the truth. Behold, there shall stand up yet three kings in Persia; and the fourth shall be far richer than *they* all: and by his strength through his riches he shall stir up all against the realm of Grecia. 3And a mighty king shall stand up, that shall rule with great dominion, and do according to his will. 4And when he shall stand up, his kingdom shall be broken, and shall be divided toward the four winds of heaven; and not to his posterity, nor according to his dominion which he ruled: for his kingdom shall be plucked up, even for others beside those.

5And the king of the south shall be strong, and *one* of his princes; and he shall be strong above him, and have dominion; his dominion *shall be* a great dominion. 6And in the end of years they shall join themselves together; for the king's daughter of the south shall come to the king of the north to make an agreement: but she shall not retain the power of the arm; neither shall he stand, nor his arm: but she shall be given up, and they that brought her, and he that begat her, and he that strengthened her in *these* times. 7But out of a branch of her roots shall *one* stand up in his estate, which shall come with an army, and shall enter into the fortress of the king of the north, and shall deal against them, and shall prevail: 8And shall also carry captives into Egypt their gods, with their princes, *and* with their precious vessels of silver and of gold; and he shall continue *more* years than the king of the north. 9So the king of the south shall come into *his* kingdom, and shall return into his own land.

10But his sons shall be stirred up, and shall assemble a multitude of great forces: and *one* shall certainly come, and overflow, and pass through: then shall he return, and be stirred up, *even* to his fortress. 11And the king of the south shall be moved with choler, and shall come forth and fight with him, *even* with the king of the north: and he shall set forth a great multitude; but the multitude shall be given into his hand. 12*And* when he hath taken away the multitude, his heart shall be lifted up; and he shall cast down *many* ten thousands: but he shall not be strengthened *by it*. 13For the king of the north shall return, and shall set forth a multitude greater than the former, and shall certainly come after certain years with a great army and with much riches.

14And in those times there shall many stand up against the king of the south: also the robbers of thy people shall exalt themselves to establish the vision; but they shall fall. 15So the king of the north shall come, and cast up a mount, and take the most fenced cities: and the arms of the south shall not withstand, neither his chosen people, neither *shall there be any* strength to withstand. 16But he that cometh against him shall do according to his own will, and none shall stand before him: and he shall stand in the glorious land, which by his hand shall be consumed. 17He shall also set his face to enter with the strength of his whole kingdom, and upright ones with him; thus shall he do: and he shall give him the daughter of women, corrupting her: but she shall not stand *on his side*, neither be for him. 18After this shall he turn his face unto the isles, and shall take many: but a prince for his own behalf shall cause the reproach offered by him to cease; without his own reproach he shall cause *it* to turn upon him. 19Then he shall turn his face toward the fort of his own land: but he shall stumble and fall, and not be found.

20Then shall stand up in his estate a raiser of taxes *in* the glory of the kingdom: but within few days he shall be destroyed, neither in anger, nor in battle. 21And in his estate shall stand up a vile person, to whom they shall not give the honour of the kingdom: but he shall come in peaceably, and obtain the kingdom by flatteries. 22And with the arms of a flood shall they be overflown from before him, and shall be broken; yea, also the prince of the covenant. 23And after the league *made* with him he shall work deceitfully: for he shall come up, and shall become strong with a small people. 24He shall enter peaceably even upon the fattest places of the province; and he shall do *that* which his fathers have not done, nor his fathers' fathers; he shall scatter among them the prey, and spoil, and riches: *yea*, and he shall forecast his devices against the strong holds, even for a time. 25And he shall stir up his power and his courage against the king of the south with a great army; and the king of the south shall be stirred up to battle with a very great and mighty army; but he shall not stand: for they shall forecast devices against him. 26Yea, they that feed of the portion of his meat shall destroy him, and his army shall overflow: and many shall fall down slain. 27And both these kings' hearts *shall be* to do mischief, and they shall speak lies at one table; but it shall not prosper: for yet the end *shall be* at the time appointed. 28Then shall he return into his land with great riches; and his heart *shall be* against the holy covenant; and he shall do *exploits*, and return to his own land.

29At the time appointed he shall return, and come toward the south; but it shall not be as the former, or as the latte

30For the ships of Chittim shall come against him: therefore he shall be grieved, and return, and have indignation against the holy covenant: so shall he do; he shall even return, and have intelligence with them that forsake the holy covenant. 31And arms shall stand on his part, and they shall pollute the sanctuary of strength, and shall take away the daily *sacrifice*, and they shall place the abomination that maketh desolate.

32And such as do wickedly against the covenant shall he corrupt by flatteries: but the people that do know their God shall be strong, and do *exploits*. **33**And they that understand among the people shall instruct many: yet they shall fall by the sword, and by flame, by captivity, and by spoil, *many* days. **34**Now when they shall fall, they shall be holpen with a little help: but many shall cleave to them with flatteries. **35**And *some* of them of understanding shall fall, to try them, and to purge, and to make *them* white, *even* to the time of the end: because *it is* yet for a time appointed.

36And the king shall do according to his will; and he shall exalt himself, and magnify himself above every god, and shall speak marvellous things against the God of gods, and shall prosper till the indignation be accomplished: for that that is determined shall be done. **37**Neither shall he regard the God of his fathers, nor the desire of women, nor regard any god: for he shall magnify himself above all. **38**But in his estate shall he honour the God of forces: and a god whom his fathers knew not shall he honour with gold, and silver, and with precious stones, and pleasant things. **39**Thus shall he do in the most strong holds with a strange god, whom he shall acknowledge *and* increase with glory: and he shall cause them to rule over many, and shall divide the land for gain.

40And at the time of the end shall the king of the south push at him: and the king of the north shall come against him like a whirlwind, with chariots, and with horsemen, and with many ships; and he shall enter into the countries, and shall overflow and pass over. **41**He shall enter also into the glorious land, and many *countries* shall be overthrown: but these shall escape out of his hand, *even* Edom, and Moab, and the chief of the children of Ammon. **42**He shall stretch forth his hand also upon the countries: and the land of Egypt shall not escape. **43**But he shall have power over the treasures of gold and of silver, and over all the precious things of Egypt: and the Libyans and the Ethiopians *shall be* at his steps. **44**But tidings out of the east and out of the north shall trouble him: therefore he shall go forth with great fury to destroy, and utterly to make away many. **45**And he shall plant the tabernacles of his palace between the seas in the glorious holy mountain; yet he shall come to his end, and none shall help him.

DANIEL CHAPTER TWELVE

"And as he sat upon the mount of Olives, the disciples came unto him privately, saying, Tell us, when shall these things be? and what *shall be* the sign of thy coming, and of the end of the world? And Jesus answered and said unto them, Take heed that no man deceive you. For many shall come in my name, saying, I am Christ; and shall deceive many." Matthew 24:3-5

Though this is a short chapter with only thirteen verses, it is loaded with much needed information necessary to help unravel the mysteries of the chapters preceding it in the book of Daniel. Also Daniel chapter twelve is very helpful in providing clues to creating a timeline concerning Daniel chapter eleven. Remember, the Bible must interpret itself.

An example of the Bible interpreting itself is seen in Daniel 12:1. We must ask:

"Who is Michael, the great prince that protects your people"?

"And at that time shall Michael stand up, the great prince which standeth for the children of thy people: and there shall be a time of trouble, such as never was since there was a nation *even* to that same time: and at that time thy people shall be delivered, every one that shall be found written in the book."

We were introduced to Michael in Daniel chapter ten with verses 13 and 21. In Daniel 10:13 Michael is called "one of the chief princes". In Daniel 10:21 he is called, "Michael, your prince." Now in Daniel 12:1 he is, Michael, "the great prince which standeth for the children of thy people."

What is a prince according to the Bible? Notice Daniel 10:20:

> "Then said he, Knowest thou wherefore I come unto thee? and now will I return to fight with the prince of Persia: and when I am gone forth, lo, the prince of Grecia shall come."

In Daniel 11:1-4 we are told that the angel or messenger contends with the king of Persia and we are also told the king of Greece was coming. So apparently a royal "prince" is a king since the "prince of Persia" and the "prince of Grecia" (Daniel 10:20) are kings. So also then, Michael the Prince is a King.

In Daniel 8:25 we are told that the "Little Horn Power" will stand up against the "Prince of princes" in the final days of this earth's history. To be a "Prince of princes" one would have to be a "King of kings".

Who in the Bible is a "King of kings"? Revelation 19:11-16 says the "Word of God" is the "King of kings and Lord of lords." And John 1:1-18 tells us the Jesus is the Word of God.

Where else does the name Michael appear in the Bible in reference to royalty?

Revelation 12:7 says,

"And there was war in heaven: Michael and his angels fought against the dragon; and the dragon fought and his angels."

And Jude 1:9 says:

"Yet Michael the archangel, when contending with the devil he disputed about the body of Moses, durst not bring against him a railing accusation, but said, The Lord rebuke thee."

In Jude 1:9 Michael is the one which resurrected Moses from the dead and refers to Himself as the Lord.

With the Biblical evidence we have above the only conclusion we can make is that Michael is Jesus before He became a man. Michael is Jesus incarnate!

Daniel 12:1:

"And at that time shall Michael stand up, the great prince which standeth for the children of thy people: and there shall be a time of trouble, such as never was since there was a nation *even* to that same time: and at that time thy people shall be delivered, every one that shall be found written in the book."

Michael stands up.

What does it mean to "stand up" in this situation?

When Jesus returned to heaven at His Ascension He took His seat at the right hand of the Father, which is a place of power.

"And when he had spoken these things, while they beheld, he was taken up; and a cloud

149

received him out of their sight. And while they looked stedfastly toward heaven as he went up, behold, two men stood by them in white apparel; Which also said, Ye men of Galilee, why stand ye gazing up into heaven? this same Jesus, which is taken up from you into heaven, shall so come in like manner as ye have seen him go into heaven." Acts 1:9-11

"Which he wrought in Christ, when he raised him from the dead, and set *him* at his own right hand in the heavenly *places*, Far above all principality, and power, and might, and dominion, and every name that is named, not only in this world, but also in that which is to come:" Ephesians 1:20,21

"Looking unto Jesus the author and finisher of *our* faith; who for the joy that was set before him endured the cross, despising the shame, and is set down at the right hand of the throne of God." Hebrews 12:2

This seating of Jesus at the right hand of the Father does not denote a specific geographic heavenly place or location, God is omnipresent, He is everywhere at one, not in one place. Notice Ephesians 2:1-6. Before Christ came into our hearts we were considered dead. But when we accept Jesus as our Saviour, we are given life and **we sit together with Him in heavenly places**, which would be at the right hand of the Father also.

"And hath raised *us* up together, and made *us* sit together in heavenly *places* in Christ Jesus" Ephesians 2:6.

To sit with Christ in heavenly places is a position of power. In Christ we have all the power we need to be all we can be in Him, if we will but surrender our all to Him. Though we are sitting at the side of Jesus in heavenly places, we are not geographically or physically at His side or in the throne room of God, we are still on this planet, abiding in Him and He in us (John 17:20-26).

In Daniel 12:1, when the soon coming future time of trouble begins, Jesus stands up. This is not to say that He has sat still at the Father's side for the last 2000 years. But it does refer to the royal position Jesus has held as time passed. When Christ stands up in the heavenly realms I believe it is letting us know that He is taking an active role in protecting the last servants of God and He is preparing to return to this earth as the angels told the disciples in Acts 1:11.

Question: AT WHAT TIME is Michael going to stand up?

Answer: Since Daniel chapters ten thru twelve are one letter, then Daniel 12:1 must follow the final verses in Daniel chapter eleven. When does Michael stand up? According to Daniel 11:40 Michael will stand up for His people, to protect them, "at the time of the end."

What else does Daniel 12:1 reveal?

1. There is a future time of trouble, such as never was, coming upon this planet, as Jesus warned in Matthew 24:21 and Daniel confirms in Daniel 9:24-27.
2. During that time of trouble, God will deliver His children. He will provide food, water, (Exodus 23:25) and shelter. We must learn to trust God for our sustenance. We learn to trust God then by trusting Him today. Now is the time to trust Him for everything we are and need, so when

that time comes we are familiar with His voice (John 10:27; Ezekiel 34:31) and comfortably confident in being cared for by Him. We must remain totally dependent on the Father NOW!

3. What book is the names of God's saved people written in? There is a book where the names of God's children are written. That book is called the BOOK OF LIFE (Psalm 69:28 and Revelation 20:15) written by God Himself before the world was created containing all the names of the saved since creation.

Daniel 12:2,3:

"And many of them that sleep in the dust of the earth shall awake, some to everlasting life, and some to shame *and* everlasting contempt. And they that be wise shall shine as the brightness of the firmament; and they that turn many to righteousness as the stars for ever and ever."

Daniel 12:1 introduces us to the near future time period which in other places is called the DAY OF THE LORD (Joel 2, Revelation 1:10), or the TIME OF GOD'S WRATH (Daniel 8:19). Revelation 20 reveals that at the end of that time of trouble there is a 1000-year judgment taking place in heaven. Daniel 12 verses 2 and 3 takes us past that 1000 years to the end of sin history just before all sin is annihilated and God makes a "new heavens and a new earth, wherein dwelleth righteousness." (2 Peter 3:13). After the 1000 years of Revelation 20, and before sin is annihilated, there is a "white throne judgement" discussed in Revelation 20:11-13. At this "great white throne judgement" a sentence is passed on every person which ever lived in consideration of each person's life choices, in their relationship with God. No person is exempt. Paul tells us in 2 Corinthians 5:10:

> "For we must **all** appear before the judgment seat of Christ; that every one may receive the things *done* in *his* body, according to that he hath done, whether *it be* good or bad."

> "And as it is appointed unto men once to die, but after this the judgment." Hebrews 9:27

Daniel 12:2,3 reveals the rewarding of those standing before the judgement seat of Christ at the end of the 1000 years. That is when God separates the sheep from the goats (Matthew 25:31-46), the wheat from the tares (Mathew 13:24-30), and the good fish from the bad fish (Matthew 13:47-50). At that time some people will be awarded eternal death and some people will be awarded eternal life. Notice Matthew 25:31-46:

"**31**When the Son of man shall come in his glory, and all the holy angels with him, then shall he sit upon the throne of his glory: **32**And before him shall be gathered all nations: and he shall separate them one from another, as a shepherd divideth *his* sheep from the goats: **33**And he shall set the sheep on his right hand, but the goats on the left.

34Then shall the King say unto them on his right hand, Come, ye blessed of my Father, inherit the kingdom prepared for you from the foundation of the world: **35**For I was an hungred, and ye gave me meat: I was thirsty, and ye gave me drink: I was a stranger, and ye took me in: **36**Naked, and ye clothed me: I was sick, and ye visited me: I was in prison, and ye came unto me. **37**Then shall the righteous answer him, saying, Lord, when saw we thee an hungred, and fed *thee*? or thirsty, and gave *thee* drink? **38**When saw we thee a stranger, and took *thee* in? or naked, and clothed *thee*? **39**Or when saw we thee sick, or in prison, and came unto thee? **40**And the King shall answer and say unto them, Verily I say unto you, Inasmuch as ye have done *it* unto one of the least of these my brethren, ye have done *it* unto me.

41Then shall he say also unto them on the left hand, Depart from me, ye cursed, into everlasting fire, prepared for the devil and his angels: **42**For I was an hungred, and ye gave me no meat: I was thirsty, and ye gave me no drink: **43**I was a stranger, and ye took me not in: naked, and ye clothed me not: sick, and in prison, and ye visited me not. **44**Then shall they also answer him, saying, Lord, when saw we thee an hungred, or athirst, or a stranger, or naked, or sick, or in prison, and did not minister unto thee? **45**Then shall he answer them, saying, Verily I say unto you, Inasmuch as ye did *it* not to one of the least of these, ye did *it* not to me. **46**And these shall go away into everlasting punishment: but the righteous into life eternal."

The day of final judgment is called **"THE LAST DAY"** in the Bible when the reward of eternal life or eternal death is handed down by the court of God. Notice John 6:39-44:

> "And this is the Father's will which hath sent me, that of all which he hath given me I should lose nothing, but should raise it up again at **the last day**. And this is the will of him that sent me, that every one which seeth the Son, and believeth on him, may have everlasting life: and I will raise him up at **the last day**. The Jews then murmured at him, because he said, I am the bread which came down from heaven. And they said, Is not this Jesus, the son of Joseph, whose father and mother we know? how is it then

that he saith, I came down from heaven? Jesus therefore answered and said unto them, Murmur not among yourselves. No man can come to me, except the Father which hath sent me draw him: and I will raise him up at **the last day**."

"Martha saith unto him, I know that he shall rise again in the resurrection at **the last day**." John 11:24

"And if any man hear my words, and believe not, I judge him not: for I came not to judge the world, but to save the world. He that rejecteth me, and receiveth not my words, hath one that judgeth him: the word that I have spoken, the same shall judge him in **the last day**." John 12:47,48.

Daniel 12:4:

"But thou, O Daniel, shut up the words, and seal the book, *even* to the time of the end: many shall run to and fro, and knowledge shall be increased."

As we near the end of the book of Daniel, God tells Daniel to "shut up the words, and seal the book, *even* to the time of the end." God has a message for each and every generation which existed since Daniel's day. He has only shown to each generation what He wanted them to know for the time in which they lived. He has reserved revealing the final mysteries for the final generation. He divulges His messages in His way and according to His appointed time. Though the Bible is available to almost every person on this planet, in one form or another, God will reveal His secrets as He has predetermined at His appointed time. We can express our ideas and our thoughts, running back and forth, about the message God is revealing for our generation, but the complete unfolding of Daniel will not take place until "the time of the end". The book of Daniel is being unsealed, but it is a progression. People living in the yesteryear were unable to understand or see the mysteries God is unveiling today.

Daniel 12:5-7:

> "Then I Daniel looked, and, behold, there stood other two, the one on this side of the bank of the river, and the other on that side of the bank of the river. And *one* said to the man clothed in linen, which *was* upon the waters of the river, How long *shall it be to* the end of these wonders? And I heard the man clothed in linen, which *was* upon the waters of the river, when he held up his right hand and his left hand unto heaven, and sware by him that liveth for ever that *it shall be* for a time, times, and an half; and when he shall have accomplished to scatter the power of the holy people, all these *things* shall be finished."

There are three heavenly participants in Daniel's vision of chapters ten through twelve. The one above the waters was described by Daniel in chapter 10 verses 4-6:

> "I was by the side of the great river, which *is* Hiddekel; Then I lifted up mine eyes, and looked, and behold a certain man clothed in linen, whose loins *were* girded with fine gold of Uphaz: His body also *was* like the beryl, and his face as the appearance of lightning, and his eyes as lamps of fire, and his arms and his feet like in colour to polished brass, and the voice of his words like the voice of a multitude."

The other two talked with and touched Daniel to give him strength and encouragement (Daniel 10:10-21). In Revelation chapter 10 a similar messenger is standing above the water pointing to "heaven" with one foot on the "sea" and the other foot on the "earth". The last day messenger of Revelation ten represents the end time servants of God that are giving the final warning message for the "heaven", "earth", and "sea" people.

During this vision Daniel is exhausted and amazed. Thinking of the right questions to ask in this time of stress and anxiety was impossible for the man of God. So one of the other heavenly angels asked the right question instead, in verse six:

"How long *shall it be to* the end of these wonders?"

Then the heavenly being above the waters replied with a time period which we have seen before in Daniel 7:25, when talking about the Little Horn Power:

> "And he shall speak *great* words against the most High, and shall wear out the saints of the most High, and think to change times and laws: and they shall be given into his hand until a time and times and the dividing of time."

Both Daniel 7:25 and Daniel 12:7 are talking about the same time period and the same Little Horn which will be waring against God's people for "a time, times, and half a time" or for three and a half years (Revelation 11:11) which is 1,260 literal days. The "he" the heavenly being is referring to in Daniel twelve verse seven is the Little Horn Power of Daniel seven and he is referring to the last three and a half years (3 ½) of the seven-year tribulation, when the Little Horn will be successful in challenging and overcoming the power of God's people.

157

What this means is that those faithful to God will continue to be faithful to Him, even in the face of imprisonment and death, and those who have not surrendered themselves to Him will be steadfastly unfaithful. Revelation 22:11 says:

> "He that is unjust, let him be unjust still: and he which is filthy, let him be filthy still: and he that is righteous, let him be righteous still: and he that is holy, let him be holy still."

A chart revealing the 1,260 days, or "time, times, and half a time" looks like this:

2,520 literal days or seven years

1,260 days	1,260 days
Pre-Little Horn	Post-Little Horn

Daniel 12:8-10:

> "And I heard, but I understood not: then said I, O my Lord, what *shall be* the end of these *things*? And he said, Go thy way, Daniel: for the words *are* closed up and sealed till the time of the end. Many shall be purified, and made white, and tried; but the wicked shall do wickedly: and none of the wicked shall understand; but the wise shall understand."

Daniel is awestruck at the vision and he wants to understand what all this means. But the heavenly messenger gently tells him to not worry about this vision because it has been sealed up and it applies to "**the time of the end**", which is two thousand six hundred years' future to the days of Daniel the prophet. And then the messenger defines his previous statement about the Little Horn Power in Daniel 12:7 when he said:

"when he shall have accomplished to scatter the power of the holy people."

The heavenly messenger explains the above quote talking about those that abide in Christ during the 7-year tribulation shaking time (Revelation 8:5) and those that do not:

"Many shall be purified, and made white, and tried; but the wicked shall do wickedly: and none of the wicked shall understand; but the wise shall understand."

The book of Daniel will be understood by those end time servants of God which have the "spirit of prophecy". Notice Revelation 19:10:

"And I fell at his feet to worship him. And he said unto me, See *thou do it* not: I am thy fellowservant, and of thy brethren that have the testimony of Jesus: worship God: for the testimony of Jesus is the spirit of prophecy."

What is the spirit of prophecy? The spirit of prophecy is a deep desire to understand and teach the prophetic messages of the Bible, especially that of Daniel and Revelation. A prophet is not necessarily one which has visions and dreams, but most assuredly is one who teaches the truth where Jesus Christ is the center of the message. Paul says in 1 Corinthians 14:1-6:

"Follow after charity, and desire spiritual *gifts*, but rather that ye may prophesy. For he that speaketh in an *unknown* tongue speaketh not unto men, but unto God: for no man understandeth *him*; howbeit in the spirit he speaketh mysteries. But he that prophesieth speaketh unto men *to* edification, and exhortation, and comfort. He that speaketh in an *unknown* tongue edifieth himself; but he that prophesieth edifieth the church. I would that ye all spake with tongues, but rather that ye prophesied: for greater *is* he that prophesieth than he that speaketh with tongues, except he interpret, that the church may receive edifying. Now, brethren, if I come unto you speaking with tongues, what shall I profit you, except I shall speak to you either by revelation, or by knowledge, or by prophesying, or by doctrine?"

THE FOLLOWING TWO VERSES ARE VITAL IN CORRECTLY PLACING ALL THE BIBLICAL PROPHETIC TIME PERIODS ON THE END TIME PROPHECY TIMELINE.

Daniel 12:11,12:

"And from the time *that* the daily *sacrifice* shall be taken away, and the abomination that maketh desolate set up, *there shall be* a thousand two hundred and ninety days. Blessed *is* he that waiteth, and cometh to the thousand three hundred and five and thirty days."

This verse is tremendously important and must be understood correctly from the original language. To be absolutely accurate, the word *sacrifice*, which is italicized in most Bibles, since it was added, must be taken out of the verse. It does not belong there.

"And from the time *that* the daily shall be taken away, and the abomination that maketh desolate set up, *there shall be* a thousand two hundred and ninety days. Blessed *is* he that waiteth, and

> cometh to the thousand three hundred and five
> and thirty days."

Not only does the word sacrifice need to be taken out of the verse, the word "daily" needs to be appropriately interpreted from the original language. The word translated as "daily" in the King James Version of the Bible is Strong's word, tamid, number 8548, pronounced (taw-meed'). The accurate translation is "perpetual" or "continual". The verse should read:

> "And from the time *that* the continual (perpetual) shall be taken away, and the abomination that maketh desolate set up, *there shall be* a thousand two hundred and ninety days. Blessed *is* he that waiteth, and cometh to the thousand three hundred and five and thirty days."

Putting this text in my own words it can read:

> "From the time the continual (perpetual) is taken away until the abomination of desolation is set up there will be 1,290 days. Blessed are they that come to the 1,335 days."

If you look at verse 11 on a horizontal time line, it would appear like this:

```
Continual          1,290 days            Abomination of
taken away I_____I desolation set up.
```

Re-read this very carefully to catch its intended meaning:

"**FROM THE TIME** the continual is taken away **UNTIL** the abomination of desolation is **SET UP** there will be **1,290 days** of time.

Verse 12 continues by saying:

"Blessed are they that come to the 1,335 days."

If you look at both verses on a horizontal time line, it would appear like this:

Continual	1,290 days	Abomination of
taken away I	_____	I desolation set up
Continual	1,335 days	God's faithful
taken away I	_____	I blessed

Throughout the book of Daniel and Revelation there are a number of prophetic time periods given. Each time period has a beginning point and an ending point. If the beginning or ending point of time can be determined, then the entire time period can be mapped.

Some of the time period beginnings were previously Biblically clarified such as when (1) the 400-year Egyptian occupation began and ended, (2) the Israelite 40 year wondering in the wilderness began, as well as (3) the timing of the 70 weeks of Daniel 9:24 which went from 457 BCE to 34 ADE.

But all the other time periods were not Biblically determined to when they began or when they ended. Many attempts have been made to try to identify the beginning time points but they have been speculative at best. But right now, to you, it is being revealed, from Daniel 12:11 and 12. We have a specific beginning time point recognized for two of the prophetic time periods. Both the 1,290 day and the 1,335 day prophecies begin when the PERPETUAL or CONTINUAL is taken away or abandoned.

Another time period that can be added to those two prophetic time periods of Daniel 12:11,12 in relationship to the CONTINUAL being taken away, is the "time, times, and half a time" of Daniel 12:7. That time period, which is three and a half years, or 1,260 literal 24 hour days, is mentioned in the same vision as the 1,290 and the 1,335 time periods. It would appear on our horizontal timeline as the following:

Continual taken away I	1,260 days I	Holy people I shattered
Continual taken away I	1,290 days I	Abomination of desolation set up
Continual taken away I	1,335 days I	God's faithful blessed

QUESTION: According to the Bible, is there another time period associated with the "doing away" with the PERPETUAL or CONTINUAL?

ANSWER: YES!!!!!

Notice Daniel 8:9-14 as quoted directly from the King James Version (KJV) of the Bible:

> "And out of one of them came forth a little horn, which waxed exceeding great, toward the south, and toward the east, and toward the pleasant *land*. And it waxed great, *even* to the host of heaven; and it cast down *some* of the host and of the stars to the ground, and stamped upon them. Yea, he magnified *himself* even to the prince of the host, and by him the **daily** *sacrifice* was taken away, and the place of his sanctuary was cast down. And an host was given *him* against the **daily** *sacrifice* by reason of transgression,

and it cast down the truth to the ground; and it practised, and prospered. Then I heard one saint speaking, and another saint said unto that certain *saint* which spake, How long *shall be* the vision *concerning* the **daily** *sacrifice*, and the transgression of desolation, to give both the sanctuary and the host to be trodden under foot? And he said unto me, Unto two thousand and three hundred days; then shall the sanctuary be cleansed." Daniel 8:9-14 KJV

(The word sacrifice was added, it does not belong in these verses.)

I have taken the liberty to correct a number of errors found in this text from the King James Version of the Bible in comparison with the original Hebrew. Following is the way Daniel 8:9-14 should be translated as per my understanding from the original language:

"And out of one of them came forth a little horn, which waxed exceeding great, toward the south, and toward the east, and toward the pleasant *land*. And it waxed great, *even* to the host of heaven; and it cast down *some* of the host and of the stars to the ground, and stamped upon them. Yea, he magnified *himself* even to the prince of the host, and by him the **continual** was taken away, and the place of his sanctuary was cast down. And an host was given *him* against the **continual** by reason of transgression, and it cast down the truth to the ground; and it practiced, and prospered. Then I heard one saint speaking, and another saint said unto that certain *saint* which spake, How long *shall be* the vision *concerning* the **continual**, and the transgression of desolation, to give both the sanctuary and the host to be trodden under foot? And he said unto me, Unto two thousand and three hundred evenings and mornings; then shall the holy be declared righteous."

It's perfectly clear that "the 2,300 evenings and mornings" time prophecy is also intimately related to the CONTINUAL (PERPETUAL) being taken away, as well as being connected with "the transgression of desolation" which is the abomination of desolation.

According to the above timelines, the 2,300 evenings and mornings, or the 2,300 literal 24 hour days, appears as follows:

Continual	1,260 days	Holy people
taken away I_____I_____I shattered		
Continual	1,290 days	Abomination of
taken away I_____I desolation set up		
Continual	1,335 days	God's faithful
taken away I_____I blessed		
Continual	2,300 evenings and mornings	Holy declared
taken away I_____I righteous		

When discussing Daniel 9:27 we proved that there is a one prophetic week of seven years coming in our future which Jesus called the "great tribulation" in Matthew 24:21.

How does that seven-year (2,520-day) time period relate with the time periods demonstrated above?

Notice the following when adding the 2,520-day tribulation to the time lines:

Continual	1,260 days	Holy people
taken away	_____	_____	shattered

Continual	1,290 days	Abomination of
taken away	_____	desolation set up

Continual	1,335 days	God's faithful
taken away	_____	blessed

Continual	2,300 evenings and mornings	Holy declared
taken away	_____	righteous

Continual	2,520 days (seven years)	Tribulation
taken away	_____	Ended

(Please note that this time line is not drawn
to scale. It is for demonstration only)

Following is a chart showing all the prophetic Biblical time periods found in the scriptures which intimately play an important role during the coming seven-year tribulation:

ALL THE END TIME BIBLICAL PROPHETIC TIME PERIODS

Time	Daniel	Revelation
X, X's, ½ X	7:25, 12:7 (1260)	12:14
2300 days	8:14	
1290 days	12:11	
1335 days	12:12	
1260 days		11:3, 12:6
42 months	(1260 days)	11:2, 13:5
5 months	(150 days)	9:5, 10
3 ½ days/years	(1260 days)	11:9, 11

As far as I know, the Biblical beginning point for the time period found in Daniel 12:11, is the key to understanding where **all** the other "appointed time of the end" time periods fit into a sensible and organized timeline.

QUESTION: Why does the Bible have numerous prophecy time periods encapsulated in the coming future seven-years of tribulation?

ANSWER: Knowing the beginning of each time period is important for the events that take place during that time period and especially at the end of that prophetic period of time. The purpose of each timeline can be ascertained by carefully and completely studying the information surrounding each of those time periods. All are for "the time of the end."

None of the particular time periods verses above can stand alone without considering the entire Biblical chapter in which they are located. No verse can be independent of the chapter in which it is found. To correctly place a time period in a timeline, all the information must be considered.

As was discussed in Daniel chapter nine, the Bible informs us of a future seven-year worldwide tribulation. Considering that a prophetic year has 360 days, a seven-year tribulation is converted in a 2,520-day period of time. When considering all the above time periods, they **all** comfortably fit into that 2,520-day timeline or time period and each has a specific purpose.

Realizing all the time periods begin when the PERPETUAL or CONTINUAL is taken away, we can begin our timeline with that information. After considering all the parameters of the time periods, the charts below clearly track the beginning and ending points of each of the below demonstrated Biblical time periods.

The following seven-year time line design will be utilized to demonstrate all the future end time prophetic time periods in the Bible. The following chart reveals:

(1) The title of the chart, (2) the event that begins the seven-year tribulation, (3) the 2,520 literal days that compose the seven years, (4) the midline which equally divides the timeline into two equal halves or wings, (5) the final 70-day period at the end of the seven years, (6) the suggested time for the second coming of Jesus, (7) the 1000 years of Revelation 20, and (8) the ETERNITY which begins after the 1000 years is finished.

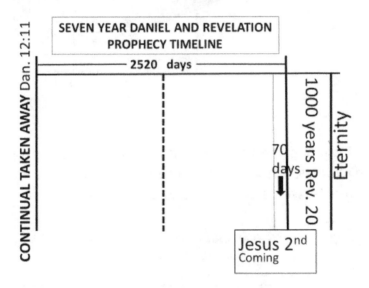

My first addition to the seven-year timeline chart is placing the **five months** of Revelation 9:5,10 on the timeline. It appears on the chart as:

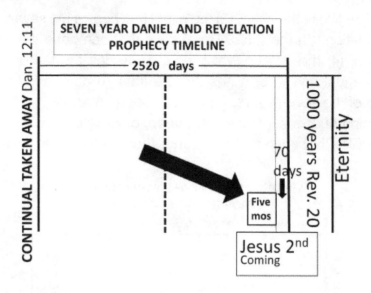

Next I will add the **three and a half (3 ½) days** of years of Revelation eleven when the two witnesses, the Old and New Testaments, will be outlawed and done away with.

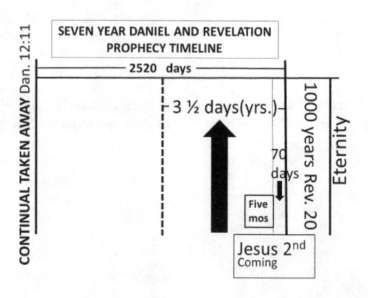

Next I will add **time, times, and half a time** (X, X'S, ½ X) of Daniel and Revelation when God's people will be trampled underfoot by the Little Horn Power (Revelation 12:12):

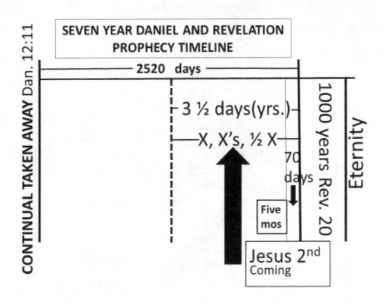

Next I will add the 42 months, when the two witnesses (Revelation 11) evangelize the world, and the 1260 days, when God's elect begin to be mistreated as the 144,000 saints reveal to the world the final gospel message about the final judgment and the kingdom of God, pointing out the people known as "heaven", "earth", and "sea" (Matthew 24:9-15):

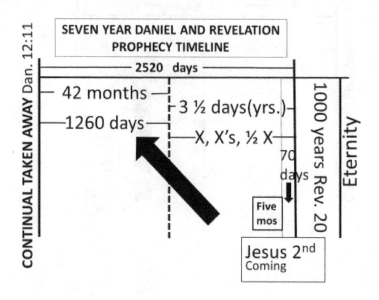

Next I will add **1,290 days** which spans the period from the time the CONTINUAL is done away until the "abomination that caused desolation" is set up.

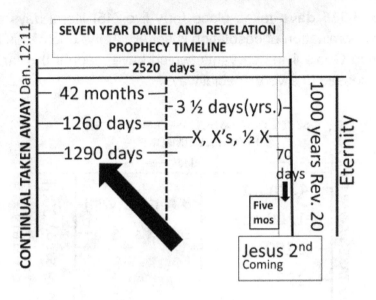

The **1,335 days** takes place forty-five (45) literal days after the abomination of desolation is set up. At the end of this time period God's living servants, which have made it this far, will be blessed in a very special way.

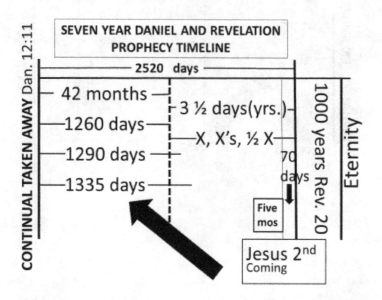

The **2,300 days** goes from the beginning of the seven-year tribulation to the time the five months of Revelation 9:5,10 begins. That is the total testing time for God's servants.

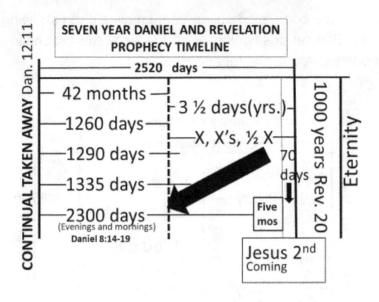

Finally, I will put the **1260 days** on our timeline when the power of the children of God will be completely shattered and "all these things shall be finished" as Daniel 12:7 tells us:

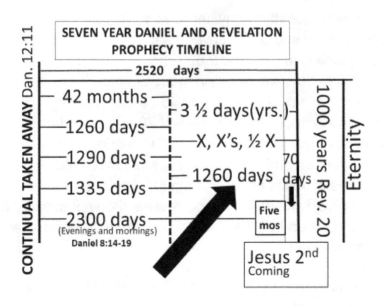

Below is the completed seven-year timeline chart showing the correct Biblical positioning of all the end time prophetic time periods located in Daniel and Revelation.

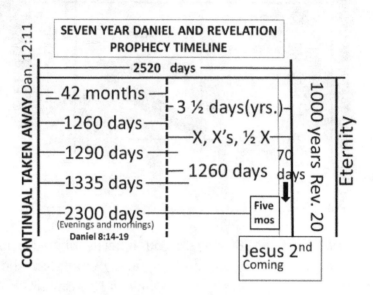

Some may question why there is a 70-day period of time located at the end of the seven-year tribulation. That is a very good question to ask. The 2,520-day tribulation time is equally divided into 36 seventy day periods of time. There are 18 70-day periods in the left wing and 18 70-day periods in the right wing. This author believes the last 70-day period of time has some very important roles to play. (1) It marks the time the sixth seal is opened and the sixth trumpet sounded. (2) Its fulfilling the words of Jesus about "cutting the time short for the elect's sake" in Mark 13:20. (3) It also reveals the final seventy days when the seven last plagues of Revelation 16 are poured out on lost mankind.

Do the math: add up the days: 2,300 + 150 (5 months) + 70 = 2520 days (7 years).

See the Youtube Video: **All the Last Day Appointed Bible Times** by Earl Schrock

BUT THAT IS NOT ALL!

This same timeline chart is used with the book of Revelation to set the suggested timing for the seven seals, seven trumpets, seven thunders, seven angels, seven woes and seven laments. All these sevens take place simultaneously, at the same time and at the same placement on the timeline, during the soon coming 7-year tribulation as follows:

Seven-year timeline revealing the timing for the opening of the seven seals, blowing of the seven trumpets, clapping of the seven thunders, shouting of the seven angels, timing of the seven woes, and the placement of the seven laments, taking place simultaneously.

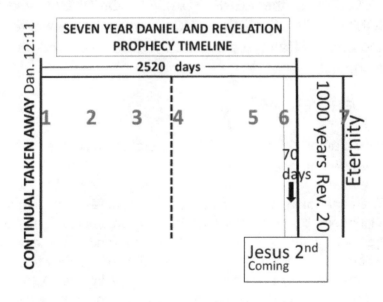

When put together with all the prophetic time periods of Daniel and Revelation it appears:

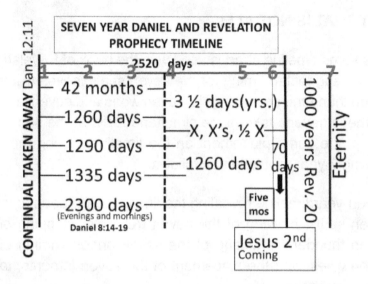

QUESTION: Is the PERPETUAL or CONTINUAL and the ABOMINATION OF DESOLATION mentioned anywhere else in the book of Daniel, other than what we discussed so far in this chapter?

ANSWER: YES.

Notice Daniel 11:20-45: (with interpretation mistakes corrected and verses numbered.)

20Then shall stand up in his estate a raiser of taxes *in* the glory of the kingdom: but within few days he shall be destroyed, neither in anger, nor in battle. **21**And in his estate shall stand up **a vile person**, to whom they shall not give the honour of the kingdom: but he shall come in peaceably, and obtain the kingdom by flatteries. **22**And with the arms of <u>a flood</u> shall they be overflown from before him, and shall be broken; yea, also the <u>prince of the covenant</u>. **23**And after the league *made* with him he shall work deceitfully: for he shall come up, and shall become strong with a small people. **24**He shall enter peaceably even upon the fattest places of the province; and he shall do *that* which his fathers have not done, nor his fathers' fathers; he shall scatter among them the prey, and spoil, and riches: *yea*, and he shall forecast his devices against the strong holds, even <u>for a time</u>.

25And he shall stir up his power and his courage against the king of the south with a great army; and the king of the south shall be stirred up to battle with a very great and mighty army; but he shall not stand: for they shall forecast devices against him. **26**Yea, they that feed of the portion of his meat shall destroy him, and his army shall overflow: and many shall fall down slain. **27**And both these kings' hearts *shall be* to do mischief, and they shall speak lies at one table; but it shall not prosper: for yet **the end *shall be* at the time appointed**. **28**Then shall he return into his land with great riches; and his heart *shall be* against <u>the holy covenant</u>; and he shall do *exploits*, and return to his own land. **29**At **the time appointed** he shall return, and come toward the south; but it shall not be as the former, or as the latter.

30For the ships of Chittim shall come against him: therefore he shall be grieved, and return, and have indignation against <u>the holy covenant</u>: so shall he do; he shall even return, and have intelligence with them that forsake <u>the holy covenant</u>. **31**And arms shall stand on his part, and they shall pollute the sanctuary of strength, and shall **take away the continual,** and they shall place **the abomination that maketh desolate**. **32**And such as do wickedly against <u>the covenant</u> shall he corrupt by flatteries: but the people that do know their God shall be strong, and do *exploits*. **33**And they that understand among the people shall instruct many: yet they shall fall by the sword, and by flame, by captivity, and by spoil, *many* days. **34**Now when they shall fall, they shall be holpen with a little help: but many shall cleave to them with flatteries. **35**And *some* of them of understanding shall fall, to try them, and to purge, and to make *them* white, *even* to **the time of the end**: because *it is* yet for **a time appointed**.

36And the king shall do according to his will; and he shall exalt himself, and magnify himself above every god, and shall speak marvellous things against the God of gods, and shall prosper till the indignation be accomplished: for that that is determined shall be done. **37**Neither shall he regard the God of his fathers, nor the desire of women, nor regard any god: for he shall magnify himself above all. **38**But in his estate shall he honour the God of forces: and a god whom his fathers knew not shall he honour with gold, and silver, and with precious stones, and pleasant things. **39**Thus shall he do in the most strong holds with a strange god, whom he shall acknowledge *and* increase with glory: and he shall cause them to rule over many, and shall divide the land for gain.

40And at **the time of the end** shall the king of the south push at him: and the king of the north shall come against him like a whirlwind, with chariots, and with horsemen, and with many ships; and he shall enter into the countries, and shall overflow and pass over. **41**He shall enter also into the glorious land, and many *countries* shall be overthrown: but these shall escape out of his hand, *even* Edom, and Moab, and the chief of the children of Ammon. **42**He shall stretch forth his hand also upon the countries: and the land of Egypt shall not escape. **43**But he shall have power over the treasures of gold and of silver, and over all the precious things of Egypt: and the Libyans and the Ethiopians *shall be* at his steps. **44**But tidings out of the east and out of the north shall trouble him: therefore he shall go forth with great fury to destroy, and utterly to make away many. **45**And he shall plant the tabernacles of his palace between the seas in the glorious holy mountain; yet he shall come to his end, and none shall help him."

Because we now know the TAKING AWAY OF THE CONTINUAL and the establishing of the ABOMINATION OF DESOLATION is part of the coming seven-year tribulation time period, we can better map the events of Daniel chapter eleven.

Up to this point, it was impossible to relate with Daniel chapter 11 because of the sparse and scattered information it provides. But verse 21 introduces us to the same power located in the rest of the book of Daniel, the Little Horn Power, which Daniel 11:21 calls "a vile person".

UNDERSTANDING THE COVENANT

Another term that has surfaced from re-reading Daniel chapter eleven is the word COVENANT. In Daniel chapter eleven it is called the HOLY COVENANT in verses 28 and 30. In this Bible study book we first saw the word "covenant" in Daniel 9:4 and 27:

> "And I prayed unto the LORD my God, and made my confession, and said, O Lord, the great and dreadful God, keeping **the covenant** and mercy to them that love him, and to them that keep his commandments."

> "And he shall confirm **the covenant** with many for one week: and in the midst of the week he shall cause the sacrifice and the oblation to cease, and for the overspreading of **abominations he shall make *it* desolate**, even until the consummation, and that determined shall be poured upon the desolate."

The word "covenant" shows up five times in Daniel 11:22-32:

"And with the arms of a flood shall they be overflown from before him, and shall be broken; yea, also <u>the prince of</u> **the covenant**. And after the league *made* with him he shall work deceitfully: for he shall come up, and shall become strong with a small people. He shall enter peaceably even upon the fattest places of the province; and he shall do *that* which his fathers have not done, nor his fathers' fathers; he shall scatter among them the prey, and spoil, and riches: *yea*, and he shall forecast his devices against the strong holds, even for a time. And he shall stir up his power and his courage against the king of the south with a great army; and the king of the south shall be stirred up to battle with a very great and mighty army; but he shall not stand: for they shall forecast devices against him. Yea, they that feed of the portion of his meat shall destroy him, and his army shall overflow: and many shall fall down slain. And both these kings' hearts *shall be* to do mischief, and they shall speak lies at one table; but it shall not prosper: for yet the end *shall be* at the time appointed. Then shall he return into his land with great riches; and his heart *shall be* against **the holy covenant**; and he shall do *exploits*, and return to his own land. At the time appointed he shall return, and come toward the south; but it shall not be as the former, or as the latter. For the ships of Chittim shall come against him: therefore he shall be grieved, and return, and have indignation against **the holy covenant**: so shall he do; he shall even return, and have intelligence with them that forsake **the holy covenant**. And arms shall stand on his part, and they shall pollute the sanctuary of strength, and shall take away the daily *sacrifice*, and they shall place the abomination that maketh desolate. And such as do wickedly against **the covenant** shall he corrupt by flatteries: but the people that do know their God shall be strong, and do *exploits*."

From the information we have above, the Little Horn Power of the book of Daniel is not only against "THE HOLY COVENANT" but the Little Horn Power is also against "THE PRINCE OF THE COVENANT", as revealed in verse 22.

QUESTIONS: (1) What is the COVENANT or HOLY COVENANT? And

(2) Who is the PRINCE OF THE COVENANT?

Definition of the word covenant: A covenant usually is a promise, agreement, or a commitment between two or more parties.

(1) What does the Bible say about the word COVENANT?

There are a number of covenants mentioned in the Bible. Most of the covenants are between God and an individual and their descendants. There are the covenants between God and Abraham, God and Isaac, God and Jacob, God and Moses, etc.

But the very first covenant or promise in the Bible was made in the Garden of Eden between God and Satan. God said in Genesis 3:14,15:

> "And the LORD God said unto the serpent, Because thou hast done this, thou *art* cursed above all cattle, and above every beast of the field; upon thy belly shalt thou go, and dust shalt thou eat all the days of thy life: And I will put enmity between thee and the woman, and between thy seed and her seed; it shall bruise thy head, and thou shalt bruise his heel."

The serpent is Satan. Revelation 12:9 and 20:2 say:

> "And the great dragon was cast out, that old serpent, called the Devil, and Satan, which deceiveth the whole world: he was cast out into the earth, and his angels were cast out with him."

"And he laid hold on the dragon, that old serpent, which is the Devil, and Satan, and bound him a thousand years."

The "seed" is Jesus Christ our Savior. Galatians 3:16 says:

"Now to Abraham and his seed were the promises made. He saith not, And to seeds, as of many; but as of one, And to thy seed, which is Christ."

Jesus Christ, our Lord and Savior, came to this earth to defeat Satan and to rescue lost humanity. He lived the perfect life we cannot live, died our eternal death on the cross of Calvary, then was resurrected; completely defeating "that old serpent, called the Devil", so that we, His kingdom, could live forever in the peace of a sinless eternity. Jesus crushed the head of the serpent, just as He promised, or covenanted.

The woman, the church, the bride, is God's kingdom of Christ. Ephesians 5:22-33 says:

"Wives, submit yourselves unto your own husbands, as unto the Lord. For the husband is the head of the wife, even as Christ is the head of the church: and he is the saviour of the body. Therefore as the church is subject unto Christ, so *let* the wives *be* to their own husbands in every thing. Husbands, love your wives, even as Christ also loved the church, and gave himself for it; That he might sanctify and cleanse it with the washing of water by the word, That he might present it to himself a glorious church, not having spot, or wrinkle, or any such thing; but that it should be holy and without blemish. So ought men to love their wives as their own bodies. He that loveth his wife loveth himself. For no man ever yet hated his own flesh; but nourisheth and cherisheth it, even as the Lord the church: For we are members of his body, of his flesh, and of his bones. For this cause shall a man leave his father and mother, and shall be joined unto his wife, and they two shall be one flesh. This is a great mystery: but I speak concerning Christ and the church. Nevertheless let every one of you in particular to love his wife even as himself; and the wife *see* that she reverence *her* husband."

There also is the covenant God made with all mankind. God said in Jeremiah 11:4, "I will be your God if you will be my people." Notice Leviticus 26:1-13:

"Ye shall make you no idols nor graven image, neither rear you up a standing image, neither shall ye set up *any* image of stone in your land, to bow down unto it: for I *am* the LORD your God. Ye shall keep my sabbaths, and reverence my sanctuary: I *am* the LORD. If ye walk in my statutes, and keep my commandments, and do them; Then I will give you rain in due season, and the land shall yield her increase, and the trees of the field shall yield their fruit. And your threshing shall reach unto the vintage, and the vintage shall reach unto the sowing time: and ye shall eat your bread to the full, and dwell in your land safely. And I will give peace in the land, and ye shall lie down, and none shall make *you* afraid: and I will rid evil beasts out of the land, neither shall the sword go through your land. And ye shall chase your enemies, and they shall fall before you by the

185

sword. And five of you shall chase an hundred, and an hundred of you shall put ten thousand to flight: and your enemies shall fall before you by the sword. For I will have respect unto you, and make you fruitful, and multiply you, and establish my **covenant** with you. And ye shall eat old store, and bring forth the old because of the new. And I will set my tabernacle among you: and my soul shall not abhor you. And I will walk among you, and will be your God, and ye shall be my people. I *am* the LORD your God, which brought you forth out of the land of Egypt, that ye should not be their bondmen; and I have broken the bands of your yoke, and made you go upright."

Notice the following:

"And he declared unto you his **covenant**, which he commanded you to perform, *even* **ten commandments**; and he wrote them upon two tables of stone." Deuteronomy 4:13

"And he was there with the LORD forty days and forty nights; he did neither eat bread, nor drink water. And he wrote upon the tables the words of the **covenant**, the **ten commandments**." Exodus 34:28

"Then verily the first *covenant* had also ordinances of divine service, and a worldly sanctuary. For there was a tabernacle made; the first, wherein *was* the candlestick, and the table, and the shewbread; which is called the sanctuary. And after the second veil, the tabernacle which is called the Holiest of all; Which had the golden censer, and the ark of the **covenant** overlaid round about with gold, wherein *was* the golden pot that had manna, and Aaron's rod that budded, and **the tables of the covenant**; And over it the cherubims of glory shadowing the mercyseat; of which we cannot now speak particularly."

Hebrews 9:1-5

Notice also that the box called the Ark, that Moses made (Exodus 25:10-22), is called the **Ark of the Covenant**. It's also called the Ark of the Testimony (Exodus 26:33).

The book of the law, the Torah, which Moses wrote with his own fingers was placed on the <u>outside</u> of the Ark of the Covenant:

"And it came to pass, when Moses had made an end of writing the words of this law in a book, until they were finished, That Moses commanded the Levites, which bare the ark of the covenant of the LORD, saying, Take this book of the law, and put it in the side of the ark of the covenant of the LORD your God, that it may be there for a witness against thee." Deuteronomy 31:24-26.

But the **Ten Commandment Covenant law**, written by the finger of God was put **inside** the Ark which is covered by the Mercy Seat, for the Shekinah Glory of God Himself.

"*There was* nothing in the ark save the two tables of stone, which Moses put there at Horeb, when the LORD made *a covenant* with the children of Israel, when they came out of the land of Egypt." 1 Kings 8:9.

The Ark of the Covenant was placed in the center of the Sanctuary or Tent of Meeting, in the Most Holy Place making the Ten Commandments the center, overshadowed by the very presence of God with the Shekinah Glory of the Mercy Seat (Exodus 26:33,34).

The **covenant**, referred to in the book of Daniel, is the **TEN COMMANDMENTS**.

(2)   Who is the PRINCE OF THE COVENANT?

In our study on Daniel chapter eight we discovered that Jesus is the Prince of princes as is mentioned in Daniel 8:25. Jesus is the Son of God the Father (1 John 5:20). God gave mankind the Ten Commandments, which He wrote Himself on two tablets of stone with His own finger.

Thus Jesus is not only our "Prince and Savior", as Acts 5:31 tells us, but Jesus Christ is also the PRINCE OF THE COVENANT.

As we discussed in our consideration of Daniel eight, the Little Horn Power will challenge Jesus, the Prince of peace, but he will not be successful and he will be defeated.

DEFINING THE PERPETUAL OR CONTINUAL

Of course the next question we must consider is:

QUESTION: WHAT IS THE **PERPETUAL** OR **CONTINUAL** THAT WILL BE TAKEN AWAY IN THE FUTURE BY THE LITTLE HORN POWER?

As with all the time periods in the Bible, we do not have the privilege or right to place these time periods just anywhere we want in human history. Each time period must be placed at the correct beginning and ending points dictated by scripture. In this case, the 1,290-day future time prophecy must begin when the PERPETUAL or CONTINUAL is abandoned. Daniel 12:11 says:

> "And from the time *that* the perpetual (continual) shall be taken away, and the abomination that maketh desolate set up, *there shall be* a thousand two hundred and ninety days."

In other words: From the time the **continual** is taken away UNTIL the abomination of desolation is set up there will be 1,290 days, or one could say, there is 1,290 days between the time the continual is taken away UNTIL the abomination of desolation is set up. In any way you look at it, the 1,290-day time period **begins** when the **CONTINUAL** is taken away and it **ends** when the abomination of desolation is established or "set up".

(3) What is the perpetual and what is the abomination of desolation?

Remember: Sola Scriptura; the Bible only. The Bible must interpret itself. 2 Peter 1:20,21 says:

> "Knowing this first, that no prophecy of the scripture is of any private interpretation. For the prophecy came not in old time by the will of man: but holy men of God spake *as they were* moved by the Holy Ghost."

Let's collect some clues in our attempt to identify the Biblical PERPETUAL or CONTINUAL:

1. It is something that can be removed, taken away, and abandoned.
2. It is something that can be replaced.
3. It will be replaced by the abomination of desolation.
4. It is something that will affect God's people since there is a special blessing to those which remain faithful from the 1,290 days up to the 1,335 days.
5. It is approved by God whereas the abomination of desolation is not approved.
6. It is related to the covenant, which is the Ten Commandments.

QUESTION: What part of the Ten Commandments Holy Covenant can be challenged, removed, abandoned, and replaced?

ANSWER: Only one of the Ten Commandments can be "taken away" and replaced with something else. That is the seventh-day Sabbath, the fourth commandment, which Biblically is from Friday night sundown to Saturday night sundown (Genesis 1:1 to 2:4).

QUESTION: Is there a text in the Bible to support the seventh-day Sabbath as being the perpetual or CONTINUAL of Daniel 12:11?

ANSWER: Yes. Notice Exodus 31:12-17:

> "And the LORD spake unto Moses, saying, Speak thou also unto the children of Israel, saying, Verily my sabbaths ye shall keep: for it *is* a sign between me and you throughout your generations; that *ye* may know that I *am* the LORD that doth sanctify you. Ye shall keep the sabbath therefore; for it *is* holy unto you: every

one that defileth it shall surely be put to death: for whosoever doeth *any* work therein, that soul shall be cut off from among his people. Six days may work be done; but in the seventh *is* the sabbath of rest, holy to the LORD: whosoever doeth *any* work in the sabbath day, he shall surely be put to death. Wherefore the children of Israel shall keep the sabbath, to observe the **sabbath** throughout their generations, *for* **a perpetual covenant**. It *is* a sign between me and the children of Israel for ever: for *in* six days the LORD made heaven and earth, and on the seventh day he rested, and was refreshed."

The CONTINUAL or PERPETUAL Sabbath will be "taken away" in the near future.

It's very important to realize what the CONTINUAL is, because all the prophetic time periods of Daniel and Revelation begin when the Sabbath is forcibly abandoned. This should not surprise us that the Sabbath will be challenged and abandoned in the near future. Look at the entire religious world around this globe. Even now the seventh-day Sabbath is not honored by the majority of religious organizations. As a matter of fact, many of them blatantly deny the Sabbath with the following false excuses which cannot be substantiated by scripture.

1. Jesus changed the Sabbath to Sunday.
2. Jesus abolished the Sabbath on the cross.
3. Paul changed the Sabbath to Sunday.
4. The apostles changed the Sabbath to Sunday.
5. The seventh-day Sabbath was abandoned and replaced with the first day of the week, Sunday, in honor of the resurrection.

191

6. Jesus is the Sabbath.

All these ridiculous excuses, manufactured by man, are used to deny honoring the seventh-day Sabbath of the Ten Commandment covenant. Notice Matthew 15:9:

"Howbeit in vain do they worship me, teaching *for* doctrines the commandments of men."

QUESTION: What is the CONTINUAL or PERPETUAL of Daniel 12:11 that will be "taken away" which marks the beginning of the time periods in Daniel and Revelation?

ANSWER: The fourth commandment of the Ten Commandment covenant, the seventh-day Sabbath, is the CONTINUAL of Daniel 12:11 which will be outlawed in the future.

QUESTION: What is the ABOMINATION OF DESOLATION that will be "set up" in its place?

IDENTIFYING THE ABOMINATION OF DESOLATION

What is an "abomination of desolation" or an "abomination that causes desolation"?

An "abomination" is that which is detestable and unacceptable by our creator God.

A "desolation" is an emptiness, void, complete destruction, without life, death.

An "abomination that causes desolation" is a detestable act against God that causes Him to react in such a way as to bring about complete destruction. Biblical examples of "abomination of desolation" or those events which brought about Gods wrath are:

1. The "abomination" was the rampant sin before the flood in Noah's day. The "desolation" was the destruction of all the living because of the sin. Genesis 6-9.
2. Destruction of sinful Sodom and Gomorrah in Abraham's day: Genesis 18,19.
3. The destruction of the rebellious ten northern tribes of Israel: 2 Kings 17,18.
4. The captivity the two unfaithful southern tribes via Nebuchadnezzar: Daniel 1.
5. The soon coming seven-year tribulation revealing God's wrath against those which refuse to trust and obey Him at the time of the end: Matthew 24:21.

BIBLICAL EXAMPLES OF THE WORD ABOMINATION:

"For the froward *is* abomination to the LORD: but his secret *is* with the righteous." Proverbs 3:32

"He that turneth away his ear from hearing the law, even his prayer *shall be* abomination." Proverbs 28:9

"A false balance *is* abomination to the LORD: but a just weight *is* his delight." Proverbs 11:1

"Judah hath dealt treacherously, and an abomination is committed in Israel and in Jerusalem; for Judah hath profaned the holiness of the LORD which he loved, and hath married the daughter of a strange god." Malachi 2:11

BIBLICAL EXAMPLES OF THE WORD DESOLATION:

> "These two *things* are come unto thee; who shall be sorry for thee? desolation, and destruction, and the famine, and the sword: by whom shall I comfort thee?" Isaiah 51:19.

> "Thy holy cities are a wilderness, Zion is a wilderness, Jerusalem a desolation. Our holy and our beautiful house, where our fathers praised thee, is burned up with fire: and all our pleasant things are laid waste." Isaiah 64:10, 11.

To set up an "abomination of desolation" is to establish something that goes against the will of God bringing about His actions of destructive anger and wrath against mankind.

The term "set up" is important to note since it refers us back to Daniel chapter three when King Nebuchadnezzar "set up" the golden image which promoted FORCED WORSHIP.

QUESTION: What is the ABOMINATION OF DESOLATION that will be "set up" in place of the Seventh-day Sabbath?

ANSWER: The end time "ABOMINATION THAT CAUSES DESOLATION" is the establishing of a false day of worship which will be demanded on all mankind, to replace the seventh-day Sabbath. Most likely that false day of worship will be the first day of the week, Sunday, since it is already popular around this globe.

Daniel 12:13:

> "But go thou thy way till the end *be*: for thou shalt rest, and stand in thy lot at the end of the days."

When Daniel heard these tremendously long time periods, noted in Daniel 12:7,11,12; the Lord must have noticed the disappointment on his facial expression. Daniel knew that the seventy years' captivity was passed and now he was anxious for his fellow countrymen to return to their home land. For him, an additional 1,290 days and 1,335 days must have been overwhelming. But the Lord told him to go about his own life. He told Daniel the time periods are for the end of the world's history. God encouraged Daniel by telling him "at the end of the days", after the 1000 years, he will receive eternal life.

This information should help us better understand the information found in Daniel 12:1-4:

> "And at that time shall Michael stand up, the great prince which standeth for the children of thy people: and there shall be a time of trouble, such as never was since there was a nation *even* to that same time: and at that time thy people shall be delivered, every one that shall be found written in the book. And many of them that sleep in the dust of the earth shall awake, some to everlasting life, and some to shame *and* everlasting contempt. And they that be wise shall shine as the brightness of the firmament; and they that turn many to righteousness as the stars for ever and ever. But thou, O Daniel, shut up the words, and seal the book, *even* to the time of the end: many shall run to and fro, and knowledge shall be increased."

Daniel was encouraged to go about his daily life and not worry about this vision because in time, at the last day, he will be resurrected from the dead, along with all the other saints, to

195

spend eternity with God. Paul believed the same thing. He writes in 2 Timothy 4:8:

> "Henceforth there is laid up for me a crown of righteousness, which the Lord, the righteous judge, shall give me at **that day**: and not to me only, but unto **all them** also that love his appearing."

QUESTION: When is the last day? Or When is the day Daniel and Paul, with all the saints, receive eternal life?

Martha, the sister of Lazarus, knew about **the last day** and the resurrection of the dead when they would receive a glorified eternal immortal body: Notice John 11:23,24:

> "Jesus saith unto her, Thy brother shall rise again. Martha saith unto him, I know that he shall rise again in the resurrection at **the last day**."

In John 6:38-40 Jesus said:

> "For I came down from heaven, not to do mine own will, but the will of him that sent me. And this is the Father's will which hath sent me, that of all which he hath given me I should lose nothing, but should raise it up again at **the last day**. And this is the will of him that sent me, that every one which seeth the Son, and believeth on him, may have everlasting life: and I will raise him up at **the last day**."

The last day, the day that eternal life and eternal death are rewarded, will be the "last day" after the 1000 years of Revelation

20, when sin is destroyed and God creates "a new heaven and a new earth".

See the **YouTube** video on **DANIEL CHAPTER TWELVE** by Earl Schrock.

DANIEL CHAPTER TWELVE (KJV)

1And at that time shall Michael stand up, the great prince which standeth for the children of thy people: and there shall be a time of trouble, such as never was since there was a nation *even* to that same time: and at that time thy people shall be delivered, every one that shall be found written in the book. 2And many of them that sleep in the dust of the earth shall awake, some to everlasting life, and some to shame *and* everlasting contempt. 3And they that be wise shall shine as the brightness of the firmament; and they that turn many to righteousness as the stars for ever and ever. 4But thou, O Daniel, shut up the words, and seal the book, *even* to the time of the end: many shall run to and fro, and knowledge shall be increased.

5Then I Daniel looked, and, behold, there stood other two, the one on this side of the bank of the river, and the other on that side of the bank of the river. 6And *one* said to the man clothed in linen, which *was* upon the waters of the river, How long *shall it be to* the end of these wonders? 7And I heard the man clothed in linen, which *was* upon the waters of the river, when he held up his right hand and his left hand unto heaven, and sware by him that liveth for ever that *it shall be* for a time, times, and an half; and when he shall have accomplished to scatter the power of the holy people, all these *things* shall be finished. 8And I heard, but I understood not: then said I, O my Lord, what *shall be* the end of these *things*? 9And he said, Go thy way, Daniel: for the words *are* closed up and sealed till the time of the end. 10Many shall be purified, and made white, and tried; but the wicked shall do wickedly: and none of the wicked shall understand; but the wise shall understand. 11And from the time *that* the daily *sacrifice* shall be taken away, and the abomination that maketh desolate set up, *there shall be* a thousand two hundred and ninety days. 12Blessed *is* he that waiteth, and cometh to the thousand three hundred and five and thirty days. 13But go thou thy way till the end *be*: for thou shalt rest, and stand in thy lot at the end of the days.

CHAPTER THIRTEEN

THE VINEGAR AT THE CROSS OF CALVARY

Many of us have read or been taught that Jesus was offered vinegar on two separate occasions while He was being crucified. Numerous Bible scholars have written about the vinegar at the cross of Calvary and have presented their personal various opinions. The <u>first</u> time Jesus was offered the bitter drink was at the third hour (9 a.m.). The <u>second</u> time it was offered to Him was at the ninth hour (3 p.m.), six hours later. He refused (Matthew 27:34) the bitter drink at the third hour, but at the ninth hour, He actually asked for it when He said, "*I thirst*" (John 19:28). When given to Him, He drank it (Matthew 27:48).
The general consensus of the numerous Bible scholars is that the vinegar was at the site of the crucifixion to be offered to those being crucified to dull their senses making the crucifixion more tolerable.

Some Bible expositors conclude that Jesus refused the vinegar the first time so He could experience the suffering and endure the cross without any benumbing assistance. On the second occasion, they teach He requested the vinegar because He was thirsty and wanted relief from the pain. These conclusions are merely opinion, and neither are substantiated by scripture.

WHY WAS THE VINEGAR AT THE CROSS?

A couple of questions to consider are: (1) Why was the vinegar at the cross in the first place? and (2) Was the vinegar there to show compassion to those impaled on the tree (Acts 10:39)?

We first must recognize that it was the soldiers (Matthew 27:27-36) that offered Jesus the vinegar (Luke 23:36) at the onset of his crucifixion and not one of his friends. Jesus was being guarded by four Roman soldiers (John 19:23). Not only were they there to crucify Jesus, but they were also there to guard Him from others who might interfere with their duty. The vinegar could not have been offered by any passers-by since they would not have been allowed to get close enough to the victim to make that humane gesture. Only the Roman soldiers had the capability to give Jesus the strong drink.

The offer of vinegar was not to show compassion to those hanging on the cross. The Romans had devised crucifixion as a terrible method of execution making it as humiliating and as painful as possible. The humiliation would come as the criminal would be stripped naked (Matthew 27:35, John 19:23) for all to see, and their crimes would be fastened on the cross (John 19:19-22) for all to read. The excruciating pain would be the natural result of first being flogged (Mark 15:15) and then hung on the cross with nails piercing the hands and feet (Psalm 22:16, Luke 24:40). The Romans hated the Jews, so showing compassion by offering medicinal assistance to the one being crucified would be incongruent and counterproductive.

The vinegar was located at Golgotha (Mark 15:22) because the Roman soldiers were there. Vinegar was a staple part of a soldier's diet. The cheap bitter drink (Matthew 27:34; Mark 15:23) was not offered in a show of compassion; it was most likely offered as a mockery (Luke 23:36).

Forcing vinegar into the broken and swollen face of Jesus would have increased His pain as the burning liquid came in contact with his bruised and bleeding face and split lips. To offer it as a cupbearer offers wine to a king (Genesis 40:21; 2 Chronicles 9:4) would add to the Roman soldiers' mockery just as they called Him *"the king of the Jews"* and jeered at Him to *"save thyself"* (Luke 23:37). So why did Jesus refuse the vinegar when it was first offered in the morning yet drank it when it was given the second time?

To realize why Jesus first refused and then later asked for the vinegar, we must understand (1) the gospel message Jesus preached while on this earth and (2) we must understand the Biblical teaching of a Nazarite vow.

THE KINGDOM OF GOD IS AT HAND (NEAR).

What was the message Jesus proclaimed while going from town to town with His disciples? Notice Mark 1:14,15 *"Now after that John was put in prison, Jesus came into Galilee, preaching the gospel of the kingdom of God, And saying, The time is fulfilled, and the kingdom of God is at hand: repent ye, and believe the gospel!"* Also in Luke 8:1, *"And it came to pass afterward, that he went throughout every city and village, preaching and shewing the glad tidings of the kingdom of God."*

The kingdom of God being near was also the message of John before baptizing Jesus. *"In those days came John the Baptist, preaching in the wilderness of Judaea, And saying, Repent ye: for the kingdom of heaven is at hand."* (Matthew 3:1,2). The promise of the kingdom of God being *"near"* or *"at hand"* means it was soon to be readily available to all mankind at that time, in their day, not delayed 2000 years later, in our day.

The kingdom of God is not a place; it's a relationship. A relationship between the created (mankind) and their Creator (John 1:1-5). The kingdom of heaven is a relationship set up or built by Jesus for all mankind by His life, death, and resurrection. The kingdom of heaven is within you (Luke 17:21). It is the kingdom *"built without hands"* (Mark 14:58) as demonstrated in Daniel chapter two.

THE KINGDOM OF GOD AND VINEGAR

What does the kingdom of God have to do with Jesus drinking the vinegar just before He died on the cross?

The question many people are asking is: *"When did the kingdom of God begin*, which Jesus prepared *"without hands"* from the *"foundation of the world?"* In other words, when was the kingdom of heaven made available for all mankind?

Answer: At the cross.

Jesus made a controversial statement when he told his disciples, *"But I tell you of a truth, there be some standing here, which shall not taste of death, till they see the kingdom of God."* (Luke 9:27). Compare that with Mark 9:1, *"And he said unto them, Verily I say unto you, That there be some of them that stand here, which shall not taste of death, till they have seen the kingdom of God come with power."* That power came fifty days after Jesus died on the cross of Calvary, in the upper room (Acts 2:1-4) at Pentacost.

There are two explanations or understandings for the Kingdom of God. The two explanations fall under the categories of (1) kingdom of grace and (2) kingdom of glory. The Kingdom of God of "GRACE" (Hebrews 12:28 KJV) was established at the cross. The eternal Kingdom of God of "GLORY" (2 Timothy

4:18) will be established at the time of the end (Matthew 16:27; 25:31-46) when sin is forever destroyed and God creates *"a new heaven and a new earth"* (Revelation 21:1) *"wherein dwelleth righteousness"* (2 Peter 3:11-13).

There are many who have been taught that God's kingdom of grace will not be created until Jesus comes the second time. For that reason, these people are under the impression Jesus lied to His disciples about some of them being alive to see the kingdom of God established (Mark 9:1). It's not that Jesus sinned by lying that they have this misunderstanding; it's that they don't realize the nature of the Kingdom of God. Remember the Kingdom of God is not a place; it's a relationship. A relationship between the created and the Creator which Jesus established with His life, death, and resurrection for you and for me. The kingdom of God of grace is available right here and right now for all who wish to have an endearing everlasting relationship with Jesus as their king with the Holy Spirit living within (2 Corinthians 1:22).

Jesus established the kingdom of grace while hanging on the cross and the power of that kingdom was demonstrated fifty days later in the upper room (Acts 2:1-4) just as He promised (Luke 9:27). The only requirement to enter this present day kingdom of grace is to have the *"wedding garment"* (Matthew 22:1-14), representing His righteousness, which is only available by accepting Jesus as one's personal savior who lived and died in our place.

How do we know that Jesus established the Kingdom of God while dying on the cross? To answer this question, we must understand the scriptural vow of a Nazarite. In the Bible, we have only three other examples of people set aside under the Nazarite oath. They are: (1) Samson in Judges 13:5-7, and

(2) Samuel in 1 Samuel 1:11, and (3) John the Baptist in Luke 1:11-17.

Consider Numbers 6:1-8.

> "And the LORD spake unto Moses, saying, Speak unto the children of Israel, and say unto them, When either man or woman shall separate themselves to vow a vow of a Nazarite, to separate themselves unto the LORD: He shall separate himself from wine and strong drink, and shall drink no vinegar of wine, or vinegar of strong drink, neither shall he drink any liquor of grapes, nor eat moist grapes, or dried. All the days of his separation shall he eat nothing that is made of the vine tree, from the kernels even to the husk. All the days of the vow of his separation there shall no rasor come upon his head: until the days be fulfilled, in the which he separateth himself unto the LORD, he shall be holy, and shall let the locks of the hair of his head grow. All the days that he separateth himself unto the LORD he shall come at no dead body. He shall not make himself unclean for his father, or for his mother, for his brother, or for his sister, when they die: because the consecration of his God is upon his head. All the days of his separation he is holy unto the LORD."

The one under a pledge of a Nazarite must fulfill three requirements. They cannot (1) drink or eat any grape or grapevine product including vinegar. (2) They cannot cut their hair or shave their head. And (3) they cannot come in contact with a dead body.

JESUS AND HIS NAZARITE VOW

At His Passover feast with His disciples, before the crucifixion, Jesus placed himself under the vow of a Nazarite. *"And he took the cup, and gave thanks, and said, Take this, and divide it among yourselves: For I say unto you, I will not drink of the fruit of the vine, until the kingdom of God shall come."* Luke 22:17, 18. Consider also Matthew 26:26-29:

> *"And as they were eating, Jesus took bread, and blessed it, and brake it, and gave it to the disciples, and said, Take, eat; this is my body. And he took the cup, and gave thanks, and gave it to them, saying, Drink ye all of it; For this is my blood of the new testament, which is shed for many for the remission of sins. But I say unto you, I will not drink henceforth of this fruit of the vine, until that day when I drink it new with you in my Father's kingdom."*

Jesus previously told them in Luke 22 verses 15 and 16, *"And he said unto them, With desire I have desired to eat this passover with you before I suffer: For I say unto you, I will not any more eat thereof, until it be fulfilled in the kingdom of God."* Verse 19 continues, *"And he took bread, and gave thanks, and brake it, and gave unto them, saying, This is my body which is given for you: this do in remembrance of me."* Not only did Jesus say He would not partake of any grape or grapevine product but He also added to the vow by saying He would not eat bread *"until the kingdom of God shall come."* (Luke 22:18).

JESUS KEPT THE VOW OF A NAZARITE

Jesus began his oath of a Nazarite at the last supper while in the upper room with His disciples (Luke 22:11,12), before they went to the Garden of Gethsemane (Matthew 26:36), and before He was taken prisoner by *"the chief priests and elders"* (Matthew 26:47-50). Jesus ended His Nazarite vow while dying on the cross.

From the time Jesus left the upper room with His disciples, until the cross, Jesus (1) did not eat or drink any product from the grapevine, (2) did not cut his hair, (3) did not come in the presence of a dead body as is demanded in Numbers chapter six; (4) nor did He eat bread, as He more specifically promised.

The first offer of vinegar was presented Jesus at the beginning of the crucifixion at the third hour or at nine o'clock in the morning (Matthew 27:1,33, 34), but Jesus refused the vinegar. Jesus knew it was not the time to establish the kingdom so when the vinegar touched His lips, He declined it. By the time the second offer of vinegar came, at the 9th hour or three in the afternoon (Matthew 27:46-48), Jesus ended or completed His Nazarite vow by drinking the vinegar, a product of the grapevine. He knew that all had been accomplished as was prophesied in the scriptures and the time had come for Him to fulfill the scripture (John 19:28), establish the Kingdom of God, and die (John 19:30).

Jesus is the sacrificial Passover lamb (1 Corinthians 5:7). He is *"the Lamb of God, which taketh away the sin of the world"* (John 1:29). The day Jesus was crucified was the day of the Biblical Jewish Passover (Mark 14:12-17). Jesus could not drink the first offer of vinegar and die at the third hour (Mark 15:25); Jesus had to die at the ninth hour which is the set time the Passover lamb was historically sacrificed (Exodus 12:6). He had to die at the specific time He drank the vinegar, at the ninth hour (Mark 15:34), in order to fulfill scripture (Psalm 69:21), honor the

Nazarite vow, and reveal the beginning of the kingdom of God which is available to you and to me right here and right now.

Think of Jesus on the cross while reading Psalm 69:17-21:

*"And hide not thy face from thy servant; for I am in trouble: hear me speedily. Draw nigh unto my soul, and redeem it: deliver me because of mine enemies. Thou hast known my reproach, and my shame, and my dishonour: mine adversaries are all before thee. Reproach hath broken my heart; and I am full of heaviness: and I looked for some to take pity, but there was none; and for comforters, but I found none. They gave me also gall for my meat; and in my **thirst** they gave me **vinegar** to drink."*

Jesus kept His vow of a Nazarite by not drinking the vinegar at the first offer. He completed His Nazarite oath by drinking it the second time it was delivered to His lips. He also further and more specifically proved the kingdom of God had come by eating bread after His resurrection. The scripture reports that on the day of His resurrection Jesus *"broke bread"* with two of His disciples (Luke 24:13,30) on the road to Emmaus. Jesus also *"ate and drank"* wine with the disciples *"after he rose from the dead."* (Acts 10:41). To better understand His Nazarite vow, keep all this in mind as you read all of Psalm 22 and Luke 23.

The Bible mentioning the two offers of vinegar at the cross is not by accident or happenstance. These two incidents are specifically included in the gospels by the will of God for our growth and understanding (2 Timothy 3:16,17). The writers of the gospels recording this event were moved by the Holy Spirit (2 Peter 1:19-21) to include the vinegar incidents for two specific reasons.

I believe one reason the vinegar at the cross was included in the Holy Bible is so we could confirm when the kingdom of God became available to all mankind and how it came into existence through the sacrifice of Jesus Himself (Genesis 22:8), *the Lamb of God, who takes away the sin of the world!"* John 1:29.

The second reason the vinegar at the cross was included in the story of salvation is because it was a fulfillment of prophecy and the Mosaic law. In the Mosaic ceremonial sacrificial law two lambs, a year old, were to be sacrificed every single day without interruption. Notice the following from Numbers 28:1-8: (emphasis is that of the author).

> "And the LORD spake unto Moses, saying, Command the children of Israel, and say unto them, My offering, and my bread for my sacrifices made by fire, for a sweet savour unto me, shall ye observe to offer unto me in their due season. And thou shalt say unto them, This is the offering made by fire which ye shall offer unto the LORD; **two lambs of the first year without spot day by day**, for a continual burnt offering. The one lamb shalt thou offer **in the morning**, and the other lamb shalt thou offer **at even**; And a tenth part of an ephah of flour for a meat offering, mingled with the fourth part of an hin of beaten oil. It is a continual burnt offering, which was ordained in mount Sinai for a sweet savour, a sacrifice made by fire unto the LORD. And **the drink offering** thereof shall be the fourth part of an hin for the one lamb: in the holy place shalt thou cause the strong **(fermented)** wine to be poured unto the LORD for a **drink offering**. And the other lamb shalt thou offer **at even**: as the meat offering of

the morning, and as the **drink offering** thereof, thou shalt offer it, a sacrifice made by fire, of a sweet savour unto the LORD."

(Strong's 7941 "shekhar" is a strong or **fermented** or **vinegar** drink offered **only** with the continual or perpetual morning and evening sacrifice.)

In the Mosaic ceremonial sacrificial law system, the **ONLY** sacrificial offering made to the Lord with **fermented drink**, or **vinegar**, was the daily food offering, made twice every day, once in the **morning** and once in the **evening**. Jesus fulfilled this ceremonial law when He was offered vinegar in the morning and vinegar in the evening. Due to His Nazarite vow, He could not drink the vinegar until just before His death, at the evening sacrifice to bring in the kingdom of God.

THE KINGDOM OF HEAVEN, KINGDOM OF GOD **

The Kingdom of God (kingdom of heaven) exists right here and right now for His people around this globe to have a place of unification under one King (Ezekiel 37:18-28); not in a building or in a single congregation but in a unifying relationship with Jesus (John 11:52). I call this large group of devoted worshippers of God located in every country in the world, "The Invisible Church." God calls them "The Kingdom of Heaven." The Invisible Church has no walls, collects no offering, and does not hold regular meetings where all the members are collectively gathered. The "Invisible Church" or the kingdom of God, is God's worldwide people, the New Jerusalem, Mt. Zion, united in one name. That one name is **Jesus** (Acts 4:12). God's desire is to have "one flock with One Shepherd."

Notice the words of Jesus found in John 10:11-18:

209

"I am the good shepherd: the good shepherd giveth his life for the sheep. But he that is an hireling, and not the shepherd, whose own the sheep are not, seeth the wolf coming, and leaveth the sheep, and fleeth: and the wolf catcheth them, and scattereth the sheep. The hireling fleeth, because he is an hireling, and careth not for the sheep. I am the good shepherd, and know my sheep, and am known of mine. As the Father knoweth me, even so know I the Father: and I lay down my life for the sheep. And other sheep I have, which are not of this fold: them also I must bring, and they shall hear my voice; and **there shall be one fold, and one shepherd**. Therefore doth my Father love me, because I lay down my life, that I might take it again. No man taketh it from me, but I lay it down of myself. I have power to lay it down, and I have power to take it again. This commandment have I received of my Father."

The kingdom of God exists so His people around this globe can praise the King of the universe in pure reverence and obedience the way He demands to be worshipped in His Word. For this reason, Daniel chapter two reveals the Invisible Church or kingdom of God, as a stone *"cut out of a mountain without hands"* (Daniel 2:34,45) which begins small, at the cross, and grows to envelop this entire planet (Daniel 2:35).

As you read the Bible, the Word of God, daily for yourself seek to discover the true pure worship God demands. *"choose you this day whom ye will serve…. but as for me and my house, we will serve the LORD."* (Joshua 24:15).

If you have not already done so, won't you give your heart, mind, and soul to God and enter into His kingdom of grace right here and right now. He prepared this kingdom for you from the foundation of the world and secured it with His death upon the cruel cross. Entering the kingdom of grace will prepare you to enter His future eternal kingdom of glory.

** Learn more about the kingdom of God by reading the eBook, "The Kingdom of Heaven and the Kingdom of God" by Earl B. Schrock, found at Xlibris,com, Amazon, Barnes and Noble, etc.

CHAPTER FOURTEEN

UNDERSTANDING THE BIBLICAL MECHANICS OF: PROPHECY LOOPS, NATURAL DIVISIONS, AND TIME LOOPS

Understanding the Biblical Mechanics; the structure of Bible writing, whether in the entire Bible, an entire book, entire chapter, or of the verses themselves, helps the Bible students correctly divide the Word of God

(2 Timothy 2:15) so the correct meaning can be ascertained.

A **PROPHECY LOOP.** or Bible Loop, is a Biblical writing style where verses following a complete thought loop back to add information to the previous verses. (I prefer to use the term PROPHECY LOOP since it's vitally important in understanding Bible prophecy.)

IN Daniel chapter two I find eighteen (18) PROPHECY LOOPS; they are as follows:

Verse 12 loops back to add information concerning verse 5.
Verse 16 loops back to add information concerning verse 2
Verse 19 loops back to add information concerning verse 2
Verse 24 loops back to add information concerning verse 16
Verse 26 loops back to add information concerning verse 5
Verse 27,28 loops back to add information concerning verse 10
Verse 31 loops back to add information concerning verse 2
Verse 37,38 loops back to add information concerning verse 32a
Verse 39 loops back to add information concerning verse 32b
Verse 40 loops back to add information concerning verse 33
Verse 40b loops back to add information concerning verse 35
Verse 41-44 loops back to add information concerning verse 33
Verse 44 loops back to add information concerning verse 42
Verse 45 loops back to add information concerning verse 34
Verse 45 loops back to add information concerning verse 40b
Verse 46 loops back to add information concerning verse 6
Verse 47 loops back to add information concerning verse 28
Verse 48 loops back to add information concerning verse 6

NATURAL DIVISIONS take place within a chapter of the Bible when there is a conversation change or a new topic is introduced. A careful OUTLINE of a Bible chapter reveals the NATURAL DIVISIONS.

In my opinion Daniel chapter two has 8 Natural Divisions. The natural divisions are: (1) verses 1-12 (2) verses 13-16 (3) verses 17-23 (4) verses 24-27 (5) verses 28-30 (6) verses 31-35 (7) verses 36-45 and (8) verses 46-49.

TIME LOOPS occur in Scripture when verses, chapter, or chapters have an <u>uninterrupted</u> beginning and an ending point <u>of time </u>then loops back to another beginning point. In this case of Daniel chapter two, there are three time loops as shown below.

The verses making up Daniel chapter two are 1 to 49.

There are three distinct time loops in Daniel chapter two.

They are put in three time loops because of where these verses fall into a historical timeline:

The three TIME LOOPS are (1) verses 1-35; (2) verses 36 to 45; and (3) verses 46 to 49.

The **first** time loop of verses 1 to 35 goes from Daniel's day to the end of the seven-year tribulation. Then the next verse, verse 36, loops back to Daniel's day.

This **second** time loop of verses 36 to 45 goes from Daniel's day to the end of the seven-year tribulation. Then the next verse, verse 46, loops back to Daniel's day.

This **third** time loop of verses 46 to 49 stays in Daniel's day on the chart.

TIME LOOP HISTORICAL CHART FOR
DANIEL CHAPTER TWO:

Babylon	Medo-Persia	Greece	Rome	Am. Bible Soc.	Time of Trouble
605 BC	**538 BC**	**330 BC**	**168 BC**	**1800 AD**	**SEVEN YEAR TRIBULATION**
Vs1-32			33a	33b	34	35
Vs 36-38	39a	39b	40	41	42-44	45
Vs 46-49						

You may have a difference of opinion about the number and placement of Prophecy Loops, Natural Divisions, and Time Loops in Daniel chapter two and that is quite alright.

THE FOLLOWING PAGE CONTAINS ALL THE
PROPHECY TIME LOOPS FOR THE
BOOK OF DANIEL

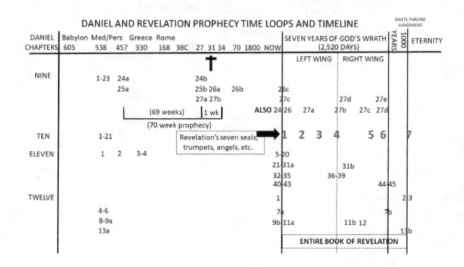

DANIEL AND REVELATION PROPHECY TIME LOOPS AND TIMELINE

WHITE THRONE JUDGEMENT

DANIEL CHAPTERS	Babylon 605	Med/Pers 538 457	Greece 330	Rome 168 3BC 27 31 34 70 1800 NOW	SEVEN YEARS OF GOD'S WRATH (2,520 DAYS)	1000 YEARS	ETERNITY

LEFT WING   RIGHT WING

ONE	1-20	21					
TWO	1-32				33b	34	35
	36-38	39a	39b	40	41	42-44	45
	46-49						
THREE	1-30						
FOUR	1-37				ENTIRE BOOK OF REVELATION		
FIVE		1-31					
SIX		1-28		Revelation's seven seals, trumpets, angels, etc. →	1 2 3 4 5 6	7
SEVEN		1-3					
	4	5	6	7	8	9,10 11
		15,16			12	13-14
				19,20a	17	18
				23	20b 21	22
		28			24	25	26 27
EIGHT		1-3 4	5-8		9-12	
		13			14	
		15-17a			17b	
		18			19	
		20	21 22		23-26	
		27				

DANIEL AND REVELATION PROPHECY TIME LOOPS AND TIMELINE

WHITE THRONE JUDGEMENT

DANIEL CHAPTERS	Babylon 605	Med/Pers 538 457	Greece 330	Rome 168 3BC 27 31 34 70 1800 NOW	SEVEN YEARS OF GOD'S WRATH (2,520 DAYS)	1000 YEARS	ETERNITY

LEFT WING   RIGHT WING

NINE		1-23 24a		24b			
		25a		25b 26a 26b	26c		
		27a 27b			27c	27d 27e
			(69 weeks)	1 wk	ALSO 24 26 27a	27b 27c 27d
			(70 week prophecy)			
TEN		1-21		Revelation's seven seals, trumpets, angels, etc. →	1 2 3 4 5 6	7
ELEVEN		1 2	3-4		5-20	
					21-31a	31b
					32-35	36-39
					40-43	44-45
TWELVE					1	2-3
		4-6			7	7b
		8-9a			9b 11a	11b 12
		13a				13b
					ENTIRE BOOK OF REVELATION	

CHAPTER FIFTEEN

THE LITTLE HORN POWER

QUESTION: What does the Bible say about the LITTLE HORN POWER?

ANSWER: The following are the locations of all the texts in the book of Daniel referring to the Little Horn Power.

1. Daniel two: verses 33-35, 41-45
2. Daniel seven: verses 7,8; 19-27
3. Daniel eight: verses 8-27
4. Daniel nine: verse 27
5. Daniel ten: verse 14
6. Daniel eleven: verses: 20-45
7. Daniel twelve: verses 4-13

Daniel 2:33-35,41-45

33His legs of iron, his feet part of iron and part of clay. **34**Thou sawest till that a stone was cut out without hands, which smote the image upon his feet *that were* of iron and clay, and brake them to pieces. **35**Then was the iron, the clay, the brass, the silver, and the gold, broken to pieces together, and became like the chaff of the summer threshingfloors; and the wind carried them away, that no place was found for them: and the stone that smote the image became a great mountain, and filled the whole earth.

41And whereas thou sawest the feet and toes, part of potters' clay, and part of iron, the kingdom shall be divided; but there shall be in it of the strength of the iron, forasmuch as thou sawest the iron mixed with miry clay. **42**And *as* the toes of the feet *were* part of iron, and part of clay, *so* the kingdom shall be partly strong, and partly broken. **43**And whereas thou sawest iron mixed with miry clay, they shall mingle themselves with the seed of men: but they shall not cleave one to another, even as iron is not mixed with clay. **44**And in the days of these kings shall the God of heaven set up a kingdom, which shall never be destroyed: and the kingdom shall not be left to other people, *but* it shall break in pieces and consume all these kingdoms, and it shall stand for ever. **45**Forasmuch as thou sawest that the stone was cut out of the mountain without hands, and that it brake in pieces the iron, the brass, the clay, the silver, and the gold; the great God hath made known to the king what shall come to pass hereafter: and the dream *is* certain, and the interpretation thereof sure.

Daniel 7:7,8; 19-27

7After this I saw in the night visions, and behold a fourth beast, dreadful and terrible, and strong exceedingly; and it had great iron teeth: it devoured and brake in pieces, and stamped the residue with the feet of it: and it *was* diverse from all the beasts that *were* before it; and it had ten horns. **8**I considered the horns, and, behold, there came up among them another little horn, before whom there were three of the first horns plucked up by the roots: and, behold, in this horn *were* eyes like the eyes of man, and a mouth speaking great things.

19Then I would know the truth of the fourth beast, which was diverse from all the others, exceeding dreadful, whose teeth *were of* iron, and his nails *of* brass; *which* devoured, brake in pieces, and stamped the residue with his feet; **20**And of the ten horns that *were* in his head, and *of* the other which came up, and before whom three fell; even *of* that horn that had eyes, and a mouth that spake very great things, whose look *was* more stout than his fellows. **21**I beheld, and the same horn made war with the saints, and prevailed against them; **22**Until the Ancient of days came, and judgment was given to the saints of the most High; and the time came that the saints possessed the kingdom. **23**Thus he said, The fourth beast shall be the fourth kingdom upon earth, which shall be diverse from all kingdoms, and shall devour the whole earth, and shall tread it down, and break it in pieces. **24**And the ten horns out of this kingdom *are* ten kings *that* shall arise: and another shall rise after them; and he shall be diverse from the first, and he shall subdue three kings. **25**And he shall speak *great* words against the most High, and shall wear out the saints of the most High, and think to change times and laws: and they shall be given into his hand until a time and times and the dividing of time. **26**But the judgment shall sit, and they shall take away his dominion, to consume and to destroy *it* unto the end. **27**And the kingdom and dominion, and the greatness of the kingdom under the whole heaven, shall be given to the people of the saints of the most High, whose kingdom *is* an everlasting kingdom, and all dominions shall serve and obey him.

Daniel eight: 8-27

8Therefore the he goat waxed very great: and when he was strong, the great horn was broken; and for it came up four notable ones toward the four winds of heaven. **9**And out of one of them came forth a little horn, which waxed exceeding great, toward the south, and toward the east, and toward the pleasant *land*. **10**And it waxed great, *even* to the host of heaven; and it cast down *some* of the host and of the stars to the ground, and stamped upon them. **11**Yea, he magnified *himself* even to the prince of the host, and by him the daily *sacrifice* was taken away, and the place of his sanctuary was cast down. **12**And an host was given *him* against the daily *sacrifice* by reason of transgression, and it cast down the truth to the ground; and it practised, and prospered. **13**Then I heard one saint speaking, and another saint said unto that certain *saint* which spake, How long *shall be* the vision *concerning* the daily *sacrifice*, and the transgression of desolation, to give both the sanctuary and the host to be trodden under foot? **14**And he said unto me, Unto two thousand and three hundred days; then shall the sanctuary be cleansed. **15**And it came to pass, when I, *even* I Daniel, had seen the vision, and sought for the meaning, then, behold, there stood before me as the appearance of a man. **16**And I heard a man's voice between *the banks of* Ulai, which called, and said, Gabriel, make this *man* to understand the vision. **17**So he came near where I stood: and when he came, I was afraid, and fell upon my face: but he said unto me, Understand, O son of man: for at the time of the end *shall be* the vision. **18**Now as he was speaking with me, I was in a deep sleep on my face toward the ground: but he touched me, and set me upright. **19**And he said, Behold, I will make thee know what shall be in the last end of the indignation: for at the time appointed the end *shall be*. **20**The ram which thou sawest having *two* horns *are* the kings of Media and Persia. **21**And the rough goat *is* the king of Grecia: and the great horn that *is* between his eyes *is* the first king. **22**Now that being broken, whereas four stood up for it, four kingdoms shall stand up out of the nation, but not in his power. **23**And in the latter time of their kingdom, when the transgressors are come to the full, a king of fierce countenance, and understanding dark sentences, shall stand up. **24**And his power shall be mighty, but not by his own power: and he shall destroy wonderfully, and shall prosper, and practise, and shall destroy the mighty and the holy people. **25**And through his policy also he shall cause craft to prosper in his hand; and he shall magnify *himself* in his heart, and by peace shall destroy many: he shall also stand up against the Prince of princes; but he shall be broken without hand. **26**And the vision of the evening and the morning which was told *is* true: wherefore shut thou up the vision; for it *shall be* for many days.

Daniel 9:27

27And he shall confirm the covenant with many for one week: and in the midst of the week he shall cause the sacrifice and the oblation to cease, and for the overspreading of abominations he shall make *it* desolate, even until the consummation, and that determined shall be poured upon the desolate.

Daniel 10:14

14Now I am come to make thee understand what shall befall thy people in the latter days: for yet the vision *is* for *many* days.

Daniel 11:14-19

(Pre-little horn activity is found in verses 14-19 as below.)

14And in those times there shall many stand up against the king of the south: also the robbers of thy people shall exalt themselves to establish the vision; but they shall fall. **15**So the king of the north shall come, and cast up a mount, and take the most fenced cities: and the arms of the south shall not withstand, neither his chosen people, neither *shall there be any* strength to withstand. **16**But he that cometh against him shall do according to his own will, and none shall stand before

221

him: and he shall stand in the glorious land, which by his hand shall be consumed. 17He shall also set his face to enter with the strength of his whole kingdom, and upright ones with him; thus shall he do: and he shall give him the daughter of women, corrupting her: but she shall not stand *on his side*, neither be for him. 18After this shall he turn his face unto the isles, and shall take many: but a prince for his own behalf shall cause the reproach offered by him to cease; without his own reproach he shall cause *it* to turn upon him. 19Then he shall turn his face toward the fort of his own land: but he shall stumble and fall, and not be found.

Daniel 11:20-45

20Then shall stand up in his estate a raiser of taxes *in* the glory of the kingdom: but within few days he shall be destroyed, neither in anger, nor in battle. 21And in his estate shall stand up a vile person, to whom they shall not give the honour of the kingdom: but he shall come in peaceably, and obtain the kingdom by flatteries. 22And with the arms of a flood shall they be overflown from before him, and shall be broken; yea, also the prince of the covenant. 23And after the league *made* with him he shall work deceitfully: for he shall come up, and shall become strong with a small people. 24He shall enter peaceably even upon the fattest places of the province; and he shall do *that* which his fathers have not done, nor his fathers' fathers; he shall scatter among them the prey, and spoil, and riches: *yea*, and he shall forecast his devices against the strong holds, even for a time. 25And he shall stir up his power and his courage against the king of the south with a great army; and the king of the south shall be stirred up to battle with a very great and mighty army; but he shall not stand: for they shall forecast devices against him. 26Yea, they that feed of the portion of his meat shall destroy him, and his army shall overflow: and many shall fall down slain. **27**And both these kings' hearts *shall be* to do mischief, and they shall speak lies at one table; but it shall not prosper: for yet the end *shall be* at the time appointed. **28**Then shall he return into his land with great riches; and his heart *shall be* against the holy covenant; and he shall do *exploits*, and return to his own land. **29**At the time appointed he shall return, and come toward the south; but it shall not be as the former, or as the latter. **30**For the ships of Chittim shall come against him: therefore he shall be grieved, and return, and have indignation against the holy covenant: so shall he do; he shall even return, and have intelligence with them that forsake the holy covenant. **31**And arms shall stand on his part, and they shall pollute the sanctuary of strength, and shall take away the daily *sacrifice*, and they shall place the abomination that maketh desolate. **32**And such as do wickedly against the covenant shall he corrupt by flatteries: but the people that do know their God shall be strong, and do *exploits*. **33**And they that understand among the people shall instruct many: yet they shall fall by the sword, and by flame, by captivity, and by spoil, *many* days. **34**Now when they shall fall, they shall be holpen with a little help: but many shall cleave to them with flatteries. **35**And *some* of them of understanding shall fall, to try them, and to purge, and to make *them* white, *even* to the time of the end: because *it is* yet for a time appointed. **36**And the king shall do according to his will; and he shall exalt himself, and magnify himself above every god, and shall speak marvellous things against the God of gods, and shall prosper till the indignation be accomplished: for that that is determined shall be done. **37**Neither shall he regard the God of his fathers, nor the desire of women, nor regard any god: for he shall magnify himself above all. **38**But in his estate shall he honour the God of forces: and a god whom his fathers knew not shall he honour with gold, and silver, and with precious stones, and pleasant things. **39**Thus shall he do in the most strong holds with a strange god, whom he shall acknowledge *and* increase with glory: and he shall cause them to rule over many, and shall divide the land for gain. **40**And at the time of the end shall the king of the south push at him: and the king of the north shall come against him like a whirlwind, with chariots, and with horsemen, and with many ships; and he shall enter into the countries, and shall overflow and pass over. **41**He shall enter also into the glorious land, and many *countries* shall be overthrown: but these shall escape out of his hand, *even* Edom, and Moab, and the chief of the children of Ammon. **42**He shall stretch forth his hand also upon the countries: and the land of Egypt shall not escape. **43**But he shall have power over the treasures of gold and of silver, and over all the precious things of Egypt: and the Libyans and the Ethiopians *shall be* at his steps. **44**But tidings out of the east and out of the north shall trouble him: therefore he shall go forth with great fury to destroy, and utterly to make away many. **45**And he shall plant the tabernacles of his palace between the seas in the glorious holy mountain; yet he shall come to his end, and none shall help him.

Daniel 12:1-13

1And at that time shall Michael stand up, the great prince which standeth for the children of thy people: and there shall be a time of trouble, such as never was since there was a nation *even* to that same time: and at that time thy people shall be delivered, every one that shall be found written in the book. **2**And many of them that sleep in the dust of the earth shall awake, some to everlasting life, and some to shame *and* everlasting contempt. **3**And they that be wise shall shine as the brightness of the firmament; and they that turn many to righteousness as the stars for ever and ever. **4**But thou, O Daniel, shut up the words, and seal the book, *even* to the time of the end: many shall run to and fro, and knowledge shall be increased. **5**Then I Daniel looked, and, behold, there stood other two, the one on this side of the bank of the river, and the other on that side of the bank of the river. **6**And *one* said to the man clothed in linen, which *was* upon the waters of the river, How long *shall it be to* the end of these wonders? **7**And I heard the man clothed in linen, which *was* upon the waters of the river, when he held up his right hand and his left hand unto heaven, and sware by him that liveth for ever that *it shall be* for a time, times, and an half; and when he shall have accomplished to scatter the power of the holy people, all these *things* shall be finished. **8**And I heard, but I understood not: then said I, O my Lord, what *shall be* the end of these *things*? **9**And he said, Go thy way, Daniel: for the words *are* closed up and sealed till the time of the end. **10**Many shall be purified, and made white, and tried; but the wicked shall do wickedly: and none of the wicked shall understand; but the wise shall understand. **11**And from the time *that* the daily *sacrifice* shall be taken away, and the abomination that maketh desolate set up, *there shall be* a thousand two hundred and ninety days. **12**Blessed *is* he that waiteth, and cometh to the thousand three hundred and five and thirty days. **13**But go thou thy way till the end *be*: for thou shalt rest, and stand in thy lot at the end of the days.

REVELATION TEXTS CONCERNING THE LITTLE HORN POWER

Revelation 12:3,4

3And there appeared another wonder in heaven; and behold a great red dragon, having seven heads and ten horns, and seven crowns upon his heads. **4**And his tail drew the third part of the stars of heaven, and did cast them to the earth: and the dragon stood before the woman which was ready to be delivered, for to devour her child as soon as it was born.

Revelation 13:

1And I stood upon the sand of the sea, and saw a beast rise up out of the sea, having seven heads and ten horns, and upon his horns ten crowns, and upon his heads the name of blasphemy. **2**And the beast which I saw was like unto a leopard, and his feet were as *the feet* of a bear, and his mouth as the mouth of a lion: and the dragon gave him his power, and his seat, and great authority. **3**And I saw one of his heads as it were wounded to death; and his deadly wound was healed: and all the world wondered after the beast. **4**And they worshipped the dragon which gave power unto the beast: and they worshipped the beast, saying, Who *is* like unto the beast? who is able to make war with him? **5**And there was given unto him a mouth speaking great things and blasphemies; and power was given unto him to continue forty *and* two months. **6**And he opened his mouth in blasphemy against God, to blaspheme his name, and his tabernacle, and them that dwell in heaven. **7**And it was given unto him to make war with the saints, and to overcome them: and power was given him over all kindreds, and tongues, and nations. **8**And all that dwell upon the earth shall worship him, whose names are not written in the book of life of the Lamb slain from the foundation of the world. **9**If any man have an ear, let him hear. **10**He that leadeth into captivity shall go into captivity: he that killeth with the sword must be killed with the sword. Here is the patience and the faith of the saints. **11**And I beheld another beast coming up out of the earth; and he had two horns like a lamb, and he spake as a dragon. **12**And he exerciseth all the power of the first beast before him, and causeth the earth and them which dwell therein to worship the first beast, whose deadly wound was healed. **13**And he doeth great wonders, so that he maketh fire come down from heaven on the earth in the sight of men, **14**And deceiveth them that dwell on the earth by *the means of* those miracles which he had power to do in the sight of the beast; saying to them that dwell on the earth, that they should make an image to the beast, which had the wound by a sword, and did live. **15**And he had power to give life unto the image of the beast, that the image of the beast should both speak, and cause that as many as would not worship the image of the beast should be killed. **16**And he causeth all, both small and great, rich and poor, free and bond, to receive a mark in their right hand, or in their foreheads: **17**And that no man might buy or sell, save he that had the mark, or the name of the beast, or the number of his name. **18**Here is wisdom. Let him that hath understanding count the number of the beast: for it is the number of a man; and his number *is* Six hundred threescore *and* six.

Revelation 17:

1And there came one of the seven angels which had the seven vials, and talked with me, saying unto me, Come hither; I will shew unto thee the judgment of the great whore that sitteth upon many waters: **2**With whom the kings of the earth have committed fornication, and the inhabitants of the earth have been made drunk with the wine of her fornication. **3**So he carried me away in the spirit into the wilderness: and I saw a woman sit upon a scarlet coloured beast, full of names of blasphemy, having seven heads and ten horns. **4**And the woman was arrayed in purple and scarlet colour, and decked with gold and precious stones and pearls, having a golden cup in her hand full of abominations and filthiness of her fornication: **5**And upon her forehead *was* a name written, MYSTERY, BABYLON THE GREAT, THE MOTHER OF HARLOTS AND ABOMINATIONS OF THE EARTH. **6**And I saw the woman drunken with the blood of the saints, and with the blood of the martyrs of Jesus: and when I saw her, I wondered with great admiration. **7**And the angel said unto me, Wherefore didst thou marvel? I will tell thee the mystery of the woman, and of the beast that carrieth her, which hath the seven heads and ten horns.

8The beast that thou sawest was, and is not; and shall ascend out of the bottomless pit, and go into perdition: and they that dwell on the earth shall wonder, whose names were not written in the book of life from the foundation of the world, when they behold the beast that was, and is not, and yet is. **9**And here *is* the mind which hath wisdom. The seven heads are seven mountains, on which the woman sitteth. **10**And there are seven kings: five are fallen, and one is, *and* the other is not yet come; and when he cometh, he must continue a short space. **11**And the beast that was, and is not, even he is the eighth, and is of the seven, and goeth into perdition. **12**And the ten horns which thou sawest are ten kings, which have received no kingdom as yet; but receive power as kings one hour with the beast. **13**These have one mind, and shall give their power and strength unto the beast. **14**These shall make war with the Lamb, and the Lamb shall overcome them: for he is Lord of lords, and King of kings: and they that are with him *are* called, and chosen, and faithful. **15**And he saith unto me, The waters which thou sawest, where the whore sitteth, are peoples, and multitudes, and nations, and tongues. **16**And the ten horns which thou sawest upon the beast, these shall hate the whore, and shall make her desolate and naked, and shall eat her flesh, and burn her with fire. **17**For God hath put in their hearts to fulfil his will, and to agree, and give their kingdom unto the beast, until the words of God shall be fulfilled. **18**And the woman which thou sawest is that great city, which reigneth over the kings of the earth.

QUESTION: WHO OR WHAT IS "THE LITTLE HORN POWER"?

ANSWER: AT THIS TIME, I DON'T REALLY KNOW FOR SURE.

There is much speculation as to the identity of the future Little Horn Power. But that is speculation since there is much information to go on, as revealed above, but very little congealing information to piece the puzzle together appropriately to actually identify the end time Little Horn Power. Since the Little Horn Power is a future event we may not know all the answers to the identity of this power until it arrives. But those familiar with the prophetic books of Daniel and Revelation will be able to properly identify it at the right time, it when it appears.

CHAPTER SIXTEEN

SUMMARY OF EACH CHAPTER

What are some of the most important prophecy lessons to be learned from each of the individual twelve chapters of Daniel?

CHAPTER ONE: The book of Daniel exposes the dilution and pollution of true worship by the mixing of the sacred with the profane as is revealed in Daniel 1:2. Nebuchadnezzar began the dilution of true worship when he mixed the worship items from the temple of God in Jerusalem with the idol worship items in his own temple. He also changed the Hebrew names to pagan names, promoted a pagan diet, and offered a pagan education. Our job today is to keep the worship of God as pure–as–gold as revealed in scripture, avoiding the amalgamation of man's traditions, culture, and ideas. We are to understand the worship God demands, as revealed in the Holy Bible, and worship Him to the best of our ability, in all we do, as we are led and guided by the indwelling Holy Spirit.

CHAPTER TWO: King Nebuchadnezzar's dream not only reveals the evolution of history over God's people from Daniel's day to the end of the world, it also reveals the source of pagan worship which infiltrated God's true worship bringing about the confusion and the variety of worship characteristics throughout the world today, especially in Christendom. His dream also reveals that the stone which strikes the image is the Kingdom of God, enlightening us where it originated and its history. This chapter also helps us understand that the term "earth", in Bible prophecy, does not apply to this total globe or planet. In Bible prophecy the term "earth" applies to God's people. That is the "earth" the four empires of Babylon, Medo-Persia, Greece, and Rome ruled over. None of them ever ruled over the entire planet. The three divisions in Bible prophecy referring to God's people are: heaven, earth, and sea. The "heaven people" serve God 100%. The "earth people" serve Him partially and the "sea people" refuse to serve Him (See Revelation 5:3; 7:3; 12:12; Exodus 20:4, etc). The dream of King Nebuchadnezzar takes us from the days of Daniel to the end of the seven-year tribulation.

The stone which strikes the statue is cut out of a mountain without hands (verse 34) and then it grows into a huge mountain and fills the entire "earth" (verse 35). QUESTION: What is the mountain that the stone is cut out of? ANSWER: The stone is cut out of the mountain which is Mount Zion (Daniel 9:16,20) the holy people of God, the Israelites. Jesus is the "chief cornerstone". The Daniel two stone represents the Kingdom of God which Jesus established with His death on the cross, after drinking the vinegar. (Read the chapter "The Vinegar at the Cross of Calvary" on page 199). The Messiah could only come out of a tribes of Israel (John 4:22), as God promised Abraham in Genesis 22:18 and He was cut out a piece of that mountain to begin the Kingdom of God. Since the cross of Calvary, the message of a merciful Savior has grown from a small group of people to now, which includes this entire planet. Everyone who has accepted Jesus as their Savior since the cross have inherited (Galatians 3:29) and dwelt in the kingdom of God (Colossians 1:9-14).

CHAPTER THREE: This chapter is important because it prepares those living in the last days to be faithful to God, even in the face of death, when the persecution time arrives. God said, "I will never leave you nor forsake you" in Hebrews 13:5. This chapter also answers the question raised in the minds of Bible students concerning Revelation 13:18 about the identity of a man, in the Bible, whose "number is 666." The "number of a man" points to King Nebuchadnezzar who represents FORCED WORSHIP which Revelation warns us of. He put up a statue, in the plain of Dura in the year 600 BC, which was 60 cubits high and 6 cubits wide (Verse one). Also see Ezra 2:13. Of the captives of King Nebuchadnezzar one is named Adonikam which had 666 ancestors return to Jerusalem. In the future an "abomination of desolation" will be "set up" and God's people will be forced to worship it in the face of death, just like that which was experienced by the 3 Hebrews.

CHAPTER FOUR: This dream again confirms that in Bible prophecy the "earth" is God's people or the land area they occupy which was Mesopotamia and surrounding nations (Psalm 80:8-11) in Daniel's era. But not only that. From this dream we come to an understanding of what a "time" is in Bible prophecy. The king was to be put out to field for "seven times". One time in Bible prophecy is one year, the time it takes for the earth to circle the sun one revolution. Later in Daniel and in Revelation "a time, times, and half a time" is mentioned. That calculates to three and a half years or 1,260 days, realizing a prophetic year is 360 days as originally determined by the Babylonians with the number 6 as their common denominator. From them we have 60 seconds in a minute, 60 minutes in an hour, 24 hours in a day, 12 months in a year with 30 days per month, and 360 days in a year. We also have 360 degrees in a circle, thanks to the Babylonians.

CHAPTER FIVE: This chapter introduces us to Belshazzar, the belligerent king of Babylon, serving as king along with his father. His is another example of Babylonian callousness in mixing the pure worship items of the true God with the false worship of idols of wood, iron, bronze, silver, and gold. It also reveals that drinking to the excess of getting drunk can cause a person to do and say things they will soon regret.

CHAPTER SIX: Daniel chapter six is a Bible story well known to people of all ages concerning Daniel and the Lion's den. Daniel's integrity preceded him and his reputation of honesty was well respected by those over him and well hated by those dishonest who served under him. In this story we are reminded to be honest in all things and be faithful to God in our worship and trust in Him under all conditions and threats, even to the threat of our lives.

CHAPTER SEVEN: The four beasts Daniel witnesses coming up out of the sea represent Babylon, Medo-Persia, Greece, and Rome. This prophecy is very important for us to understand concerning the symbolism of the combination beast of Revelation 13 as well as other important prophecy interpretations in the book of Revelation. In this chapter the "sea" represents the rebellious Hebrew people which had turned their backs on God. The four winds represent strife, turmoil, and conflict. This dream takes us from Daniel's day to the end of the 1000 years of Revelation 20, which includes the heavenly judgment mentioned in verses 13,14,26,27 taking place during that 1000 years. We are also introduced to the Little Horn Power, in verse 8, which will play a major role in "the appointed time of the end". In this chapter we have the first mention of "the time, times, and half a time" in verse 25 which comes out to be three and a half years or 1,260 literal days.

CHAPTER EIGHT: This chapter is important because it confirms that the two empires which will follow after the Babylonian Empire is that of the Medo-Persians and the Greeks. At the end of the Greek empire the pagan worship ideas from the three ruling nations will spread throughout the then known world in all the directions of the compass as God's people are disseminated. Also much more information is provided concerning the Little Horn Power and its catastrophic influence over God's last day people. In verse 13 the term CONTINUAL or PERPETUAL is introduced along with the phase "the abomination or transgression of desolation". This particular verse speaks of the "holy" and the "host" being defeated or trampled upon. Daniel 8:9-26 deals mainly with the appointed time of the end, which is still future (verses 16,19,23,26). Verse 14 is important because it provides the amount of time in which the "holy" and the "host" will be abused. It states that the holy will be abused for a little over 6 years but will be reconciled or vindicated at the end of "the 2,300 evenings and mornings", which are 2,300 literal 24 hour days. In this chapter we realize a horn can represent a kingdom but it also represents power. A single huge horn is more powerful than two separate horns. In the "appointed time of the end" the Little Horn Power will be allied with three of the 10 horns and the combination of four united horns facing 7 independent horns will make it the strongest bully on the block.

CHAPTER NINE: In this chapter Daniel is reminiscing on the prophecies he had in Daniel 7 and 8, seeking to comprehend them. He had written them down, but did not understand them, especially considering the seventy years of captivity were almost completed. From Daniel 9:3-23 Daniel is in prayer with an example of one of the best prayers in the Bible. As he nears the end of his petition the angel Gabriel visits him to provide answers to his questions. In Daniel 9:24-27 the angel gives

Daniel more information to add to that which he previously had. The Bible does not say if Daniel understood this added information or not and it is highly unlikely that anyone else did until this current generation. This 70-week prophecy is 490 years long and it began in 457 BC, almost 80 years after Daniel had the vision. Those familiar with Daniel were most likely dead by the time 457 BC came along and the only ones which did come across it were those who actually read his letters. The book of Daniel did not become available in English until 1535 and to the general public until the 1816 when the American Bible Society was formed with the goal of putting the Bible in every home in the entire world. The first person to promote an understanding to the public about the prophecy of Daniel 9:24-27 was a Baptist preacher named William Miller (1782-1849) in 1823. The seventy-week prophecy pinpoints the year Jesus was baptized and crucified as well as the year Stephen, the first Christian martyr, would die. The seventy-week prophecy goes from 457 BC to 34 AD. The prophecy is actually more advantageous to this generation than any other because the message rings loud and clear to us, we have access to it and understand it, and it applies directly to us. The 70-week prophecy was not only directed at the children of Israel but it's for us also to prepare our lives in accordance with God's will, before the second coming of Jesus. **

It tells us, two separate times, that a seven-year tribulation of God's people is real and it is coming in the near future. That seven-year tribulation is 2,520 days in duration. 70 X 7 = 490. 490 X 360 = 176,400. 176,400 divided by 70 = 2,520. 2,520 divided by 360 = 7 years.

** Read the eBook or hard copy book "The 3 Visible Advents of Jesus" by Earl B. Schrock from Xlibris.com, Amazon, Barnes and Nobles, etc.

CHAPTER TEN: Daniel chapter ten is the introduction to the visions of Daniel 11 and 12. The messenger in the conversation reminds Daniel in verse 14 that the information he is about to receive concerns the "latter days" which is way in the future for Daniel, but not too far in the future for us. In verse 20 the messenger tells Daniel that in his future the Persians will defeat the Babylonians and will rule over the people of God. He also reinforces the point that the nation of Greece will overtake the Persians at a later date which agrees with the dream of King Nebuchadnezzar in chapter two.

CHAPTER ELEVEN: Verses 1-4 is not difficult to understand. The messenger is reminding Daniel that the Persians will reign over the Hebrew captives and that the Grecians will defeat the Persians in the future. As was mentioned in Daniel chapter 7 the Grecian empire, along with their pagan teachings, will be circulated to the four directions of the compass. In verses 5-42 the information is fragmented, scattered, and difficult to understand or interpret, without understanding Daniel chapter twelve.

CHAPTER TWELVE: By the end of Daniel 11:42 the conditions in the entire world are drastic and God's end time people are about to be completely tested. At that point God's last day servants will be placed in turmoil and as Daniel 12:1 states "there will be a time of trouble such as never was." Michael, the name of Jesus in heaven, will stand up for His elect and will deliver His people providing for their needs and defense. Verses two and three takes us further up in the future to the end of the 1000 years of Revelation 20 at the point of time called "the last day" or "end of the days" as stated in verse 13. Verse 7 lets us know that during the 1260 days of the coming 2520 days, "the holy people" will be "completely shattered". In verse 9 Daniel is reminded that this vision is not for his day but for "the time of the end" when the vision will be understood. Verse 10 reveals the results of the time of trouble, and the following seven-year time of tribulation, in that the obedient servants of God, and the rebellious followers of God, will be clearly separated and defined.

Chapter twelve verse eleven (12:11) is probably the most important verse in the Bible when it comes to placing the time periods, mentioned in the books of Daniel and Revelation, on a timeline. The prophetic "time, times, and half a time", the 1260, 1290, 1335, 2300, 3 1/2 days and the 42 months of the end time will be estabished when "the continual is taken away."

The 4 events intimately attached to all of these above prophetic time periods are:

1. The **covenant** or holy covenant: which is the Ten Commandments of Exodus 20:1-17, which the Little Horn Power despises.
2. The **continual**: which is the 7th day Sabbath of the fourth commandment (Exodus 20:8-11) which the Little Horn Power will do away with and replace with another false day of worship.
3. The **abomination of desolation**. The false day of worship the Little Horn Power will "set up" in place of the seventh-day Sabbath and force people to bow to it.
4. The **Little Horn Power** is connected to all of these time periods because all of them are fulfilled during the soon coming seven-year tribulation.

No individual verse of the Bible stands independent of the chapter in which it is found. The entire chapter must be realized to correctly understand and site the time periods.

The chart below demonstrates all the prophetic Biblical time periods associated with the soon coming seven-year tribulation along with the single position of the seven seals, trumpets, angels, thunders, woes, and laments which take place simultaneously.

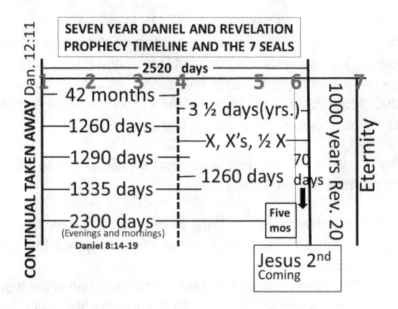

REVELATION CHAPTER 10 (KJV)

1And I saw another mighty angel come down from heaven, clothed with a cloud: and a rainbow was upon his head, and his face was as it were the sun, and his feet as pillars of fire: 2And he had in his hand a little book open: and he set his right foot upon the sea, and his left foot on the earth, 3And cried with a loud voice, as when a lion roareth: and when he had cried, seven thunders uttered their voices.

4And when the seven thunders had uttered their voices, I was about to write: and I heard a voice from heaven saying unto me, Seal up those things which the seven thunders uttered, and write them not. 5And the angel which I saw stand upon the sea and upon the earth lifted up his hand to heaven, 6And sware by him that liveth for ever and ever, who created heaven, and the things that therein are, and the earth, and the things that therein are, and the sea, and the things which are therein, that there should be time no longer: 7But in the days of the voice of the seventh angel, when he shall begin to sound, the mystery of God should be finished, as he hath declared to his servants the prophets.

8And the voice which I heard from heaven spake unto me again, and said, Go and take the little book which is open in the hand of the angel which standeth upon the sea and upon the earth. 9And I went unto the angel, and said unto him, Give me the little book. And he said unto me, Take it, and eat it up; and it shall make thy belly bitter, but it shall be in thy mouth sweet as honey. 10And I took the little book out of the angel's hand, and ate it up; and it was in my mouth sweet as honey: and as soon as I had eaten it, my belly was bitter. 11And he said unto me, Thou must prophesy again before many peoples, and nations, and tongues, and kings.

(MAY THE ENDTIME ELECT SERVANTS OF GOD
UNDERSTAND THE ABOVE MESSAGE.)

BIBLICAL "APPOINTED TIME OF THE END" PROPHETIC TIME PERIODS

Time	Daniel	Revelation
X, X's, ½ X	7:25, 12:7 (1260)	12:14
2300 days	8:14	
1290 days	12:11	
1335 days	12:12	
1260 days		11:3, 12:6
42 months	(1260 days)	11:2, 13:5
5 months	(150 days)	9:5, 10
3 ½ days/years	(1260 days)	11:9, 11

DANIEL AND REVELATION SEVEN-YEAR TRIBULATION TIMELINE

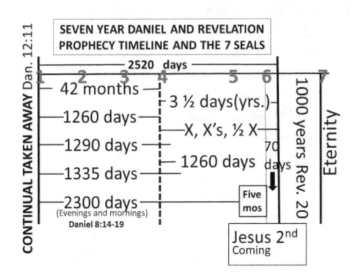

TABLA DE CONTENIDO

Un texto clave para entender el libro de Daniel:

"Y el Señor entregó en sus manos á Joacim rey de Judá, y parte de los vasos de la casa de Dios, y trájolos á tierra de Sinar, á la casa de su dios: y metió los vasos en la casa del tesoro de su dios." Daniel 1:2

Mezclando lo sagrado con la profana

¿Quién subirá al monte de Jehová? ¿Y quién estará en el lugar de su santidad? El limpio de manos, y puro de corazón: El que no ha elevado su alma á la vanidad, Ni jurado con engaño. El recibirá bendición de Jehová, Y justicia del Dios de salud. Tal es la generación de los que le buscan, De los que buscan tu rostro, oh Dios de Jacob. (Selah.)" Salmos 24:3-6

Por favor, tómate el tiempo para orar para la guía de Dios mientras busca Su verdad revelada en el Sagrada Biblia.

A personal message to my readers enjoying the following pages in Spanish.

You will certainly discover many vocabulary errors and word misusage in the following pages. Though I enjoy communicating with my friends and family in your beautiful language, I'm not fluent enough or have a large enough vocabulary to communicate in writing appropriately. My desire is that, beyond the humor you may discover in the way things are said or explained, hopefully you will be able to understand the message I'm attempting to share concerning the current important revelations from the prophetic book of Daniel which has a direct bearing on you and the near future generations.

The following translation is from the online Google Translation Application which I have leaned on heavily to bring the following to your attention. Be blessed.

Un mensaje personal para mis lectores disfrutando de las siguientes páginas en español.

Seguramente descubrirás muchos errores de vocabulario y uso indebido de palabras en las siguientes páginas. Aunque disfruto comunicarme con mis amigos y familiares en su hermoso idioma, no hablo con la suficiente fluidez ni tengo un vocabulario lo suficientemente amplio como para comunicarme por escrito de manera adecuada. Mi deseo es que, más allá del humor que puedas descubrir en la forma en que se dicen o explican las cosas, ojalá puedas entender el mensaje que intento compartir sobre las importantes revelaciones actuales del libro profético de Daniel que tiene un impacto directo. sobre ti y las próximas generaciones.

La siguiente traducción es de la aplicación de traducción de Google en línea, en la que me he apoyado mucho para llamar su atención sobre lo siguiente. Se bendecido.

"Y el Señor entregó en sus manos á Joacim rey de Judá, y parte de los vasos de la casa de Dios, y trájolos á tierra de Sinar, á la casa de su dios: y metió los vasos en la casa del tesoro de su dios." Daniel 1:2

Los libros escritos por Earl B. Schrock son:

The Three Secrets of Success and Happiness
Los Tres Secretos del Éxito y Felicidad
Hodgepodge: Thoughts and Tales from Davidson County, North Carolina
The Kingdom of Heaven and the Kingdom of God
The 3 Visible Advents of Jesus
Las 3 Venidas de Jesús
Understanding the book of Daniel for this Generation
Entendiendo el libro de Daniel para esta generación
PRÓXIMAMENTE, EN BREVE, PRONTO:
Understanding the book of Revelation for this Generation
Entendiendo el libro de Apocalipsis para esta Generación

Vídeos de YouTube de la presentación de profecías de Earl Schrock:

1. Discusión capítulo por capítulo sobre el libro de Daniel
2. Explicación del libro de Apocalipsis (abreviado)Contact Information

Earl B. Schrock, P.O. Box 2302, Thomasville, NC 27361
ProphecyPresentation@gmail.com

Sitio de estudio bíblico en línea sugerido
http://studies.itiswritten.com/discover/
Earl Benjamin Schrock se graduó en
1969 de Pioneer Valley Academy
y un graduado de 1979 en Teología del
Southern Missionary College (SAU)
Dado que la interpretación de la profecía es un arte y no
una ciencia, el autor se reserva el derecho de cambiar
o enmendar todas y cada una de las ideas de sus
interpretaciones según lo indique el Espíritu de Dios.

Mención especial y agradecimiento a http://
referencebible.org/ por su sitio web de búsqueda e
información de la Biblia Biblos.com, que me ayudó
enormemente a escudriñar las Escrituras.

Leer este pequeño libro una sola vez no consolidará la información que necesita para comprender y enseñar el material que se está discutiendo. Por favor, tómese su tiempo para absorber el contenido de este librito, tomar notas y volver a leerlo tan a menudo como pueda para comprender y enseñar los conceptos proféticos revelados en el interior según se apliquen a esta generación.

INTRODUCCIÓN

PROFECÍA BÍBLICA: TODO SE TRATA DE ADORACIÓN

Nuestro Padre celestial no se sorprende por las miles de organizaciones religiosas diferentes en todo el mundo hoy. En el libro de Daniel, Dios revela una imagen cuyos pies están hechos de fragmentos de hierro y arcilla cerámica. Cada una de las miles de organizaciones religiosas diferentes está representada por un solo trozo de hierro incrustado en la arcilla endurecida de los pies. Estas organizaciones son inflexibles como el hierro y se niegan a ser modificadas o mejoradas.

¿De dónde vino toda la confusión mundial en la religión hoy?

Tenemos un libro, el libro 66 de la Santa Biblia, que dice una cosa a un pueblo, pero tenemos miles de sistemas de creencias diferentes. ¿Por qué?

El libro de Daniel ayuda a revelar la respuesta a esa pregunta.

Intentar comprender e interpretar la profecía bíblica ha sido el objetivo de todas las generaciones desde que las profecías se escribieron, leyeron y se hicieron públicas por primera vez. Cada generación sucesiva interpretó la profecía bíblica con el conocimiento y la mentalidad que poseía. Cada generación, desde que el libro de Daniel estuvo disponible para el público, intentó hacer personal cada profecía, aplicándola a ellos mismos para el día en que vivieron y vivieron, creyendo que se aplicaba a ellos "viviendo en los últimos días".

Todos creemos lo que nos han enseñado los que vivieron en la generación anterior a nosotros. Hoy en día, muchas personas están satisfechas con las interpretaciones y entendimientos pasados de la profecía bíblica que aprendieron de otros y no tienen interés en buscar una posible mejor conclusión o interpretación profética. Pero, ¿qué pasa con esta generación? ¿Deberíamos estar contentos de permanecer por debajo del entendimiento de las personas que vivieron generaciones antes que nosotros? A menos que una persona deje de lado las ideas preconcebidas de la profecía bíblica, entonces lo que le han enseñado aquellos que fueron enseñados por otros, continuará creyendo y enseñando la misma verdad y los mismos errores a las generaciones futuras. Necesitamos estudiar la Biblia por nosotros mismos para estar seguros de que lo que creemos es la verdad según la Biblia, según se aplica a nuestra generación. El día oportuno en el que vivimos no nos permite simplemente aceptar la opinión de los demás.

Cada uno de nosotros somos producto de nuestro entorno. Solo sabemos lo que nos han enseñado o aprendido de los demás y de las influencias que nos rodean. Estamos influenciados por los líderes en nuestras vidas, como padres, maestros, pastores y otras personas. Nos influencian los libros que leemos, la televisión y las películas que vemos, internet, la radio que escuchamos, así como las revistas, los videojuegos, etc. Nos influencian nuestros amigos y, a veces, nuestros enemigos, ya sea de forma directa. o comunicación indirecta o conversación casual. Pero para estudiar y comprender la Biblia correctamente, debemos dejar de lado todo lo que sabemos y entendemos, para acercarnos a la Biblia con una mente abierta. Debemos entender que la Biblia es la única fuente de verdad en la que podemos confiar. Sola Scriptura: La Biblia solamente. Debemos poder defender la Biblia mediante la Biblia y ningún otro material extrabíblico.

Debemos interpretar la Biblia por nosotros mismos como somos guiados por el Espíritu Santo que mora en nosotros y que nos guiará a toda la verdad:

> "Pero cuando viniere aquel Espíritu de verdad, él os guiará á toda verdad; porque no hablará de sí mismo, sino que hablará todo lo que oyere, y os hará saber las cosas que han de venir." Juan 16:13

Para ser un vaso de Dios, es necesario tener una mente abierta y un corazón receptivo, ya que somos moldeados como arcilla en Sus manos a través de Su Palabra. Ser cabeza dura promueve la dureza del corazón.

> "Ahora pues, Jehová, tú eres nuestro padre; nosotros lodo, y tú el que nos formaste; así que obra de tus manos, todos nosotros." Isaías 64:8.

A veces debemos desafiarnos a nosotros mismos y a nuestro entendimiento de la Biblia. Podemos desafiar nuestras propias ideas sobre la interpretación de las profecías bíblicas si consideramos un punto de vista opcional. Una vez que se ha considerado una vista opcional de la interpretación de la profecía bíblica, cada persona tiene la opción de continuar con su interpretación original o enmendar su forma de entender la profecía bíblica a la luz del tiempo actual en el que vive.

Por favor, no cierre este librito en ningún momento porque no fluye con sus propias ideas preconcebidas. Pon a prueba tus conceptos con este librito y con la Palabra de Dios. Que se diga de ti lo que se dijo acerca de los bereanos en los días de Pablo en Hechos 17:11:

"Y fueron estós más nobles que los que estaban en Tesalónica, pues recibieron la palabra con toda solicitud, escudriñando cada día las Escrituras, si estas cosas eran así."

Cada capítulo de la Biblia del libro de Daniel se encuentra al final de cada capítulo de este librito para su conveniencia. Es aconsejable y prudente leer también a Daniel de la Biblia de su elección para cada capítulo que se representa a medida que lee este librito.

Esta no es una explicación versículo por versículo del libro de Daniel. La idea de este escrito es extraer de cada capítulo la lección o lecciones principales necesarias para comprender cada capítulo y, a su vez, todo el libro y también el libro de Apocalipsis. Es imposible comprender correctamente el libro de Apocalipsis sin comprender primero a Daniel. La profecía bíblica tiene que ver con la ADORACIÓN.

El libro de Daniel no trata tanto sobre reyes gobernantes e imperios en ascenso y caída como sobre ADORACIÓN. Cada generación que leyó y estudió los libros de Daniel y Apocalipsis ha sido bendecida de una manera u otra al aplicar las lecciones de vida obtenidas de su estudio y hacer una aplicación práctica con ellos. Pero en realidad, los libros de Daniel y Apocalipsis son en realidad más importantes y más aplicables a la última generación de la historia de este mundo que a cualquier otra generación desde los días de Daniel. Es con la última generación que tanto los libros de Daniel como Apocalipsis tendrán su cumplimiento completo y final.

La lección que se debe aprender de todo el libro de Daniel es reconocer cómo la adoración sólida como el oro hacia y para Dios, en los días de Daniel, se diluyó y se contaminó con las enseñanzas del paganismo, a través del tiempo hasta nuestros días, a través de los imperios que gobernaban sobre el pueblo de Dios. Así como el rey Nabucodonosor mezcló los "vasos de Dios" con su propia adoración pagana en "la casa del tesoro de su dios", la adoración al Dios verdadero se ha deteriorado desde la adoración sólida que era en los días de Daniel hasta lo que es en el mundo. hoy, no solo en el cristianismo, sino en todas las religiones actuales en todo el mundo. La influencia pagana, ya sea poco o mucho, quita la ADORACIÓN del verdadero Dios Creador y la dirige a Satanás, el que quiere ser adorado como Dios:

> "Sobre las alturas de las nubes subiré, y seré semejante al Altísimo. Mas tú derribado eres en el sepulcro, á los lados de la huesa. Inclinarse han hacia ti los que te vieren, te considerarán diciendo: ¿Es este aquel varón que hacía temblar la tierra, que trastornaba los reinos; Que puso el mundo como un desierto, que asoló sus ciudades; que á sus presos nunca abrió la cárcel? Todos los reyes de las gentes, todos ellos yacen con honra cada uno en su casa. Mas tú echado eres de tu sepulcro como tronco abominable, como vestido de muertos pasados á cuchillo, que descendieron al fondo de la sepultura; como cuerpo muerto hollado. No serás contado con ellos en la sepultura: porque tú destruiste tu tierra, mataste tu pueblo. No será nombrada para siempre la simiente de los malignos." Isaías 14: 12-14.

La gran controversia en este planeta desde la primera semana, cuando Dios creó este mundo y todo lo que contiene, fue responder a la pregunta de quién merece el derecho de adoración y alabanza de la humanidad. Dios claramente reclama el derecho a ser adorado como nuestro Creador, Redentor y Sustentador. Sin embargo, Satanás dice que Dios es injusto y que si la gente lo adorara a él en lugar del Creador, él sería un mejor líder con una vida mejor para todos los que lo siguen (Isaías 14: 12-14). Por supuesto, la historia, desde la caída de Adán y Eva, ha probado una y otra vez que Satanás es un mentiroso y un asesino (Juan 8:44), y que nuestro Dios Creador es digno (Apocalipsis 4:11) de toda la adoración. podemos reunirnos.

En Su Santa Biblia, Dios revela claramente Su carácter y la adoración que Él requiere de las personas que lo aceptan como Señor y Maestro de sus vidas. El objetivo de Satanás es robarle esa adoración a Dios y dirigirla hacia él mismo infiltrándose en la verdadera adoración bíblica de Dios y mezclándola con información falsa y prácticas paganas. Los siervos de Dios de los últimos días quieren conocerlo y escudriñarán las Escrituras todos los días para alcanzar esa meta y aprender la forma correcta de adorar al Creador tal como Él lo ha revelado. Se bendecido.

Vea el video de YouTube **INTRODUCCIÓN A DANIEL EN ESPAÑOL** por Earl Schrock

DANIEL CAPÍTULO UNO

Nuestro estilo de vida debe recordarnos a nuestro Dios Creador por los lugares a los que vamos, las cosas que hacemos, las palabras que usamos y la comida que comemos.

> "Si pues coméis, ó bebéis, ó hacéis otra cosa, haced lo todo á gloria de Dios." 1 Corintios 10:31.

El texto clave en el libro de Daniel, que ofrece una pista de lo que trata todo el libro, se encuentra en Daniel 1:2:

> "Y el Señor entregó en sus manos á Joacim rey de Judá, y parte de los vasos de la casa de Dios, y trájolos á tierra de Sinar, á la casa de su dios: y metió los vasos en la casa del tesoro de su dios."

Así como el rey Nabucodonosor mezcló los artículos sagrados de Jerusalén con los vasos babilónicos paganos profanos en el templo de su dios, el capítulo uno revela además que intentó diluir la confianza y el amor en el Dios Creador de los cautivos hebreos, mezclando la verdad con el error. Hay tres áreas principales que el rey atacó en su intento de distraer a Daniel, Hananiah, Misael y Azariah de ser fieles a su Dios Diseñador.

1. Cambió sus nombres de aquellos que apuntaban al Dios Creador a nombres que enfatizaban a sus dioses paganos.
2. Cambió su dieta de la que les recordaba al Dios Soberano por la dieta que alababa a sus dioses paganos.
3. Promovió una educación pagana que enfatizaba su lenguaje, sus conceptos y sus ideas para hacerlos dignos de servir en su gobierno.

Este fue un plan deliberado del rey porque en Daniel 1:3,4 la Biblia dice:

"Y dijo el rey á Aspenaz, príncipe de sus eunucos, que trajese de los hijos de Israel, del linaje real de los príncipes, Muchachos en quienes no hubiese tacha alguna, y de buen parecer, y enseñados en toda sabiduría, y sabios en ciencia, y de buen entendimiento, é idóneos para estar en el palacio del rey; y que les enseñase las letras y la lengua de los Caldeos."

CAMBIO DE NOMBRE

El rey Nabucodonosor les quitó los nombres piadosos y les dio nombres paganos relacionados con los dioses a los que servía.

"A los cuales el príncipe de los eunucos puso nombres: y puso á Daniel, Beltsasar; y á Ananías, Sadrach; y á Misael, Mesach; y á Azarías, Abednego." Daniel 1:7

Daniel significa "Dios es mi juez". Beltsasar significa "tesorero de Bel".

Hananías significa "a quien Jehová favoreció". Sadrac significa "mensajero del sol".

Misael significa "comparable a Dios". Mishach significa "del dios Shach".

Azarías significa "a quien Jehová ayuda". Obednego significa "adorador de Nego".

DIETA

Nabucodonosor también es culpable de intentar cambiarlos introduciendo su dieta en sus vidas en oposición a la dieta kosher establecida por Dios (Levítico 11) que separa lo limpio de lo inmundo, incluso en la comida que comían. Sin embargo, Daniel 1:8 dice:

> "Y Daniel propuso en su corazón de no contaminarse en la ración de la comida del rey, ni en el vino de su beber: pidió por tanto al príncipe de los eunucos de no contaminarse."

Comer, según las indicaciones de Dios, no es solo un problema de salud, es un problema de obediencia. ¿Vamos a obedecer a Dios o lo vamos a desobedecer? Las pocas cosas que se mencionan en la Biblia como inmundas para el consumo humano son superadas en número por todos los alimentos maravillosos que Dios dice que podemos comer. Aparte de las zonas de hambruna, las personas de todo el mundo tienen alimentos disponibles para comer sin comer alimentos inmundos. Es una elección. ¿Obedecer o desobedecer?

La comida ha sido un tema de adoración desde el Jardín del Edén. Dios les dijo a Adán y Eva que no comieran del fruto del "árbol del conocimiento del bien y del mal" o morirían (Génesis 2:15-17). Pero Satanás llamó a Dios mentiroso y le dijo a Eva (Génesis 3:4) que Dios la había engañado:

> "Entonces la serpiente dijo á la mujer: No moriréis."

Eva le creyó y la Biblia dice en Génesis 3:6:

> "Y vió la mujer que el árbol era bueno para comer, y que era agradable á los ojos, y árbol codiciable para alcanzar la sabiduría; y tomó de su fruto, y comió; y dió también á su marido, el cual comió así como ella."

La mentira de Satanás sigue viva y coleando hoy y muchos miembros de la familia de Dios todavía le creen. Están convencidos de que comer alimentos inmundos no conducirá a la muerte, como Dios advirtió a Adán y Eva. Pero la Biblia es clara. Obedece a Dios y vive, desobedece a Dios y muere. Se llama pecado.

No había nada intrínsecamente malo o malo en la fruta que a Adán y Eva se les prohibió comer. La fruta de aspecto delicioso no era venenosa o de lo contrario habrían muerto inmediatamente después de comerla, no novecientos años después. Pero fue una prueba de fe, una prueba de obediencia. La prueba es la misma hoy para nosotros que para ellos. ¿La voluntad de Dios o la nuestra?

Desobedecer a Dios, incluso en las cosas que no podemos explicar, dirige nuestra adoración a Satanás. Es triste decir que hoy, no solo en el cristianismo, sino en todo el mundo, se ignora a Dios ya que los seres humanos consumen alimentos inmundos de todo tipo. Y el argumento que da la gente, incluso aquellos que saben lo que Dios ha exigido, es que Dios cambió de opinión.

Dios es omnisciente, nunca cambia. Sus planes se establecen de manera oportuna:

"Porque yo Jehová, no me mudo." Malaquías 3:6.

"Jesucristo es el mismo ayer, y hoy, y por los siglos." Hebreos 13:8.

En ninguna parte de las Escrituras, cuando se entiende correctamente, Dios se retracta de sus valores o los nuestros acerca de lo que es limpio e inmundo en lo que respecta a la comida. Las razones por las que la gente desobedece a Dios son las mismas razones a las que Eva se aferró cuando desobedeció a Dios: ORGULLO:

> "Porque todo lo que hay en el mundo, la concupiscencia de la carne, y la concupiscencia de los ojos, y la soberbia de la vida, no es del Padre, mas es del mundo." 1 Juan 2:16

Algunas personas bien intencionadas leen mal la Biblia o aceptan el razonamiento infundado de otros para satisfacer su estilo de vida particular. ¿No sería mejor para los siervos del Dios viviente dedicar su tiempo a la Biblia para entenderla correctamente en lugar de emplear un tiempo valioso tratando de distorsionar las Escrituras para satisfacer su propia lujuria y orgullo? Recuerde el dicho: "Si Dios lo dice, yo lo creo, y eso me resuelve".

EDUCACIÓN

Nabucodonosor no solo intentó distraer la atención de los hebreos de su Dios con cambios de nombre, y al tentarlos con alimentos inmundos y prohibidos, también patrocinó una beca de la Universidad Babilónica de tres años para cada uno de ellos. Afortunadamente, para los devotos cuatro campeones hebreos, una educación babilónica no les permitió alejarse de su querido Creador. Una buena educación, entonces y ahora, es algo que debe valorarse y apreciarse. Con una buena educación, controlas el mundo que te rodea, pero con una mala educación, el mundo que te rodea te controla a ti. Pero a veces una buena educación pública puede ser una trampa para los hijos de Dios.

Históricamente, para muchos, cuanto mejor educada se vuelve una persona, de acuerdo con las normas del mundo, más se aleja de Dios. Para algunas personas, cuanto más saben, menos útiles se vuelven al servicio del Rey. Por eso debemos mantener la mirada en Dios en todas las cosas, incluso durante los ejercicios educativos. Pasa tiempo con Dios todos los días para mantenerte enfocado en Él, incluso con un horario de trabajo / escuela demasiado ocupado.

En estas tres áreas, Daniel y sus tres compañeros nos dieron un ejemplo: Daniel 1:8:

> "Y Daniel propuso en su corazón de no contaminarse en la ración de la comida del rey, ni en el vino de su beber: pidió por tanto al príncipe de los eunucos de no contaminarse."

Debemos vivir una vida determinada para entregarnos diariamente a Dios al entregar nuestra voluntad, a fin de vivir el estilo de vida en nuestra conversación, nuestra dieta, nuestras opciones de educación y todas las demás partes de nuestra existencia para vivir totalmente para Dios. Esta debe ser una decisión diaria desde el momento en que nos despertamos hasta el momento en que nos vamos a dormir porque el diablo hará todo lo posible para distraernos de servir a Dios. Note lo que dice en 1 Pedro 5:5-11:

"Igualmente, mancebos, sed sujetos á los ancianos; y todos sumisos unos á otros, revestíos de humildad; porque Dios resiste á los soberbios, y da gracia á los humildes. Humillaos pues bajo la poderosa mano de Dios, para que él os ensalce cuando fuere tiempo; Echando toda vuestra solicitud en él, porque él tiene cuidado de vosotros. Sed templados, y velad; porque vuestro adversario el diablo, cual león rugiente, anda alrededor buscando á quien devore: Al cual resistid firmes en la fe, sabiendo que las mismas aflicciones han de ser cumplidas en la compañía de vuestros hermanos que están en el mundo. Mas el Dios de toda gracia, que nos ha llamado á su gloria eterna por Jesucristo, después que hubiereis un poco de tiempo padecido, él mismo os perfeccione, coforme, corrobore y establezca. A él sea gloria é imperio para siempre. Amén."

Los cambios que el rey Nabucodonosor trajo a la vida de Daniel y sus tres compañeros son advertencias a todos los hijos de Dios para que estén alerta a aquellas cosas en nuestras vidas que pueden separarnos de Dios. Pero eso no es todo lo que encontramos en el capítulo uno de Daniel.

Entender el Libro de Daniel nos abre la puerta a entender el Libro de Apocalipsis. Existe una conexión entre estos dos libros que debemos conocer.

Observe la conexión de Apocalipsis en Daniel 1:12-16 mientras observa cuántas veces se usan las palabras "**diez días**" en el siguiente texto:

> "Prueba, te ruego, tus siervos **diez días**, y dennos legumbres á comer, y agua á beber. Parezcan luego delante de ti nuestros rostros, y los rostros de los muchachos que comen de la ración de la comida del rey; y según que vieres, harás con tus siervos. Consintió pues con ellos en esto, y probó con ellos **diez días**. Y al cabo de los **diez días** pareció el rostro de ellos mejor y más nutrido de carne, que los otros muchachos que comían de la ración de comida del rey. Así fué que Melsar tomaba la ración de la comida de ellos, y el vino de su beber, y dábales legumbres."

Cuando Dios se repite en la Biblia, es el momento de animarnos y prestar especial atención porque normalmente Él está tratando de decirnos algo importante. José, en el libro de Génesis, nos llama la atención sobre esto cuando habla con el faraón, rey de Egipto, acerca de sus dos sueños (Génesis 41:1-7). José le dijo al faraón:

> "Y el suceder el sueño á Faraón dos veces, significa que la cosa es firme de parte de Dios, y que Dios se apresura á hacerla." Génesis 41:32

Recuerde, si no está familiarizado con el libro de Daniel, no podrá comprender adecuadamente el libro de Apocalipsis. De hecho, el libro de Apocalipsis respaldalo que estoy diciendo al dejar caer pistas a lo largo de sí mismo que nos alientan a mirar, familiarizarnos y conocer el libro de Daniel.

Tres veces se nos dice en Daniel 1:12-16 que los hijos de Israel, los prisioneros del rey Nabucodonosor, recibieron una prueba que duró "**diez días**". ¿Por qué es tan importante?

Es importante porque todos debemos llegar al punto en nuestra experiencia cristiana, en nuestra búsqueda de la verdad, en nuestro deseo de comprender y conocer la Biblia, que DEBEMOS DEJAR QUE LA BIBLIA SE INTERPRETE A SÍ MISMA. Cada vez que vayamos a los libros de historia o al periódico o las últimas redes sociales, o alguna otra influencia literaria externa, para descubrir la verdad bíblica, eventualmente nos decepcionaremos. La Biblia y la Biblia solo pueden interpretarse a sí mismas. Note lo siguiente:

> "Tenemos también la palabra profética más permanente, á la cual hacéis bien de estar atentos como á una antorcha que alumbra en lugar oscuro hasta que el día esclarezca, y el lucero de la mañana salga en vuestros corazones: Entendiendo primero esto, que ninguna profecía de la Escritura es de particular interpretación; Porque la profecía no fué en los tiempos pasados traída por voluntad humana, sino los santos hombres de Dios hablaron siendo inspirados del Espíritu Santo.2 Pedro 1:19-21

Entonces, ¿qué es tan importante en cuanto a que Dios se repita tres veces en Daniel 1: 12-16? Note Apocalipsis 2:10:

> "No tengas ningún temor de las cosas que has de padecer. He aquí, el diablo ha de enviar algunos de vosotros á la cárcel, para que seáis probados,

y tendréis tribulación de **diez días**. Sé fiel hasta
la muerte, y yo te daré la corona de la vida."

Esta declaración de "**diez días en prisión**" en Apocalipsis 2:10
es una referencia directa al libro de Daniel. ¿POR QUÉ? Por
varias razones: (1) Para comprender correctamente el libro
Apocalipsis, debe conocer y comprender el libro de Daniel.
(2) Mateo 24 y Apocalipsis 13 nos permiten saber que vendrá
un tiempo en que el pueblo de Dios será perseguido, incluso
encarcelado, como Daniel, y algunos serán asesinados. Para
permanecer firmes por Dios en tiempos de extrema dificultad,
debemos estar firmes por Él hoy en tiempos más fáciles.
Debemos ser como Daniel, quien "se propuso en su corazón"
que él sería fiel a Dios, para lo que sea que Él requiera, sin
importar qué. (3) Hoy en día, Dios todavía tiene una dieta
particular para sus hijos como prueba de fe similar a la del
jardín del Edén y de Babilonia. Debemos ser obedientes a Dios
hoy, incluso en nuestras elecciones de alimentos, si vamos a
serle fieles en tiempos difíciles.

Lea el mensaje del Espíritu Santo a la iglesia de Esmirna en
Apocalipsis 2: 8-11. Un grupo o asamblea de siervos de Dios
de los últimos días necesita este mensaje. ¿Es ese un mensaje
para que prestes más atención a obedecer la Palabra de Dios
con respecto a comer carne y alimentos limpios?

La dieta limpia e inmunda de Levítico once no ha cambiado,
ni Dios tampoco (Malaquías 3: 6, Hebreos 13: 8). Dios todavía
requiere que le obedezcamos con respecto a lo que comemos.
No es el hecho de que la comida inmunda sea dañina para
nosotros, es solo una simple prueba de fe. ¿Obedecer o no
obedecer? Esa es la pregunta. ¡Intentalo! ¡Pruébalo! Pasar "tres
semanas completas" (Daniel 10: 2,3), 21 días, sin comer ningún
alimento inmundo y ver qué pasa. Daniel demostró estar **diez**

veces (Daniel 1:20) mejor que aquellos que desobedecieron, tú también puedes ser así, especialmente con una conciencia limpia de la obediencia a la clara Palabra de Dios.

El libro de Daniel, como todas las profecías bíblicas, tiene que ver con la ADORACIÓN. Daniel revela el debilitamiento de la religión pura por la introducción de influencias paganas desde su día hasta nuestros días. El capítulo uno de Daniel revela las formas en que el Imperio babilónico, bajo el rey Nabucodonosor, tomó medidas para entrar en las mentes y corromper los cuerpos del pueblo de Dios.

Este capítulo también revela la mentalidad decidida que debe tener el pueblo de Dios para poder protegerse de las influencias que enfrentamos a diario y que están diseñadas para alejarnos de nuestro Dios Creador. El cumplimiento del libro de Daniel se logrará "en el tiempo señalado del fin" (Daniel 8:19), como nos recuerdan continuamente los doce capítulos. Esa es la razón por la que la generación final será en realidad la única generación que comprenderá completamente el libro de Daniel y verá sus profecías reveladas en persona por sí mismos.

Bosquejo del capítulo uno de Daniel:

> Versículos 1,2: El rey Nabucodonosor comenzó a debilitar y diluir la adoración verdadera de Dios mezclando la verdad con el error cuando colocó los "artículos de Dios" de Su santo templo con los artículos paganos en el templo de sus dioses paganos.

> Versículos 3-18: Daniel y sus tres compañeros están decididos a ser fieles al Dios Altísimo en todas las formas posibles en sus propios pensamientos, palabras y acciones.

Vea el video de YouTube **DANIEL CAPÍTULO UNO EN ESPAÑOL** por Earl Schrock

DANIEL CAPÍTULO UNO (RVR)

1 EN el año tercero del reinado de Joacim rey de Judá, vino Nabucodonosor rey de Babilonia á Jerusalem, y cercóla. 2 Y el Señor entregó en sus manos á Joacim rey de Judá, y parte de los vasos de la casa de Dios, y trájolos á tierra de Sinar, á la casa de su dios: y metió los vasos en la casa del tesoro de su dios. 3 Y dijo el rey á Aspenaz, príncipe de sus eunucos, que trajese de los hijos de Israel, del linaje real de los príncipes, 4 Muchachos en quienes no hubiese tacha alguna, y de buen parecer, y enseñados en toda sabiduría, y sabios en ciencia, y de buen entendimiento, é idóneos para estar en el palacio del rey; y que les enseñase las letras y la lengua de los Caldeos. 5 Y señalóles el rey ración para cada día de la ración de la comida del rey, y del vino de su beber: que los criase tres años, para que al fin de ellos estuviesen delante del rey. 6 Y fueron entre ellos, de los hijos de Judá, Daniel, Ananías, Misael y Azarías: 7 A los cuales el príncipe de los eunucos puso nombres: y puso á Daniel, Beltsasar; y á Ananías, Sadrach; y á Misael, Mesach; y á Azarías, Abed-nego. 8 Y Daniel propuso en su corazón de no contaminarse en la ración de la comida del rey, ni en el vino de su beber: pidió por tanto al príncipe de los eunucos de no contaminarse. 9 (Y puso Dios á Daniel en gracia y en buena voluntad con el príncipe de los eunucos.) 10 Y dijo el príncipe de los eunucos á Daniel: Tengo temor de mi señor el rey, que señaló vuestra comida y vuestra bebida; pues luego que él habrá visto vuestros rostros más tristes que los de los muchachos que son semejantes á vosotros, condenaréis para con el rey mi cabeza. 11 Entonces dijo Daniel á Melsar, que estaba puesto por el príncipe de los eunucos sobre Daniel, Ananías, Misael, y Azarías: 12 Prueba, te ruego, tus siervos

diez días, y dennos legumbres á comer, y agua á beber. 13 Parezcan luego delante de ti nuestros rostros, y los rostros de los muchachos que comen de la ración de la comida del rey; y según que vieres, harás con tus siervos. 14 Consintió pues con ellos en esto, y probó con ellos diez días. 15 Y al cabo de los diez días pareció el rostro de ellos mejor y más nutrido de carne, que los otros muchachos que comían de la ración de comida del rey. 16 Así fué que Melsar tomaba la ración de la comida de ellos, y el vino de su beber, y dábales legumbres. 17 Y á estos cuatro muchachos dióles Dios conocimiento é inteligencia en todas letras y ciencia: mas Daniel tuvo entendimiento en toda visión y sueños. 18 Pasados pues los días al fin de los cuales había dicho el rey que los trajesen, el príncipe de los eunucos los trajo delante de Nabucodonosor. 19 Y el rey habló con ellos, y no fué hallado entre todos ellos otro como Daniel, Ananías, Misael, y Azarías: y así estuvieron delante del rey. 20 Y en todo negocio de sabiduría é inteligencia que el rey les demandó, hallólos diez veces mejores que todos los magos y astrólogos que había en todo su reino. 21 Y fué Daniel hasta el año primero del rey Ciro.

DANIEL CAPÍTULO DOS

"Porque nadie puede poner otro fundamento que el que está puesto, el cual es Jesucristo. Y si alguno edificare sobre este fundamento oro, plata, piedras preciosas, madera, heno, hojarasca; La obra de cada uno será manifestada: porque el día la declarará; porque por el fuego será manifestada; y la obra de cada uno cuál sea, el fuego hará la prueba."

1 Corintios 3:11-13.

El capítulo uno de Daniel revela que la adoración del Dios verdadero se diluyó con ideas e influencias paganas bajo el rey Nabucodonosor. El capítulo dos de Daniel revela que la fusión de ideas paganas en la verdadera adoración de Dios no terminó cuando cayó el Imperio Babilónico. Daniel 2 revela la fuente de las prácticas e ideas paganas que se han filtrado hasta nuestros días y que han contaminado la adoración verdadera en todo el mundo bajo los imperios que gobernaron sobre el pueblo de Dios desde los días de Daniel.

En este capítulo, el rey Nabucodonosor tiene un sueño interesante. Al día siguiente, sabe que el sueño es importante, pero no lo recuerda. Dado que sus consejeros paganos, los sabios, que supuestamente son capaces de revelar secretos y misterios, no pudieron contarle al rey su sueño, declara un decreto de muerte para todos los consejeros, que incluían a Daniel y sus tres compañeros.

Daniel le pidió al rey con respeto y tacto más tiempo y el rey Nabucodonosor le concedió su pedido. Con sus tres amigos, Daniel llevó a cabo una reunión de oración pidiendo a Dios que les revelara el sueño para que pudieran satisfacer la petición del rey y salvar sus vidas. Durante la noche Dios le mostró a Daniel el sueño y al día siguiente Daniel le contó el sueño al rey dándole a Dios toda la gloria.

En el sueño, el rey Nabucodonosor ve una estatua. Tiene cabeza de oro, pecho y brazos de plata, vientre y muslos de bronce, piernas de hierro, con sus pies y diez dedos una mezcla de hierro y barro. Mientras el rey está contemplando la imagen, se corta una pequeña piedra de una montaña sin manos y se estrella contra los pies de la estatua, haciendo que se desmorone en una pila de polvo que el viento se lleva. Después de que el polvo se aclara, la piedra se convierte en una gran montaña y llena toda la tierra.

Daniel luego revela el significado del sueño. Le explica al rey que la cabeza de oro representa al rey y al imperio babilónico que gobierna sobre hombres y bestias. Continúa revelando al rey que el pecho y los brazos de plata, el vientre y los muslos de bronce, las piernas de hierro, los pies de hierro y barro y los dedos de los pies de hierro y barro representan otros imperios o reinos que seguirían a su y también gobernaría sobre toda la tierra. Así, la estatua en su sueño representaba siete reinos en total, Babilonia y otros cinco que surgirán después del suyo, así como el reino representado por la piedra destructiva. Daniel nos dice que la piedra que destruye la estatua es un reino que aniquilará la estatua, se hará enorme, cubrirá toda la tierra y durará para siempre. De este sueño del rey Nabucodonosor se representan en total siete reinos.

En los siguientes capítulos de Daniel, Dios revela la identidad de los otros tres reinos que "gobiernan sobre toda la tierra" después del imperio babilónico. En Daniel 2:37 y 38, Daniel le dice al rey que la cabeza de oro lo representa a él o, en otras palabras, al reino de Babilonia. Daniel 5: 30,31 y Daniel 8:20 revela que el cofre y los brazos de plata representan el reino de los medos y persas. Daniel 8:21 revela que el vientre y los muslos de bronce representan el reino de Grecia bajo Alejandro Magno. El cuarto reino se describe en Daniel dos y siete, pero no se nombra explícitamente. La historia revela que el imperio que venció al Imperio griego fue el Imperio Romano, que era el reino gobernante cuando nació Cristo. Se supone que el Imperio Romano está representado por las piernas de Hierro.

Los pies y los dedos de los pies también representan dos reinos separados. Note Daniel 2:41-43:

> "Y lo que viste de los pies y los dedos, en parte de barro cocido de alfarero, y en parte de hierro, el reino será dividido; mas habrá en él algo de fortaleza de hierro, según que viste el hierro mezclado con el tiesto de barro."

> Y por ser los dedos de los pies en parte de hierro, y en parte de barro cocido, en parte será el reino fuerte, y en parte será frágil. Cuanto á aquello que viste, el hierro mezclado con tiesto de barro, mezcláranse con simiente humana, mas no se pegarán el uno con el otro, como el hierro no se mistura con el tiesto."

LA IMAGEN DE SUEÑO DEL REY NEBUCHADNEZZAR DE DANIEL DOS

CABEZA DE ORO   BABILONIA

PECHO / BRAZOS DE PLATA   MEDO-PERSIA

VIENTRE / MUSLOS DE LATÓN   GRECIA

PATAS DE HIERRO   ROMA

PIES DE HIERRO / ARCILLA   ÚLTIMO DÍA (X 2)

PIEDRA DE MONTAÑA   REINO DE DIOS

Muchos creen que en este momento, el pueblo de Dios está viviendo en el tiempo del "hierro mezclado con barro fangoso" o el tiempo de los pies. Hay diferentes opiniones sobre esto, ya que la Biblia no es perfectamente clara para distinguirlo. Algunos enseñan que estamos viviendo en el tiempo de los pies y algunos creen que estamos viviendo en el tiempo de los dedos de los pies. Para este autor, creo que vivimos en la época en que los pies se unen a los dedos, es decir, donde el pie distal se encuentra con los dedos proximales. El Apocalipsis revela esto cuando dice:

"Y son siete reyes. Los cinco son caídos; el uno es, el otro aun no es venido; y cuando viniere, es necesario que dure breve tiempo." Apocalipsis 17:10

"Y los diez cuernos que has visto, son diez reyes, que aun no han recibido reino; mas tomarán

potencia por una hora como reyes con la bestia."
Apocalipsis 17:12

Creo que los "diez dedos de los pies" y los "diez cuernos" representan el mismo reino del tiempo del fin, que tiene una vida útil corta. Pero tenga en cuenta; la estatua de Daniel dos trata más de la influencia corruptora de la adoración pagana, que se infiltró en la adoración del Dios verdadero, que de la identificación de naciones. La adoración de Dios era "pura" como el oro cuando el rey atacó Jerusalén y el templo de Jerusalén. Pero con el tiempo esa adoración fue diluida y contaminada por las ideas y enseñanzas paganas de la adoración de los imperios babilónico, medopersa, griego y romano. El hierro en las piernas y los pies representa la culminación del paganismo de todos esos reinos que influyen en la adoración de Dios, entonces y ahora.

PREGUNTA:

¿Por qué dice en Daniel 2:38 y 39 que estos cuatro reinos, representados por los cuatro metales diferentes, "gobernarán sobre toda la tierra"? En consideración a estos cuatro reinos, ninguno de ellos gobernó jamás sobre "toda la tierra". Los dos imperios que en realidad se puede decir que gobernaron la mayor parte de este mundo son el de Inglaterra y España, pero no se mencionan en el sueño del rey Nabucodonosor. Entonces, la pregunta debe hacerse,

"¿Qué significa gobernar sobre toda la tierra?"

Debemos recordar que el libro de Daniel es más que una simple lección de historia mundial. También revela que nuestro Dios es omnisciente porque lo sabe todo, conoce el fin desde el principio (Isaías 46: 9,10). Él sabe qué reinos se levantarán y caerán y, sobre todo, de acuerdo con la intención del libro de

Daniel, también sabe qué imperios tendrían la mayor influencia para introducir ideas y prácticas paganas en Su adoración pura como el oro que Él establecida a través de la nación hebrea de Israel. Note que en estos reinos la única gente mencionada de ser gobernada es el pueblo de Dios.

RESPUESTA:

Aunque estos reinos nunca gobernaron cada sección de este planeta, todos estos reinos gobernaron Mesopotamia y los territorios circundantes (Salmo 80: 8-11) donde vivía el pueblo de Dios en ese momento. Con eso en mente, debemos concluir que, en la mayoría de los casos, en la profecía bíblica, cuando la Biblia habla de la "tierra", se refiere al pueblo de Dios, a Su reino y no a todo este planeta. En Deuteronomio, Moisés se dirige a los hijos de Israel, el pueblo de Dios, y les da consejos sobre cómo permanecer cerca de Dios. Note Deuteronomio 32:1-4:

> "ESCUCHAD, cielos, y hablaré; Y oiga **la tierra** los dichos de mi boca. Goteará como la lluvia mi doctrina; Destilará como el rocío mi razonamiento; Como la llovizna sobre la grama, Y como las gotas sobre la hierba: Porque el nombre de Jehová invocaré: Engrandeced á nuestro Dios. El es la Roca, cuya obra es perfecta, Porque todos sus caminos son rectitud: Dios de verdad, y ninguna iniquidad en él: Es justo y recto."

Tenga en cuenta: Al leer y estudiar la Biblia, se deben considerar una serie de cosas para llegar a la comprensión adecuada de lo que se está leyendo. Debemos considerar el contexto, el contenido y la historia. Debemos saber: quién está hablando, a quién se dirige, cuál es la ocasión, cuál es el mensaje en ese momento y cómo se relaciona ese mensaje con nosotros en nuestros días. Lo mismo se aplica cada vez que leemos sobre la "tierra" en la Biblia. Necesitamos determinar, durante nuestra lectura, ¿se refiere a este planeta o se refiere al pueblo de Dios, a Su reino?

Note el siguiente texto que se encuentra en Isaías 66:1,2:

> "JEHOVA dijo así: El cielo es mi solio, y la **tierra** estrado de mis pies: ¿dónde está la casa que me habréis de edificar, y dónde este lugar de mi reposo? Mi mano hizo todas estas cosas, y así todas estas cosas fueron, dice Jehová: mas á aquél miraré que es pobre y humilde de espíritu, y que tiembla á mi palabra."

El cielo es donde habita Dios. Donde Dios habita ese es el cielo. La **tierra** bajo sus pies es lo que Dios gobierna y controla. Aquellas personas que alegre y voluntariamente permiten que Dios viva en sus corazones y se establezca en sus vidas, es donde Dios habita, eso es el cielo.

Aquellas personas que deben ser controladas y constantemente restringidas de seguir sus propios caminos, esa es la gente de la **tierra**. Es triste decirlo, la mayoría de nosotros caemos en la categoría de "gente de la tierra". Pero la diferencia entre la "gente de la tierra" y la "gente del mar" es que la "gente de la **tierra**" busca activamente al Señor, como se revela en el Salmo 24. También observe el versículo seis: "Esta es la generación de los que lo buscan, que buscan tu rostro ".

Entiende que la palabra hebrea para "**tierra**" es el número 772 de Strong:"ara" (se pronuncia ar-ah '), que también se puede traducir como "tierra" o "suelo". Y en griego, la palabra "tierra". "Es el número 1093 de Strong:" gé "(se pronuncia" ghay ") y también se puede traducir como tierra, suelo, región y país.

En su investigación y estudio bíblico, cuando encuentre la palabra" tierra "o" tierra ", considere la contexto y contenido y pregúntese qué palabra es la más apropiada, "tierra" o "tierra" y si la palabra "tierra" o "tierra" se refiere al pueblo de Dios, Su reino, Su "pueblo terrenal" o no.

¿Por qué Dios llamaría **"tierra"** al pueblo de su reino para distinguirlo de la gente que no está en su reino? Considera lo siguiente:

> "Formó, pues, Jehová Dios al hombre del polvo de la tierra, y alentó en su nariz soplo de vida; y fué el hombre en alma viviente." Génesis 2:7

> "En el sudor de tu rostro comerás el pan hasta que vuelvas á la tierra; porque de ella fuiste tomado: pues polvo eres, y al polvo serás tornado." Génesis 3:19

Hay una marca distintiva entre los que creen en Dios y los que no. Aquellos que creen en Dios saben que Él existe (Hebreos 11: 6) y que Él es el Creador de todas las cosas (Efesios 3: 9). Aquellos que niegan a Dios no creen en Él y no creen que Él sea el Creador de todas las cosas. La diferencia entre los dos es que un grupo, creyendo que Dios creó al hombre de la tierra, está en la "ciudad" o "reino" de Dios y el otro grupo está fuera de la "ciudad" o "reino" de Dios. Un grupo habita en la ciudad espiritual de Jerusalén y el otro en la ciudad espiritual de Babilonia.

> "Bienaventurados los que guardan sus mandamientos, para que su potencia sea en el árbol de la vida, y que entren por las puertas en la ciudad. Mas los perros estarán fuera, y los hechiceros, y los disolutos, y los homicidas, y los

idólatras, y cualquiera que ama y hace mentira."
Apocalipsis 22:14,15.

"ESTO también sepas, que en los postreros días
vendrán tiempos peligrosos: Que habrá hombres
amadores de sí mismos, avaros, vanagloriosos,
soberbios, detractores, desobedientes á los
padres, ingratos, sin santidad, Sin afecto,
desleales, calumniadores, destemplados,
crueles, aborrecedores de lo bueno, Traidores,
arrebatados, hinchados, amadores de los
deleites más que de Dios; Teniendo apariencia
de piedad, mas habiendo negado la eficacia de
ella: y á éstos evita. Porque de éstos son los
que se entran por las casas, y llevan cautivas
las mujercillas cargadas de pecados, llevadas
de diversas concupiscencias; Que siempre
aprenden, y nunca pueden acabar de llegar
al conocimiento de la verdad. Y de la manera
que Jannes y Jambres resistieron á Moisés, así
también estos resisten á la verdad; hombres
corruptos de entendimiento, réprobos acerca de
la fe. Mas no prevalecerán; porque su insensatez
será manifiesta á todos, como también lo fué la
de aquéllos." 2 Timoteo 3:1-9.

La gente de la "**Tierra**", los que viven en el reino de Dios, aquí
y ahora, saben que fueron creados del suelo tal como Dios
dice. Los que viven fuera del reino de Dios no creen que fueron
creados de la tierra. **

La gente del reino de Dios vive la vida que Él ordena. A lo largo
de la Biblia, Dios nos dice que nuestras acciones desobedientes
pueden contaminar la tierra (Isaías 24: 4-6), Su pueblo. El estilo

de vida y las elecciones de vida del pueblo de Dios reflejan su fe, confianza y fe en Él. El deseo del pueblo del reino es ser como Jesús, entregando completamente su voluntad a Dios en obediencia a Su voluntad. Note Apocalipsis 11:18:

> "Y se han airado las naciones, y tu ira es venida, y el tiempo de los muertos, para que sean juzgados, y para que des el galardón á tus siervos los profetas, y á los santos, y á los que temen tu nombre, á los pequeñitos y á los grandes, y para que destruyas los que destruyen **la tierra**."

Dios tiene amor y deseo por Su pueblo, la tierra, y Su ira en el tiempo del fin será contra aquellos que desean destruir a Su pueblo. Aquellos que persiguen a su pueblo, incluso matándolos, al final serán juzgados, destruidos y aniquilados. Note Malaquías 4:1-3:

> "PORQUE he aquí, viene el día ardiente como un horno; y todos los soberbios, y todos los que hacen maldad, serán estopa; y aquel día que vendrá, los abrasará, ha dicho Jehová de los ejércitos, el cual no les dejará ni raíz ni rama. Mas á vosotros los que teméis mi nombre, nacerá el Sol de justicia, y en sus alas traerá salud: y saldréis, y saltaréis como becerros de la manada. Y hollaréis á los malos, los cuales serán ceniza bajo las plantas de vuestros pies, en el día que yo hago, ha dicho Jehová de los ejércitos."

¿Hay otros ejemplos en la Biblia donde la palabra "tierra" se refiere claramente a las personas que componen el actual reino de Dios en este planeta?

Note lo siguiente:

"Y he aquí, Jehová estaba en lo alto de ella, el cual dijo: Yo soy Jehová, el Dios de Abraham tu padre, y el Dios de Isaac: la tierra en que estás acostado te la daré á ti y á tu simiente. Y será tu simiente como el polvo de la tierra, y te extenderás al occidente, y al oriente, y al aquilón, y al mediodía; y todas las familias de la tierra serán benditas en ti y en tu simiente. Y he aquí, yo soy contigo, y te guardaré por donde quiera que fueres, y te volveré á esta **tierra**; porque no te dejaré hasta tanto que haya hecho lo que te he dicho." Génesis 28:13-15

"De cierto os digo que todo lo que ligareis en **la tierra**, será ligado en el cielo; y todo lo que desatareis en la tierra, será desatado en el cielo. Otra vez os digo, que si dos de vosotros se convinieren en la tierra, de toda cosa que pidieren, les será hecho por mi Padre que está en los cielos." Mateo 18:19,20

"Pero los mansos heredarán la tierra, Y se recrearán con abundancia de paz."

Salmos 37:11.

"Bienaventurados los mansos: porque ellos recibirán **la tierra** por heredad." Mateo 5:5.

"Y les fué mandado que no hiciesen daño á la hierba de **la tierra**, ni á ninguna cosa verde, ni á ningún árbol, sino solamente á **los hombres**

que no tienen la señal de Dios en sus frentes."
Apocalipsis 9:4

"Y vi otro ángel volar por en medio del cielo, que
tenía el evangelio eterno para predicarlo á los
que moran en la **tierra**, y á toda nación y tribu y
lengua y pueblo, Diciendo en alta voz: Temed á
Dios, y dadle honra; porque la hora de su juicio
es venida; y adorad á aquel que ha hecho el
cielo y la **tierra** y el **mar** y las fuentes de las
aguas." Apocalipsis 14:6,7

No debería sorprendernos saber que la palabra "**tierra**" se
refiere al pueblo de Dios. La palabra "mar" o "agua" también
se refiere **a personas**:

"Y él me dice: Las **aguas** que has visto donde la
ramera se sienta, son **pueblos** y muchedumbres
y naciones y lenguas." Apocalipsis17:15

Observe el siguiente versículo que utiliza "cielo", "tierra" y "mar"
como el pueblo de Dios que habita Su reino aquí y ahora:

"Por lo cual alegraos, **cielos**, y los que moráis
en ellos. ¡Ay de los moradores de **la tierra** y del
mar! porque el diablo ha descendido á vosotros,
teniendo grande ira, sabiendo que tiene poco
tiempo." Apocalipsis 12:12.

** Aprenda más sobre el reino de Dios leyendo el libro
electrónico, "The Kingdom of Heaven and the Kingdom of God"
de Earl B. Schrock, que se encuentra en Xlibris.com, Amazon.
com, Barnes and Noble, etc.

CONCLUSIÓN: El sueño del rey Nabucodonosor no se trata solo de imperios que surgen y caen o de reyes que van y vienen, o incluso de la omnisciencia de Dios. El sueño del capítulo dos de Daniel trata sobre la influencia pagana que salió de estas naciones, que gobernaron sobre el pueblo de Dios. Estos imperios introdujeron ideas paganas en la adoración pura de Dios que Él había establecido a lo largo del tiempo durante la historia de la humanidad.

Contempla los metales en la estatua en consideración a la pureza en la adoración a Dios. Al principio, durante los días de Daniel, la adoración de Dios era pura porque las interferencias paganas anteriores de Egipto fueron tratadas con severidad y eliminadas ante el rey Nabucodonosor. La gente tenía la Palabra de Dios para guiarlos en su adoración. Pero a medida que cada reino pagano sucesivo agregó su influencia pagana a la mezcla, la adoración pura de Dios se deterioró, por lo que los metales se volvieron más duros y menos flexibles, y de menos valor. Y finalmente, en los últimos días, los pies y los dedos de los pies representan la miríada de grupos de adoración que ocupan este planeta, cada uno de los cuales no está dispuesto a ceder ante el otro en la manera de adorar a Dios correcta y correctamente de la manera que Él exige. Pero la historia no se detiene ahí.

En los últimos días, los días de los pies y los dedos de los pies, Dios tendrá un pueblo que se familiarizará tanto con Él y Su adoración que dejará de lado todas las influencias paganas que debilitaron la adoración de Dios a través de los siglos y no solo Adórelo "en espíritu y en verdad" (Juan 4:23) pero enseñará a otros lo mismo.

"Porque reprendiéndolos dice: He aquí vienen días, dice el Señor, Y consumaré para con la casa de Israel y para con la casa de Judá un nuevo pacto; No como el pacto que hice con sus padres El día que los tomé por la mano para sacarlos de la tierra de Egipto: Porque ellos no permanecieron en mi pacto, Y yo los menosprecié, dice el Señor. Por lo cual, este es el pacto que ordenaré á la casa de Israel Después de aquellos días, dice el Señor: Daré mis leyes en el alma de ellos, Y sobre el corazón de ellos las escribiré; Y seré á ellos por Dios, Y ellos me serán á mí por pueblo: Y ninguno eneseñará á su prójimo, Ni ninguno á su hermano, diciendo: Conoce al Señor: Porque todos me conocerán, Desde el menor de ellos hasta el mayor. Porque seré propicio á sus injusticias, Y de sus pecados y de sus iniquidades no me acordaré más. Diciendo, Nuevo pacto, dió por viejo al primero; y lo que es dado por viejo y se envejece, cerca está de desvanecerse." Hebreos 8:8-13.

DESCUBRIENDO LA VERDAD SOBRE LA PIEDRA QUE HUELGA LA ESTATUA:

Suele haber diferencias de opinión sobre lo que representa la piedra que golpea la estatua en el sueño del rey Nabucodonosor. Como en todos los casos de consideración de cosas bíblicas, el mejor lugar al que acudir para descubrir este secreto es la Biblia misma. La tradición o los conceptos e ideas previos de otros, o incluso lo que dice el pastor o el instructor bíblico, debe dejarse de lado hasta que se descubra y aclare toda la información de la Biblia. La Biblia y la Biblia solo deben interpretarse a sí mismas.

Algunos consideran que la imagen es la historia del pecado o de la humanidad. Por lo tanto, asumen que la piedra es la segunda venida de Jesús al final de los tiempos que borra la historia de la humanidad pecadora. Pero los versículos 35 y 45 de Daniel 2 revelan que la estatua está en su forma completa de la cabeza a los pies cuando la piedra la golpea. La cabeza no desapareció cuando murió el rey Nabucodonosor o cuando los medopersas se apoderaron del reino. La estatua no representa la historia del pecado y la piedra no es la segunda venida de Jesús.

Debemos recordar: la profecía bíblica tiene que ver con la ADORACIÓN. Así que tenemos que preguntarnos: "¿Qué tiene que ver la piedra del sueño del rey Nabucodonosor con la adoración?"

A CONTINUACIÓN ESTÁN LOS TEXTOS DE DANIEL TWO SOBRE LA PIEDRA DESTRUCTIVA

33 Sus piernas de hierro; sus pies, en parte de hierro, y en parte de barro cocido.

34 Estabas mirando, hasta que una piedra fué cortada, no con mano, la cual hirió á la imagen en sus pies de hierro y de barro cocido, y los desmenuzó. **35** Entonces fué también desmenuzado el hierro, el barro cocido, el metal, la plata y el oro, y se tornaron como tamo de las eras del verano: y levantólos el viento, y nunca más se les halló lugar. Mas la piedra que hirió á la imagen, fué hecha un gran monte, que hinchió toda la tierra.

42 Y por ser los dedos de los pies en parte de hierro, y en parte de barro cocido, en parte será el reino fuerte, y en parte será frágil. **43** Cuanto á aquello que viste, el hierro mezclado con tiesto de barro, mezclaránse con simiente humana, mas no se pegarán el uno con el otro, como el hierro no se mistura con el tiesto. **44** Y en los días de estos reyes, levantará el Dios del cielo un reino que nunca jamás se corromperá: y no será dejado á otro pueblo este reino; el cual desmenuzará y consumirá todos estos reinos, y él permanecerá para siempre. **45** De la manera que viste que del monte fué cortada una piedra, no con manos, la cual desmenuzó al hierro, al metal, al tiesto, á la plata, y al oro; el gran Dios ha mostrado al rey lo que ha de acontecer en lo por venir: y el sueño es verdadero, y fiel su declaración.

INFORMACIÓN OBTENIDA DE LOS TEXTOS ANTERIORES:

1. La piedra golpea los dedos de los pies en algún momento después del reino de los pies (versículo 33).
2. La piedra se corta sin manos (versículo 34)
3. Golpea los pies y los dedos de los pies, que están hechos de hierro y barro (versículo 34).
4. Cuando golpea, los diferentes metales se pulverizan juntos, al mismo tiempo (Vs 35).
5. Los metales de hierro, arcilla, bronce, plata y oro se vuelven como paja de trigo (v. 35).
6. El viento aleja el polvo metálico (versículo 35).
7. Una vez destruido, el polvo metálico no se puede encontrar (Versículo 35).
8. La piedra se convierte en una gran montaña (versículo 35).
9. Llena por completo toda la tierra (versículo 35).
10. Los diez dedos de los pies representan un reino (versículo 42).
11. Los pies y los dedos de los pies son dos reinos separados (versículos 41, 42).
12. El hierro y el barro en los pies representan grupos de personas divididos (versículo 43).

13. Las multitudes representadas en los pies y los dedos de los pies nunca estarán de acuerdo (Versículo 43).

14. El reino de los dedos del pie permanecerá dividido hasta que la estatua sea demolida (versículo 44).

15. El reino de Dios está formado por personas (versículo 44).

16. Golpea la imagen específicamente durante el tiempo del reino de los dedos del pie (versículos 42-44).

17. Durante el tiempo del "reino de los pies", Dios establece Su reino (versículo 44).

18. El reino de Dios nunca será destruido (versículo 44).

19. El reino de Dios nunca cambiará de dueño (versículo 44).

20. El reino de Dios destruirá y consumirá todos los reinos anteriores (versículo 44).

21. El reino de Dios durará para siempre (versículo 44).

22. La piedra está tallada en una montaña (versículo 45).

23. Está cortado de la montaña sin manos (versículo 45).

24. El reino de Dios pulveriza la imagen metálica de pies a cabeza (versículo 45).

25. La piedra que destruye la imagen es un futuro muy lejano del rey (versículo 45).

26. Daniel le dice al rey que el sueño sucederá tal como fue revelado (versículo 45).

¿Qué significa que la piedra fue "cortada de un monte" (versículo 45)? Esta pregunta se responderá con más detalle durante la discusión sobre el capítulo nueve de Daniel.

¿Qué significa "sin manos" (versículo 34)? Dios ha desarrollado un pueblo que forma Su reino por Sus propios métodos y no por los del hombre. Ha desarrollado a su pueblo del reino para que sea un templo o un santuario para albergar a su Espíritu. Algo desarrollado por Dios, a su manera, se construye sin manos.

"¿O ignoráis que vuestro cuerpo es templo del Espíritu Santo, el cual está en vosotros, el cual tenéis de Dios, y que no sois vuestros?" 1 Corintios 6:19.

¿Qué significa que la piedra se convirtió en una gran montaña (versículo 35)? El reino de los cielos ha ido creciendo desde los días de Jesús. El monte espiritual de Sion se ha convertido en una enorme montaña a partir de hoy. Vea el Salmo 74:1,2; Hechos 17:24; Éxodo 25:8; 1 Corintios 3:16; Lucas 17:21; Miqueas 4:1-5; e Isaías 2:1-5.

Nosotros, su pueblo del reino, somos el monte Sion, su pueblo, su montaña. Efesios 2: 11-22:

"Por tanto, acordaos que en otro tiempo vosotros los Gentiles en la carne, que erais llamados incircuncisión por la que se llama circuncisión, hecha con mano en la carne; Que en aquel tiempo estabais sin Cristo, alejados de la república de Israel, y extranjeros á los pactos de la promesa, sin esperanza y sin Dios en el mundo. Mas ahora en Cristo Jesús, vosotros que en otro tiempo estabais lejos, habéis sido hechos cercanos por la sangre de Cristo. Porque él es nuestra paz, que de ambos hizo uno, derribando la pared intermedia de separación; Dirimiendo en su carne las enemistades, la ley de los mandamientos en orden á ritos, para edificar en sí mismo los dos en un nuevo hombre, haciendo la paz, Y reconciliar por la cruz con Dios á ambos en un mismo cuerpo, matando en ella las enemistades. Y vino, y anunció la paz á vosotros que estabais lejos, y á los que estaban cerca: Que por él los unos y los otros tenemos entrada por un mismo Espíritu al Padre. Así que ya no sois extranjeros ni advenedizos, sino juntamente ciudadanos con los santos, y domésticos de Dios; Edificados sobre el fundamento de los apóstoles y profetas, siendo la principal piedra del ángulo Jesucristo mismo; En el cual, compaginado todo el edificio, va creciendo para ser un templo santo en el Señor: En el cual vosotros también sois juntamente edificados, para morada de Dios en Espíritu."

¿Qué significa que "llenó toda la tierra" (versículo 35)? La "tierra" en la profecía bíblica representa el "reino terrenal de Dios". Está compuesto por los "grandes" y los "pequeños" (Apocalipsis 20:12), que son personas familiarizadas con Jesús de todas las naciones de este mundo.

¿QUÉ SIGNIFICA: "MEZCLARSE CON LA SEMILLA DE HOMBRES" en el versículo 43? ¿CUÁL ES LA DEFINICIÓN DE LA "SEMILLA DE LOS HOMBRES"? Note lo siguiente:

Jesús es la "simiente" de Abraham, que era un hombre (Gálatas 3:15).

La simiente de Abraham será como el polvo, las estrellas y la arena (Génesis 13:16, 22:17, 32:12).

La Palabra de Dios, la Biblia, es la "semilla" (Lucas 8:11). La buena semilla representa a los justos; la mala semilla representa a los perdidos (Mat. 13: 24-30, 38).

La semilla se usa para determinar el valor de la tierra (Levítico 27:16).

La semilla se usa para mantener la vida (Génesis 47:23).

La semilla representa la justicia (Oseas 10:12).

Semilla puede referirse a descendientes (palabra griega Sperma: Strong's 4690) (Hechos 7: 5).

La semilla representa "descendencia" o descendientes (en hebreo zera: Strong's 2234) (Dan. 2:43).

Muchos asumen que esta frase "mezclarse con la simiente de los hombres" significa casarse entre sí para generar solidaridad entre reinos. ¿Pero es eso lo que realmente significa?

¿Quiénes son "ellos" y "ellos mismos" en el versículo 43 cuando dice:

> "Cuanto á aquello que viste, el hierro mezclado con tiesto de barro, mezcláranse con simiente humana, mas no se pegarán el uno con el otro, como el hierro no se mistura con el tiesto."

El "ellos" y "ellos mismos" significan personas, el pueblo de Dios, que viven en Su reino, aquí y ahora, no imperios o reinos. El pueblo de Dios de hoy, en diferentes denominaciones o grupos de adoración, en todo el mundo es muy firme en el cambio. Es como "una vez bautista, siempre bautista", no importa lo que digan nada ni nadie. La mayoría de las personas discutirán su forma de pensar y adorar hasta la muerte, porque esa es la forma en que fueron criados para adorar. Así, las comunidades de adoración fragmentadas de hierro se niegan a unirse.

CONCLUSIÓN DE LA PIEDRA: De lo anterior sabemos que la piedra representa el "reino de Dios" que Él desarrolló o formó sin manos humanas, cuando Jesús murió en la cruz, luego de beber el "fruto de la vid", el vinagre (Lea el capítulo

"El vinagre en la cruz del Calvario" en la página 450). A la muerte de Jesús, la principal piedra angular (Efesios 2: 19-22), el reino de los cielos, o de Dios, estaba formado por unas pocas personas, pero durante los últimos 2000 años el reino de Cristo ha llegado a incluir todas las partes. de este planeta. Creo que la montaña en la que se cortó la piedra fue el monte Sión, el reino que Dios desarrolló durante los 4000 años anteriores, desde los días de Adán hasta los de Cristo. Jesús dijo: "La salvación es de los judíos" (Juan 4:22) porque Él salió del árbol genealógico que se describe en el capítulo uno de Mateo y el capítulo dos de Lucas, que va desde Dios el Padre hasta Jesús el Hijo.

Desde los días de Daniel en el reino de Babilonia hasta los días de Jesús, el reino de Dios se había contaminado con el paganismo de Babilonia, Medo-Persia, Grecia y Roma. Esas enseñanzas paganas todavía están incrustadas en la adoración en todo el mundo hoy. Pero el desarrollo del reino de Cristo, "piedra cortada sin manos", desde los días de Jesús hasta nuestros días ha ido reconociendo lentamente las enseñanzas paganas y ahora en los últimos días hay un pueblo que sirve a Dios "en espíritu y en verdad" mientras se dedican a ser guiados por el Espíritu Santo a través de la Palabra de Dios, el 66 libro de la Santa Biblia. Estos siervos de Dios, de todos los ámbitos de la vida y de cada comunidad religiosa, son llamados Sus elegidos y están dispuestos a "seguir al Cordero por dondequiera que vaya" (Apocalipsis 14: 4) para realizar Su voluntad, no la suya propia. Quieren servir a Dios totalmente, según Su Palabra, y no según las tradiciones de los hombres. Estas son las personas del "cielo". Hay otros que se niegan a obedecer completamente a Dios en Su Palabra, la gente de la "tierra" y la del "mar": estos tres grupos ocupan el Reino de Dios. **

"Así habéis invalidado el mandamiento de Dios por vuestra tradición. Hipócritas, bien profetizó de vosotros Isaías, diciendo: Este pueblo de labios me honra; Mas su corazón lejos está de mí. 9 Mas en vano me honran, Enseñando doctrinas y mandamientos de hombres." Matthew 15:6-9.

Vea el video de YouTube **DANIEL CAPÍTULO DOS EN ESPAÑOL** por Earl Schrock

Vea el video de YouTube **LA PIEDRA DE DANIEL CAPÍTULO DOS EN ESPAÑOL** por Earl Schrock

** Obtenga más información sobre el reino de Dios en el libro electrónico, "The Kingdom of Heaven and the Kingdom of God" de Earl B. Schrock; en Xlibris.com, Amazon.com, Barnes and Noble, etc.

DANIEL CAPÍTULO DOS (RVR)

1 Y EN el segundo año del reinado de Nabucodonosor, soñó Nabucodonosor sueños, y perturbóse su espíritu, y su sueño se huyó de él. 2 Y mandó el rey llamar magos, astrólogos, y encantadores, y Caldeos, para que mostrasen al rey sus sueños. Vinieron pues, y se presentaron delante del rey. 3 Y el rey les dijo: He soñado un sueño, y mi espíritu se ha perturbado por saber del sueño. 4 Entonces hablaron los Caldeos al rey en lengua aramea: Rey, para siempre vive: di el sueño á tus siervos, y mostraremos la declaración. 5 Respondió el rey y dijo á los Caldeos: El negocio se me fué: si no me mostráis el sueño y su declaración, seréis hechos cuartos, y vuestras casas serán puestas por muladares. 6 Y si mostrareis el sueño y su declaración, recibiréis de mí dones y mercedes y grande honra: por tanto, mostradme el sueño y su declaración. 7 Respondieron la segunda vez, y dijeron: Diga el rey el sueño á

sus siervos, y mostraremos su declaración. 8 El rey respondió, y dijo: Yo conozco ciertamente que vosotros ponéis dilaciones, porque veis que el negocio se me ha ido. 9 Si no me mostráis el sueño, una sola sentencia será de vosotros. Ciertamente preparáis respuesta mentirosa y perversa que decir delante de mí, entre tanto que se muda el tiempo: por tanto, decidme el sueño, para que yo entienda que me podéis mostrar su declaración. 10 Los Caldeos respondieron delante del rey, y dijeron: No hay hombre sobre la tierra que pueda declarar el negocio del rey: demás de esto, ningún rey, príncipe, ni señor, preguntó cosa semejante á ningún mago, ni astrólogo, ni Caldeo. 11 Finalmente, el negocio que el rey demanda, es singular, ni hay quien lo pueda declarar delante del rey, salvo los dioses cuya morada no es con la carne. 12 Por esto el rey con ira y con grande enojo, mandó que matasen á todos los sabios de Babilonia. 13 Y publicóse el mandamiento, y los sabios eran llevados á la muerte; y buscaron á Daniel y á sus compañeros para matarlos. 14 Entonces Daniel habló avisada y prudentemente á Arioch, capitán de los de la guarda del rey, que había salido para matar los sabios de Babilonia. 15 Habló y dijo á Arioch capitán del rey: ¿Qué es la causa que este mandamiento se publica de parte del rey tan apresuradamente? Entonces Arioch declaró el negocio á Daniel. 16 Y Daniel entró, y pidió al rey que le diese tiempo, y que él mostraría al rey la declaración. 17 Fuése luego Daniel á su casa, y declaró el negocio á Ananías, Misael, y Azarías, sus compañeros, 18 Para demandar misericordias del Dios del cielo sobre este misterio, y que Daniel y sus compañeros no pereciesen con los otros sabios de Babilonia. 19 Entonces el arcano fué revelado á Daniel en visión de noche; por lo cual bendijo Daniel al Dios del cielo. 20 Y Daniel habló, y dijo: Sea bendito el nombre de Dios de siglo hasta siglo: porque suya es la sabiduría y la fortaleza: 21 Y él es el que muda los tiempos y las oportunidades: quita reyes, y pone reyes: da la sabiduría á los sabios, y la ciencia á los entendidos: 22 El revela lo profundo y lo escondido: conoce lo que está en tinieblas, y la luz mora con él. 23 A ti, oh Dios de mis padres, confieso y te alabo, que me diste sabiduría y fortaleza, y ahora me enseñaste lo que te pedimos; pues nos has enseñado el negocio del rey. 24 Después de esto Daniel entró á Arioch, al cual el rey había puesto para matar á los sabios de Babilonia; fué, y díjole así: No mates á los sabios de Babilonia: llévame delante del rey, que yo mostraré al rey la declaración. 25 Entonces Arioch llevó prestamente á Daniel delante del rey, y díjole así: Un varón de los trasportados de Judá he hallado, el cual declarará al rey la interpretación. 26 Respondió el rey, y dijo á Daniel, al cual llamaban Beltsasar: ¿Podrás tú hacerme entender el sueño que vi, y su declaración? 27 Daniel respondió delante del rey, y dijo: El misterio que el rey demanda, ni sabios, ni astrólogos, ni magos, ni adivinos lo pueden enseñar al rey. 28 Mas hay un Dios en los cielos, el cual revela los misterios, y él ha hecho saber al rey Nabucodonosor lo que ha de acontecer á cabo de días. Tu sueño, y las visiones de tu cabeza sobre tu cama, es esto: 29 Tú, oh rey, en tu cama subieron tus pensamientos por saber lo que había de ser en lo por venir; y el que revela los misterios te mostró lo que ha de ser. 30 Y á mí ha sido revelado este misterio, no por sabiduría que en mí haya, más que en todos los vivientes, sino para que yo notifique al rey la declaración, y que entiendieses los pensamientos de tu corazón. 31 Tú, oh rey, veías, y he aquí una grande imagen. Esta imagen, que era muy grande, y cuya gloria era muy sublime, estaba en pie delante de ti, y su aspecto era terrible. 32 La cabeza de esta imagen era de fino oro; sus pechos y sus brazos, de plata; su vientre y sus muslos, de metal; 33 Sus piernas de hierro; sus pies, en parte de hierro, y en parte de barro cocido. 34 Estabas mirando, hasta que una piedra fué cortada, no con mano, la cual hirió á la imagen en sus pies de hierro y de barro cocido, y los desmenuzó. 35 Entonces fué también desmenuzado el hierro, el barro cocido, el metal, la plata y el oro, y se tornaron como tamo de las eras del verano: y levantólos el viento, y nunca más se les halló lugar. Mas la piedra que hirió á la imagen, fué hecha un gran monte, que hinchió toda la tierra. 36 Este es el sueño: la declaración de él diremos también en presencia del rey. 37 Tú, oh rey, eres rey de reyes; porque el Dios del cielo te ha dado reino, potencia, y fortaleza, y majestad. 38 Y todo lo que habitan hijos de hombres, bestias del campo, y aves del cielo, él ha entregado en tu mano, y te ha hecho enseñorear sobre todo: tú eres aquella cabeza de oro. 39 Y después de ti se levantará otro reino menor que tú; y otro tercer reino de metal, el cual se enseñoreará de toda la tierra. 40 Y el reino cuarto será fuerte como hierro; y como el hierro desmenuza y doma todas las cosas, y como el hierro que quebranta todas estas cosas, desmenuzará y quebrantará. 41 Y lo que viste de los pies y los dedos, en parte de barro cocido de alfarero, y en parte de hierro, el reino será dividido; mas habrá en él algo de fortaleza de hierro, según que viste el hierro mezclado con el tiesto de barro. 42 Y por ser los dedos de los pies en parte de hierro, y en parte de barro cocido, en parte será el reino fuerte, y en parte será frágil. 43 Cuanto á aquello que viste, el hierro mezclado con tiesto de barro, mezcláranse con simiente humana, mas no se pegarán el uno con el otro, como el hierro no se mistura con el tiesto. 44 Y en los días de estos reyes, levantará el Dios del cielo un reino que nunca jamás se corromperá: y no será dejado á otro pueblo este reino; el cual desmenuzará y consumirá todos estos reinos, y él permanecerá para siempre. 45 De la manera que viste que del monte fué cortada una piedra, no con manos, la cual desmenuzó al hierro, al metal, al tiesto, á la plata, y al oro; el gran Dios ha mostrado al rey lo que ha de acontecer en lo por venir: y el sueño es verdadero, y fiel su declaración. 46 Entonces el rey Nabucodonosor cayó sobre su rostro, y humillóse á Daniel, y mandó que le sacrificasen presentes y perfumes. 47 El rey habló á Daniel, y dijo: Ciertamente que el Dios vuestro es Dios de dioses, y el Señor de los reyes, y el descubridor de los misterios, pues pudiste revelar este arcano. 48 Entonces el rey engrandeció á Daniel, y le dió muchos y grandes dones, y púsolo por gobernador de toda la provincia de Babilonia, y por príncipe de los gobernadores sobre todos los sabios de Babilonia. 49 Y Daniel solicitó del rey, y él puso sobre los negocios de la provincia de Babilonia á Sadrach, Mesach, y Abed-nego: y Daniel estaba á la puerta del rey.

DANIEL CAPÍTULO TRES

"Por lo demás, hermanos, todo lo que es verdadero, todo lo honesto, todo lo justo, todo lo puro, todo lo amable, todo lo que es de buen nombre; si hay virtud alguna, si alguna alabanza, en esto pensad." Filipenses 4:8

El rey Nabucodonosor tomó cautivo a Daniel y sus tres compañeros en el año 605 a. C. Después de los tres años completos de asistir a la universidad de Babilonia, según lo establecido por el rey (Daniel 1:3-5), los cuatro amigos se graduaron con honores (Daniel 1:17-20). Aproximadamente en el 602 a. C., el rey tuvo su sueño multimetal como se registra en el capítulo dos de Daniel. Daniel le reveló al rey que Babilonia era la cabeza de oro y que otros tres imperios surgirían después del suyo.

Al parecer, no contento con ser solo la cabeza de oro en su sueño, el rey Nabucodonosor encargó la construcción de una escultura, similar a la imagen de su sueño, pero esta vez toda la estatua sería de oro, lo que significa que su imperio duraría para siempre.

La estatua debía ser enorme para que pudiera verse a kilómetros de distancia. Tendría 60 codos de alto y 6 codos de ancho (100 pies de alto y 10 pies de ancho). La imagen fue preparada bajo las especificaciones del rey y en el año 600 a.

C. la imagen fue revelada en la llanura de Dura, en la provincia de Babilonia (Daniel 3:1). La inauguración se llevó a cabo con una gran cantidad de fanfarrias que incluyeron mucha música (versículo 5) y celebraciones. Había una gran multitud que incluía a todos los funcionarios que formaban el gabinete del rey (versículo 2) y el gobierno.

Pero sucedió más en todo esto de lo que parece.

El jefe del reino del rey Nabucodonosor fue Daniel debido a su honestidad e integridad. A los otros funcionarios del gobierno no les gustó que Daniel y sus tres compañeros honestos los cuidaran a ellos y a todos sus arreglos comerciales (Daniel 2: 48,49). Creo que los consejeros celosos no solo alentaron al rey a construir la imagen, sino que también establecieron el castigo para cualquiera que no estuviera dispuesto a adorarla. Los sabios no pudieron encontrar nada malo en Daniel y sus tres amigos cuando se trataba de negocios o de su servicio al rey, pero también se dieron cuenta de que estos cuatro hombres nunca, nunca, nunca se inclinarían ante la estatua del rey. La pena por no adorar la imagen del rey fue la muerte inmediata al ser arrojado a uno de los hornos de fundición circundantes (versículos 4-6).

No creo que el rey se haya dado cuenta de su traición hasta el día de la revelación y las festividades, cuando los sabios se acercaron a él y le dijeron que algunas personas de la multitud se negaban a inclinarse y adorar su imagen. Tan pronto como le dijeron que eran Sadrac, Mesac y Abednego, reconoció su engaño e inmediatamente se enojó consigo mismo y con ellos (versículos 12,13). La trampa estaba tendida, lo habían engañado y ahora no tenía salida para salvar a los tres jóvenes. El rey había aceptado que se llevaran a cabo todos los arreglos y ahora todos los ojos de todo su gobierno estaban puestos en él. Solo tenía una opción y una oportunidad para salvar a sus tres líderes de confianza.

El rey Nabucodonosor llamó a los jóvenes a sí mismo, a la vista de todos los funcionarios de su gobierno, y les dio una oportunidad más de adorar la imagen o ser arrojados al horno ardiente (versículos 14,15). Daniel no estuvo presente en esta celebración para calmar al rey o defender a sus tres compañeros. Solo puedo imaginar que los sabios habían dispuesto que él estuviera lejos del área cuando pusieron su plan en acción. Si hubiera estado allí, probablemente las cosas hubieran sido bastante diferentes. Pero por ahora, las vidas de sus tres compañeros estaban en juego y estaban solos.

Quizás Daniel hubiera tenido más tacto al responder al rey que sus tres compañeros, pero no revelaron ningún tacto en su respuesta al rey ya frustrado.

"Sadrach, Mesach, y Abed-nego respondieron y dijeron al rey Nabucodonosor: no cuidamos de responderte sobre este negocio. He aquí nuestro Dios á quien honramos, puede librarnos del horno de fuego ardiendo; y de tu mano, oh rey, nos librará. Y si no, sepas, oh rey, que tu dios no adoraremos, ni tampoco honraremos la estatua que has levantado." Daniel 3:16-18.

Ante esta respuesta arrogante, el rey no solo estaba enojado consigo mismo por no ver el truco del sabio, ahora realmente estaba extremadamente enojado (versículo 19) con sus tres principales supervisores por responderle tan despiadadamente frente al mundo entero. En su furiosa prisa, hizo calentar el horno más allá de su límite legal. Esto también pudo haber sido un movimiento de misericordia por parte del rey para hacer que la muerte de sus amados sirvientes fuera instantánea. Cuando los soldados fuertes arrojaron a los tres hombres a la boca del horno, hacía tanto calor que los soldados murieron por estar demasiado cerca del calor (versículo 22).

Pero el rey pronto olvidó su rabia cuando notó que alguien se había unido a Sadrac, Mesac y Abednego en las furiosas llamas. Ahora contó cuatro figuras en el horno caminando ilesas y una era "como el hijo de Dios" (versículo 25). Tan pronto como pudo, el rey se acercó lo más que pudo al horno y llamó a los jóvenes para que se acercaran a él. Cuando salieron de la trampa mortal, no se les chamuscó ni un pelo de la cabeza y no había olor a humo en sus ropas, para sorpresa de asombro de todos los hombres presentes, incluidos los astutos sabios y los asistentes "sátrapas, administradores, gobernadores y consejeros del rey" (versículo 27).

Después de ver esto, que aparentemente le quitó la mente de su frustración y enojo, el rey alabó al Dios de Sadrac, Mesac y Abednego (versículo 28), pero no olvidó el engaño de sus oficiales, por lo que dijo en el versículo 29:

> "Por mí pues se pone decreto, que todo pueblo, nación, ó lengua, que dijere blasfemia contra el Dios de Sadrach, Mesach, y Abed-nego, sea descuartizado, y su casa sea puesta por muladar; por cuanto no hay dios que pueda librar como éste."

Al parecer este truco gigantesco, que casi funcionó, se quedó grabada en la mente de los sabios, o en la de sus compañeros, porque en el futuro (Daniel 6) volverán a intentarlo. ¿Por qué no? Lo lograron la primera vez ilesos, ¿por qué no intentarlo de nuevo bajo un liderazgo diferente? El problema es que el resultado la próxima vez será muy diferente de lo esperado.

CONCLUSIÓN:

La historia del "horno de fuego ardiendo" (versículo 23) es mucho más que una interesante historia bíblica de tres valientes dedicados a Dios. Es una lección de vida para la generación que vive en los últimos días de la historia de este mundo. Hay un tiempo futuro de tribulación que Jesús nos advirtió en Mateo 24:21-25:

"Porque habrá entonces grande aflicción, cual no fué desde el principio del mundo hasta ahora, ni será. Y si aquellos días no fuesen acortados, ninguna carne sería salva; mas por causa de los escogidos, aquellos días serán acortados. Entonces, si alguno os dijere: He aquí está el Cristo, ó allí, no creáis. Porque se levantarán falsos Cristos, y falsos profetas, y darán señales grandes y prodigios; de tal manera que engañarán, si es posible, aun á los escogidos. He aquí os lo he dicho antes."

Esta información que se entiende hoy no es por accidente. Dios dijo que revelaría Sus secretos a Sus siervos antes del evento prometido, en el momento y lugar correctos:

"Porque no hará nada el Señor Jehová, sin que revele su secreto á sus siervos los profetas." Amós 3:7.

Apocalipsis trece continúa con esta advertencia mencionando con mayor detalle lo que esos días de tribulación implicarán para toda la humanidad. Note Apocalipsis 13:11-18:

"Después vi otra bestia que subía de la tierra; y tenía dos cuernos semejantes á los de un cordero, mas hablaba como un dragón. Y ejerce todo el poder de la primera bestia en presencia de ella; y hace á la tierra y á los moradores de ella adorar la primera bestia, cuya llaga de muerte fué curada. Y hace grandes señales, de tal manera que aun hace descender fuego del cielo á la tierra delante de los hombres. Y engaña á los moradores de la tierra por las señales que le ha sido dado hacer en presencia de la bestia, mandando á los moradores de la tierra que hagan la imagen de la bestia que tiene la herida de cuchillo, y vivió. Y le fué dado que diese espíritu á la imagen de la bestia, para que la imagen de la bestia hable; y hará que cualesquiera que no adoraren la imagen de la bestia sean muertos. Y hacía que á todos, á los pequeños y grandes, ricos y pobres, libres y siervos, se pusiese una marca en su mano derecha, ó en sus frentes: Y que ninguno pudiese comprar ó vender, sino el que tuviera la señal, ó el nombre de la bestia, ó el número de su nombre. Aquí hay sabiduría. El que tiene entendimiento, cuente el número de la bestia; porque es el número de hombre: y el número de ella, seiscientos sesenta y seis.”

La bestia de Apocalipsis trece desea adorar para sí misma. Por eso, se instituirá la ADORACIÓN FORZADA, con el pretexto de lograr algo más. Por esa razón, el versículo 18 nos remite al capítulo tres de Daniel. Note lo que dice:

“Aquí hay sabiduría. El que tiene entendimiento, cuente el número de la bestia; porque es el número de hombre: y el número de ella, seiscientos sesenta y seis.”

Creo que el número 666 nos remite al capítulo tres de Daniel porque “el número de un hombre” en este versículo, tiene que referirse a un hombre en la Biblia, no fuera de la Biblia. El rey

Nabucodonosor instaló la imagen y obligó a todos a adorar esa imagen o morirían. Note que la imagen fue colocada en 600 a. EC, y tenía 60 codos de alto y 6 codos de ancho: por lo tanto, seiscientos sesenta y seis (666).

Esdras 2:13 apoya esta premisa de que el rey Nabucodonosor es el hombre en la Biblia cuyo número es 666. Uno de los cautivos hebreos del rey Nabucodonosor, en 605 a. EC, era un hombre llamado Adonikam que tenía 666 descendientes que regresaron a Jerusalén desde Babilonia año de Ciro, rey de Persia" (Esdras 1: 1). De los tres lugares en la Biblia que incluyen 1 Reyes 10:14 que pueden estar relacionados con el número 666, Daniel 3:1 y Esdras 2:13, señale al rey Nabucodonosor que mezcló la adoración falsa con la adoración verdadera y que forzó la adoración falsa a todos. la gente, ante la amenaza de muerte, como lo que Jesús predijo que sucedería en el período de tribulación venidera.

Es muy importante que nos demos cuenta de que algunos de nosotros podemos estar en la misma situación que Sadrac, Mesac y Abednego. Podemos estar en posición de ser amenazados por la fuerza para alejarnos de nuestro Creador y adorar a lo creado. Recuerde: la profecía bíblica se trata de ADORACIÓN.

Para estar preparados y ser capaces de defender a Dios, cada uno de nosotros debe vivir cada momento, cada día, siendo fiel a Dios en todo. De esa manera, cuando venga la tentación de obedecer o desobedecer a Dios, la elección no será difícil para aquellos que viven sus vidas ahora siendo completamente obedientes a Dios y a Su voluntad.

¿Cómo sabemos la voluntad de Dios para nosotros? Dedicamos un tiempo precioso en la oración DIARIA con la lectura y el estudio de la Palabra de Dios, la Biblia. Es una cuestión de vida o muerte.

Vea el video de YouTube **DANIEL CAPÍTULO TRES EN ESPAÑOL** por Earl Schrock

DANIEL CAPÍTULO TRES (RVR)

1 EL rey Nabucodonosor hizo una estatua de oro, la altura de la cual era de sesenta codos, su anchura de seis codos: levantóla en el campo de Dura, en la provincia de Babilonia. 2 Y envió el rey Nabucodonosor á juntar los grandes, los asistentes y capitanes, oidores, receptores, los del consejo, presidentes, y á todos los gobernadores de las provincias, para que viniesen á la dedicación de la estatua que el rey Nabucodonosor había levantado. 3 Fueron pues reunidos los grandes, los asistentes y capitanes, los oidores, receptores, los del consejo, los presidentes, y todos los gobernadores de las provincias, á la dedicación de la estatua que el rey Nabucodonosor había levantado: y estaban en pie delante de la estatua que había levantado el rey Nabucodonosor. 4 Y el pregonero pregonaba en alta voz: Mándase á vosotros, oh pueblos, naciones, y lenguas, 5 En oyendo el son de la bocina, del pífano, del tamboril, del arpa, del salterio, de la zampoña, y de todo instrumento músico, os postraréis y adoraréis la estatua de oro que el rey Nabucodonosor ha levantado: 6 Y cualquiera que no se postrare y adorare, en la misma hora será echado dentro de un horno de fuego ardiendo. 7 Por lo cual, en oyendo todos los pueblos el son de la bocina, del pífano, del tamboril, del arpa, del salterio, de la zampoña, y de todo instrumento músico, todos los pueblos, naciones, y lenguas, se postraron, y adoraron la estatua de oro que el rey Nabucodonosor había levantado. 8 Por esto en el mismo tiempo algunos varones Caldeos se llegaron, y denunciaron de los Judíos. 9 Hablando

y diciendo al rey Nabucodonosor: Rey, para siempre vive. 10 Tú, oh rey, pusiste ley que todo hombre en oyendo el son de la bocina, del pífano, del tamboril, del arpa, del salterio, de la zampoña, y de todo instrumento músico, se postrase y adorase la estatua de oro: 11 Y el que no se postrase y adorase, fuese echado dentro de un horno de fuego ardiendo. 12 Hay unos varones Judíos, los cuales pusiste tú sobre los negocios de la provincia de Babilonia; Sadrach, Mesach, y Abed-nego: estos varones, oh rey, no han hecho cuenta de ti; no adoran tus dioses, no adoran la estatua de oro que tú levantaste. 13 Entonces Nabucodonosor dijo con ira y con enojo que trajesen á Sadrach, Mesach, y Abed-nego. Al punto fueron traídos estos varones delante del rey. 14 Habló Nabucodonosor, y díjoles: ¿Es verdad Sadrach, Mesach, y Abed-nego, que vosotros no honráis á mi dios, ni adoráis la estatua de oro que he levantado? 15 Ahora pues, ¿estáis prestos para que en oyendo el son de la bocina, del pífano, del tamboril, del arpa, del salterio, de la zampoña, y de todo instrumento músico, os postréis, y adoréis la estatua que he hecho? Porque si no la adorareis, en la misma hora seréis echados en medio de un horno de fuego ardiendo: ¿y qué dios será aquel que os libre de mis manos? 16 Sadrach, Mesach, y Abed-nego respondieron y dijeron al rey Nabucodonosor: no cuidamos de responderte sobre este negocio. 17 He aquí nuestro Dios á quien honramos, puede librarnos del horno de fuego ardiendo; y de tu mano, oh rey, nos librará. 18 Y si no, sepas, oh rey, que tu dios no adoraremos, ni tampoco honraremos la estatua que has levantado. 19 Entonces Nabucodonosor fué lleno de ira, y demudóse la figura de su rostro sobre Sadrach, Mesach, y Abed-nego: así habló, y ordenó que el horno se encendiese siete veces tanto de lo que cada vez solía. 20 Y mandó á hombres muy vigorosos que tenía en su ejército, que atasen á Sadrach, Mesach, y Abed-nego, para echarlos en el horno de fuego ardiendo. 21 Entonces estos varones fueron atados con sus mantos, y sus calzas, y sus turbantes, y sus vestidos, y fueron echados dentro del horno de fuego ardiendo. 22 Y porque la palabra del rey daba priesa, y había procurado que se encendiese mucho, la llama del fuego mató á aquellos que habían alzado á Sadrach, Mesach, y Abed-nego. 23 Y estos tres varones, Sadrach, Mesach, y Abed-nego, cayeron atados dentro del horno de fuego ardiendo. 24 Entonces el rey Nabucodonosor se espantó, y levantóse apriesa, y habló, y dijo á los de su consejo: ¿No echaron tres varones atados dentro del fuego? Ellos respondieron y dijeron al rey: Es verdad, oh rey. 25 Respondió él y dijo: He aquí que yo veo cuatro varones sueltos, que se pasean en medio del fuego, y ningún daño hay en ellos: y el parecer del cuarto es semejante á hijo de los dioses. 26 Entonces Nabucodonosor se acercó á la puerta del horno de fuego ardiendo, y habló y dijo: Sadrach, Mesach, y Abed-nego, siervos del alto Dios, salid y venid. Entonces Sadrach, Mesach, y Abed-nego, salieron de en medio del fuego. 27 Y juntáronse los grandes, los gobernadores, los capitanes, y los del consejo del rey, para mirar estos varones, como el fuego no se enseñoreó de sus cuerpos, ni cabello de sus cabezas fué quemado, ni sus ropas se mudaron, ni olor de fuego había pasado por ellos. 28 Nabucodonosor habló y dijo: Bendito el Dios de ellos, de Sadrach, Mesach, y Abed-nego, que envió su ángel, y libró sus siervos que esperaron en él, y el mandamiento del rey mudaron, y entregaron sus cuerpos antes que sirviesen ni adorasen otro dios que su Dios. 29 Por mí pues se pone decreto, que todo pueblo, nación, ó lengua, que dijere blasfemia contra el Dios de Sadrach, Mesach, y Abed-nego, sea descuartizado, y su casa sea puesta por muladar; por cuanto no hay dios que pueda librar como éste. 30 Entonces el rey engrandeció á Sadrach, Mesach, y Abed-nego en la provincia de Babilonia.

DANIEL CAPÍTULO CUATRO

"Antes del quebrantamiento es la soberbia; Y antes de la caída la altivez de espíritu." Proverbios 16:18

Cosas importantes a tener en cuenta al considerar el capítulo cuatro de Daniel:

1. En el capítulo 2 de Daniel, el rey no se acordó del sueño.
2. En Daniel 4 recuerda el sueño pero no comprende lo que significa.
3. El capítulo cuatro está dirigido a la gente que "habita en toda la tierra" (vs.1), no a este planeta porque el rey no era el gobernante de este planeta, sino que gobernaba el reino de Dios, Su pueblo
4. En Daniel 4: 2,3 el rey alaba al Dios Altísimo, el Dios de Daniel, y luego comienza a explicar por qué está alabando al Padre Celestial.
5. En el sueño de Daniel cuatro, el rey ve un árbol "en medio de la tierra" (versículo 10).
6. El árbol llega hasta el cielo y se ve desde los confines de la tierra (11).
7. Todas las criaturas de la "tierra" fueron sostenidas por el árbol (versículo 12).
8. En los versículos 13-18, el rey describe a un ser celestial al que llama "el vigilante" que desciende del cielo y ordena que el árbol sea cortado y desmantelado.

9. El muñón tendrá "sus raíces en la tierra" para dejarlo en su lugar con una banda de hierro y una banda de bronce envuelto alrededor para sostenerlo y mantenerlo vivo.

10. En los versículos 15 y 16 al muñón se le dan características humanas que dicen: "Sea su porción con las bestias en la hierba de la tierra: Sea cambiado su corazón de hombre, y le sea dado corazón de bestia; y siete tiempos pasen sobre él ".

11. El versículo 16 menciona un período de tiempo de "siete tiempos" para pasar.

12. En el versículo 17, el "vigilante" dice la razón de las acciones futuras que se realizarán, "para que los vivientes sepan que el Altísimo gobierna en el reino de los hombres, y a quien quiere lo da, y establece sobre ella el más vil de los hombres ".

13. En los versículos 19-27, Daniel explica el sueño.

14. El árbol representa al rey Nabucodonosor.

15. Es una advertencia para que ajuste su forma de pensar y tratar a otras personas.

16. Si se niega a aceptar la advertencia, el Dios Altísimo lo alejará de los hombres y vivirá como un animal hasta que siete veces pase sobre él (versículo 23).

17. En los versículos 28-33 se nos dice que el rey no cambió sus caminos y que se jactó de que todo el éxito que tuvo en la vida se debió a sus propias acciones. En ese momento una voz le recuerda el sueño y se le da la mentalidad de una bestia salvaje. Vive como un animal, comiendo hierba y viviendo en la naturaleza, hasta que pasen los siete tiempos.

18. En los versículos 34-37 el rey explica que sus poderes de razonamiento regresaron a él al final de los siete tiempos (siete años) y que fue restaurado a su posición real.

19. El rey alaba al Dios del cielo y dice que los "habitantes de la tierra" no son nada y que Dios controla los asuntos de la gente en la tierra (versículo 35) y Dios está por encima de ser interrogado acerca de las cosas que hace.

Los siete tiempos son en realidad siete años. Una sola vez es el tiempo que tarda nuestro planeta en dar la vuelta al sol. Además de revelar el poder y la gloria de Dios, y el efecto humillante que tiene en las personas que lo alaban, es importante revelar esta visión de Daniel cuatro en la profecía bíblica de que:

1. Los árboles y las plantas pueden representar a una persona o personas. Apocalipsis 9:4 dice:
   "Y les fué mandado que no hiciesen daño á **la hierba** de la tierra, ni á ninguna cosa **verde**, ni á ningún **árbol**, sino solamente á los hombres que no tienen la señal de Dios en sus frentes.
2. Dios es el Señor de la "gente de la tierra", que es Su pueblo, que forma Su reino, aquí y ahora.
3. Un solo "tiempo" es un año completo.

CONCLUSIÓN: El orgullo es una ruina de la humanidad (Proverbios 11:2; 16:18). A menudo, las personas anteponen sus propios deseos, necesidades y deseos a los de los demás y a los de Dios. Pero debemos recordar que todo lo que poseemos, administramos, velamos y cuidamos proviene de Dios. Somos sus embajadores y sus mayordomos. Cuando desarrollamos la actitud orgullosa de que nos hemos convertido en lo que somos gracias a nuestros propios esfuerzos, Dios intervendrá y podrá romper nuestro desafío orgulloso. Mantener nuestros ojos en Jesús, diariamente, en Su Palabra nos ayudará a seguir siendo testigos humildes y efectivos de nuestro Padre Celestial.

Vea el video de YouTube **DANIEL CAPÍTULO CUATRO EN ESPAÑOL** por Earl Schrock

DANIEL CAPÍTULO CUATRO (RVR)

1 NABUCODONOSOR rey, á todos los pueblos, naciones, y lenguas, que moran en toda la tierra: Paz os sea multiplicada: 2 Las señales y milagros que el alto Dios ha hecho conmigo, conviene que yo las publique. 3 ¡Cuán grandes son sus señales, y cuán potentes sus maravillas! Su reino, reino sempiterno, y su señorío hasta generación y generación. 4 Yo Nabucodonosor estaba quieto en mi casa, y floreciente en mi palacio. 5 Vi un sueño que me espantó, y las imaginaciones y visiones de mi cabeza me turbaron en mi cama. 6 Por lo cual yo puse mandamiento para hacer venir delante de mí todos los sabios de Babilonia, que me mostrasen la declaración del sueño. 7 Y vinieron magos, astrólogos, Caldeos, y adivinos: y dije el sueño delante de ellos, mas nunca me mostraron su declaración; 8 Hasta tanto que entró delante de mí Daniel, cuyo nombre es Beltsasar, como el nombre de mi dios, y en el cual hay espíritu de los dioses santos, y dije el sueño delante de él, diciendo: 9 Beltsasar, príncipe de los magos, ya que he entendido que hay en ti espíritu de los dioses santos, y que ningún misterio se te esconde, exprésame las visiones de mi sueño que he visto, y su declaración. 10 Aquestas las visiones de mi cabeza en mi cama: Parecíame que veía un árbol en medio de la tierra, cuya altura era grande. 11 Crecía este árbol, y hacíase fuerte, y su altura llegaba hasta el cielo, y su vista hasta el cabo de toda la tierra. 12 Su copa era hermosa, y su fruto en abundancia, y para todos había en él mantenimiento. Debajo de él se ponían á la sombra las bestias del campo, y en sus ramas hacían morada las aves del cielo, y manteníase de él toda carne. 13 Veía en las visiones de mi cabeza en mi cama, y he aquí que un vigilante y santo descendía del cielo. 14 Y clamaba fuertemente y decía

así: Cortad el árbol, y desmochad sus ramas, derribad su copa, y derramad su fruto: váyanse las bestias que están debajo de él, y las aves de sus ramas. 15 Mas la cepa de sus raíces dejaréis en la tierra, y con atadura de hierro y de metal entre la hierba del campo; y sea mojado con el rocío del cielo, y su parte con las bestias en la hierba de la tierra. 16 Su corazón sea mudado de corazón de hombre, y séale dado corazón de bestia, y pasen sobre él siete tiempos. 17 La sentencia es por decreto de los vigilantes, y por dicho de los santos la demanda: para que conozcan los vivientes que el Altísimo se enseñorea del reino de los hombres, y que á quien él quiere lo da, y constituye sobre él al más bajo de los hombres. 18 Yo el rey Nabucodonosor he visto este sueño. Tú pues, Beltsasar, dirás la declaración de él, porque todos los sabios de mi reino nunca pudieron mostrarme su interpretación: mas tú puedes, porque hay en ti espíritu de los dioses santos. 19 Entonces Daniel, cuyo nombre era Beltsasar, estuvo callando casi una hora, y sus pensamientos lo espantaban: El rey habló, y dijo: Beltsasar, el sueño ni su declaración no te espante. Respondió Beltsasar, y dijo: Señor mío, el sueño sea para tus enemigos, y su declaración para los que mal te quieren. 20 El árbol que viste, que crecía y se hacía fuerte, y que su altura llegaba hasta el cielo, y su vista por toda la tierra; 21 Y cuya copa era hermosa, y su fruto en abundancia, y que para todos había mantenimiento en él; debajo del cual moraban las bestias del campo, y en sus ramas habitaban las aves del cielo, 22 Tú mismo eres, oh rey, que creciste, y te hiciste fuerte, pues creció tu grandeza, y ha llegado hasta el cielo, y tu señorío hasta el cabo de la tierra. 23 Y cuanto á lo que vió el rey, un vigilante y santo que descendía del cielo, y decía: Cortad el árbol y destruidlo: mas la cepa de sus raíces dejaréis en la tierra, y con atadura de hierro y de metal en la hierba del campo; y sea mojado con el rocío del cielo, y su parte sea con las bestias del campo, hasta que pasen sobre él siete tiempos: 24 Esta es la declaración, oh rey, y la sentencia del Altísimo, que ha venido sobre el rey mi señor: 25 Que te echarán de entre los hombres, y con las bestias del campo será tu morada, y con hierba del campo te apacentarán como á los bueyes, y con rocío del cielo serás bañado; y siete tiempos pasarán sobre ti, hasta que entiendas que el Altísimo se enseñorea en el reino de los hombres, y que á quien él quisiere lo dará. 26 Y lo que dijeron, que dejasen en la tierra la cepa de las raíces del mismo árbol, significa que tu reino se te quedará firme, luego que entiendas que el señorío es en los cielos. 27 Por tanto, oh rey, aprueba mi consejo, y redime tus pecados con justicia, y tus iniquidades con misericordias para con los pobres; que tal vez será eso una prolongación de tu tranquilidad. 28 Todo aquesto vino sobre el rey Nabucodonosor. 29 A cabo de doce meses, andándose paseando sobre el palacio del reino de Babilonia, 30 Habló el rey, y dijo: ¿No es ésta la gran Babilonia, que yo edifiqué para casa del reino, con la fuerza de mi poder, y para gloria de mi grandeza? 31 Aun estaba la palabra en la boca del rey, cuando cae una voz del cielo: A ti dicen, rey Nabucodonosor; el reino es traspasado de ti: 32 Y de entre los hombres te echan, y con las bestias del campo será tu morada, y como á los bueyes te apacentarán: y siete tiempos pasarán sobre ti, hasta que conozcas que el Altísimo se enseñorea en el reino de los hombres, y á quien él quisiere lo da. 33 En la misma hora se cumplió la palabra sobre Nabucodonosor, y fué echado de entre los hombres; y comía hierba como los bueyes, y su cuerpo se bañaba con el rocío del cielo, hasta que su pelo creció como de águila, y sus uñas como de aves. 34 Mas al fin del tiempo yo Nabucodonosor alcé mis ojos al cielo, y mi sentido me fué vuelto; y bendije al Altísimo, y alabé y glorifiqué al que vive para siempre; porque su señorío es sempiterno, y su reino por todas las edades. 35 Y todos los moradores de la tierra por nada son contados: y en el ejército del cielo, y en los habitantes de la tierra, hace según su voluntad: ni hay quien estorbe su mano, y le diga: ¿Qué haces? 36 En el mismo tiempo mi sentido me fué vuelto, y la majestad de mi reino, mi dignidad y mi grandeza volvieron á mí, y mis gobernadores y mis grandes me buscaron; y fuí restituído á mi reino, y mayor grandeza me fué añadida. 37 Ahora yo Nabucodonosor alabo, engrandezco y glorifico al Rey del cielo, porque todas sus obras son verdad, y sus caminos juicio; y humillar puede á los que andan con soberbia.

DANIEL CAPÍTULO CINCO

"Y para poder discernir entre lo santo y lo profano,
y entre lo inmundo y lo limpio." Levítico 10:10

El rey Belsasar es nieto del rey Nabucodonosor. Su padre es Nabonido, hijo del rey Nabucodonosor. Para entonces, el rey Nabucodonosor ha muerto y el reino de Babilonia está en manos tanto del rey Nabonido como de su hijo, Belsasar.

Fuera de la fortaleza de Babilonia está el ejército de los medos. Dado que los habitantes de Babilonia se consideraban a salvo del ejército enemigo, el rey Belsasar patrocina una fiesta. Este capítulo de Daniel demuestra de qué se trata el libro de Daniel. Se trata de adorar y mezclar el paganismo con la adoración pura del Dios Altísimo. La influencia debilitante en la unificación de lo sagrado con lo secular en la adoración ha durado todos estos años y es muy viva y evidente en la adoración de Dios incluso hoy. La mezcla de lo sagrado con lo profano comenzó en el imperio de Babilonia y continuó bajo el dominio de todos los reinos que surgieron después del Imperio de Babilonia.

El rey Belsasar, que fue levantado a las rodillas de Daniel, decide traer los vasos de oro y plata de la "casa del tesoro de sus dioses". Estos vasos sagrados son los que su abuelo había tomado de Jerusalén y "colocado en el templo de sus dioses" (Daniel 1: 2). Belsasar impulsó arrogantemente sus búsquedas para beber vino de ellos. El rey Nabucodonosor se había humillado ante Dios y aceptado Su soberanía, no se puede decir lo mismo de su nieto. Aparentemente, no tenía respeto por las cosas sagradas. Mientras las esposas, concubinas e invitados del rey bebían vino de los vasos sagrados, "alabaron a los dioses de oro, plata, bronce, hierro, madera y piedra" (versículo 4), el mismo idolatría señalada por los mismos metales en el capítulo dos de Daniel.

De repente aparece una mano sin sangre y comienza a escribir palabras en la distante pared enlucida que detiene la fiesta. El rey tiene mucho miedo e inmediatamente exige la presencia de todos los sabios y consejeros del reino con la promesa de que:

> "El rey clamó en alta voz que hiciesen venir magos, Caldeos, y adivinos. Habló el rey, y dijo á los sabios de Babilonia: Cualquiera que leyere esta escritura, y me mostrare su declaración, será vestido de púrpura, y tendrá collar de oro á su cuello; y en el reino se enseñoreará el tercero." (Versículo 7).

Para disgusto del rey, ninguno de los sabios o magos pudo explicar la escritura.

El orgulloso y arrogante rey se convirtió en una masa débil, frágil, que lloraba y sus rodillas chocaban entre sí por el miedo (versículo 6). Su madre, la reina, escuchó el alboroto y acudió en ayuda de su hijo. Calmó a su hijo y le sugirió que llamara a Daniel, quien históricamente resolvió problemas como este en el pasado.

Para cuando Daniel llegó, el asustado rey había recuperado algo de su compostura y nuevamente mostró su arrogancia al preguntarle a Daniel si él era de quien había escuchado que podría resolver el misterio y si resolvía el acertijo sería enormemente recompensado. No hace falta decir que Daniel, en su sabiduría envejecida, puso valientemente al rey en su lugar recordándole que sabía quién era Daniel y que también estaba al tanto de las historias que lo rodeaban a él y al rey Nabucodonosor. Daniel rechazó los regalos, pero dijo que le diría al rey por qué apareció la mano, qué estaba escrito y el significado de las palabras.

En Daniel 5:25-28 Daniel dijo:

> "Y la escritura que esculpió es: MENE, MENE, TEKEL, UPHARSIN. La declaración del negocio es: MENE: Contó Dios tu reino, y halo rematado. TEKEL: Pesado has sido en balanza, y fuiste hallado falto. PERES: Tu reino fué rompido, y es dado á Medos y Persas."

Esa noche, el ejército mediano desvió el río Éufrates, que atravesaba la ciudad, y entró en la ciudad en aguas poco profundas. Las compuertas se habían dejado abiertas por descuido, lo que permitió que el ejército entrara en la ciudad y tomara el control de ella, matando al rey Belsasar en el proceso.

El orgullo y la arrogancia tienen poco lugar en el reino de Dios. Se prefiere un espíritu obediente humilde y manso, que reconoce y alaba al Creador del universo. Una porción de Daniel dos se cumplió esa noche. La demostración de oro seguido de plata en el sueño del rey del capítulo dos de Daniel se convirtió en una realidad. La influencia secular de los babilonios sobre la adoración de oro puro que Dios había exigido fue plantada y ahora la influencia pagana del imperio medopersa también cobraría su precio, diluyendo y contaminando aún más la adoración verdadera. Esas influencias paganas se extenderían y crecerían durante siglos.

Aunque el rey Belsasar y muchas otras personas que gobernaron el reino de Dios no aceptaron al Dios Altísimo, aparentemente hubo algunos que sí lo hicieron. Quinientos años después de Daniel, los magos vienen del este en busca del Rey que nació en Belén. ¿Eran estos descendientes de los judíos cautivos de la época de Nabucodonosor o eran descendientes de los siguientes imperios gobernantes? No lo sabemos. Pero Dios siempre ha tenido su pueblo remanente que lo buscó. ¿Te encontrarás en ese remanente hoy?

¿Estás interesado en buscar al Rey?

Entrégate a Él hoy. Escuche Su voz mientras le habla diariamente en Su Palabra.

Vea el video de YouTube **DANIEL CAPÍTULO CINCO EN ESPAÑOL** por Earl Schrock

DANIEL CAPÍTULO CINCO (RVR)

1 EL rey Belsasar hizo un gran banquete á mil de sus príncipes, y en presencia de los mil bebía vino. 2 Belsasar, con el gusto del vino, mandó que trajesen los vasos de oro y de plata que Nabucodonosor su padre había traído del templo de Jerusalem; para que bebiesen con ellos el rey y sus príncipes, sus mujeres y sus concubinas. 3 Entonces fueron traídos los vasos de oro que habían traído del templo de la casa de Dios que estaba en Jerusalem, y bebieron con ellos el rey y sus príncipes, sus mujeres y sus concubinas. 4 Bebieron vino, y alabaron á los dioses de oro y de plata, de metal, de hierro, de madera, y de piedra. 5 En aquella misma hora salieron unos dedos de mano de hombre, y escribían delante del candelero sobre lo encalado de la pared del palacio real, y el rey veía la palma de la mano que escribía. 6 Entonces el rey se demudó de su color, y sus pensamientos lo turbaron, y desatáronse

las ceñiduras de sus lomos, y sus rodillas se batían la una con la otra. 7 El rey clamó en alta voz que hiciesen venir magos, Caldeos, y adivinos. Habló el rey, y dijo á los sabios de Babilonia: Cualquiera que leyere esta escritura, y me mostrare su declaración, será vestido de púrpura, y tendrá collar de oro á su cuello; y en el reino se enseñoreará el tercero. 8 Entonces fueron introducidos todos los sabios del rey, y no pudieron leer la escritura, ni mostrar al rey su declaración. 9 Entonces el rey Belsasar fué muy turbado, y se le mudaron sus colores y alteráronse sus príncipes. 10 La reina, por las palabras del rey y de sus príncipes, entró á la sala del banquete. Y habló la reina, y dijo: Rey, para siempre vive, no te asombren tus pensamientos, ni tus colores se demuden: 11 En tu reino hay un varón, en el cual mora el espíritu de los dioses santos; y en los días de tu padre se halló en él luz é inteligencia y sabiduría, como ciencia de los dioses: al cual el rey Nabucodonosor, tu padre, el rey tu padre constituyó príncipe sobre todos los magos, astrólogos, Caldeos, y adivinos: 12 Por cuanto fué hallado en él mayor espíritu, y ciencia, y entendimiento, interpretando sueños, y declarando preguntas, y deshaciendo dudas, es á saber, en Daniel; al cual el rey puso por nombre Beltsasar. Llámese pues ahora á Daniel, y él mostrará la declaración. 13 Entonces Daniel fué traído delante del rey. Y habló el rey, y dijo á Daniel: ¿Eres tú aquel Daniel de los hijos de la cautividad de Judá, que mi padre trajo de Judea? 14 Yo he oído de ti que el espíritu de los dioses santos está en ti, y que en ti se halló luz, y entendimiento y mayor sabiduría. 15 Y ahora fueron traídos delante de mí, sabios, astrólogos, que leyesen esta escritura, y me mostrasen su interpretación: pero no han podido mostrar la declaración del negocio. 16 Yo pues he oído de ti que puedes declarar las dudas, y desatar dificultades. Si ahora pudieres leer esta escritura, y mostrarme su interpretación, serás vestido de púrpura, y collar de oro tendrás en tu cuello, y en el reino serás el tercer señor. 17 Entonces Daniel respondió, y dijo

317

delante del rey: Tus dones sean para ti, y tus presentes dalos á otro. La escritura yo la leeré al rey, y le mostraré la declaración. 18 El altísimo Dios, oh rey, dió á Nabucodonosor tu padre el reino, y la grandeza, y la gloria, y la honra: 19 Y por la grandeza que le dió, todos los pueblos, naciones, y lenguas, temblaban y temían delante de él. Los que él quería mataba, y daba vida á los que quería: engrandecía á los que quería, y á los que quería humillaba. 20 Mas cuando su corazón se ensoberbeció, y su espíritu se endureció en altivez, fué depuesto del trono de su reino, y traspasaron de él la gloria: 21 Y fué echado de entre los hijos de los hombres; y su corazón fué puesto con las bestias, y con los asnos monteses fué su morada. Hierba le hicieron comer, como á buey, y su cuerpo fué bañado con el rocío del cielo, hasta que conoció que el altísimo Dios se enseñorea del reino de los hombres, y que pondrá sobre él al que quisiere. 22 Y tú, su hijo Belsasar, no has humillado tu corazón, sabiendo todo esto: 23 Antes contra el Señor del cielo te has ensoberbecido, é hiciste traer delante de ti los vasos de su casa, y tú y tus príncipes, tus mujeres y tus concubinas, bebisteis vino en ellos: demás de esto, á dioses de plata y de oro, de metal, de hierro, de madera, y de piedra, que ni ven, ni oyen, ni saben, diste alabanza: y al Dios en cuya mano está tu vida, y cuyos son todos tus caminos, nunca honraste. 24 Entonces de su presencia fué enviada la palma de la mano que esculpió esta escritura. 25 Y la escritura que esculpió es: MENE, MENE, TEKEL, UPHARSIN. 26 La declaración del negocio es: MENE: Contó Dios tu reino, y halo rematado. 27 TEKEL: Pesado has sido en balanza, y fuiste hallado falto. 28 PERES: Tu reino fué rompido, y es dado á Medos y Persas. 29 Entonces, mandándolo Belsasar, vistieron á Daniel de púrpura, y en su cuello fué puesto un collar de oro, y pregonaron de él que fuese el tercer señor en el reino. 30 La misma noche fué muerto Belsasar, rey de los Caldeos. 31 Y Darío de Media tomó el reino, siendo de sesenta y dos años.

DANIEL CAPÍTULO SEIS

"EL que habita al abrigo del Altísimo, Morará bajo la sombra del Omnipotente. Diré yo á Jehová: Esperanza mía, y castillo mío; Mi Dios, en él confiaré. Y él te librará del lazo del cazador: De la peste destruidora." Salmos 91:1,2

Bajo el liderazgo de Darío, el primer rey medo que gobernó al pueblo de Dios después de la caída de Babilonia, los sabios, adivinos, magos, consejeros y príncipes del gobierno enfrentaron el mismo problema amenazante que habían experimentado antes. La amenaza para ellos era el profeta Daniel como su supervisor inmediato. Bajo su cuidadoso cuidado, aunque eran el principal consejero del rey Nabucodonosor, no pudieron salirse con la suya con ninguna travesura que pudiera hacer que el rey perdiera una parte de sus bienes.

Darius estaba consciente de la infidelidad de los sabios y de la integridad de Daniel. Quería proteger sus activos para que no se distribuyeran sin su conocimiento. Su plan era sencillo. Pondría tres presidentes sobre los asuntos del reino y Daniel sería el primero. Todos tendrían que responder nuevamente ante Daniel por sus gastos. Esto no le fue bien al resto del gabinete del rey.

Creo que los consejeros corruptos reflexionaron sobre el "fiasco del horno de fuego" del capítulo tres de Daniel y los sabios planearon dejar que la historia se repitiera. Esta vez engañaron al rey para que firmara una ley que establecía que ninguna persona podía invocar a ningún dios durante los siguientes treinta días, excepto al rey mismo (versículo 7). Su orgullo fue usado en su contra y estuvo de acuerdo con la idea, diciéndole que TODOS los consejeros habían estado de acuerdo en esto. No le dijeron que Daniel no había sido parte de este plan.

El castigo para cualquiera que le rezara a cualquier otro dios, que no fuera el rey, sería ser arrojado a la guarida del León. No se nos informa por qué el rey tenía un foso de leones, pero aparentemente sirvieron para algo. Los sabios sabían que Daniel no cumpliría con este arreglo y supongo que permitieron que las feroces bestias se quedaran sin comer durante un período de tiempo en preparación para la muerte rápida, segura y humana de Daniel.

Aunque Daniel fue informado del plan, después de que se firmó la petición, no le impidió comunicarse con el Dios Altísimo, como lo hacía tres veces al día, todos los días. Los sabios planearon esto y colocaron testigos para poder testificar ante el rey contra Daniel.

Cuando se acercó al rey con valentía en relación con la oración de Daniel a otro dios, que no era el rey, se dio cuenta de inmediato de que había sido engañado y engañado. Todos los sabios corruptos se complacieron en seguir informando al rey que una ley firmada por el rey no podía ser retractada. Aunque el rey trató de todas las formas posibles para liberar a Daniel, fue en vano.

Cuando Daniel fue arrojado al foso de los leones, el rey estaba allí y le dijo a Daniel:

"El Dios tuyo, á quien tú continuamente sirves, él te libre."
(verso 16).

Después de sellar la cubierta de la entrada con su anillo de
sello, el rey pasó el resto de la noche sin dormir preocupándose
por Daniel. Aunque la Biblia no lo dice, creo que el rey
probablemente oró al Dios de Daniel pidiendo Su protección
para Su siervo especial.

A la mañana siguiente, el rey corrió al foso y, al quitar la piedra,
el rey preguntó:

> "Y llegándose cerca del foso llamó á voces á
> Daniel con voz triste: y hablando el rey dijo á
> Daniel: Daniel, siervo del Dios viviente, el Dios
> tuyo, á quien tú continuamente sirves ¿te ha
> podido librar de los leones? (verso 20).

Entonces Daniel respondió al rey con uno de los primeros
versículos de memoria que mi hermosa hija de dos años,
Wendi, memorizó:

"El Dios mío envió su ángel, el cual cerró la boca de los leones."
(verso 22).

El rey se alegró de escuchar la voz de Daniel y lo hizo retirar
inmediatamente del foso de los leones.

Aparentemente, el truco que los sabios le hicieron al rey
Nabucodonosor, en el capítulo tres de Daniel, estaba tan bien
planeado y orquestado que el rey no pudo tomar represalias
contra ellos, aunque en ese momento estoy bastante seguro
de que el rey se dio cuenta de que lo habían engañado. Su ira
inicial contra ellos lo demostró. Pero aparentemente cuando
los tres hebreos le respondieron tan crudamente, la ira hacia

los consejeros fue un trampolín que aumentó la ira del rey contra Sadrac, Mesac y Abednego por su insolencia. En el capítulo tres, en los días del rey Nabucodonosor, los astutos sabios se habían salido con la suya casi asesinando a Sadrac, Mesac y Abednego.

Pero ese no iba a ser el caso con el rey Darío.

Tan pronto como Daniel estuvo libre, el rey puso en marcha su propio plan. Reunió a todos los consejeros inteligentes que lo habían engañado, junto con sus familias. Sin fanfarrias ni demoras, los hizo arrojar a todos a la guarida de las bestias hambrientas. El versículo 24 dice:

> "Y mandándolo el rey fueron traídos aquellos hombres que habían acusado á Daniel, y fueron echados en el foso de los leones, ellos, sus hijos, y sus mujeres; y aun no habían llegado al suelo del foso, cuando los leones se apoderaron de ellos, y quebrantaron todos sus huesos."

Entonces el rey envió un decreto. Los versículos 26 y 27 dicen:

> "De parte mía es puesta ordenanza, que en todo el señorío de mi reino todos teman y tiemblen de la presencia del Dios de Daniel: porque él es el Dios viviente y permanente por todos los siglos, y su reino tal que no será desecho, y su señorío hasta el fin. Que salva y libra, y hace señales y maravillas en el cielo y en la tierra; el cual libró á Daniel del poder de los leones."

Al igual que el rey Nabucodonosor, el rey Darío reconoció el poder del Dios de Daniel y compartió su convicción con todo el pueblo de su reino. Y nuevamente, al igual que con el rey Nabucodonosor, el rey Darío emitió órdenes de adoración forzada al Dios del cielo (Daniel 3:29). Dios no promueve la adoración forzada. Quiere que su pueblo le adore voluntariamente por respeto y admiración por quién es y lo que ha hecho. Para comprender más de lo que Dios ha hecho por nosotros y nuestra obediente respuesta a Él, lea los capítulos dos y tres de Efesios.

CONCLUSIÓN: ¿Cuáles son las lecciones que se pueden aprender del capítulo seis de Daniel?

1. Dios traza una clara línea de distinción entre lo sagrado y lo profano. Es nuestra responsabilidad estudiar y conocer Su Palabra para darnos cuenta de cuáles son.
2. Nosotros, el reino de Dios, tenemos la responsabilidad de demostrar integridad pura con todas las personas con las que interactuamos. No hay lugar para la deshonestidad en Su reino (Apocalipsis 22:15) ni siquiera en las cosas más pequeñas.
   "El que es fiel en lo muy poco, también en lo más es fiel: y el que en lo muy poco es injusto, también en lo más es injusto." Lucas 16:10.
3. Otras personas miran a los hijos de Dios y los notan. Ninguno de nosotros vive en una burbuja. Nuestro testimonio a los demás puede llevarlos al Salvador o alejarlos. Nuestra elección 24/7.
4. En tiempos de estrés y calamidad, debemos mantener nuestra fe en Dios. Es posible que perdamos la vida en nuestro esfuerzo por ser fieles, pero debemos permanecer fuertes y saber que si eso sucede, estamos en buena compañía cuando consideramos a los fieles en la Biblia que dieron todo por Cristo.
5. Se acerca un tiempo de angustia y tribulación. Debemos vivir nuestras vidas siendo completamente fieles a

Dios ahora. No podemos esperar hasta que llegue el momento de la angustia para desarrollar el tipo de fe necesaria para sufrir en el nombre de Dios. Debemos vivir totalmente dependientes de Dios.

Vea el video de YouTube **DANIEL CAPÍTULO SEIS EN ESPAÑOL** por Earl Schrock

DANIEL CAPÍTULO SEIS (RVR)

1 PARECIO bien á Darío constituir sobre el reino ciento veinte gobernadores, que estuviesen en todo el reino. 2 Y sobre ellos tres presidentes, de los cuales Daniel era el uno, á quienes estos gobernadores diesen cuenta, porque el rey no recibiese daño. 3 Pero el mismo Daniel era superior á estos gobernadores y presidentes, porque había en él más abundancia de espíritu: y el rey pensaba de ponerlo sobre todo el reino. 4 Entonces los presidentes y gobernadores buscaban ocasiones contra Daniel por parte del reino; mas no podían hallar alguna ocasión ó falta, porque él era fiel, y ningún vicio ni falta fué en él hallado. 5 Entonces dijeron aquellos hombres: No hallaremos contra este Daniel ocasión alguna, si no la hallamos contra él en la ley de su Dios. 6 Entonces estos gobernadores y presidentes se juntaron delante del rey, y le dijeron así: Rey Darío, para siempre vive: 7 Todos los presidentes del reino, magistrados, gobernadores, grandes y capitanes, han acordado por consejo promulgar un real edicto, y confirmarlo, que cualquiera que demandare petición de cualquier dios ú hombre en el espacio de treinta días, sino de ti, oh rey, sea echado en el foso de los leones. 8 Ahora, oh rey, confirma el edicto, y firma la escritura, para que no se pueda mudar, conforme á la ley de Media y de Persia, la cual no se revoca. 9 Firmó pues el rey Darío la escritura y el edicto. 10 Y Daniel, cuando supo que la escritura estaba firmada, entróse en su casa, y abiertas las ventanas de

su cámara que estaban hacia Jerusalem, hincábase de rodillas tres veces al día, y oraba, y confesaba delante de su Dios, como lo solía hacer antes. 11 Entonces se juntaron aquellos hombres, y hallaron á Daniel orando y rogando delante de su Dios. 12 Llegáronse luego, y hablaron delante del rey acerca del edicto real: ¿No has confirmado edicto que cualquiera que pidiere á cualquier dios ú hombre en el espacio de treinta días, excepto á ti, oh rey, fuese echado en el foso de los leones? Respondió el rey y dijo: Verdad es, conforme á la ley de Media y de Persia, la cual no se abroga. 13 Entonces respondieron y dijeron delante del rey: Daniel que es de los hijos de la cautividad de los Judíos, no ha hecho cuenta de ti, oh rey, ni del edicto que confirmaste; antes tres veces al día hace su petición. 14 El rey entonces, oyendo el negocio, pesóle en gran manera, y sobre Daniel puso cuidado para librarlo; y hasta puestas del sol trabajó para librarle. 15 Empero aquellos hombres se reunieron cerca del rey, y dijeron al rey: Sepas, oh rey, que es ley de Media y de Persia, que ningún decreto ú ordenanza que el rey confirmare pueda mudarse. 16 Entonces el rey mandó, y trajeron á Daniel, y echáronle en el foso de los leones. Y hablando el rey dijo á Daniel: El Dios tuyo, á quien tú continuamente sirves, él te libre. 17 Y fué traída una piedra, y puesta sobre la puerta del foso, la cual selló el rey con su anillo, y con el anillo de sus príncipes, porque el acuerdo acerca de Daniel no se mudase. 18 Fuése luego el rey á su palacio, y acostóse ayuno; ni instrumentos de música fueron traídos delante de él, y se le fué el sueño. 19 El rey, por tanto, se levantó muy de mañana, y fué apriesa al foso de los leones: 20 Y llegándose cerca del foso llamó á voces á Daniel con voz triste: y hablando el rey dijo á Daniel: Daniel, siervo del Dios viviente, el Dios tuyo, á quien tú continuamente sirves ¿te ha podido librar de los leones? 21 Entonces habló Daniel con el rey: oh rey, para siempre vive. 22 El Dios mío envió su ángel, el cual cerró la boca de los leones, para que no me hiciesen mal: porque delante de él se halló en mí justicia: y aun delante de ti, oh rey, yo no he hecho lo que no debiese. 23 Entonces se alegró el rey en gran manera á causa de él, y mandó sacar á Daniel del foso: y fué Daniel sacado del foso, y ninguna lesión se halló en él, porque creyó en su Dios. 24 Y mandándolo el rey fueron traídos aquellos hombres que habían acusado á Daniel, y fueron echados en el foso de los leones, ellos, sus hijos, y sus mujeres; y aun no habían llegado al suelo del foso, cuando los leones se apoderaron de ellos, y quebrantaron todos sus huesos. 25 Entonces el rey Darío escribió á todos los pueblos, naciones, y lenguas, que habitan en toda la tierra: Paz os sea multiplicada: 26 De parte mía es puesta ordenanza, que en todo el señorío de mi reino todos teman y tiemblen de la presencia del Dios de Daniel: porque él es el Dios viviente y permanente por todos los siglos, y su reino tal que no será desecho, y su señorío hasta el fin. 27 Que salva y libra, y hace señales y maravillas en el cielo y en la tierra; el cual libró á Daniel del poder de los leones. 28 Y este Daniel fué prosperado durante el reinado de Darío, y durante el reinado de Ciro, Persa.

DANIEL CAPÍTULO SIETE

"¿O no sabéis que los santos han de juzgar al mundo? Y si el mundo ha de ser juzgado por vosotros, ¿sois indignos de juzgar cosas muy pequeñas? 3 ¿O no sabéis que hemos de juzgar á los angeles? ¿cuánto más las cosas de este siglo? 1 Corintios 6:2,3

Daniel tiene un sueño. En el sueño, ve un gran mar sacudido de un lado a otro por los cuatro vientos del cielo. Mientras observa el mar revuelto, cuatro bestias diferentes salen del mar, una tras otra. En los versículos 1 al 8, Daniel ve:

1. Un **león** con dos alas de águila unidas a su espalda sale del mar. Mientras observa al león que le arrancan las dos alas, se pone de pie sobre sus patas traseras y se le da el corazón de un hombre.
2. Después del león, Daniel ve a un **oso** salir del mar. Un lado del oso es más alto que el otro y tiene tres costillas en la boca entre los dientes. Al oso se le dice: "Levántate, devora mucha carne". (La explicación de las costillas de los árboles se revela en el libro de Ester del Antiguo Testamento).
3. Después del oso, Daniel ve un **leopardo** que sale del mar. El leopardo tiene cuatro alas y cuatro cabezas. Se le da dominio.

4. La cuarta **bestia** que salió del mar era diferente al resto. Fue "espantoso y terrible, y extremadamente fuerte; y tenía grandes dientes de hierro: devoró y partió en pedazos, y pisoteó el residuo con sus pies: y era diferente de todas las bestias que habían antes de él; y tenía diez cuernos ". Mientras Daniel miraba los diez cuernos, un cuerno pequeño creció entre ellos. A medida que crecía el cuerno pequeño, tres de los diez cuernos fueron desarraigados. Daniel nota que el cuerno pequeño tiene los ojos de un hombre y una boca que habla cosas audaces.

En los versículos 9 al 14, Daniel ve la escena del juicio, revelada en Apocalipsis 20, que tiene lugar durante los 1000 años futuros, después de la segunda venida de Jesús. Él observa hasta que las cuatro bestias son destruidas y el reino eterno y sin pecado de Dios se establece para siempre.

En los versículos 15 al 18 se le revela a Daniel que las cuatro bestias que vio salir del mar son en realidad cuatro reinos. Estos cuatro reinos gobernarán sobre el pueblo de Dios, pero al final perderán su dominio y su pueblo será eternamente victorioso.

Es muy interesante notar que en el versículo diecisiete se le dice a Daniel que las cuatro bestias salieron de "la tierra". ¿Qué significa cuando al principio suben del "mar" (versículo tres) y luego salen de "la tierra" (versículo diecisiete)?

En los versículos 23 al 27, la atención de Daniel se dirige a la cuarta bestia que tiene diez cuernos, dientes de hierro y uñas de bronce que derrota y ataca violentamente "la tierra". Se da cuenta de un cuerno pequeño que (1) arranca tres de los diez cuernos, (2) pronuncia grandes palabras "contra el Altísimo", (3) persigue a "los santos del Altísimo", (4) intenta "cambiar los tiempos y leyes ", y (5) gobierna sobre el pueblo de Dios, Sus santos, por" un tiempo y tiempos y la división del tiempo ". En el juicio, el poder del cuerno pequeño (6) es quitado y (7) es destruido para siempre. (8) Después de lo cual los santos de Dios heredarán el reino y reinarán con Dios en paz por los siglos de los siglos.

En el versículo 28, Daniel confiesa que aunque estaba preocupado por lo que veía, se dedicó a sus asuntos, guardando estas cosas en su corazón.

INTERPRETACIÓN:

Daniel vio que las cuatro bestias, o cuatro reinos, se corresponden con los cuatro reinos del capítulo dos de Daniel. Los cuatro reinos que gobernaron sobre la "tierra" o el pueblo de Dios son Babilonia, Medo-Persia, Grecia y, supuestamente, Roma.

Babilonia está representada por la cabeza de oro de la estatua y el león alado.

Medo-Persia está representada por el torso superior plateado de la imagen y por el oso.

Grecia está representada por el vientre y el muslo de bronce y el leopardo de cuatro alas.

Roma está representada por las piernas de hierro y la terrible bestia con diez cuernos.

Aunque hay muchas sugerencias convincentes en cuanto a la identidad del "cuerno pequeño", este autor cree que es un enemigo de Dios que aún no ha aparecido durante la futura tribulación de siete años por razones que se detallarán en nuestra discusión sobre la venida. los capítulos de Daniel 8 al 12 incluyen la discusión de los "tiempos, el tiempo y la división del tiempo".

PREGUNTA: ¿Por qué los cuatro imperios, que dominaron al pueblo de Dios desde los días del rey Nabucodonosor hasta los tiempos de los emperadores romanos, están representados por los metales de Daniel dos y las bestias de Daniel siete?

RESPUESTA: Recuerde que la profecía bíblica tiene que ver con la adoración. Daniel 2 revela las fuentes empíricas de las debilitantes influencias paganas que diluyeron y contaminaron la forma en que Dios desea ser adorado. Daniel siete nos ayuda a identificar mejor esos imperios gobernantes, pero también proporciona información vital adicional que es necesaria para comprender e interpretar el libro de Apocalipsis.

Note Apocalipsis 13:1, 2 Juan dice:

> "Y YO me paré sobre la arena del mar, y vi una bestia subir del mar, que tenía siete cabezas y diez cuernos; y sobre sus cuernos diez diademas; y sobre las cabezas de ella nombre de blasfemia. Y la bestia que vi, era semejante á un leopardo, y sus pies como de oso, y su boca como boca de león. Y el dragón le dió su poder, y su trono, y grande potestad."

En Apocalipsis, mientras está de pie sobre la arena de la playa, la tierra, el apóstol Juan ve **una bestia** que se levanta del mar. Esta única bestia se compone de diferentes partes de las cuatro bestias que vio Daniel en el capítulo siete. Tiene **siete cabezas**, **diez cuernos**, cuerpo de **leopardo**, pies de **oso**, boca de **león**, y obtiene su autoridad del **dragón**.

PREGUNTA: ¿Quién es el dragón del que esta criatura obtiene su autoridad, poder y vida?

RESPUESTA: El dragón que le da vida y poder a la bestia es Satanás, el diablo. Apocalipsis 12: 9 dice: "And the great dragon was cast out, that old serpent, called the Devil, and Satan, which deceiveth the whole world."

Note el concepto del artista de esta bestia de siete cabezas que Juan ve en Apocalipsis trece:

Apocalipsis 13 bestia combinada de Daniel siete

Las siete cabezas de esta única bestia se componen de las siete cabezas de las cuatro bestias del capítulo siete de Daniel. Cuéntelos: León: una cabeza; Oso: una cabeza; Leopardo: cuatro cabezas; y bestia monstruo: una cabeza.

León: uno = 1
Oso: uno = 1
Leopardo: cuatro = 4
Bestia: <u>uno = 1</u>
Total: 7 cabezas de una bestia que representan el culto pagano mezclado con lo sagrado.

PREGUNTA: ¿Por qué aparece la única bestia en el libro de Apocalipsis compuesta de diferentes partes de las cuatro bestias del capítulo siete de Daniel?

RESPUESTA: La imagen en el capítulo dos de Daniel revela el proceso histórico por el cual las prácticas religiosas paganas se integraron en la adoración de hoy. Los cuatro reinos de Babilonia, Medo-Persia, Grecia y Roma jugaron cada uno un papel en la promoción de la mentalidad religiosa pagana que ocupa la mentalidad religiosa actual. A medida que los metales se volvieron menos valiosos, también se volvieron más duraderos, hasta que las prácticas paganas están tan impregnadas en las religiones del mundo que las prácticas paganas son irreconocibles. Algunos adoradores están decididos a defender estas prácticas paganas pensando que están viviendo y adorando de la manera que Dios desea, hasta el punto de ignorar y desobedecer la Palabra escrita de Dios. Prefieren cerrar los ojos, los oídos y la mente para defender su propia adoración.

La bestia combinada representa todas las prácticas paganas que se han infiltrado en la verdadera adoración de Dios desde los días de Daniel. Esa bestia está viva y coleando en nuestros días y pronto jugará un papel importante en el "tiempo señalado del fin".

PREGUNTA: ¿Por qué las cuatro bestias del capítulo siete de Daniel salen del "mar" en el versículo 3, y de "la tierra" en el versículo 17?

RESPUESTA: Las cuatro bestias que salen del "mar" nos remiten a los días de Daniel cuando las prácticas paganas se introdujeron en la verdadera adoración de Dios desde cada uno de los cuatro reinos diferentes comenzando con Babilonia en los días del rey Nabucodonosor. Las cuatro bestias que salen de la "tierra" nos remite al tiempo del fin cuando las prácticas paganas son una parte normal de la adoración del tiempo del fin como la practica el pueblo de Dios en todo el mundo. En el futuro, el pueblo de Dios equivocado provocará la adoración forzada para satisfacer las demandas que se le imponen a la humanidad en todo el mundo, durante el terrible "tiempo del fin".Notice the single combination beast of Revelation 13:1,2 comes up out of the sea.

PREGUNTA: ¿Qué representa el agua o "mar" en la Biblia?

RESPUESTA: Note que Apocalipsis 17:15 dice:

> "Y él me dice: Las aguas que has visto donde la ramera se sienta, son pueblos y muchedumbres y naciones y lenguas."

El "mar" representa las personas de todas las naciones y lenguas. Pero no cualquier pueblo. Estas son personas que creen en Dios, pero se niegan a seguirlo como Él dicta en la Biblia, así como el "mar" representó a los israelitas rebeldes en los días de Daniel (Daniel 7:2,3).

Recuerde, en la profecía bíblica:

El "cielo" representa al pueblo de Dios que le sirve con todo su corazón, mente y alma. La "gente del cielo" sirve a Dios al 100%.

La "tierra" representa las personas de todas las naciones y lenguas que están familiarizadas con los mandamientos de Dios, pero que se niegan a seguirlo por completo, haciendo TODO lo que Él requiere. La "gente de la tierra" sirve a Dios parcialmente, eligiendo y eligiendo lo que hará y lo que no hará.

La "gente del mar" cree en Dios pero se niegan a obedecerle.

Note Apocalipsis 21:1 que dice "y no había más mar". Esta frase no tiene nada que ver con el agua literal, está hablando en sentido figurado. Los cuerpos de agua tienen un efecto calmante relajante en las personas. Seguramente habrá cuerpos de agua asombrosos y literales en la tierra nueva. Pero en sentido figurado, no hay "mar" en la tierra nueva porque no hay rebelión en el reino glorioso, eterno y sin pecado venidero. Todas las personas conocerán a Dios y lo adorarán voluntariamente como Él lo exija. Note Jeremías 31:31-34:

> "He aquí que vienen días, dice Jehová, en los cuales haré nuevo pacto con la casa de Jacob y la casa de Judá: No como el pacto que hice con sus padres el día que tomé su mano para sacarlos de tierra de Egipto; porque ellos invalidaron mi pacto, bien que fuí yo un marido para ellos, dice Jehová: Mas éste es el pacto que haré con la casa de Israel después de aquellos días, dice Jehová: Daré mi ley en sus entrañas, y escribiréla en sus corazones; y seré yo á ellos por Dios, y ellos me serán por pueblo. Y no enseñará más ninguno á su prójimo, ni ninguno á

su hermano, diciendo: Conoce á Jehová: porque todos me conocerán, desde el más pequeño de ellos hasta el más grande, dice Jehová: porque perdonaré la maldad de ellos, y no me acordaré más de su pecado."

Note también Apocalipsis 12:12 que se refiere a la gente del cielo, la tierra y el mar:

"Por lo cual alegraos, cielos, y los que moráis en ellos. ¡Ay de los moradores de la tierra y del mar! porque el diablo ha descendido á vosotros, teniendo grande ira, sabiendo que tiene poco tiempo."

En el futuro, justo antes y durante la tribulación de siete años, Dios tendrá un pueblo que lo adorará y honrará como dice la Biblia, entregándose al 100% a Él, obedeciéndole en todo lo que Él requiera. A estos se les llama gente del "cielo". Se acerca un tiempo futuro en el que Dios impedirá que Satanás pueda entrar en la mente y la vida de estas personas porque estarán rodeadas por la protección de Dios. Tendrán "el sello de Dios" (Apocalipsis 7:3; 9:4). Pero la gente de la "tierra" y la del "mar" no tendrán esa protección. Cuando el diablo se dé cuenta de que ha perdido su influencia sobre la "gente del cielo", dirigirá su odio diabólico hacia la "tierra" y la gente del "mar". Lea cuidadosamente:

"Por lo cual alegraos, cielos, y los que moráis en ellos. ¡Ay de los moradores de la tierra y del mar! porque el diablo ha descendido á vosotros, teniendo grande ira, sabiendo que tiene poco tiempo." Apocalipsis 12:12.

PREGUNTA: ¿Cómo se prepara uno para estar en el grupo de personas de los últimos días llamado "cielo", aquellos sellados con el "sello de Dios" (Apocalipsis 7: 3; 9: 4)?

RESPUESTA: Al entregar nuestro todo a Dios hoy, buscándolo con todo nuestro corazón, mente y alma (Jeremías 29:13; Mateo 22:37), con el deseo de entregarnos totalmente a Él en todo lo que pensamos, decimos y hacer, nos preparamos para estar en el grupo de personas llamado "cielo". En el libro de Apocalipsis, la "gente del cielo" forma el grupo de personas conocido como los "144.000" de Apocalipsis 7:1-8 y 14:1-5. Aquellos que esperan entregar todo a Dios, hasta que llegue el momento de la angustia, serán los que tendrán las experiencias más difíciles durante los próximos siete años de la gran tribulación (Mateo 24:21), ya que su entrega se debe a la coacción. no porque voluntariamente dieron todo a Jesús antes de que comenzara el tiempo de angustia.

Ahora considere los metales de Daniel dos en comparación con Apocalipsis 9:20,21:

> "Y los otros hombres que no fueron muertos con estas plagas, aun no se arrepintieron de las obras de sus manos, para que no adorasen á los demonios, y á las imágenes de oro, y de plata, y de metal, y de piedra, y de madera; las cuales no pueden ver, ni oir, ni andar: Y no se arrepintieron de sus homicidios, ni de sus hechicerías, ni de su fornicación, ni de sus hurtos."

Para comprender el Libro de Apocalipsis en el Nuevo Testamento, una persona debe primero comprender la interpretación del libro de Daniel en el Antiguo Testamento. Todo el libro de Apocalipsis se cumplirá durante la próxima tribulación de siete años y no antes.

La intención de todo el libro de Apocalipsis es proporcionar a la generación de los últimos días de Dios la información que necesitan justo antes y durante la próxima tribulación de siete años, para explicar los eventos que tienen lugar a su alrededor y preparar a otros para lo que está por venir. . Las personas familiarizadas con sus Biblias y con los mensajes de Daniel y Apocalipsis adorarán a Dios de la manera que Él dicta. Conocerán a su Dios y lo que Él quiere.

Hasta este punto de la historia humana, todas las profecías cumplidas en la Biblia han sido reconocidas en retrospectiva. Pero el libro de Apocalipsis prepara al pueblo de Dios para lo que vendrá en el futuro si pueden interpretarlo correctamente.

Recuerde: la profecía bíblica: TODO SE TRATA DE ADORACIÓN.

Vea el video de YouTube **DANIEL CAPÍTULO SIETE EN ESPAÑOL** por Earl Schrock

DANIEL CAPÍTULO SIETE (RVR)

1 EN el primer año de Belsasar rey de Babilonia, vió Daniel un sueño y visiones de su cabeza en su cama: luego escribió el sueño, y notó la suma de los negocios. 2 Habló Daniel y dijo: Veía yo en mi visión de noche, y he aquí que los cuatro vientos del cielo combatían en la gran mar. 3 Y cuatro bestias grandes, diferentes la una de la otra, subían de la mar. 4 La primera era como león, y tenía alas de águila. Yo estaba mirando hasta tanto que sus alas fueron arrancadas, y fué quitada de la tierra; y púsose enhiesta sobre los pies á manera de hombre, y fuéle dado corazón de hombre. 5 Y he aquí otra segunda bestia, semejante á un oso, la cual se puso al un lado, y tenía en su boca tres costillas entre sus dientes; y fuéle dicho así: Levántate, traga carne mucha. 6 Después de esto yo miraba, y

he aquí otra, semejante á un tigre, y tenía cuatro alas de ave en sus espaldas: tenía también esta bestia cuatro cabezas; y fuéle dada potestad. 7 Después de esto miraba yo en las visiones de la noche, y he aquí la cuarta bestia, espantosa y terrible, y en grande manera fuerte; la cual tenía unos dientes grandes de hierro: devoraba y desmenuzaba, y las sobras hollaba con sus pies: y era muy diferente de todas las bestias que habían sido antes de ella, y tenía diez cuernos. 8 Estando yo contemplando los cuernos, he aquí que otro cuerno pequeño subía entre ellos, y delante de él fueron arrancados tres cuernos de los primeros; y he aquí, en este cuerno había ojos como ojos de hombre, y una boca que hablaba grandezas. 9 Estuve mirando hasta que fueron puestas sillas: y un Anciano de grande edad se sentó, cuyo vestido era blanco como la nieve, y el pelo de su cabeza como lana limpia; su silla llama de fuego, sus ruedas fuego ardiente. 10 Un río de fuego procedía y salía de delante de él: millares de millares le servían, y millones de millones asistían delante de él: el Juez se sentó, y los libros se abrieron. 11 Yo entonces miraba á causa de la voz de las grandes palabras que hablaba el cuerno; miraba hasta tanto que mataron la bestia, y su cuerpo fué deshecho, y entregado para ser quemado en el fuego. 12 Habían también quitado á las otras bestias su señorío, y les había sido dada prolongación de vida hasta cierto tiempo. 13 Miraba yo en la visión de la noche, y he aquí en las nubes del cielo como un hijo de hombre que venía, y llegó hasta el Anciano de grande edad, é hiciéronle llegar delante de él. 14 Y fuéle dado señorío, y gloria, y reino; y todos los pueblos, naciones y lenguas le sirvieron; su señorío, señorío eterno, que no será transitorio, y su reino que no se corromperá. 15 Mi espíritu fué turbado, yo Daniel, en medio de mi cuerpo, y las visiones de mi cabeza me asombraron. 16 Lleguéme á uno de los que asistían, y preguntéle la verdad acerca de todo esto. Y hablóme, y declaróme la interpretación de las cosas. 17 Estas grandes bestias, las cuales son cuatro,

cuatro reyes son, que se levantarán en la tierra. 18 Después tomarán el reino los santos del Altísimo, y poseerán el reino hasta el siglo, y hasta el siglo de los siglos. 19 Entonces tuve deseo de saber la verdad acerca de la cuarta bestia, que tan diferente era de todas las otras, espantosa en gran manera, que tenía dientes de hierro, y sus uñas de metal, que devoraba y desmenuzaba, y las sobras hollaba con sus pies: 20 Asimismo acerca de los diez cuernos que tenía en su cabeza, y del otro que había subido, de delante del cual habían caído tres: y este mismo cuerno tenía ojos, y boca que hablaba grandezas, y su parecer mayor que el de sus compañeros. 21 Y veía yo que este cuerno hacía guerra contra los santos, y los vencía, 22 Hasta tanto que vino el Anciano de grande edad, y se dió el juicio á los santos del Altísimo; y vino el tiempo, y los santos poseyeron el reino. 23 Dijo así: La cuarta bestia será un cuarto reino en la tierra, el cual será más grande que todos los otros reinos, y á toda la tierra devorará, y la hollará, y la despedazará. 24 Y los diez cuernos significan que de aquel reino se levantarán diez reyes; y tras ellos se levantará otro, el cual será mayor que los primeros, y á tres reyes derribará. 25 Y hablará palabras contra el Altísimo, y á los santos del Altísimo quebrantará, y pensará en mudar los tiempos y la ley: y entregados serán en su mano hasta tiempo, y tiempos, y el medio de un tiempo. 26 Empero se sentará el juez, y quitaránle su señorío, para que sea destruído y arruinado hasta el extremo; 27 Y que el reino, y el señorío, y la majestad de los reinos debajo de todo el cielo, sea dado al pueblo de los santos del Altísimo; cuyo reino es reino eterno, y todos los señoríos le servirán y obedecerán. 28 Hasta aquí fué el fin de la plática. Yo Daniel, mucho me turbaron mis pensamientos, y mi rostro se me mudó: mas guardé en mi corazón el negocio.

DANIEL CAPÍTULO OCHO

"Por tanto, cuando viereis la abominación del asolamiento, que fué dicha por Daniel profeta, que estará en el lugar santo, (el que lee, entienda), 16 Entonces los que están en Judea, huyan á los montes." Mateo 24:15,16

La primera visión que tuvo Daniel, en el capítulo siete, fue en el primer año del rey Belsasar. Ahora, la visión para el capítulo ocho es durante el tercer año del rey, co-reinando con su padre, Nabonido. En este sueño, desde el punto de vista de Daniel, se ve a sí mismo en el palacio de Shushan junto al río de Ulai. Ve un carnero con dos cuernos, uno más alto que el otro, abriéndose camino desde el este hacia el oeste, el norte y el sur. Este ariete corría libre y no era desafiado, haciendo lo que quería. Observe que este ariete se mueve en todas las direcciones de la brújula a la vez. Esto debería ser una pista para nosotros de que es la influencia pagana de este animal extendiéndose en todas direcciones y no el animal en sí.

Luego, del oeste viene un macho cabrío que tenía un cuerno enorme entre los ojos. El macho cabrío estaba furioso y se movía hacia el este tan rápido que sus pies no tocaban el suelo. Se acercó al carnero con tanta furia que le rompió los dos cuernos, dejándolo impotente, y el macho cabrío pisoteó al carnero bajo sus pies. Después, la cabra se volvió tan poderosa que nadie pudo desafiarla. Luego, una vez que la cabra se volvió muy poderosa, su único cuerno grande se rompió y cuatro cuernos más pequeños crecieron en su lugar y la influencia pagana de la cabra también creció hacia las cuatro direcciones de la brújula.

Luego, desde el norte, un cuerno pequeño comenzó a crecer y creció hacia el sur, hacia el este y hacia el oeste. También creció en todas las direcciones de la brújula como el Imperio Medo-Persa y el Imperio Griego. Se hizo muy grande incluso hasta los cielos y arrojó algunas de las huestes y las estrellas del cielo, las arrojó a la tierra y las pisoteó. Se magnificó al príncipe de las huestes del cielo y por él lo CONTINUO fue quitado y lo santo fue derribado. Un ejército de personas lo apoyó quitando el CONTINUO y la verdad fue arrojada al suelo y prosperó y creció.

Daniel 8:13,14 says:

> "Y oí un santo que hablaba; y otro de los santos dijo á aquél que hablaba: ¿Hasta cuándo durará la visión del continuo sacrificio, y la prevaricación asoladora que pone el santuario y el ejército para ser hollados? Y él me dijo: Hasta dos mil y trescientos días de tarde y mañana; y el santuario será purificado."

Debemos entender que la palabra "sacrificio" no pertenece a este versículo. Se agregó por error. Además, la palabra "santuario" es en realidad una mala interpretación de la palabra "santo". La palabra "ejército" se refiere a la palabra "anfitrión". No es una mala traducción de la palabra "anfitrión" una vez que se entiende mejor el texto. La palabra "anfitrión" en este caso se refiere a un grupo de personas.

En realidad, del hebreo original, los versículos 13 y 14 deberían traducirse de manera diferente. Lo siguiente es en mis propias palabras, ya que una traducción correcta no está disponible.

> "Entonces oí a un santo hablar con el otro santo que estaba hablando y él preguntó: '¿Hasta cuándo la visión del continuo (perpetuo) y la transgresión de la desolación para que el santo y el ejército sean pisoteados? Y él me dijo, hasta dos mil trescientas tardes y mañanas, entonces lo santo será hecho justo (justificado o vindicado)."

NOTA ESPECIAL: En el libro de Daniel, la palabra hebrea tamid (taw-meed '), Strong's 8548, significa CONTINUO o PERPETUO. La palabra "sacrificio" fue agregada porque los traductores erróneamente razonaron que la palabra "perpetuo" o "continuo" se refería a los sacrificios perpetuos diarios que Dios estableció en el libro de Moisés. No entendían cómo se podía "quitar" lo "perpetuo" o lo "continuo". No sabían a qué se refería la palabra "tamid". Asumieron que la palabra "tamid" de Daniel 8:13 se refería al sacrificio perpetuo de la tarde y la mañana de Éxodo 29: 38-42, ya que un sacrificio "continuo" podía literalmente detenerse o abandonarse. Pero su suposición ha creado un tremendo malentendido durante siglos. Este librito revelará cuál es el mensaje de Daniel 8:13; y Daniel 12:11 en realidad representa, con respecto al "perpetuo" o "continuo" que se quita.

ENTENDIENDO A DANIEL 8:14

> "Entonces oí a un santo hablar con el otro santo que estaba hablando y él preguntó: '¿Hasta cuándo la visión del perpetuo (o continuo) y la transgresión de la desolación para el santo y el anfitrión serán pisoteados? Y él me dijo, hasta

dos mil trescientas tardes y mañanas, entonces lo santo será hecho justo (justificado o vindicado)." (Daniel 8:13,14 en mis palabras.)

En Daniel 8:14 los 2,300 días (tardes y mañanas) son días literales de 24 horas ya que se les llama los 2,300 "tardes y mañanas" así como los días de la semana de la creación eran una tarde y una mañana cada uno (Génesis uno). También los 2.300 días serán una realidad durante el tiempo de la ira de Dios, en el tiempo del fin, cuando el pecado haya alcanzado su máxima expresión. Los 2.300 días también fueron "cerrados" (Daniel 8:26) o sellados o encerrados para que su misterio no se entendiera hasta que Dios estuviera listo para revelar lo que realmente son, justo antes del tiempo que serían aplicados durante el período de siete años. tribulación de 2.520 días.

PREGUNTA: ¿Qué iba a pasar durante los 2.300 días, que es un poco más de 6 años?

RESPUESTA: Durante los 2.300 días literales (1) se acabará el CONTINUO, (2) se establecerá la "transgresión de la desolación", (3) se faltará el respeto al "santo", (4) el "anfitrión" o el pueblo santo será pisoteado o perseguido, (5) al final de los 2,300 días, el pueblo "santo", la gente fiel a Dios, será reivindicado y se les mostrará que tomaron la decisión correcta de ser obedientes a Dios en la cara. de persecución y muerte.

Cuando terminó la visión, Daniel trató de comprender el significado de la visión, pero no pudo. Luego escuchó la voz de un hombre que decía: "Gabriel, haz que este hombre entienda la visión". Gabriel se acercó a Daniel y le dijo: "Entiende, hijo de hombre, que esta visión se refiere **al tiempo del fin**". Daniel 8:16, 17.

Daniel se sintió muy débil, asustado y solo. El mensajero lo tocó, forteleciendo a Daniel, luego Gabriel continuó hablando. Dijo en el versículo 19:

"Y dijo: He aquí yo te enseñaré lo ha de venir en el fin de la ira: porque al tiempo se cumplirá"

Gabriel le dijo a Daniel que le explicaría la visión, pero que Daniel necesitaba entender que esta visión se aplica a los últimos días de la historia de esta tierra, durante el tiempo de la ira de Dios, en el tiempo señalado del fin, mucho después de que su vida había terminado. .

Gabriel continuó explicando que el Carnero representa el reino de los medos y los persas, mientras que la cabra representa el reino de Grecia. Dijo que el cuerno grande es su primer rey, que es Alejandro el Grande, y que después de su muerte su reino se dividiría en cuatro reinos. La historia revela que eso es exactamente lo que sucedió como predijo la visión de Daniel.

Es necesario reconocer que un cuerno representa poder. Cuanto más grande es el cuerno o más cuernos tiene una criatura, más fuerte es. El enorme cuerno de cabra era más poderoso que los dos cuernos más pequeños del carnero. Cuando se rompieron los cuernos del carnero, no tenía fuerza (Daniel 8:6-8). Además, se necesitaron cuatro cuernos nuevos para crecer para igualar el poder del cuerno grande que representaba a Alejandro Magno. Cuantos más cuernos, más poder. En Daniel 7, la bestia monstruo tiene diez cuernos. Luego aparece un cuerno pequeño que le da 11 cuernos individuales. Pero 3 de los diez cuernos ceden su poder al Cuerno Pequeño, lo que lo convierte en cuatro cuernos aliados contra 7 cuernos individuales, lo que hace que el Poder del Cuerno Pequeño sea el más fuerte.

Los versículos 23 al 25 están dedicados a explicar más sobre el Poder del Cuerno Pequeño. Gabriel dice que durante los últimos días, cuando el pecado haya alcanzado su plenitud, se levantará un rostro de rey fiero que comprende sentencias oscuras. Será poderoso pero no en su propio poder. Prosperará y practicará y destruirá al pueblo santo y poderoso y se engrandecerá ante el Príncipe de los príncipes. Entonces será quebrantado, pero no por una mano humana.

> "Y con su sagacidad hará prosperar el engaño en su mano; y en su corazón se engrandecerá, y con paz destruirá á muchos: y contra el príncipe de los príncipes se levantará; mas sin mano será quebrantado." Daniel 8:25.

¿Quién es el príncipe de los príncipes?

> "El Dios de nuestros padres levantó á Jesús, al cual vosotros matasteis colgándole de un madero. 31 A éste ha Dios ensalzado con su diestra por Príncipe y Salvador, para dar á Israel arrepentimiento y remisión de pecados." Hechos 5:30,31.

Jesús es el Príncipe de los príncipes. El futuro venidero del tiempo del fin Little Horn Power desafiará a Jesús, pero tendrá un éxito parcial en su intento, pero al final se romperá. En el versículo 26 Gabriel dice:

> "Y la visión de la tarde y la mañana que está dicha, es verdadera: y tú guarda la visión, porque es para muchos días."

Gabriel, por lo tanto Dios, le asegura a Daniel que "la profecía de las 2.300 tardes y mañanas" se llevará a cabo tal como se le dijo, pero que él debía "callar" la visión porque tendría lugar en el futuro. El significado de la visión sería "encerrado" o sellado, por lo que permanecería como un misterio hasta el mismo momento del final cuando sería una realidad. Muchas son las interpretaciones actuales del versículo catorce, pero no deben identificarse correctamente hasta el tiempo del fin. Daniel se enfermó después de la visión y no pudo encontrar a nadie que pudiera explicarlo.

CONCLUSIÓN: El capítulo ocho de Daniel brinda más información que nos ayuda a comprender mejor el sueño del rey Nabucodonosor en el capítulo dos de Daniel y la visión de Daniel en el capítulo siete. Medo-Persia está representada por (1) los hombros de plata, (2) el oso torcido y (3) el carnero. El imperio de Grecia está representado por (1) el vientre de bronce, (2) el leopardo de cuatro cabezas y (3) la cabra furiosa.

También tenemos más información sobre el cuerno pequeño de Daniel siete y ocho. Aparecerá al final de los tiempos, durante el tiempo señalado del fin, durante el tiempo de la ira de Dios. Será decisivo para acabar con lo CONTINUO o perpetuo (lo cotidiano) y producirá "la abominación desoladora". Será poderoso y popular y será fundamental en la persecución contra el pueblo de Dios, hasta el punto de desafiar al Príncipe de los príncipes, que es el mismo Jesús.

En Isaías 9: 6 Jesús es llamado Príncipe de paz. Hechos 5:31 dice que Jesús es nuestro Príncipe y nuestro Salvador. Apocalipsis 1: 5 dice que Jesús es el Príncipe de los reyes de la tierra.

Todas las cosas mencionadas anteriormente sucederán durante los 2,300 días literales que ocupan una gran parte de los 2,520 días, o siete años de tribulación. El capítulo ocho de Daniel debe considerarse como un todo. Daniel 8:14 no está ni puede estar solo. Ese período de tiempo no se puede colocar en cualquier lugar que elija una persona. Dios tiene un tiempo específico para que comience y descubriremos ese punto de inicio cuando estudiemos el capítulo doce de Daniel.

Vea el video de YouTube **DANIEL CAPÍTULO OCHO EN ESPAÑOL** por Earl Schrock

DANIEL CAPÍTULO OCHO (RVR)

1 EN el año tercero del reinado del rey Belsasar, me apareció una visión á mí, Daniel, después de aquella que me había aparecido antes. 2 Vi en visión, (y aconteció cuando vi, que yo estaba en Susán, que es cabecera del reino en la provincia de Persia;) vi pues en visión, estando junto al río Ulai, 3 Y alcé mis ojos, y miré, y he aquí un carnero que estaba delante del río, el cual tenía dos cuernos: y aunque eran altos, el uno era más alto que el otro; y el más alto subió á la postre. 4 Vi que el carnero hería con los cuernos al poniente, al norte, y al mediodía, y que ninguna bestia podía parar delante de él, ni había quien escapase de su mano: y hacía conforme á su voluntad, y engrandecíase. 5 Y estando yo considerando, he aquí un macho de cabrío venía de la parte del poniente sobre la haz de toda la tierra, el cual no tocaba la tierra: y tenía aquel macho de cabrío un cuerno notable entre sus ojos: 6 Y vino hasta el carnero que tenía los dos cuernos, al cual había yo visto que estaba delante del río, y corrió contra él con la ira de su fortaleza. 7 Y vilo que llegó junto al carnero, y levantóse contra él, é hiriólo, y quebró sus dos cuernos, porque en el carnero no había fuerzas para parar delante de él: derribólo por tanto en tierra, y hollólo; ni hubo quien librase al carnero de su mano. 8 Y engrandecióse en gran manera el macho de cabrío; y estando en su mayor fuerza, aquel gran cuerno fué quebrado, y en su lugar subieron otros cuatro maravillosos

hacia los cuatro vientos del cielo. 9 Y del uno de ellos salió un cuerno pequeño, el cual creció mucho al mediodía, y al oriente, y hacia la tierra deseable. 10 Y engrandecióse hasta el ejército del cielo; y parte del ejército y de las estrellas echó por tierra, y las holló. 11 Aun contra el príncipe de la fortaleza se engrandeció, y por él fué quitado el continuo sacrificio, y el lugar de su santuario fué echado por tierra. 12 Y el ejército fué le entregado á causa de la prevaricación sobre el continuo sacrificio: y echó por tierra la verdad, é hizo cuanto quiso, y sucedióle prósperamente. 13 Y oí un santo que hablaba; y otro de los santos dijo á aquél que hablaba: ¿Hasta cuándo durará la visión del continuo sacrificio, y la prevaricación asoladora que pone el santuario y el ejército para ser hollados? 14 Y él me dijo: Hasta dos mil y trescientos días de tarde y mañana; y el santuario será purificado. 15 Y acaeció que estando yo Daniel considerando la visión, y buscando su inteligencia, he aquí, como una semejanza de hombre se puso delante de mí. 16 Y oí una voz de hombre entre las riberas de Ulai, que gritó y dijo: Gabriel, enseña la visión á éste. 17 Vino luego cerca de donde yo estaba; y con su venida me asombré, y caí sobre mi rostro. Empero él me dijo: Entiende, hijo del hombre, porque al tiempo se cumplirá la visión. 18 Y estando él hablando conmigo, caí dormido en tierra sobre mi rostro: y él me tocó, é hízome estar en pie. 19 Y dijo: He aquí yo te enseñaré lo ha de venir en el fin de la ira: porque al tiempo se cumplirá: 20 Aquel carnero que viste, que tenía cuernos, son los reyes de Media y de Persia. 21 Y el macho cabrío es el rey de Javán: y el cuerno grande que tenía entre sus ojos es el rey primero. 22 Y que fué quebrado y sucedieron cuatro en su lugar, significa que cuatro reinos sucederán de la nación, mas no en la fortaleza de él. 23 Y al cabo del imperio de éstos, cuando se cumplirán los prevaricadores, levantaráse un rey altivo de rostro, y entendido en dudas. 24 Y su poder se fortalecerá, mas no con fuerza suya, y destruirá maravillosamente, y prosperará;

y hará arbitrariamente, y destruirá fuertes y al pueblo de los santos. 25 Y con su sagacidad hará prosperar el engaño en su mano; y en su corazón se engrandecerá, y con paz destruirá á muchos: y contra el príncipe de los príncipes se levantará; mas sin mano será quebrantado. 26 Y la visión de la tarde y la mañana que está dicha, es verdadera: y tú guarda la visión, porque es para muchos días. 27 Y yo Daniel fuí quebrantado, y estuve enfermo algunos días: y cuando convalecí, hice el negocio del rey; mas estaba espantado acerca de la visión, y no había quien la entendiese.

DANIEL CAPITULO NUEVE

Cantad á Jehová, toda **la tierra**, Anunciad de día en día su salud. Cantad entre las gentes su gloria, Y en todos los pueblos sus maravillas. Temed en su presencia, toda **la tierra**: El mundo será aún establecido, para que no se conmueva. Alégrense los cielos, y gócese **la tierra**, Y digan en las naciones: Reina Jehová. Resuene la mar, y la plenitud de ella: Alégrese el campo, y todo lo que contiene. Entonces cantarán los árboles de los bosques delante de Jehová, Porque viene á juzgar **la tierra**." 1 Crónicas 16:23,24; 30-33

El "reino de los caldeos" y la "tierra" se refieren al mismo pueblo o territorio.

"EN el año primero de Darío hijo de Assuero, de la nación de los Medos, el cual fué puesto por rey sobre el reino de los Caldeos." Daniel 9:1

¡¡TIERRA!! ¿A qué se aplica la palabra "TIERRA" en la profecía bíblica? Daniel 2:39 dice:

"Y después de ti se levantará otro reino menor que tú; y otro tercer reino de metal, el cual se enseñoreará de toda la tierra."

Y Daniel 4:22:

> "Tú mismo eres, oh rey, que creciste, y te hiciste fuerte, pues creció tu grandeza, y ha llegado hasta el cielo, y tu señorío hasta el cabo de la tierra."

Daniel le dijo al rey Nabucodonosor que gobernaría sobre toda la tierra y también los reinos que le siguieron. Pero la historia revela que ninguno de estos reyes gobernó jamás sobre toda la tierra al referirse a este globo; nuestro planeta. El rey Nabucodonosor, gobernante de Babilonia, ni los otros reyes de los tres imperios siguientes del capítulo dos de Daniel, tenían una propiedad geográfica tan grande como algunas otras naciones del mundo, no mencionadas en el libro de Daniel. Entonces, ¿a qué oa quién se aplica la palabra "tierra"?

Daniel 9: 2 nos da la respuesta. Dice:

> "En el año primero de su reinado, yo Daniel miré atentamente en los libros el número de los años, del cual habló Jehová al profeta Jeremías, que había de concluir la asolación de Jerusalem en setenta años."

La "tierra" en el libro de Daniel, en la mayoría de los casos, se refiere al "reino de los caldeos".

¿Qué o quién era el encargado de Nabucodonosor, el caldeo? Note Daniel 4:35:

> "Y de entre los hombres te echan, y con las bestias del campo será tu morada, y como á los bueyes te apacentarán: y siete tiempos pasarán sobre ti, hasta que conozcas que el Altísimo se enseñorea en el reino de los hombres, y á quien él quisiere lo da."

¿Quiénes son los "pueblos de la tierra"? Note el Salmo 98:4-6:

> "Cantad alegres á Jehová, **toda la tierra**;
> Levantad la voz, y aplaudid, y salmead. Salmead
> á Jehová con arpa; Con arpa y voz de cántico.
> Aclamad con trompetas y sonidos De bocina
> delante del rey Jehová."

Los "pueblos de la tierra" o la "gente de la tierra" son todas las personas que componen la "iglesia invisible" de todo el mundo; el reino de Dios. Cualquiera y todos los que creen en el Dios Creador entran en la categoría de la "gente de la tierra."

DANIEL 9:2-6

En 605 a. EC, el rey Nabucodonosor atacó a la tribu de Judá y se llevó a muchas personas a Babilonia. Después de que llegaron a Babilonia, Dios les envió mensajes a través de cartas del profeta Jeremías.

Cuando Daniel tenía ochenta años, estaba leyendo las cartas enviadas a Babilonia por el profeta Jeremías. Mientras leía las cartas, hizo un importante descubrimiento oportuno. En Jeremías 29:1-9, Dios le dice al pueblo capturado de Israel que se establezca en el lugar donde han sido llevados. Deben construir casas, plantar huertos y ampliar sus familias porque van a estar allí por mucho tiempo. Luego, en el versículo diez, Dios dice:

> "Porque así dijo Jehová: Cuando en Babilonia
> se cumplieren los setenta años, yo os visitaré,
> y despertaré sobre vosotros mi buena palabra,
> para tornaros á este lugar."

En 605 a. EC, el rey Nabucodonosor atacó a la tribu de Judá y se llevó a muchas personas a Babilonia. Después de que llegaron a Babilonia, Dios les envió mensajes a través de cartas del profeta Jeremías.

Cuando Daniel tenía más de ochenta años, estaba leyendo el libro. Este descubrimiento debe haber llenado de gozo el corazón de Daniel. A pesar de que lo habían llevado lejos de casa a una edad temprana, el deseo de regresar, para él y sus compatriotas, hombres y mujeres, era un maravilloso sueño de esperanza que todos compartían. Ahora Daniel se dio cuenta de que los setenta años, de los que hablaba Jeremías, estaban casi completos.

PREGUNTA: ¿Por qué setenta (70) años para que los hijos de Israel estuvieran cautivos en Babilonia?

Note 2 Crónicas 36:20,21:

> "Los que quedaron del cuchillo, pasáronlos á Babilonia; y fueron siervos de él y de sus hijos, hasta que vino el reino de los Persas; Para que se cumpliese la palabra de Jehová por la boca de Jeremías, hasta que la tierra hubo gozado sus sábados: porque todo el tiempo de su asolamiento reposó, hasta que los setenta años fueron cumplidos."

Se nos dice que la razón por la que Dios envió a la tribu de Judá al cautiverio durante setenta años fue porque los hijos de Israel no habían guardado los años sabáticos para la tierra, santa como Dios les había dicho.

PREGUNTA: ¿Qué es un año sabático? Note Levítico 25:3,4:

"Seis años sembrarás tu tierra, y seis años podarás tu viña, y cogerás sus frutos; 4 Y el séptimo año la tierra tendrá sábado de holganza, sábado á Jehová: no sembrarás tu tierra, ni podarás tu viña."

En Levítico 25, Dios les dijo específicamente a los hijos de Israel que una vez que hubieran entrado en la tierra prometida, debían trabajar la tierra durante seis años, pero en el séptimo año debían dejar reposar la tierra. Los versículos 1-7 dicen muy claramente que no debían arar, plantar o cosechar como lo habían hecho durante los seis años anteriores de agricultura. Debían dejar la tierra en paz para que descansara el sábado. Dios les prometió que los cuidaría durante ese tiempo, si tan solo confiaran en Él. No pudieron hacer esto. Aparentemente, los hijos de Israel no habían dado a la tierra el año de reposo que Dios exigía. Así que los hijos de Judá fueron enviados al cautiverio durante setenta años, un año por cada año sabático que no se honraba.

¡HAGAMOS UN POCO DE MATEMÁTICAS!

PREGUNTA: Si los hijos de Israel habían descuidado guardar u honrar 70 de los séptimos años como sábado de reposo, ¿cuántos años en total habían desobedecido a Dios?

70 años sabáticos multiplicados por 7 años = 490 años. AS: 70 años sabáticos x 7 años son 490 años. Los hijos de Israel habían desobedecido a Dios y no habían confiado en Él durante 490 años de desafío.

Daniel 9:7-14

En Daniel 9: 7-14, Daniel hace una oración de contrición. En esta hermosa oración, Daniel pide el perdón de Dios y confiesa por todas las personas que no obedecen los mandamientos de Dios. Daniel menciona los pecados que los hijos de Israel cometieron contra Dios al no obedecer la ley de Moisés.

¿Cuál es la parte específica de la ley de Moisés que los hijos de Israel desobedecieron? ¿Y cuál es el castigo por esa desobediencia? Note Levítico 26:14-16: Dios dijo:

> "Empero si no me oyereis, ni hiciereis todos estos mis mandamientos, Y si abominareis mis decretos, y vuestra alma menospreciare mis derechos, no ejecutando todos mis mandamientos, é invalidando mi pacto; Yo también haré con vosotros esto: enviaré sobre vosotros terror, extenuación y calentura, que consuman los ojos y atormenten el alma: y sembraréis en balde vuestra simiente, porque vuestros enemigos la comerán."

Luego Levítico 26:32-35:

> "Yo asolaré también la tierra, y se pasmarán de ella vuestros enemigos que en ella moran: Y á vosotros os esparciré por las gentes, y desenvainaré espada en pos de vosotros: y vuestra tierra estará asolada, y yermas vuestras ciudades. Entonces la tierra holgará sus sábados todos los días que estuviere asolada, y vosotros en la tierra de vuestros enemigos: la tierra descansará entonces y gozará sus sábados. Todo el tiempo que estará asolada, holgará lo

que no holgó en vuestros sábados mientras habitabais en ella."

Daniel estaba muy familiarizado con la ley de Moisés y por esto oró fervientemente para que Dios perdonara los pecados pasados de su pueblo por desobedecerlo al no guardar la ley de Moisés con respecto al descanso anual del séptimo sábado que él demandaba.

Daniel 9:15-19

En Daniel 9:15-19, Daniel suplica humildemente a Dios que recuerde al pueblo, Su pueblo, Su ciudad santa, Su Jerusalén, Su montaña, y recuerde que han sufrido estos últimos setenta años como ningún otro pueblo lo ha hecho y que han pagado el castigo por sus pecados como lo estableció. Daniel suplica fervientemente por la misericordia de Dios. El versículo 19 dice:

"Oye, Señor; oh Señor, perdona; presta oído, Señor, y haz; no pongas dilación, por amor de ti mismo, Dios mío: porque tu nombre es llamado sobre tu ciudad y sobre tu pueblo."

Daniel 9:20-23

Durante esta oración, Daniel usa varios términos para describir al pueblo de Dios, "los pueblos de la tierra". Él nombra al pueblo de Dios como: los hombres de Judá, el pueblo de Jerusalén, todo Israel, tu pueblo, tu ciudad Jerusalén, tu montaña santa, tu santuario desolado, la ciudad que lleva tu nombre, tu ciudad, tu pueblo, mi pueblo Israel. y su santo monte. Aunque algunos de estos términos se pueden aplicar a ubicaciones geográficas físicas; también se aplican al pueblo de Dios, Su reino, no solo en los días de Daniel, sino también en nuestros días.

Recuerde la visión del rey Nabucodonosor en el capítulo dos de Daniel. En la visión, el rey ve una piedra tallada en la montaña. ¿Cuál es la montaña de la que está tallada la piedra del reino que destruye la imagen pagana? Ese monte no era otro que el monte Sion, el monte de Dios, los israelitas en los días de Jesús. Jesús es del pueblo israelita que Dios estableció y desarrolló comenzando con un hombre, Abraham (Génesis 12). Jesús es la Roca, la principal piedra del ángulo (1 Pedro 2: 4-9), que fue excavada en esa montaña, el Monte Sión, y de Él surgió el reino de Dios comenzando como una pequeña piedra, colgando de una cruel cruz, hasta el punto de envolver todo este planeta, creando el reino de Dios que está vivo y coleando hoy. El monte Sión, la montaña que llenó toda la tierra, desde los días de Jesús, no es solo un lugar en la región palestina, también es un pueblo; un pueblo de la tierra, el pueblo de Dios que está esparcido por este globo en cada continente, nación, lengua y pueblo que acepta a Jesucristo como su Salvador personal: el reino de Dios.

(Obtenga más información sobre el reino de Dios en un libro electrónico titulado: "The Kingdom of Heaven and the Kingdom of God" por Earl Schrock de Xlibris.com, Amazon, Barnes and Nobles, etc.)

La promesa de Dios a Abraham se ha cumplido. Dios le dijo a Abraham, Isaac y Jacob que serían los padres de muchas naciones, no solo la nación de Israel. Las personas de todas las naciones del mundo, que aceptan y siguen a Jesucristo, son el monte Sión, Su reino.

Note Gálatas 3:26-29:

> "Porque todos sois hijos de Dios por la fe en Cristo Jesús. Porque todos los que habéis sido bautizados en Cristo, de Cristo estáis vestidos.

No hay Judío, ni Griego; no hay siervo, ni libre; no hay varón, ni hembra: porque todos vosotros sois uno en Cristo Jesús. Y si vosotros sois de Cristo, ciertamente la simiente de Abraham sois, y conforme á la promesa los herederos."

El deseo de Daniel es que Dios perdone a su pueblo, su santo monte, y les permita regresar a su país. Mientras oraba, se le apareció el ángel Gabriel. Los versículos 22 y 23 dicen:

"É hízome entender, y habló conmigo, y dijo: Daniel, ahora he salido para hacerte entender la declaración. Al principio de tus ruegos salió la palabra, y yo he venido para enseñártela, porque tú eres varón de deseos. Entiende pues la palabra, y entiende la visión."

Entonces el ángel Gabriel llena de esperanza el corazón de Daniel. La súplica de oración original de Daniel era que su pueblo fuera perdonado y se le permitiera regresar a casa. Gabriel le dice a Daniel que su gente podrá regresar a casa en 70 semanas. Note lo siguiente:

Daniel 9:24

"Setenta semanas están determinadas sobre tu pueblo y sobre tu santa ciudad, para acabar la prevaricación, y concluir el pecado, y expiar la iniquidad; y para traer la justicia de los siglos, y sellar la visión y la profecía, y ungir al Santo de los santos."

Desde la perspectiva de Daniel, él pudo haber pensado que Dios iba a liberar a los hijos de Israel en 490 días (70 semanas literales son 490 días literales) que es aproximadamente un año y medio desde el momento de la oración de Daniel nueve. Eso habría llenado su corazón de esperanza. Cuando Ciro, rey de Persia, dio el decreto de libertad en 538 a. EC, (Esdras 1: 1-4) Daniel podría haber calculado que los 70 años se completaron.

Daniel 9:24-27

"Setenta semanas están determinadas sobre tu pueblo y sobre tu santa ciudad, para acabar la prevaricación, y concluir el pecado, y expiar la iniquidad; y para traer la justicia de los siglos, y sellar la visión y la profecía, y ungir al Santo de los santos. Sepas pues y entiendas, que desde la salida de la palabra para restaurar y edificar á Jerusalem hasta el Mesías Príncipe, habrá siete semanas, y sesenta y dos semanas; tornaráse á edificar la plaza y el muro en tiempos angustiosos. Y después de las sesenta y dos semanas se quitará la vida al Mesías, y no por sí: y el pueblo de un príncipe que ha de venir, destruirá á la ciudad y el santuario; con inundación será el fin de ella, y hasta el fin de la guerra será talada con asolamientos. Y en otra semana confirmará el pacto á muchos, y á la mitad de la semana hará cesar el sacrificio y la ofrenda: después con la muchedumbre de las abominaciones será el desolar, y esto hasta una entera consumación; y derramaráse la ya determinada sobre el pueblo asolado."

Desde la perspectiva de Daniel, él pudo haber pensado que Dios iba a liberar a los hijos de Israel en 490 días (70 semanas literales son 490 días literales) que es aproximadamente un año y medio desde el momento de la oración de Daniel nueve. Eso habría llenado su corazón de esperanza. Cuando Ciro, rey de Persia, dio el decreto de libertad en 538 a. EC, (Esdras 1: 1-4) Daniel podría haber calculado que los 70 años eran. Entonces, ¿qué quiso decir el ángel Gabriel con toda la visión de Daniel nueve que le dio a Daniel?

¿De qué se tratan las 70 semanas en referencia a toda la profecía?

Como en todas las cosas, la retrospectiva es 20/20. Siempre entendemos más cuando miramos hacia atrás que cuando miramos hacia adelante, especialmente cuando se trata de la profecía bíblica. Dios tiene su tiempo particular designado para que todas las cosas sucedan y siempre serán acertadas. No podemos cumplir con las Escrituras asignando períodos de tiempo a eventos aleatorios para los que no fueron intencionados, planeados o programados. Pero nosotros, los humanos, en un intento por resolver todos los misterios de la Biblia, aplicándolos a nuestro propio período de vida, a menudo cometemos ese error.

Por ejemplo, Pablo entendió mal cuándo terminaría el mundo. Pensó que sería en su día. En 1 Corintios 7:1-9 y 25-31 anima a las personas a no casarse, a ser como él, ya que el tiempo es corto. Pero agrega, no es pecado casarse si quisieran. Dios no lo corrigió con este malentendido de que el fin de la era fue durante su vida.

Juan, el discípulo de Jesús, entendió mal cuándo terminaría el mundo; pensó que también terminaría en su día. Dijo en 1 Juan 2:18:

> "Hijitos, ya es el último tiempo: y como vosotros habéis oído que el anticristo ha de venir, así también al presente han comenzado á ser

muchos anticristos; por lo cual sabemos que es el último tiempo."

No deberíamos sentirnos mal si hemos hecho lo mismo. La humanidad ha sido culpable de adivinar o tratar de poner un tiempo o evento en las profecías de Dios en relación con el día en que viven desde que las profecías se hicieron públicas. Muchos han probado ecuaciones matemáticas, datos científicos e incluso eventos históricos para explicar la profecía bíblica y la mayoría de ellos han sido inexactos al revelar la interpretación correcta de la profecía bíblica o el momento del fin del mundo. La ÚNICA manera de interpretar la profecía bíblica y de comprenderla correctamente es a partir de la Biblia y únicamente de la Biblia. Los libros de historia, Internet y las noticias locales y mundiales siempre fallarán en revelar la verdad bíblica, especialmente la profecía.

PREGUNTA: ¿A qué apunta la profecía de las setenta semanas de Daniel 9:24-27?

Una clave para entender esta profecía es aplicar la interpretación de "día por un año" como Dios lo hizo con los hijos de Israel. Dios les dijo a los israelitas, recién salidos de la tierra de Egipto, que fueran a Canaán, y Él estaría con ellos y lucharía por ellos. Se negaron a confiar en Él. Después de cuarenta días de espiar la tierra, diez de los doce espías dudaron y causaron que toda la comunidad dudara de Dios (Números 13). Debido a esta duda, por cada día que estaban en la tierra como espías, Dios los hizo servir un año en el desierto: un día por un año según Números 14:34:

> "Conforme al número de los días, de los cuarenta días en que reconocisteis la tierra, llevaréis vuestras iniquidades cuarenta años, un año por cada día; y conoceréis mi castigo."

El principio de día por año se usa al considerar la profecía de tiempo de Daniel 9: 24-27. Si tomamos 70 X 7 obtenemos 490. Cuando se usa el principio de día por año, eso resulta en 490 años. Desde el momento en que comenzó la profecía hasta que se completó, serían cuatrocientos noventa años de historia.

Cuatrocientos noventa años. ¿Te suena familiar el número 490? Cuando decimos "cuatrocientos noventa años", eso debería llevar nuestra atención de regreso a nuestra discusión anterior de Daniel nueve versículos dos al seis. ¿Recuerda la discusión sobre el año sabático? La razón por la que los hijos de Israel estuvieron en cautiverio en Babilonia durante 70 años es porque se habían negado a reconocer 70 de los años sabáticos de Dios. Como hay 7 años en cada semana de años, entonces 7 X 70 = 490 años literales. Los hijos de Israel habían desobedecido a Dios durante 490 años, y ahora, de acuerdo con la profecía de Daniel nueve, Él les está dando otros 490 años de gracia, la misma cantidad de tiempo que los israelitas desobedecieron a Dios con el séptimo año de reposo anual para la tierra. para descansar en los días anteriores a Daniel, para volverse de sus malos caminos.

Todas las profecías del tiempo bíblico tienen dos puntos de interés. Existe el punto inicial del tiempo y el final. Cuando se conoce cualquiera de estos dos puntos de tiempo, entonces se puede realizar el otro. Cuando consideramos las profecías del tiempo bíblico cumplidas en el pasado, podemos ver sus puntos de inicio y final en retrospectiva. Lo mismo ocurre con la profecía de las 70 semanas de Daniel nueve.

Pensemos racionalmente por un momento con respecto a la profecía de las 70 semanas del capítulo nueve de Daniel. Mirándolo en el reverso, desde la perspectiva de Daniel,

¿cuándo comenzó la profecía? Pudo haber pensado que la profecía comenzó dos años después de que el imperio medopersa se apoderara de Babilonia. Pero el tiempo reveló que ese no era el caso. Aparentemente nadie descubrió el verdadero significado de la profecía de las 70 semanas hasta nuestros días. Por lo tanto, la profecía de las 70 semanas realmente solo se entiende en retrospectiva, 20/20.

Así que la profecía de las 70 semanas del capítulo nueve de Daniel se perdió en la historia desde los días de Daniel hasta los nuestros. Las únicas personas, antes de que se hiciera pública la Biblia, que hubieran tropezado con ella habrían sido aquellas personas que tenían acceso a los rollos del templo. E incluso entonces, ¿qué sentido le habría dado? No, esta profecía solo debía ser reconocida como satisfecha al principio de la historia, mucho después de que se hubiera cumplido. Seguramente, si alguna persona, durante esos cinco siglos, antes de Cristo, hubiera tenido interés en esta profecía, habría perdido su importancia durante las generaciones que le siguieron.

Hagamos lo mismo que se aconsejó anteriormente. Usemos la retrospectiva para determinar el cumplimiento de la profecía del tiempo de las setenta semanas del capítulo nueve de Daniel. Hay pistas que se presentan que solo nosotros, en nuestros días, podemos identificar clara y positivamente en esta profecía. Primero, releamos la profecía antes de enumerar las pistas: Daniel 9:24-27:

> "Setenta semanas están determinadas sobre tu pueblo y sobre tu santa ciudad, para acabar la prevaricación, y concluir el pecado, y expiar la iniquidad; y para traer la justicia de los siglos, y sellar la visión y la profecía, y ungir al Santo de

los santos. Sepas pues y entiendas, que desde la salida de la palabra para restaurar y edificar á Jerusalem hasta el Mesías Príncipe, habrá siete semanas, y sesenta y dos semanas; tornaráse á edificar la plaza y el muro en tiempos angustiosos. Y después de las sesenta y dos semanas se quitará la vida al Mesías, y no por sí: y el pueblo de un príncipe que ha de venir, destruirá á la ciudad y el santuario; con inundación será el fin de ella, y hasta el fin de la guerra será talada con asolamientos. Y en otra semana confirmará el pacto á muchos, y á la mitad de la semana hará cesar el sacrificio y la ofrenda: después con la muchedumbre de las abominaciones será el desolar, y esto hasta una entera consumación; y derramaráse la ya determinada sobre el pueblo asolado."

Pistas para resolver el comienzo de la profecía de las setenta semanas, nosotros:

1. Necesita un momento en el que se emitió un decreto para reconstruir y restaurar Jerusalén (versículo 25).
2. Necesita un tiempo en el que el "santísimo" sea ungido (versículo 24).
3. Necesita un tiempo para la llegada del Mesías, el Príncipe (versículo 25).
4. Necesita un tiempo en el que el Mesías sea "cortado" o asesinado (versículo 26).

Empecemos con los números dos y tres anteriores. ¿Cuándo fue ungido el "santísimo" o cuándo llegó el Mesías, el Príncipe? Según Marcos 1: 9-11 Jesús fue ungido por el Padre y el Espíritu Santo el día de Su bautismo.

"Y aconteció en aquellos días, que Jesús vino de Nazaret de Galilea, y fué bautizado por Juan en el Jordán. Y luego, subiendo del agua, vió abrirse los cielos, y al Espíritu como paloma, que descendía sobre él. Y hubo una voz de los cielos que decía: Tú eres mi Hijo amado; en ti tomo contentamiento."

Históricamente, Jesús fue bautizado por Juan en el 27 d.C. Entonces tenemos la respuesta a los números 2 y 3 anteriores. Después de Su bautismo, Jesús enseñó durante 3 años y medio y luego murió llevándonos a 31 ADE. Así que ahora tenemos la respuesta al número 4. Entonces, ¿qué hacemos con estos números?

Note la profecía. Decía en Daniel 9 los versículos 25 y 26:

"Sepas pues y entiendas, que desde la salida de la palabra para restaurar y edificar á Jerusalem hasta el Mesías Príncipe, habrá siete semanas, y sesenta y dos semanas; tornaráse á edificar la plaza y el muro en tiempos angustiosos. Y después de las sesenta y dos semanas se quitará la vida al Mesías, y no por sí: y el pueblo de un príncipe que ha de venir, destruirá á la ciudad y el santuario; con inundación será el fin de ella, y hasta el fin de la guerra será talada con asolamientos."

Una sola puntuación de semanas equivale a 20 semanas. Setenta semanas son 60 semanas. Siete semanas más sesenta semanas más 2 semanas son 69 semanas. Sesenta y nueve semanas multiplicadas por 7 días a la semana equivale a 483 días o 483 días de años, o 483 años. Entonces, algo tuvo que suceder 483 años antes de que el Mesías fuera bautizado

para comenzar la profecía en el frente de la visión de Daniel.
Hagamos los cálculos: 27 ADE

        -483 años

        457 a. C.

Entonces, ¿qué sucedió en el 457 a. C.? Para esta respuesta, consideremos otra pista en la profecía misma: Note el versículo 25 nuevamente:

> "Sepas pues y entiendas, que desde la salida de la palabra para restaurar y edificar á Jerusalem hasta el Mesías Príncipe, habrá siete semanas, y sesenta y dos semanas; tornaráse á edificar la plaza y el muro en tiempos angustiosos."

¿En qué parte de la Biblia habla del mandamiento de restaurar y reconstruir Jerusalén? Note que en el libro de Esdras hay tres decretos diferentes dados en las Escrituras para que los hijos de Israel regresen a Jerusalén desde Babilonia.

1. 537 o 538 a. EC por el rey Ciro que se encuentra en Esdras 1: 2-4.
2. 519 AEC por Darío I Hystaspes (No Darío el Medo) Esdras 6: 1-12.
3. 457 AEC por Artajerjes I en Esdras 7: 11-26.

Estos tres reyes se mencionan en Esdras 6:14:

> "Y los ancianos de los Judíos edificaban y prosperaban, conforme á la profecía de Haggeo profeta, y de Zacarías hijo de Iddo. Edificaron pues, y acabaron, por el mandamiento del Dios de Israel, y por el mandamiento de Ciro, y de Darío, y de Artajerjes rey de Persia."

Tenemos dos formas de señalar cuándo comenzó la profecía de las 70 semanas. (1) Fíjense en nuestras matemáticas, considerando el bautismo de Jesús y restando 483 años, llegamos al 457 a. C. para que comenzara la profecía de las 70 semanas de Daniel. (2) También en la Biblia y los registros históricos, nos damos cuenta de que Artajerjes emitió un decreto para que los hijos de Israel regresaran a reconstruir Jerusalén en el 457 a. C. Pero, ¿hay otra forma de determinar si la fecha del 457 a. C. es precisa? ¡Sí hay!

Observe cómo las primeras 69 semanas se dividen en dos secciones de tiempo diferentes en Daniel 9 el versículo 25.

> *"Sepas pues y entiendas, que desde la salida de la palabra para restaurar y edificar á Jerusalem hasta el Mesías Príncipe, habrá siete semanas, y sesenta y dos semanas; tornaráse á edificar la plaza y el muro en tiempos angustiosos."*

¿Por qué Dios dividió las setenta semanas en 7 semanas, 62 semanas y finalmente 1 semana en el versículo 27?

Es porque nuestro Dios es muy inteligente. La razón por la que Dios comenzó esta profecía de tiempo con un período de tiempo de siete semanas es porque quería dar una pista adicional que solo alguien familiarizado con Sus años de reposo sabático podría entender verdaderamente.

Anteriormente discutimos el año de reposo que Dios estableció en Levítico 25: 1-7. Pero eso no es todo lo que Dios estableció en Levítico 25. También estableció el Calendario del Jubileo que revela el momento del muy importante año del Jubileo para Su pueblo.

Funciona así: Cada séptimo año es un año de reposo para la tierra y, por lo tanto, también para la gente. Entonces Dios dijo que después de siete años de reposo, siete años multiplicado por siete años de reposo, la tierra y el pueblo deben tener un descanso especial durante el siguiente año de Jubileo. El año de Jubileo sería el próximo año después del séptimo año sabático, que es el año 49. Así que el quincuagésimo año sería un año de jubileo. Tenga en cuenta que el 50º año del Jubileo del ciclo anterior del Calendario Jubilar también sería el primer año del próximo calendario Jubilar o ciclo del Jubileo. Se vería así en un calendario:

Siete años sabáticos seguidos

El año 50 es el próximo primer año
... El año del Jubileo !!!!

PREGUNTA: ¿Por qué es importante comprender el diseño del Calendario Jubilar?

RESPUESTA: Es importante entender cómo se calcula el año del Jubileo debido a la enorme pista importante que Dios dio cuando comenzaría la profecía de las 70 semanas de Daniel nueve. La razón por la que Dios dividió las sesenta y nueve semanas en siete semanas y sesenta y dos semanas, para llegar al momento en que el Mesías fue bautizado o ungido, fue porque Él quería que Su gente de la tierra entendiera que el decreto para comenzar la profecía de las 70 semanas debe decretarse en un año jubilar. De los tres decretos o mandatos diferentes para "restaurar y reconstruir Jerusalén" en el libro de Esdras, el único que se da en un año de Jubileo es la fecha del 457 a. C. (Por cierto, el próximo año jubilar para nosotros es el año 2043).

Entonces: en pocas palabras. La profecía de las setenta semanas comenzó en un año de Jubileo en el 457 a. C. El Mesías fue bautizado sesenta y nueve semanas después, en el 27 a. EC. Pero la profecía no se detiene ahí. También dice en los versículos 26 y 27:

> ""Y después de las sesenta y dos semanas se quitará la vida al Mesías, y no por sí… Y en otra semana confirmará el pacto á muchos, y á la mitad de la semana hará cesar el sacrificio y la ofrenda."

Jesús fue bautizado en el 27 d.C., al comienzo de la semana 70. Murió tres años y medio después, a mediados de la septuagésima semana, a los 31 d.C. Tres años y medio después, en el año 34 d.C., Steven fue apedreado (Hechos 6, 7) como mártir, asesinado por los líderes religiosos judíos, porque creía en Jesús como el Mesías. Por lo tanto, la profecía de las 70 semanas se completó en 34 ADE. 457 a. C. a 34 d. C. implica la profecía completa de las setenta semanas.

¿Qué significa cuando dice el versículo 27?

> "y á la mitad de la semana hará cesar el sacrificio y la ofrenda."

Cuando Jesús murió a la mitad de la semana 70, cumplió con los requisitos de la ley ceremonial y los sábados ceremoniales que se encuentran en Levítico 23 para un sacrificio de sangre. Jesús es el "Cordero de Dios que quita los pecados del mundo" (Juan 1:29). Los sábados ceremoniales de Levítico 23 podrían caer en cualquier día de la semana, incluido el séptimo.

Hebreos 9:22 dice:

> "Y casi todo es purificado según la ley con sangre; y sin derramamiento de sangre no se hace remisión."

La sangre de Jesús muriendo en la cruz es donde el tipo se encuentra con el antitipo. Todas las ceremonias del Antiguo Testamento y los sábados festivos que apuntaban al Mesías, que exigían un sacrificio de sangre, se cumplieron en Cristo Jesús. Dijo en Mateo 5:17:

> "No penséis que he venido para abrogar la ley ó los profetas: no he venido para abrogar, sino á cumplir."

Note lo que Pablo dice acerca de la ley ceremonial en Colosenses 2:6-17:

> "Por tanto, de la manera que habéis recibido al Señor Jesucristo, andad en él: Arraigados y sobreedificados en él, y confirmados en la fe, así como habéis aprendido, creciendo en ella con hacimiento de gracias. Mirad que ninguno os engañe por filosofías y vanas sustilezas, según las tradiciones de los hombres, conforme á los elementos del mundo, y no según Cristo: Porque en él habita toda la plenitud de la divinidad

corporalmente: Y en él estáis cumplidos, el cual es la cabeza de todo principado y potestad: En el cual también sois circuncidados de circuncisión no hecha con manos, con el despojamiento del cuerpo de los pecados de la carne, en la circuncisión de Cristo; Sepultados juntamente con él en la bautismo, en el cual también resucitasteis con él, por la fe de la operación de Dios que le levantó de los muertos. Y á vosotros, estando muertos en pecados y en la incircuncisión de vuestra carne, os vivificó juntamente con él, perdonándoos todos los pecados, Rayendo la cédula de los ritos que nos era contraria, que era contra nosotros, quitándola de en medio y enclavándola en la cruz; Y despojando los principados y las potestades, sacólos á la vergüenza en público, triunfando de ellos en sí mismo. Por tanto, nadie os juzgue en comida, ó en bebida, ó en parte de día de fiesta, ó de nueva luna, ó de sábados: Lo cual es la sombra de lo por venir; mas el cuerpo es de Cristo."

Debo aconsejarle en este punto. No confunda el séptimo día sábado de la semana con los sábados ceremoniales de Levítico 23. El séptimo día sábado está entretejido en el tejido de los Diez Mandamientos, que son una expresión del carácter de Dios, que Él estableció en la creación, para todos los pueblos, en todas partes, para siempre. El cuarto mandamiento nunca se puede eliminar o sacar del Decálogo ni se puede cambiar su tiempo. El sábado del séptimo día, desde el atardecer del viernes hasta el atardecer del sábado, permanece para siempre, perpetua o continuamente, y será honrado por toda la eternidad incluso después de que este mundo sea destruido y renovado:

"Porque como los cielos nuevos y la nueva tierra, que yo hago, permanecen delante de mí, dice Jehová, así permanecerá vuestra simiente y vuestro nombre. Y será que de mes en mes, y de sábado en sábado, vendrá toda carne á adorar delante de mí, dijo Jehová." Isaías 66:22,23.

El sábado del séptimo día es honrado por "los pueblos de la tierra", Su reino, por la misma razón que los otros nueve mandamientos son honrados, respetados y guardados. Las personas que aceptan a Jesucristo como su Creador, Redentor y Sustentador guardan los Diez Mandamientos porque aman al Señor. Note lo que Jesús dice en Juan 14:15 y en Lucas 6:46:

"Si me amáis, guardad mis mandamientos."

"¿Por qué me llamáis, Señor, Señor, y no hacéis lo que digo?"

El pueblo de Dios, que le obedece y guarda sus Diez Mandamientos, no lo hace para ser salvo, porque nadie se salva por obedecer la ley (Gálatas 3:11,12), sino que guarda los Diez Mandamientos porque es salvo y quieren obedecer a Dios en todas las cosas.

"Mas por cuanto por la ley ninguno se justifica para con Dios, queda manifiesto: Que el justo por la fe vivirá. La ley también no es de la fe; sino, El hombre que los hiciere, vivirá en ellos."

Algunas personas afirman que guardar el sábado del séptimo día es legalismo. Si honrar el cuarto mandamiento es legalismo, ¿cómo se llama honrar los otros nueve mandamientos?

Además... Aunque los sábados ceremoniales se cumplieron durante y después de la muerte y resurrección de Jesús, no está mal reconocerlos. Como dice Paul, no nos corresponde a nosotros juzgar a una persona si todavía desea celebrarla o no. Creo que todos los estudiantes de la Biblia dedicados a Dios deben darse cuenta íntimamente de la belleza y la intención de cada uno de los sábados ceremoniales y lo que representan. Algunos tienen la impresión de que todavía tienen un contexto futuro hacia el fin de este mundo. ¿Y usted?

PERO HAY MÁS ...

¿Cuál fue la intención o la razón de la profecía de las setenta semanas?

¿Qué quería Dios que su pueblo, los hijos de Israel, hiciera antes del final de la profecía de las setenta semanas de los 490 años? Note el versículo 24:

> "Setenta semanas están determinadas sobre tu pueblo y sobre tu santa ciudad, para acabar la prevaricación, y concluir el pecado, y expiar la iniquidad; y para traer la justicia de los siglos, y sellar la visión y la profecía, y ungir al Santo de los santos."

¿Cuáles son las siete cosas que Dios quería que su pueblo lograra?

La profecía de las setenta semanas y los 490 años era para que el pueblo de Dios, los israelitas, hiciera siete cosas:

1. Termina la transgression
2. Acaba con los pecados
3. Haz la reconciliación por la iniquidad
4. Trae justicia eterna.
5. Selle la vision

6. Selle la profecía
7. Unge al Santísimo.

¿Qué significan esas siete cosas anteriores? Vamos a reescribirlos para resaltar su significado:

1. Reconozca su error y rebelión contra Dios y arrepiéntase.
2. Deje de pecar y planee pecar contra Dios.
3. Devolver o devolver todo lo que puedan para reconciliarse por su desobediencia.
4. Empiece a vivir una vida de rectitud o de hacer el bien.
5. Comprender la visión de Daniel.
6. Reconocer la importancia y los aspectos de la profecía.
7. Dé la bienvenida al Mesías cuando venga por primera vez, como un bebé.

PERO AÚN HAY MAS...

La profecía de Daniel 9: 24-27 no termina con la lapidación de Esteban. Note todos los versículos 26 y 27:

> "Y después de las sesenta y dos semanas se quitará la vida al Mesías, y no por sí: y el pueblo de un príncipe que ha de venir, destruirá á la ciudad y el santuario; con inundación será el fin de ella, y hasta el fin de la guerra será talada con asolamientos. Y en otra semana confirmará el pacto á muchos, y á la mitad de la semana hará cesar el sacrificio y la ofrenda: después con la muchedumbre de las abominaciones será el desolar, y esto hasta una entera consumación; y derramaráse la ya determinada sobre el pueblo asolado."

Para captar más información de esta importante visión, vamos a desglosarla más:

1. Después de 69 semanas, el Mesías moriría (sería cortado) por toda la humanidad.
2. Vendría la gente del príncipe.
3. Destruirían la ciudad y el santuario.
4. El final vendría como una inundación destructiva.
5. Hacia el fin de los tiempos se determinarían las desolaciones y las guerras.
6. El pacto se confirmaría con muchos durante una semana.
7. A mediados de esa semana cesarían los sacrificios y las oblaciones.
8. Se establecería una abominación desoladora.
9. La abominación desoladora duraría hasta el fin de los tiempos.
10. Esa abominación precederá al derramamiento de la ira de Dios sobre la humanidad.

Observe la cronología de los eventos que tienen lugar para que podamos captarlos y comprenderlos.

1. Después de 69 semanas, el Mesías moriría por toda la humanidad:	31 ADE
2. Vendría la gente del príncipe.	70 ADE
3. Destruirían la ciudad y el santuario.	70 ADE
4. El final vendría como una inundación destructiva.	Ahora y en el futuro
5. Hacia el final se determinan las desolaciones y las guerras.	Ahora y futuro
6. El pacto se confirmaría por una semana.	Nuestro futuro

7. A mitad de semana cesarían los sacrificios y las oblaciones. Nuestro futuro

8. Habría una abominación desoladora. Nuestro futuro

9. La abominación desoladora duraría hasta el final. Nuestro futuro

10. La ira de Dios se derramaría sobre la humanidad (Apocalipsis 16). Futuro

Explicación adicional de lo anterior señalando la cronología perfecta de eventos:

1. El Mesías murió por toda la humanidad en el año 31 DC como fue profetizado. Después:
2. En el año 70 d.C. el ejército romano, en este caso el príncipe, atacó Jerusalén y derribó todos sus muros.
3. El ejército romano también derribó el templo de Jerusalén "sin dejar piedra sobre piedra", como Jesús predijo en Mateo 24: 2.
4. Ahora vivimos en los tiempos del número 4.
5. Ahora vivimos en los tiempos del número 5.
6. Viene una tribulación de una semana, o siete años, que Jesús predijo en Mateo 24:21 durante la cual el pacto será confirmado.
7. En medio de la próxima tribulación de siete años, 1260 días después de que comience, los servicios de la iglesia y la enseñanza de la Biblia se suspenderán en todo el mundo.
8. 1290 días después de que comience la tribulación de siete años, se establecerá o establecerá un día falso de adoración como se predice en Daniel 12:11.
9. La abominación desoladora permanecerá hasta que se complete el tiempo del fin.

10. La ira de Dios se derramará sobre aquellas personas que apoyan la abominación desoladora, que se niegan a obedecerle, como se revela en Apocalipsis 16.

PERO HAY MUCHO MÁS ...

Desde el momento en que Daniel tuvo la visión de Daniel nueve, hasta el decreto del rey Artajerjes en 457 a. EC de "reconstruir y restaurar Jerusalén", ya habían pasado unos 80 años. Daniel y toda la gente de su época habían muerto hacía mucho tiempo. Luego agregue los 490 años reales de la profecía, que totalizan 537 años desde que la profecía se puso por escrito en los libros. Durante ese tiempo, lo más probable es que se hubiera abandonado el descubrimiento de la interpretación de la profecía. Nadie estaba al tanto de la profecía ni de los requisitos que Dios había establecido para su pueblo cuando la profecía estaba viva y se estaba cumpliendo. Nadie podría haber sabido o habría sabido esperar al Mesías en el 27 d.C. de esta profecía.

Entonces, ¿por qué Dios le dio la visión de 70 semanas a Daniel?

Nuestro Padre Celestial entendió que Su visión y la interpretación de la visión no serían entendidas ni conocidas hasta después de que se cumpliera la profecía. También se dio cuenta de que el 66 libro Santa Biblia, la Palabra de Dios, que contiene Daniel nueve, no se imprimiría para que todo el mundo lo viera hasta alrededor de 1800 ADE cuando se estableció la Sociedad Bíblica Estadounidense. Dios le dio la profecía de las setenta semanas a Daniel, no para que los hijos de Israel la entendieran, sino para que nosotros, la generación del último día de Dios, la entendiéramos.

Los israelitas no podrían haber entendido esta profecía o descifrarla. No tenían concepto de BCE y ADE. Entonces ... ¿Cómo nos impacta esa profecía? Hagamos algunas matemáticas.

En la profecía bíblica hay 24 horas en un día, 30 días por mes y 360 días por año, como fue desarrollado por Dios y reconocido por los babilonios y adaptado por el mundo. Así que siga con atención:

70 semanas X 7 días a la semana, equivale a 490 semanas de años.

490 años X 360 días por año, equivale a 176,400 días literales.

176,400 días literales divididos por 70, equivale a 2,520 días literales.

2.520 días literales divididos por 360 días por año, equivale a 7 años.

7 años en Daniel 9:27 es una semana profética, como lo apoya Daniel 9:24,27.

"Y en otra semana confirmará el pacto á muchos, y á la mitad de la semana hará cesar el sacrificio y la ofrenda." Daniel 9:27

A veces, la Biblia usa una aplicación dual en la profecía bíblica, lo que significa que una sola profecía se puede aplicar en dos o más lugares, situaciones o períodos de tiempo diferentes. Este es el caso del texto anterior.

Esta profecía de la "una semana" que se encuentra en Daniel 9:27:

1. Aplicado a la semana 70 entre el 27 ADE y el 34 ADE como discutimos anteriormente.
2. Dijo el día exacto en que Jesús moriría en el año 31 d.C., que era el miércoles, y
3. Se aplica al tiempo del fin, nuestro futuro cercano.
4. Dos veces esta profecía revela una tribulación de 7 años venidera.

Dios ha establecido un período de tribulación de una semana o siete años antes de que Él regrese por segunda vez. Note lo siguiente de Mateo 24:

"Entonces os entregarán para ser afligidos, y os matarán; y seréis aborrecidos de todas las gentes por causa de mi nombre. Y muchos entonces serán escandalizados; y se entregarán unos á otros, y unos á otros se aborrecerán. Y muchos falsos profetas se levantarán y engañarán á muchos. Y por haberse multiplicado la maldad, la caridad de muchos se resfriará. Mas el que perseverare hasta el fin, éste será salvo." Versos 9-13.

"Porque habrá entonces grande aflicción, cual no fué desde el principio del mundo hasta ahora, ni será." Verso 21.

"Empero del día y hora nadie sabe, ni aun los ángeles de los cielos, sino mi Padre solo. Mas como los días de Noé, así será la venida del Hijo del hombre. Porque como en los días antes del diluvio estaban comiendo y bebiendo, casándose y dando en casamiento, hasta el día que Noé entró en el arca, Y no conocieron hasta que vino el diluvio y llevó á todos, así será también la venida del Hijo del hombre." Versos 36-39.

¿Qué quiso decir Jesús cuando dijo en Mateo 9:37?

"Mas como los días de Noé, así será la venida del Hijo del hombre"

La respuesta a esa pregunta se puede descubrir si observamos cuidadosamente qué más dijo Jesús antes de ir al capítulo siete de Génesis para comprender más acerca de "los días de Noé". Considere el texto nuevamente, pero esta vez con ciertas palabras resaltadas.

"Empero del **día** y hora nadie sabe, ni aun los ángeles de los cielos, sino mi Padre solo. Mas como los **días** de Noé, así será la venida del Hijo del hombre. Porque como en los **días** antes del diluvio estaban comiendo y bebiendo, casándose y dando en casamiento, hasta el **día** que Noé entró en el arca, Y no conocieron hasta que vino el diluvio y llevó á todos, así será también la venida del Hijo del hombre." Versos 36-39.

Note que Jesús enfatiza los días de Noé desde el momento en que entró en el Arca hasta el momento en que realmente comenzó el diluvio.

Observe cuántas veces se usa la palabra día o días en el versículo de Mateo 24. Jesús se repite a sí mismo con un propósito específico.

¿Qué significa cuando Dios se repite en la Biblia?

José le dijo al Faraón que cuando Dios se repite, eso significa prestar mucha atención y la profecía seguramente se llevará a cabo, tal como él dijo que sucedería. Note Génesis 41:32:

> "Y el suceder el sueño á Faraón dos veces, significa que la cosa es firme de parte de Dios, y que Dios se apresura á hacerla."

También mire cuidadosamente lo que Jesús está diciendo en el texto anterior. Él está hablando de la diferencia de tiempo desde que Noé **entró** en el Arca **hasta** que llegaron las aguas del diluvio. ¿Cómo descubrimos cuántos **días** pasaron desde que Noé **entró** en el arca **hasta** que comenzó la lluvia que trajo el diluvio? Note lo siguiente, en mis palabras, de Génesis 7: 1, 4, 5, 10.

> "Entren en el arca, usted y toda su familia…. Dentro de **siete días** enviaré lluvia sobre la tierra durante cuarenta días y cuarenta noches, y borraré de la faz de la tierra todo ser viviente que he creado…. Y Noé hizo todo lo que el SEÑOR le mandó ... Y después de los **siete días**, las aguas del diluvio cayeron sobre la tierra ".

Así como Noé y su familia estuvieron a salvo en el Arca durante siete días antes de la destrucción de toda la humanidad, Dios ha planeado una tribulación de siete años con el pueblo de Su último día a salvo bajo Su cuidado durante ese tiempo. Al pensar en la semana de Daniel 9:27, debemos recordar que un día profético en la profecía bíblica equivale a un año literal. Jesús nos está diciendo en Mateo 24 que vendrá un tiempo de tribulación que durará siete años antes de que regrese para Su segunda venida. **

Así como Jesús alimentó a los israelitas con maná en el desierto (Éxodo 16:35) y llevó a Elías al arroyo burbujeante, alimentándolo por medio de los cuervos (1 reyes 17: 1-6), Él velará por Sus siervos elegidos durante este período. tiempo para satisfacer sus necesidades también. Un período de siete años para la ira de Dios (Daniel 11:36; Romanos 1:18; Apocalipsis 15:17) contra el pecado y la desobediencia no debería sorprendernos. Dios a menudo ha dividido los tiempos en grupos de siete años.

La Biblia enumera numerosas veces que Dios usó un período de tiempo de siete años:

1. Siete años de abundancia en los días de José: Génesis 41.
2. Siete años de hambre en los días de José: Génesis 41.
3. Siete años de locura con el rey Nabucodonosor: Daniel 4.
4. Jacob sirvió durante siete años por cada una de sus dos esposas: Génesis 29.
5. Hubo una hambruna de siete años en los días de Eliseo: 2 Reyes 8: 1.
6. La mujer viuda regresó a su casa después de siete años: 2 Reyes 8: 1-6.
7. Joás tenía siete años cuando comenzó a reinar: 2 Reyes 11:21.
8. Salomón tardó siete años en construir el templo de Dios: 1 Reyes 6:38.
9. Un hebreo podría ser esclavo de un hebreo sólo durante siete años: Jeremías 34:14.
10. Los israelitas debían quemar las armas de sus enemigos durante siete años: Ezequiel 39: 9.
11. Ana la profetisa estuvo casada durante siete años: Lucas 2:36.

12. Jesús ha prometido una tribulación de siete años antes de que venga por segunda vez.

La profecía de las 70 semanas revela dos veces que habrá una tribulación de siete años o 2.520 días antes de la segunda venida de Jesús. ¿Para qué es ese período de tiempo? La tribulación de siete años tiene exactamente las mismas metas para nosotros que se enumeran para Israel durante sus 490 años.

** Lea el libro electrónico o el libro impreso "Los 3 advenimientos visibles de Jesús" de Earl B. Schrock de Xlibris.com, Amazon, Barnes and Nobles, etc.

La profecía de las setenta semanas y los 490 años era para que el pueblo de Dios, los israelitas, hicieran siete (7) cosas. Esas mismas metas también se establecen para los siervos de Dios de los últimos días:

Antes y durante la tribulación de siete años, Dios quiere que su "gente de la tierra":

1. Termina la transgression
2. Acaba con los pecados
3. Haz la reconciliación por la iniquidad
4. Trae justicia eterna.
5. Selle la vision
6. Selle la profecía
7. Unge al Santísimo.

¿Qué significan esas siete cosas anteriores en nuestra lengua vernácula? Vamos a reescribirlos para resaltar su significado:

1. Reconoce nuestros errores y nuestra rebelión contra Dios y arrepiéntete.

2. Deje de pecar y desobedecer a Dios.
3. Devolución o devolución de todo lo que podamos para reconciliarnos por nuestra desobediencia.
4. Empiece a vivir una vida de rectitud o de hacer el bien.
5. Completar y comprender la visión de Daniel.
6. Reconozca la importancia y los aspectos de la profecía bíblica.
7. Dé la bienvenida al Mesías cuando venga por segunda vez como Redentor.

Los israelitas no entendieron ni calcularon la profecía de las setenta semanas, a pesar de que Dios cumplió esa profecía tal como dijo que lo haría y justo a tiempo. Pero esa profecía de tiempo es más importante para nosotros de lo que era aplicable a ellos. Es más importante para nosotros porque nos ayuda a comprender cuán maravilloso y puntual es Dios, además, dado que lo sabemos, podemos entenderlo y podemos aplicarlo a nuestra situación aquí y ahora. La decisión de servir a Dios, como Él dicta, o de desobedecerlo y hacer nuestras propias cosas, es nuestra. Como dijo Joshua:

> "Y si mal os parece servir á Jehová, escogeos hoy á quién sirváis; si á los dioses á quienes siervieron vuestros padres, cuando estuvieron de esotra parte del río, ó á los dioses de los Amorrheos en cuya tierra habitáis: que yo y mi casa serviremos á Jehová. Josué 24:15

Ahora es el momento para que todos los hijos de Dios, Su "montaña" moderna, Sus siervos, Sus elegidos, tomen una decisión determinada de entregarlo todo a Él en cada pensamiento, palabra y acción.

Aquellos que no adapten su estilo de vida ahora, voluntariamente, para ser siervos obedientes de Dios, serán forzados a hacerlo bajo coacción, durante los futuros 2.520 días o siete años de tribulación.

Si aún no lo ha hecho, ¿hoy, ahora mismo, entregará su vida a Jesús y vivir la vida que Dios el Padre ha dispuesto para usted, a través del poder del Espíritu Santo que mora en usted?

Vea el video de YouTube **DANIEL CAPÍTULO NUEVE EN ESPAÑOL** por Earl Schrock

DANIEL CAPÍTULO NUEVE (RVR)

1 EN el año primero de Darío hijo de Assuero, de la nación de los Medos, el cual fué puesto por rey sobre el reino de los Caldeos; 2 En el año primero de su reinado, yo Daniel miré atentamente en los libros el número de los años, del cual habló Jehová al profeta Jeremías, que había de concluir la asolación de Jerusalem en setenta años. 3 Y volví mi rostro al Señor Dios, buscándole en oración y ruego, en ayuno, y cilicio, y ceniza. 4 Y oré á Jehová mi Dios, y confesé, y dije: Ahora Señor, Dios grande, digno de ser temido, que guardas el pacto y la misericordia con los que te aman y guardan tus mandamientos; 5 Hemos pecado, hemos hecho iniquidad, hemos obrado impíamente, y hemos sido rebeldes, y nos hemos apartado de tus mandamientos y de tus juicios. 6 No hemos obedecido á tus siervos los profetas, que en tu nombre hablaron á nuestros reyes, y á nuestros príncipes, á nuestros padres, y á todo el pueblo de la tierra. 7 Tuya es, Señor, la justicia, y nuestra la confusión de rostro, como en el día de hoy á todo hombre de Judá, y á los moradores de Jerusalem, y á todo Israel, á los de cerca y á los de lejos, en todas las tierras á donde los has echado á causa de su rebelión con que contra ti se rebelaron. 8 Oh Jehová, nuestra es la confusión de rostro, de nuestros reyes, de nuestros príncipes, y de nuestros

padres; porque contra ti pecamos. 9 De Jehová nuestro Dios es el tener misericordia, y el perdonar, aunque contra él nos hemos rebelado; 10 Y no obedecimos á la voz de Jehová nuestro Dios, para andar en sus leyes, las cuales puso él delante de nosotros por mano de sus siervos los profetas. 11 Y todo Israel traspasó tu ley apartándose para no oir tu voz: por lo cual ha fluído sobre nosotros la maldición, y el juramento que está escrito en la ley de Moisés, siervo de Dios; porque contra él pecamos. 12 Y él ha verificado su palabra que habló sobre nosotros, y sobre nuestros jueces que nos gobernaron, trayendo sobre nosotros tan grande mal; que nunca fué hecho debajo del cielo como el que fué hecho en Jerusalem. 13 Según está escrito en la ley de Moisés, todo aqueste mal vino sobre nosotros: y no hemos rogado á la faz de Jehová nuestro Dios, para convertirnos de nuestras maldades, y entender tu verdad. 14 Veló por tanto Jehová sobre el mal, y trájolo sobre nosotros; porque justo es Jehová nuestro Dios en todas sus obras que hizo, porque no obedecimos á su voz. 15 Ahora pues, Señor Dios nuestro, que sacaste tu pueblo de la tierra de Egipto con mano poderosa, y te hiciste nombre cual en este día; hemos pecado, impíamente hemos hecho. 16 Oh Señor, según todas tus justicias, apártese ahora tu ira y tu furor de sobre tu ciudad Jerusalem, tu santo monte: porque á causa de nuestros pecados, y por la maldad de nuestros padres, Jerusalem y tu pueblo dados son en oprobio á todos en derredor nuestro. 17 Ahora pues, Dios nuestro, oye la oración de tu siervo, y sus ruegos, y haz que tu rostro resplandezca sobre tu santuario asolado, por amor del Señor. 18 Inclina, oh Dios mío, tu oído, y oye; abre tus ojos, y mira nuestros asolamientos, y la ciudad sobre la cual es llamado tu nombre: porque no derramamos nuestros ruegos ante tu acatamiento confiados en nuestras justicias, sino en tus muchas miseraciones. 19 Oye, Señor; oh Señor, perdona; presta oído, Señor, y haz; no pongas dilación, por amor de ti mismo, Dios mío: porque tu nombre es llamado sobre tu ciudad y sobre tu pueblo. 20 Aun estaba hablando, y orando, y confesando mi pecado y el pecado de mi pueblo Israel, y derramaba mi ruego delante de Jehová mi Dios por el monte santo de mi Dios; 21 Aun estaba hablando en oración, y aquel varón Gabriel, al cual había visto en visión al principio, volando con presteza, me tocó como á la hora del sacrificio de la tarde. 22 É hízome entender, y habló conmigo, y dijo: Daniel, ahora he salido para hacerte entender la declaración. 23 Al principio de tus ruegos salió la palabra, y yo he venido para enseñártela, porque tú eres varón de deseos. Entiende pues la palabra, y entiende la visión. 24 Setenta semanas están determinadas sobre tu pueblo y sobre tu santa ciudad, para acabar la prevaricación, y concluir el pecado, y expiar la iniquidad; y para traer la justicia de los siglos, y sellar la visión y la profecía, y ungir al Santo de los santos. 25 Sepas pues y entiendas, que desde la salida de la palabra para restaurar y edificar á Jerusalem hasta el Mesías Príncipe, habrá siete semanas, y sesenta y dos semanas; tornaráse á edificar la plaza y el muro en tiempos angustiosos. 26 Y después de las sesenta y dos semanas se quitará la vida al Mesías, y no por sí: y el pueblo de un príncipe que ha de venir, destruirá á la ciudad y el santuario; con inundación será el fin de ella, y hasta el fin de la guerra será talada con asolamientos. 27 Y en otra semana confirmará el pacto á muchos, y á la mitad de la semana hará cesar el sacrificio y la ofrenda: después con la muchedumbre de las abominaciones será el desolar, y esto hasta una entera consumación; y derramaráse la ya determinada sobre el pueblo asolado.

DANIEL CAPITULO DIEZ

"ESTO también sepas, que en los postreros días vendrán tiempos peligrosos: Que habrá hombres amadores de sí mismos, avaros, vanagloriosos, soberbios, detractores, desobedientes á los padres, ingratos, sin santidad, Sin afecto, desleales, calumniadores, destemplados, crueles, aborrecedores de lo bueno, Traidores, arrebatados, hinchados, amadores de los deleites más que de Dios; Teniendo apariencia de piedad, mas habiendo negado la eficacia de ella: y á éstos evita. Porque de éstos son los que se entran por las casas, y llevan cautivas las mujercillas cargadas de pecados, llevadas de diversas concupiscencias; Que siempre aprenden, y nunca pueden acabar de llegar al conocimiento de la verdad. Y de la manera que Jannes y Jambres resistieron á Moisés, así también estos resisten á la verdad; hombres corruptos de entendimiento, réprobos acerca de la fe. Mas no prevalecerán; porque su insensatez será manifiesta á todos, como también lo fué la de aquéllos." 2 Timoteo 3:1-9.

Los últimos tres capítulos de Daniel están unidos como una letra, agregando información a Daniel nueve. Son como tres piezas de rompecabezas diferentes que forman un rompecabezas completo cuando se combinan. El capítulo diez es la introducción a los capítulos once y doce. A partir de esta introducción de estos tres capítulos, es muy importante comprender el momento en que se cumplirá la visión. Note el siguiente énfasis en Daniel diez de los siguientes versículos:

1. Versículo uno: "la cosa era verdad, pero el **tiempo señalado fue largo**"
2. Versículo catorce: "Ahora he venido para hacerte entender lo que sucederá a tu pueblo en los últimos días; porque aún la visión **es para muchos días**".

Todo el libro de Daniel fue escrito con la intención de informar a la última generación que vivirá "**en los últimos días**" en "**el tiempo señalado**". Note otras referencias a la última generación de los capítulos anteriores que hemos discutido:

1. Daniel 2:28: "Pero hay un Dios en el cielo que revela secretos y da a conocer al rey Nabucodonosor lo que sucederá **en los últimos días**".
2. Daniel 2:29: "lo que sucederá **después**".
3. Daniel 2:45: "el gran Dios ha dado a conocer al rey lo **que sucederá después**; y el sueño es cierto, y segura su interpretación".
4. Daniel 8:17: "Entiende, hijo de hombre: porque en **el tiempo del fin será** la visión".
5. Daniel 8:19: "Te haré saber lo que será en el **último fin de la indignación**: porque en el **tiempo señalado** será el fin."
6. Daniel 8:23: "Y en **el postrer tiempo de su reino**, cuando **los transgresores hayan llegado a la plenitud**, se levantará un rey de semblante feroz y entendido en oraciones oscuras.
7. Daniel 8:26: "Por tanto, cierra la visión; porque **será por muchos días** ".
8. Daniel 9: 26,27: "y su **fin será** con un diluvio, y hasta **el fin** de la guerra se determinarán las desolaciones. Y confirmará el pacto con muchos **durante una semana**; y a la mitad de la semana hará cesar el sacrificio y la oblación, y por la propagación de abominaciones la

desolará, hasta **la consumación**, y lo determinado. **será derramado sobre los desolados**."

A través de los siglos, muchos han intentado resolver los misterios y desentrañar los secretos del libro de Daniel a través de eventos históricos, noticias actuales y acciones políticas, pero todos eran propensos al fracaso. La verdad de entender e interpretar todo el libro de Daniel está reservada para la generación que experimentará lo que se le muestra a Daniel; la generación que precede a la tribulación de siete años. La apertura de Daniel ha estado en progresión durante siglos, sin embargo, hay más misterios que se revelan a cada generación sucesiva, incluida esta. No podemos contentarnos con conclusiones pasadas.

Vea el video de YouTube **DANIEL CAPÍTULO DIEZ EN ESPAÑOL** por Earl Schrock

DANIEL CAPÍTULO DIEZ (RVR)

1 EN el tercer año de Ciro rey de Persia, fué revelada palabra á Daniel, cuyo nombre era Beltsasar; y la palabra era verdadera, mas el tiempo fijado era largo: él empero comprendió la palabra, y tuvo inteligencia en la visión. 2 En aquellos días yo Daniel me contristé por espacio de tres semanas. 3 No comí pan delicado, ni entró carne ni vino en mi boca, ni me unté con ungüento, hasta que se cumplieron tres semanas de días. 4 Y á los veinte y cuatro días del mes primero estaba yo á la orilla del gran río Hiddekel; 5 Y alzando mis ojos miré, y he aquí un varón vestido de lienzos, y ceñidos sus lomos de oro de Uphaz: 6 Y su cuerpo era como piedra de Tarsis, y su rostro parecía un relámpago, y sus ojos como antorchas de fuego, y sus brazos y sus pies como de color de metal resplandeciente, y la voz de sus palabras

como la voz de ejército. 7 Y sólo yo, Daniel, vi aquella visión, y no la vieron los hombres que estaban conmigo; sino que cayó sobre ellos un gran temor, y huyeron, y escondiéronse. 8 Quedé pues yo solo, y vi esta gran visión, y no quedó en mí esfuerzo; antes mi fuerza se me trocó en desmayo, sin retener vigor alguno. 9 Empero oí la voz de sus palabras: y oyendo la voz de sus palabras, estaba yo adormecido sobre mi rostro, y mi rostro en tierra. 10 Y, he aquí, una mano me tocó, é hizo que me moviese sobre mis rodillas, y sobre las palmas de mis manos. 11 Y díjome: Daniel, varón de deseos, está atento á las palabras que te hablaré, y levántate sobre tus pies; porque á ti he sido enviado ahora. Y estando hablando conmigo esto, yo estaba temblando. 12 Y díjome: Daniel, no temas: porque desde el primer día que diste tu corazón á entender, y á afligirte en la presencia de tu Dios, fueron oídas tus palabras; y á causa de tus palabras yo soy venido. 13 Mas el príncipe del reino de Persia se puso contra mí veintiún días: y he aquí, Miguel, uno de los principales príncipes, vino para ayudarme, y yo quedé allí con los reyes de Persia. 14 Soy pues venido para hacerte saber lo que ha de venir á tu pueblo en los postreros días; porque la visión es aún para días; 15 Y estando hablando conmigo semejantes palabras, puse mis ojos en tierra, y enmudecí. 16 Mas he aquí, como una semejanza de hijo de hombre tocó mis labios. Entonces abrí mi boca, y hablé, y dije á aquel que estaba delante de mí: Señor mío, con la visión se revolvieron mis dolores sobre mí, y no me quedó fuerza. 17 ¿Cómo pues podrá el siervo de mi señor hablar con este mi señor? porque al instante me faltó la fuerza, y no me ha quedado aliento. 18 Y aquella como semejanza de hombre me tocó otra vez, y me confortó; 19 Y díjome: Varón de deseos, no temas: paz á ti; ten buen ánimo, y aliéntate. Y hablando él conmigo cobré yo vigor, y dije: Hable mi señor, porque me has fortalecido. 20 Y dijo: ¿Sabes por qué he venido á ti? Porque luego tengo de volver para pelear con el príncipe de los Persas; y en saliendo yo, luego viene el príncipe de Grecia. 21 Empero yo te declararé lo que está escrito en la escritura de verdad: y ninguno hay que se esfuerce conmigo en estas cosas, sino Miguel vuestro príncipe.

DANIEL CAPITULO ONCE

"Y HABLO Dios todas estas palabras, diciendo: Yo soy JEHOVA tu Dios, que te saqué de la tierra de Egipto, de casa de siervos. No tendrás dioses ajenos delante de mí." Éxodo 20:1-3

Los primeros cuatro versículos de este capítulo se corresponden claramente con lo que hemos aprendido de los diez capítulos anteriores:

1. El pueblo de Dios, "la tierra", será gobernado por muchas naciones debido a la desobediencia.
2. Esas naciones gobernantes son Babilonia, Medo-Persia y Grecia; más, uno más.
3. El reino griego será gobernado por Alejandro Magno y después de su muerte se dividirá en cuatro reinos diferentes cuya influencia pagana se extenderá a los cuatro puntos cardinales para abarcar todo el planeta.

Después del versículo cuatro, el resto del capítulo once de Daniel se vuelve difícil de entender o interpretar. La información en Daniel 11 desde el versículo cinco en adelante, es vaga y dispersa. Debido a su vaguedad, muchos han etiquetado con éxito su propia interpretación en el capítulo, engañando a muchos que aceptaron su explicación sin cuestionar porque era la única solución o interpretación viable disponible o que se ofreció.

Debemos entender que la Biblia debe interpretarse a sí misma. Los libros de historia, las fuentes de noticias e Internet no son la base para descubrir la interpretación de las profecías bíblicas. Aunque no se explica en este capítulo, en esta página, entenderemos mejor el capítulo once después de considerar los secretos descubiertos en el capítulo doce de Daniel.

Pero no se desanime. Una gran parte del capítulo once de Daniel se revelará cuando terminemos nuestra discusión bíblica sobre el libro de Daniel.

DESGLOSE LOS VERSÍCULOS EN DANIEL CAPÍTULO ONCE:

Con respecto al capítulo once de Daniel, mencionamos anteriormente que los versículos 1-4 proporcionan información sobre los pasados imperios medopersa y griego. Y anteriormente discutimos el poder del cuerno pequeño que viene en los capítulos siete y ocho que Daniel once en los versículos 21-45 menciona nuevamente.

El misterio actual que debe entenderse mejor en Daniel once se encuentra entre los versículos 5-20.

Los versículos 5-15 tratan sobre el Rey del Sur sin nombre y el Rey del Norte.

Luego, en el versículo 16 se introduce un protagonista diferente. Él es el centro de atención desde los versículos 16 al 19, que mencionan "tropezará y caerá, y no será hallado".

El versículo 20 introduce a otro protagonista que surge pero no dura mucho porque "dentro de unos días será destruido, ni en la ira ni en la batalla".

El bosquejo versículo por versículo del capítulo once de Daniel es el siguiente:

Versos 1-4: Los imperios medopersa y griego.

Versos 5-15: El Rey del Sur y el Rey del Norte.

Versos 16-19: Un protagonista que "tropezará y caerá, y no será hallado".

Versículo 20: Otro protagonista diferente de corta duración que "será destruido".

Versos 21-45: Información relacionada con el futuro Little Horn Power.

En este momento, mi conjetura sobre la identidad de los reyes del norte y del sur son:

Rey del Norte: las personas con mentalidad espiritual de todo el mundo.

Rey del Sur: las personas no religiosas del mundo con mentalidad política.

Supongo que en la descripción anterior de estos dos reyes porque en nuestro futuro hay un problema o una catástrofe mundial. Esos problemas podrían estar relacionados con las crisis climáticas globales que se están produciendo actualmente a medida que nuestra atmósfera, masas de agua y masas de tierra aumentan de temperatura. Este cambio climático está provocando muchos problemas mundiales de sequía, hambruna, terremotos, erupciones volcánicas, enormes tormentas devastadoras, grandes incendios forestales destructivos, enfermedades y problemas de salud, así como pandemias médicas en todo el mundo.

Aunque el cambio climático mortal es una opción para el futuro problema global que enfrenta toda la humanidad, puede haber una serie de eventos imprevistos que podrían amenazar la existencia humana y llevar a unir al mundo en un problema común hasta un punto en el que el mundo religioso y el no religioso. El mundo religioso podría estar en desacuerdo el uno con el otro al encontrar una solución viable para prevenir la extinción de la humanidad.

Con el tiempo, el mundo se unirá para intentar reconocer y resolver los problemas que afectan negativamente a todos los hombres, mujeres y niños de este planeta. Las personas con mentalidad política buscarán una respuesta a través de la ciencia o de alguna otra forma. Los religiosos de mentalidad espiritual buscarán una respuesta a través de la intervención del poder de Dios. Cada uno de estos grupos promulgará leyes para forzar un cambio en la forma de vida de las personas en un intento por mejorar las condiciones de vida del mundo entero. Mi conjetura es flexible a medida que ocurren y cambian los eventos mundiales.

En un momento, los de mentalidad política estarán poniendo el listón para los hijos de Dios y cuando eso falle, los de mentalidad espiritual incluirán sus propias reglas y regulaciones, incluso hasta el punto de ir en contra de la Palabra escrita y la voluntad de Dios al forzar la adoración. La gente se verá obligada a ir en contra de su propia conciencia para obedecer la regla de la mayoría. Se establecerán consecuencias para obligar a las personas a ceñirse a la voluntad de la mayoría. Los fieles a la voluntad de Dios quedarán atrapados en medio de estas dos facciones. Las historias de los capítulos tres y seis de Daniel son lecciones prácticas para nosotros y se repetirán. Entonces debemos permanecer fieles.

Vea el video de YouTube **DANIEL CAPÍTULO ONCE EN ESPAÑOL** por Earl Schrock

DANIEL CAPÍTULO ONCE (RVR)

1 Y EN el año primero de Darío el de Media, yo estuve para animarlo y fortalecerlo. 2 Y ahora yo te mostraré la verdad. He aquí que aun habrá tres reyes en Persia, y el cuarto se hará de grandes riquezas más que todos; y fortificándose con sus riquezas, despertará á todos contra el reino de Javán. 3 Levantaráse luego un rey valiente, el cual se enseñoreará sobre gran dominio, y hará su voluntad. 4 Pero cuando estará enseñoreado, será quebrantado su reino, y repartido por los cuatro vientos del cielo; y no á sus descendientes, ni según el señorío con que él se enseñoreó: porque su reino será arrancado, y para otros fuera de aquellos. 5 Y haráse fuerte el rey del mediodía: mas uno de los príncipes de aquél le sobrepujará, y se hará poderoso; su señorío será grande señorío. 6 Y al cabo de años se concertarán, y la hija del rey del mediodía vendrá al rey del norte para hacer los conciertos. Empero ella no podrá retener la fuerza del brazo: ni permanecerá él, ni su brazo; porque será entregada ella, y los que la habían traído, asimismo su hijo, y los que estaban de parte de ella en aquel tiempo. 7 Mas del renuevo de sus raíces se levantará uno sobre su silla, y vendrá con ejército, y entrará en la fortaleza del rey del norte, y hará en ellos á su arbitrio, y predominará. 8 Y aun los dioses de ellos, con sus príncipes, con sus vasos preciosos de plata y de oro, llevará cautivos á Egipto: y por años se mantendrá él contra el rey del norte. 9 Así entrará en el reino el rey del mediodía, y volverá á su tierra. 10 Mas los hijos de aquél se airarán y reunirán multitud de

grandes ejércitos: y vendrá á gran priesa, é inundará, y pasará, y tornará, y llegará con ira hasta su fortaleza. 11 Por lo cual se enfurecerá el rey del mediodía, y saldrá, y peleará con el mismo rey del norte; y pondrá en campo gran multitud, y toda aquella multitud será entregada en su mano. 12 Y la multitud se ensoberbecerá, elevaráse su corazón, y derribará muchos millares; mas no prevalecerá. 13 Y el rey del norte volverá á poner en campo mayor multitud que primero, y á cabo del tiempo de años vendrá á gran priesa con grande ejército y con muchas riquezas. 14 Y en aquellos tiempos se levantarán muchos contra el rey del mediodía; é hijos de disipadores de tu pueblo se levantarán para confirmar la profecía, y caerán. 15 Vendrá pues el rey del norte, y fundará baluartes, y tomará la ciudad fuerte; y los brazos del mediodía no podrán permanecer, ni su pueblo escogido, ni habrá fortaleza que pueda resistir. 16 Y el que vendrá contra él, hará á su voluntad, ni habrá quien se le pueda parar delante; y estará en la tierra deseable, la cual será consumida en su poder. 17 Pondrá luego su rostro para venir con el poder de todo su reino; y hará con aquél cosas rectas, y daríle una hija de mujeres para trastornarla: mas no estará ni será por él. 18 Volverá después su rostro á las islas, y tomará muchas; mas un príncipe le hará parar su afrenta, y aun tornará sobre él su oprobio. 19 Luego volverá su rostro á las fortalezas de su tierra: mas tropezará y caerá, y no parecerá más. 20 Entonces sucederá en su silla uno que hará pasar exactor por la gloria del reino; mas en pocos días será quebrantado, no en enojo, ni en batalla. 21 Y sucederá en su lugar un vil, al cual no darán la honra del reino: vendrá empero con paz, y tomará el reino con halagos. 22 Y con los brazos de inundación serán inundados delante de él, y serán quebrantados; y aun también el príncipe del pacto. 23 Y después de los conciertos con él, él hará engaño, y subirá, y saldrá vencedor con poca gente. 24 Estando la provincia en paz y en abundancia, entrará y hará lo que no hicieron sus padres, ni los padres de sus padres; presa, y despojos, y riquezas repartirá á sus soldados; y contra las fortalezas formará sus designios: y esto por tiempo. 25 Y despertará sus fuerzas y su corazón contra el rey del mediodía con grande ejército: y el rey del mediodía se moverá á la guerra con grande y muy fuerte ejército; mas no prevalecerá, porque le harán traición. 26 Aun los que comerán su pan, le quebrantarán; y su ejército será destruído, y caerán muchos muertos. 27 Y el corazón de estos dos reyes será para hacer mal, y en una misma mesa tratarán mentira: mas no servirá de nada, porque el plazo aun no es llegado. 28 Y volveráse á su tierra con grande riqueza, y su corazón será contra el pacto santo: hará pues, y volveráse á su tierra. 29 Al tiempo señalado tornará al mediodía; mas no será la postrera venida como la primera. 30 Porque vendrán contra él naves de Chîttim, y él se contristará, y se volverá, y enojaráse contra el pacto santo, y hará: volveráse pues, y pensará en los que habrán desamparado el santo pacto. 31 Y serán puestos brazos de su parte; y contaminarán el santuario de fortaleza, y quitarán el continuo sacrificio, y pondrán la abominación espantosa. 32 Y con lisonjas hará pecar á los violadores del pacto: mas el pueblo que conoce á su Dios, se esforzará, y hará. 33 Y los sabios del pueblo darán sabiduría á muchos: y caerán á cuchillo y á fuego, en cautividad y despojo, por días. 34 Y en su caer serán ayudados de pequeño socorro: y muchos se juntarán á ellos con lisonjas. 35 Y algunos de los sabios caerán para ser purgados, y limpiados, y emblanquecidos, hasta el tiempo determinado: porque aun para esto hay plazo. 36 Y el rey hará á su voluntad; y se ensoberbecerá, y se engrandecerá sobre todo dios: y contra el Dios de los dioses hablará maravillas, y será prosperado, hasta que sea consumada la ira: porque hecha está determinación. 37 Y del Dios de sus padres no se cuidará, ni del amor de las mujeres: ni se cuidará de dios alguno, porque sobre todo se engrandecerá. 38 Mas honrará en su lugar al dios Mauzim, dios que sus padres no conocieron: honrarálo con oro, y plata, y piedras preciosas, y con cosas de gran precio. 39 Y con el dios ajeno que conocerá, hará á los baluartes de Mauzim crecer en gloria: y harálos enseñorear sobre muchos, y por interés repartirá la tierra. 40 Empero al cabo del tiempo el rey del mediodía se acorneará con él; y el rey del norte levantará contra él como tempestad, con carros y gente de á caballo, y muchos navíos; y entrará por las tierras, é inundará, y pasará. 41 Y vendrá á la tierra deseable, y muchas provincias caerán; mas éstas escaparán de su mano: Edom, y Moab, y lo primero de los hijos de Ammón. 42 Asimismo extenderá su mano á las otras tierras, y no escapará el país de Egipto. 43 Y se apoderará de los tesoros de oro y plata, y de todas las cosas preciosas de Egipto, de Libia, y Etiopía por donde pasará. 44 Mas nuevas de oriente y del norte lo espantarán; y saldrá con grande ira para destruir y matar muchos. 45 Y plantará la tiendas de su palacio entre los mares, en el monte deseable del santuario; y vendrá hasta su fin, y no tendrá quien le ayude.

DANIEL CAPITULO DOCE

"Y sentándose él en el monte de las Olivas, se llegaron á él los discípulos aparte, diciendo: Dinos, ¿cuándo serán estas cosas, y qué señal habrá de tu venida, y del fin del mundo? 4 Y respondiendo Jesús, les dijo: Mirad que nadie os engañe. 5 Porque vendrán muchos en mi nombre, diciendo: Yo soy el Cristo; y á muchos engañarán." Mateo 24:3-5

Aunque este es un capítulo corto con solo trece versículos, está cargado de información muy necesaria para ayudar a desentrañar los misterios de los capítulos que lo preceden en el libro de Daniel. También el capítulo doce de Daniel es muy útil para proporcionar pistas para crear una línea de tiempo con respecto al capítulo once de Daniel. Recuerde, la Biblia debe interpretarse a sí misma.

Un ejemplo de la Biblia que se interpreta a sí misma se ve en Daniel 12:1. Debemos preguntar:

"¿Quién es Miguel, el gran príncipe que protege a tu pueblo"?

"Y EN aquel tiempo se levantará Miguel, el gran príncipe que está por los hijos de tu pueblo; y será tiempo de angustia, cual nunca fué después que hubo gente hasta entonces: mas en aquel tiempo será libertado tu pueblo, todos los que se hallaren escritos en el libro."

Nos presentaron a Miguel en el capítulo diez de Daniel con los versículos 13 y 21. En Daniel 10:13, a Miguel se le llama "uno de los principales príncipes". En Daniel 10:21 se le llama, "Miguel, tu príncipe". Ahora en Daniel 12: 1 él es, Miguel, "el gran príncipe que está a favor de los hijos de tu pueblo".

¿Qué es un príncipe según la Biblia? Note Daniel 10:20:

"Y dijo: ¿Sabes por qué he venido á ti? Porque luego tengo de volver para pelear con el príncipe de los Persas; y en saliendo yo, luego viene el príncipe de Grecia."

En Daniel 11: 1-4 se nos dice que el ángel o mensajero contiende con el rey de Persia y también se nos dice que vendría el rey de Grecia. Entonces, aparentemente, un "príncipe" real es un rey, ya que el "príncipe de Persia" y el "príncipe de Grecia" (Daniel 10:20) son reyes. Entonces también, Miguel el Príncipe es un Rey.

En Daniel 8:25 se nos dice que el "Poder del Cuerno Pequeño" se enfrentará al "Príncipe de los príncipes" en los últimos días de la historia de esta tierra. Para ser un "Príncipe de príncipes" habría que ser un "Rey de reyes".

¿Quién en la Biblia es un "Rey de reyes"? Apocalipsis 19: 11-16 dice que la "Palabra de Dios" es el "Rey de reyes y Señor de señores". Y Juan 1: 1-18 nos dice que Jesús es la Palabra de Dios.

¿Dónde más aparece el nombre Michael en la Biblia en referencia a la realeza?

Apocalipsis 12:7 dice:

"Y fué hecha una grande batalla en el cielo: Miguel y sus ángeles lidiaban contra el dragón; y lidiaba el dragón y sus ángeles."

Y Judas 1:9 dice:

> "Pero cuando el arcángel Miguel contendía con el diablo, disputando sobre el cuerpo de Moisés, no se atrevió á usar de juicio de maldición contra él, sino que dijo: El Señor te reprenda."

En Judas 1:9, Miguel es el que resucitó a Moisés de entre los muertos y se refiere a sí mismo como el Señor.

Con la evidencia bíblica que tenemos arriba, la única conclusión que podemos hacer es que Miguel es Jesús antes de convertirse en hombre. ¡Miguel es Jesús encarnado!

Daniel 12:1:

> "Y EN aquel tiempo se levantará Miguel, el gran príncipe que está por los hijos de tu pueblo; y será tiempo de angustia, cual nunca fué después que hubo gente hasta entonces: mas en aquel tiempo será libertado tu pueblo, todos los que se hallaren escritos en el libro."

Michael se pone de pie.

¿Qué significa "ponerse de pie" en esta situación?

Cuando Jesús regresó al cielo en Su Ascensión, se sentó a la diestra del Padre, que es un lugar de poder.

"Y habiendo dicho estas cosas, viéndo lo ellos, fué alzado; y una nube le recibió y le quitó de sus ojos. Y estando con los ojos puestos en el cielo, entre tanto que él iba, he aquí dos varones se pusieron junto á ellos en vestidos blancos; Los cuales también les dijeron: Varones Galileos, ¿qué estáis mirando al cielo? este mismo Jesús que ha sido tomado desde vosotros arriba en el cielo, así vendrá como le habéis visto ir al cielo."

Hechos 1:9-11

"La cual obró en Cristo, resucitándole de los muertos, y colocándole á su diestra en los cielos, Sobre todo principado, y potestad, y potencia, y señorío, y todo nombre que se nombra, no sólo en este siglo, mas aun en el venidero." Efesios 1:20,21

"Puestos los ojos en al autor y consumador de la fe, en Jesús; el cual, habiéndole sido propuesto gozo, sufrió la cruz, menospreciando la vergüenza, y sentóse á la diestra del trono de Dios." Hebreos 12:2

Este asiento de Jesús a la diestra del Padre no denota un lugar o ubicación celestial geográfica específica, Dios es omnipresente, Él está en todas partes en uno, no en un solo lugar. Note Efesios 2:1-6. Antes de que Cristo entrara en nuestros corazones, se nos consideraba muertos. Pero cuando aceptamos a Jesús como nuestro Salvador, se nos da vida y **nos sentamos con Él en los lugares celestiales**, que también estaría a la diestra del Padre.

"Y juntamente nos resucitó, y asimismo nos hizo sentar en los cielos con Cristo Jesús." Efesios 2:6.

Sentarse con Cristo en los lugares celestiales es una posición de poder. En Cristo tenemos todo el poder que necesitamos para ser todo lo que podamos ser en Él, si le entregamos todo a Él. Aunque estamos sentados al lado de Jesús en los lugares celestiales, no estamos geográfica o físicamente a Su lado o en el salón del trono de Dios, todavía estamos en este planeta, permaneciendo en Él y Él en nosotros (Juan 17: 20- 26).

En Daniel 12: 1, cuando comienza el próximo tiempo futuro de problemas, Jesús se pone de pie. Esto no quiere decir que se haya sentado al lado del Padre durante los últimos 2000 años. Pero sí se refiere a la posición real que Jesús ha tenido con el paso del tiempo. Cuando Cristo se levanta en los reinos celestiales, creo que nos hace saber que está tomando un papel activo en la protección de los últimos siervos de Dios y que se está preparando para regresar a esta tierra, como los ángeles les dijeron a los discípulos en Hechos 1:11.

Pregunta: ¿A QUÉ HORA se pondrá de pie Michael?

Respuesta: Dado que los capítulos diez al doce de Daniel son una sola letra, entonces Daniel 12:1 debe seguir a los versículos finales del capítulo once de Daniel. ¿Cuándo se pone de pie Michael? Según Daniel 11:40, Miguel defenderá a su pueblo, para protegerlo, "en el tiempo del fin".

¿Qué más revela Daniel 12:1?

1. Hay un tiempo futuro de problemas, como nunca lo hubo, que vendrá sobre este planeta, como Jesús advirtió en Mateo 24:21 y Daniel lo confirma en Daniel 9: 24-27.

2. Durante ese tiempo de angustia, Dios librará a sus hijos. Él proporcionará comida, agua (Éxodo 23:25) y refugio. Debemos aprender a confiar en Dios para nuestro sustento. Aprendemos a confiar en Dios entonces confiando en Él hoy. Ahora es el momento de confiar en Él para todo lo que somos y necesitamos, para que, cuando llegue ese momento, estemos familiarizados con Su voz (Juan 10:27; Ezequiel 34:31) y confiados cómodamente en ser cuidados por Él. ¡Debemos permanecer totalmente dependientes del Padre AHORA!

3. ¿En qué libro están escritos los nombres de los salvos de Dios? Hay un libro donde están escritos los nombres de los hijos de Dios. Ese libro se llama el LIBRO DE LA VIDA (Salmo 69:28 y Apocalipsis 20:15) escrito por Dios mismo antes de que el mundo fuera creado y contiene todos los nombres de los salvos desde la creación.

Daniel 12:2,3:

"Y muchos de los que duermen en el polvo de la tierra serán despertados, unos para vida eterna, y otros para vergüenza y confusión perpetua. 3 Y los entendidos resplandecerán como el resplandor del firmamento; y los que enseñan á justicia la multitud, como las estrellas á perpetua eternidad."

Daniel 12: 1 nos presenta el período de tiempo futuro cercano que en otros lugares se llama el DÍA DEL SEÑOR (Joel 2, Apocalipsis 1:10), o el TIEMPO DE LA IRA DE DIOS (Daniel 8:19). Apocalipsis 20 revela que al final de ese tiempo de angustia habrá un juicio de 1000 años que tendrá lugar en el cielo. Daniel 12, versículos 2 y 3, nos lleva más allá de esos

1000 años hasta el final de la historia del pecado, justo antes de que todo pecado sea aniquilado y Dios haga un "cielo nuevo y una tierra nueva, en los cuales mora la justicia". (2 Pedro 3:13). Después de los 1000 años de Apocalipsis 20, y antes de que el pecado sea aniquilado, hay un "juicio del trono blanco" que se discute en Apocalipsis 20: 11-13. En este "juicio del gran trono blanco" se dicta una sentencia sobre cada persona que haya vivido en consideración de las decisiones de vida de cada persona, en su relación con Dios. Nadie está exento. Pablo nos dice en 2 Corintios 5:10:

> "Porque es menester que **todos** nosotros parezcamos ante el tribunal de Cristo, para que cada uno reciba según lo que hubiere hecho por medio del cuerpo, ora sea bueno ó malo."

"Y de la manera que está establecido á los hombres que mueran una vez, y después el juicio." Hebreos 9:27

Daniel 12: 2,3 revela la recompensa de los que están de pie ante el tribunal de Cristo al final de los 1000 años. Es entonces cuando Dios separa las ovejas de las cabras (Mateo 25: 31-46), el trigo de la cizaña (Mateo 13: 24-30) y el pescado bueno del pescado malo (Mateo 13: 47-50). En ese momento, a algunas personas se les otorgará la muerte eterna y a algunas personas se les otorgará la vida eterna. Note Mateo 25:31-46:

"31 Y cuando el Hijo del hombre venga en su gloria, y todos los santos ángeles con él, entonces se sentará sobre el trono de su gloria. 32 Y serán reunidas delante de él todas las gentes: y los apartará los unos de los otros, como aparta el pastor las ovejas de los cabritos. 33 Y pondrá las ovejas á su derecha, y los cabritos á la izquierda. 34 Entonces el Rey dirá á los que estarán á su derecha: Venid, benditos de mi Padre, heredad el reino preparado para vosotros desde la fundación del mundo. 35 Porque tuve hambre, y me disteis de comer; tuve sed, y me disteis de beber; fuí huésped, y me recogisteis; 36 Desnudo, y me cubristeis; enfermo, y me visitasteis; estuve en la cárcel, y vinisteis á mí. 37 Entonces los justos le responderán, diciendo: Señor, ¿cuándo te vimos hambriento, y te sustentamos? ¿ó sediento, y te dimos de beber? 38 ¿Y cuándo te vimos huésped, y te recogimos? ¿ó desnudo, y te cubrimos? 39 ¿O cuándo te vimos enfermo, ó en la cárcel, y vinimos á ti? 40 Y respondiendo el Rey, les dirá: De cierto os digo que en cuanto lo hicisteis á uno de estos mis hermanos pequeñitos, á mí lo hicisteis. 41 Entonces dirá también á los que estarán á la izquierda: Apartaos de mí, malditos, al fuego eterno preparado para el diablo y para sus ángeles: 42 Porque tuve hambre, y no me disteis de comer; tuve sed, y no me disteis de beber; 43 Fuí huésped, y no me recogisteis; desnudo, y no me cubristeis; enfermo, y en la cárcel, y no me visitasteis. 44 Entonces también ellos le responderán, diciendo: Señor, ¿cuándo te vimos hambriento, ó sediento, ó huésped, ó desnudo, ó enfermo, ó en la cárcel, y no te servimos? 45 Entonces les responderá, diciendo: De cierto os digo que en cuanto no lo hicisteis á uno de estos pequeñitos, ni á mí lo hicisteis. 46 E irán éstos al tormento eterno, y los justos á la vida eterna."

Este período de tiempo se llama "**EL ÚLTIMO DÍA**" en la Biblia es cuando la recompensa de la vida eterna o la muerte eterna es dictada por la corte de Dios. Note Juan 6:39-44:

> "Y esta es la voluntad del que me envió, del Padre: Que todo lo que me diere, no pierda de ello, sino que lo resucite en el **día postrero**. Y esta es la voluntad del que me ha enviado: Que todo aquel que ve al Hijo, y cree en él, tenga vida eterna: y yo le resucitaré en el **día postrero**.

Murmuraban entonces de él los Judíos, porque había dicho: Yo soy el pan que descendí del cielo. Y decían: ¿No es éste Jesús, el hijo de José, cuyo padre y madre nosotros conocemos? ¿cómo, pues, dice éste: Del cielo he descendido? Y Jesús respondió, y díjoles: No murmuréis entre vosotros. Ninguno puede venir á mí, si el Padre que me envió no le trajere; y yo le resucitaré en el **día postrero**."

"Marta le dice: Yo sé que resucitará en la resurrección en el **día postrero**." Juan 11:24

"Y el que oyere mis palabras, y no las creyere, yo no le juzgo; porque no he venido á juzgar al mundo, sino á salvar al mundo. 48 El que me desecha, y no recibe mis palabras, tiene quien le juzgue: la palabra que he hablado, ella le juzgará en el **día postrero**."

Juan 12:47,48.

Daniel 12:4:

"Tú empero Daniel, cierra las palabras y sella el libro hasta el tiempo del fin: pasarán muchos, y multiplicaráse la ciencia."

A medida que nos acercamos al final del libro de Daniel, Dios le dice a Daniel que "cierre las palabras y selle el libro hasta el tiempo del fin". Dios tiene un mensaje para todas y cada una de las generaciones que existió desde los días de Daniel. Solo ha mostrado a cada generación lo que quería que supieran para el tiempo en que vivieron. Se ha reservado revelar los misterios finales para la generación final. Divulga

Sus mensajes a Su manera y según Su tiempo señalado. Aunque la Biblia está disponible para casi todas las personas en este planeta, de una forma u otra, Dios revelará Sus secretos como lo ha predeterminado en Su tiempo señalado. Podemos expresar nuestras ideas y nuestros pensamientos, yendo y viniendo, sobre el mensaje que Dios está revelando para nuestra generación, pero el desarrollo completo de Daniel no tendrá lugar hasta "el tiempo del fin". El libro de Daniel se está abriendo, pero es una progresión. Las personas que vivían en el pasado no podían entender o ver los misterios que Dios está desvelando hoy.

Daniel 12:5-7:

> "Y yo, Daniel, miré, y he aquí otros dos que estaban, el uno de esta parte á la orilla del río, y el otro de la otra parte á la orilla del río. Y dijo uno al varón vestido de lienzos, que estaba sobre las aguas del río: ¿Cuándo será el fin de estas maravillas? Y oía al varón vestido de lienzos, que estaba sobre las aguas del río, el cual alzó su diestra y su siniestra al cielo, y juró por el Viviente en los siglos, que será por tiempo, tiempos, y la mitad. Y cuando se acabare el esparcimiento del escuadrón del pueblo santo, todas estas cosas serán cumplidas."

Hay tres participantes celestiales en la visión de Daniel de los capítulos diez al doce. El que está sobre las aguas fue descrito por Daniel en el capítulo 10 versículos 4-6:

> "Y á los veinte y cuatro días del mes primero estaba yo á la orilla del gran río Hiddekel; Y alzando mis ojos miré, y he aquí un varón vestido de lienzos, y ceñidos sus lomos de oro de

> Uphaz: Y su cuerpo era como piedra de Tarsis,
> y su rostro parecía un relámpago, y sus ojos
> como antorchas de fuego, y sus brazos y sus
> pies como de color de metal resplandeciente, y
> la voz de sus palabras como la voz de ejército."

Los otros dos hablaron con Daniel y lo tocaron para darle fuerza y aliento (Daniel 10: 10-21). En el capítulo 10 de Apocalipsis, un mensajero similar está parado sobre el agua apuntando al "cielo" con un pie en el "mar" y el otro pie en la "tierra". El mensajero del último día de Apocalipsis diez representa a los siervos de Dios del tiempo del fin que están dando el mensaje de advertencia final para la gente del "cielo", la "tierra" y el "mar".

Durante esta visión, Daniel está exhausto y asombrado. Pensar en las preguntas correctas para hacer en este momento de estrés y ansiedad era imposible para el hombre de Dios. Entonces, uno de los otros ángeles celestiales hizo la pregunta correcta en cambio, en Daniel 12 versículo seis:

"¿Cuándo será el fin de estas maravillas?"

Entonces el ser celestial sobre las aguas respondió con un período de tiempo que hemos visto antes en Daniel 7:25, cuando hablamos del Poder del Cuerno Pequeño:

> "Y oía al varón vestido de lienzos, que estaba
> sobre las aguas del río, el cual alzó su diestra
> y su siniestra al cielo, y juró por el Viviente en
> los siglos, que será por tiempo, tiempos, y la
> mitad. Y cuando se acabare el esparcimiento del
> escuadrón del pueblo santo, todas estas cosas
> serán cumplidas." Daniel 12:7

Tanto Daniel 7:25 como Daniel 12: 7 están hablando del mismo período de tiempo y el mismo Cuerno Pequeño que estará en guerra contra el pueblo de Dios por "un tiempo, tiempos y medio tiempo" o por tres años y medio (Apocalipsis 11:11) que son 1260 días literales. El "él" al que se refiere el ser celestial en Daniel doce versículo siete es el Poder del Cuerno Pequeño de Daniel siete y se está refiriendo a los últimos tres años y medio (3 ½) de la tribulación de siete años, cuando el Cuerno Pequeño tendrá éxito en desafiar y vencer el poder del pueblo de Dios.

Lo que esto significa es que los fieles a Dios seguirán siendo fieles a Él, incluso frente al encarcelamiento y la muerte, y los que no se hayan rendido a Él serán infieles firmemente. Apocalipsis 22:11 dice:

> "El que es injusto, sea injusto todavía: y el que es sucio, ensúciese todavía: y el que es justo, sea todavía justificado: y el santo sea santificado todavía."

n gráfico que muestra los 1260 días o "tiempo, tiempos y medio tiempo" se ve así:

2.520 días literales o siete años

1260 días	1260 días
Pre-cuerno pequeño	Post-cuerno pequeño

Daniel 12:8-10:

> "Y yo oí, mas no entendí. Y dije: Señor mío, ¿qué será el cumplimiento de estas cosas? Y dijo: Anda, Daniel, que estas palabras están cerradas y selladas hasta el tiempo del cumplimiento. Muchos serán

limpios, y emblanquecidos, y purificados; mas los impíos obrarán impíamente, y ninguno de los impíos entenderá, pero entenderán los entendidos."

Daniel está asombrado por la visión y quiere entender qué significa todo esto. Pero el mensajero celestial le dice gentilmente que no se preocupe por esta visión porque ha sido sellada y se aplica al **"tiempo del fin"**, que es el futuro de dos mil seiscientos años hasta los días del profeta Daniel. Y luego el mensajero define su declaración anterior sobre el Poder del Cuerno Pequeño en Daniel 12: 7 cuando dijo:

"Y cuando se acabare el esparcimiento del escuadrón del pueblo santo, todas estas cosas serán cumplidas."

El mensajero celestial explica la cita anterior hablando de aquellos que permanecen en Cristo durante el tiempo de sacudida de la tribulación de 7 años (Apocalipsis 8:5) y aquellos que no:

"Muchos serán limpios, y emblanquecidos, y purificados; mas los impíos obrarán impíamente, y ninguno de los impíos entenderá, pero entenderán los entendidos."

El libro de Daniel será entendido por aquellos siervos de Dios de los últimos tiempos que tienen el "espíritu de profecía". Note Apocalipsis 19:10:

"Y yo me eché á sus pies para adorarle. Y él me dijo: Mira que no lo hagas: yo soy siervo contigo, y con tus hermanos que tienen el testimonio de Jesús: adora á Dios; porque el testimonio de Jesús es el espíritu de la profecía."

¿Qué es el espíritu de profecía? El espíritu de profecía es un profundo deseo de comprender y enseñar los mensajes proféticos de la Biblia, especialmente el de Daniel y Apocalipsis. Un profeta no es necesariamente uno que tiene visiones y sueños, pero ciertamente es uno que enseña la verdad donde Jesucristo es el centro del mensaje. Pablo dice en 1 Corintios 14:1-6:

> "SEGUID la caridad; y procurad los dones espirituales, mas sobre todo que profeticéis. Porque el que habla en lenguas, no habla á los hombres, sino á Dios; porque nadie le entiende, aunque en espíritu hable misterios. Mas el que profetiza, habla á los hombres para edificación, y exhortación, y consolación. El que habla lengua extraña, á sí mismo se edifica; mas el que porfetiza, edifica á la iglesia. Así que, quisiera que todos vosotros hablaseis lenguas, empero más que profetizaseis: porque mayor es el que profetiza que el que habla lenguas, si también no interpretare, para que la iglesia tome edificación. Ahora pues, hermanos, si yo fuere á vosotros hablando lenguas, ¿qué os aprovecharé, si no os hablare, ó con revelación, ó con ciencia, ó con profecía, ó con doctrina?"

LOS DOS VERSÍCULOS SIGUIENTES SON VITALES PARA COLOCAR CORRECTAMENTE TODOS LOS PERÍODOS DE TIEMPO PROFÉTICO BÍBLICO EN LA LÍNEA DE TIEMPO DE LA PROFECÍA DEL TIEMPO FINAL.

Daniel 12:11,12:

> "Y desde el tiempo que fuere quitado el continuo sacrificio hasta la abominación espantosa, habrá mil doscientos y noventa días. Bienaventurado el que esperare, y llegare hasta mil trescientos treinta y cinco días."

Este versículo es tremendamente importante y debe entenderse correctamente desde el idioma original. Para ser absolutamente exactos, la palabra sacrificio, que está en cursiva en la mayoría de las Biblias, ya que fue agregada, debe eliminarse del versículo. No pertenece allí.

> "Y desde el tiempo que fuere quitado el continuo hasta la abominación espantosa, habrá mil doscientos y noventa días. Bienaventurado el que esperare, y llegare hasta mil trescientos treinta y cinco días."

Poniendo este texto en mis propias palabras, se puede leer:

> "Desde el momento en que lo continuo (perpetuo) sea quitado hasta que se establezca la abominación desoladora, habrá 1.290 días. Bienaventurados los que llegan a los 1335 días."

Si observa el versículo 11 en una línea de tiempo horizontal, se vería así:

```
Continuo          1.290 dias                    Abominación
quitado I_____I espantosa
```

Vuelva a leer esto con mucho cuidado para captar su significado previsto:

"**DESDE EL TIEMPO** que el continuo sea quitado **HASTA** que la abominación desoladora sea **ESTABLECIDA**, habrá 1.290 días de tiempo.

El versículo 12 continúa diciendo:

"Bienaventurados los que llegan a los 1335 días."

Si observa ambos versículos en una línea de tiempo horizontal, aparecería así:

```
Continuo        1.290 dias       Abominación
quitado I_____I espantosa

Continuo        1.335 dias                Los fieles de dios
quitado I_____I bendecidos
```

A lo largo del libro de Daniel y Apocalipsis se dan varios períodos proféticos. Cada período de tiempo tiene un punto de inicio y un punto final. Si se puede determinar el punto inicial o final del tiempo, entonces se puede mapear el período de tiempo completo.

Algunos de los comienzos del período de tiempo fueron previamente aclarados bíblicamente, como cuando (1) la ocupación egipcia de 400 años comenzó y terminó, (2) los 40 años israelitas comenzaron a maravillarse en el desierto, así como (3) el tiempo de los 70 años. semanas de Daniel 9:24 que fueron del 457 a. C. al 34 d. C.

Pero todos los demás períodos de tiempo no estaban determinados Bíblicamente a cuándo comenzaron o cuándo terminaron. Se han hecho muchos intentos para tratar de identificar los puntos de tiempo de inicio, pero en el mejor de los casos han sido especulativos. Pero ahora mismo, para ti, se está revelando, de Daniel 12:11 y 12. Tenemos un punto de tiempo de inicio específico reconocido para dos de los períodos de tiempo proféticos. Tanto las profecías de los 1290 días como las de los 1335 días comienzan cuando lo PERPETUO o CONTINUO es quitado o abandonado.

Otro período de tiempo que se puede agregar a esos dos períodos de tiempo proféticos de Daniel 12:11,12 en relación con el CONTINUO siendo quitado, es el "tiempo, tiempos y medio tiempo" de Daniel 12:7. Ese período de tiempo, que es de tres años y medio, o 1.260 días literales de 24 horas, se menciona en la misma visión que los períodos de tiempo 1.290 y 1.335. Aparecería en nuestra línea de tiempo horizontal de la siguiente manera:

Continuo   1,260 dias   Gente santa
quitado I_____I_____I destrozado

Continuo   1.290 dias   Abominación
quitado I_____ _I espantosa

Continuo   1.335 dias   Los fieles de dios
quitado I_____I bendecidos

PREGUNTA: Según la Biblia, ¿hay otro período de tiempo asociado con la "eliminación" de lo PERPETUO o CONTINUO?

RESPUESTA: ¡¡¡¡SI !!!!!

Note Daniel 8:9-14 como se cita directamente de la Biblia:

"Y del uno de ellos salió un cuerno pequeño, el cual creció mucho al mediodía, y al oriente, y hacia la tierra deseable. Y engrandecióse hasta el ejército del cielo; y parte del ejército y de las

417

estrellas echó por tierra, y las holló. Aun contra el príncipe de la fortaleza se engrandeció, y por él fué quitado **el continuo** sacrificio, y el lugar de su santuario fué echado por tierra. Y el ejército fué le entregado á causa de la prevaricación sobre **el continuo** sacrificio: y echó por tierra la verdad, é hizo cuanto quiso, y sucedióle prósperamente. Y oí un santo que hablaba; y otro de los santos dijo á aquél que hablaba: ¿Hasta cuándo durará la visión del **continuo** sacrificio, y la prevaricación asoladora que pone el santuario y el ejército para ser hollados? Y él me dijo: Hasta dos mil y trescientos días de tarde y mañana; y el santuario será purificado."

(Se agregó la palabra sacrificio, no pertenece a estos versículos).

EN el siguiente texto de Daniel 8: 9-14, he eliminado la palabra "sacrificio", ya que no pertenece allí, y he traducido con mayor precisión el final del versículo catorce para que se lea más de cerca al hebreo original:

"Y del uno de ellos salió un cuerno pequeño, el cual creció mucho al mediodía, y al oriente, y hacia la tierra deseable. Y engrandecióse hasta el ejército del cielo; y parte del ejército y de las estrellas echó por tierra, y las holló. Aun contra el príncipe de la fortaleza se engrandeció, y por él fué quitado **el continuo**, y el lugar de su santuario fué echado por tierra. Y el ejército fué le entregado á causa de la prevaricación sobre **el continuo**: y echó por tierra la verdad, é hizo cuanto quiso, y sucedióle prósperamente. Y oí un santo que hablaba; y otro de los santos dijo á aquél que hablaba: ¿Hasta cuándo durará la visión del **continuo**, y la prevaricación asoladora que pone el santuario y el ejército para ser hollados? Y él me dijo: Hasta dos mil y trescientos días de tarde y mañana; **y el santo es vindicado**."

Está perfectamente claro que la profecía del tiempo de "las 2.300 tardes y mañanas" también está íntimamente relacionada con el hecho de que el CONTINUO (PERPETUO) sea quitado, así como con "la transgresión de la desolación", que es la abominación de la desolación.

De acuerdo con las líneas de tiempo anteriores, las 2.300 tardes y mañanas, o los 2.300 días literales de 24 horas, aparecen de la siguiente manera:

Continuo   1,260 dias   Gente santa
quitado I_____I_____I destrozado

Continuo   1.290 dias   Abominación
quitado I_____ _I espantosa

Continuo   1.335 dias   Los fieles de dios
quitado I_____I bendecidos

Continuo   2.300 tardes y mañanas   Pueblo santo
quitado I_____I reivindicado

Cuando hablamos de Daniel 9:27, probamos que hay una semana profética de siete años en nuestro futuro que Jesús llamó la "gran tribulación" en Mateo 24:21.

¿Cómo se relaciona ese período de siete años (2.520 días) con los períodos de tiempo demostrados anteriormente?

Observe lo siguiente al agregar la tribulación de 2.520 días a las líneas de tiempo:

Continuo   1,260 dias   Gente santa
quitado I_____I_____I destrozado

Continuo   1.290 dias   Abominación
quitado I_____ _I espantosa

Continuo   1.335 dias   Los fieles de dios
quitado I_____I bendecidos

Continuo   2.300 tardes y mañanas   Pueblo santo
quitado I_____I reivindicado

Continuo   2.520 dias (siete años)   La tribulación
quitado I_____I terminó

(Tenga en cuenta que estas líneas de tiempo no están dibujadas a escala. Es solo para demostración).

A continuación se muestra un cuadro que muestra todos los períodos de tiempo bíblicos proféticos que se encuentran en las escrituras que íntimamente juegan un papel importante durante la próxima tribulación de siete años:

TODOS LOS PERÍODOS DE TIEMPO PROFÉTICO BÍBLICO DEL TIEMPO FINAL

TIEMPO	DANIEL	REVELACIÓN
Tiempo, tiempos, medio tiempo	7:25 & 12:7 (1.260 dias)	12:14
2.300 dias	8:14	
1.290 dias	12:11	
1,335 dias	12:12	
1,260 dias		11:3 & 12:6
42 meses (1.260 dias)		11:2 & 13:5
5 meses (150 dias)		9:5,10
3 ½ dias (1.260 dias)		11:9,11

Hasta donde yo sé, el punto de inicio bíblico para el período de tiempo que se encuentra en Daniel 12:11, es la clave para comprender dónde encajan **todos** los demás períodos de tiempo del "tiempo señalado del fin" en una línea de tiempo sensata y organizada.

PREGUNTA: ¿Por qué la Biblia tiene numerosos períodos de tiempo de profecía encapsulados en los próximos siete años de tribulación?

RESPUESTA: Conocer el comienzo de cada período de tiempo es importante para los eventos que tienen lugar durante ese período de tiempo y especialmente al final de ese período de tiempo profético. El propósito de cada línea de tiempo se puede determinar mediante el estudio cuidadoso y completo de la información que rodea a cada uno de esos períodos de tiempo. Todos son para "el tiempo del fin".

Ninguno de los períodos de tiempo en particular, los versículos anteriores pueden ser independientes sin considerar todo el capítulo bíblico en el que se encuentran. Ningún versículo puede ser independiente del capítulo en el que se encuentra. Para colocar correctamente un período de tiempo en una línea de tiempo, se debe considerar toda la información.

Como se discutió en el capítulo nueve de Daniel, la Biblia nos informa de una futura tribulación mundial de siete años. Considerando que un año profético tiene 360 días, una tribulación de siete años se convierte en un período de tiempo de 2.520 días. Al considerar todos los períodos de tiempo anteriores, todos encajan cómodamente en esa línea de tiempo o período de tiempo de 2.520 días y cada uno tiene un propósito específico.

Al darnos cuenta de que **todos** los períodos de tiempo comienzan cuando se quita el PERPETUO o CONTINUO, podemos comenzar nuestra línea de tiempo con esa información. Después de considerar todos los parámetros de los períodos de tiempo, las tablas a continuación rastrean claramente los puntos de inicio y finalización de cada uno de los períodos de tiempo bíblicos demostrados a continuación.

El siguiente diseño de línea de tiempo de siete años se utilizará para demostrar todos los períodos proféticos del tiempo del fin en la Biblia. La siguiente tabla revela:

(1) El título de la tabla, (2) el evento que comienza la tribulación de siete años, (3) los 2.520 días literales que componen los siete años, (4) la línea media que divide igualmente la línea de tiempo en dos mitades o alas iguales, (5) el período final de 70 días al final de los siete años, (6) el tiempo sugerido para la segunda venida de Jesús, (7) los 1000 años de Apocalipsis 20, y (8) la ETERNIDAD que comienza después del 1000 los años se acaban.

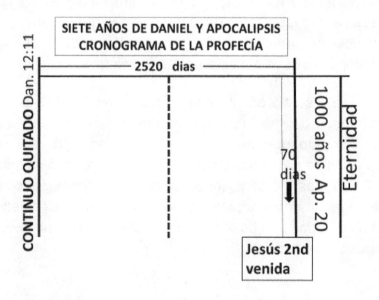

Mi primera adición a la tabla de la línea de tiempo de siete años es colocar los cinco meses de Apocalipsis 9:5,10 en la línea de tiempo. Aparece en el gráfico como:

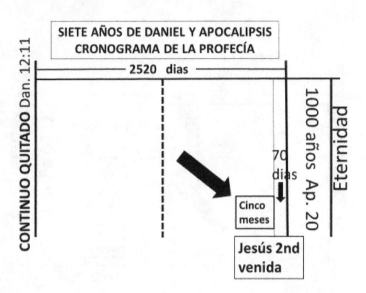

A continuación, agregaré los tres días y medio (3 ½) de los años de Apocalipsis once cuando los dos testigos, el Antiguo y el Nuevo Testamento, serán proscritos y eliminados.

A continuación, agregaré tiempo, tiempos y medio tiempo (X, X'S, ½ X) de Daniel y Apocalipsis cuando el pueblo de Dios será pisoteado por el Poder del Cuerno Pequeño (Apocalipsis 12:12):

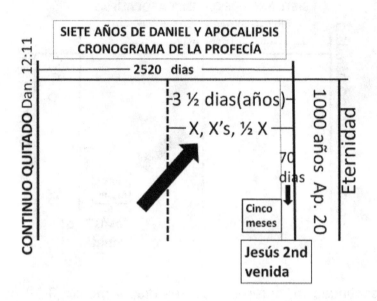

A continuación agregaré los 42 meses, cuando los dos testigos (Apocalipsis 11) evangelizan el mundo, y los 1260 días, cuando los elegidos de Dios comienzan a ser maltratados cuando los 144.000 santos revelan al mundo el mensaje final del evangelio sobre el juicio final y el reino de Dios, señalando a las personas conocidas como "cielo", "tierra" y "mar" (Mateo 24: 9-15):

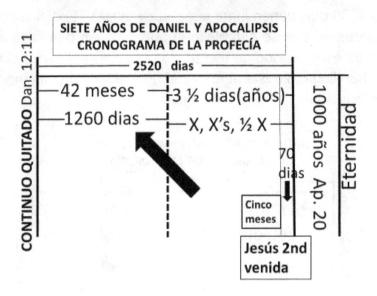

A continuación, agregaré 1,290 días que abarcan el período desde el momento en que se termina el CONTINUAL hasta que se establece la "abominación que causó la desolación".

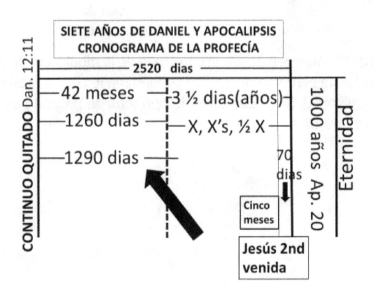

Los 1335 días tienen lugar cuarenta y cinco (45) días literales después de que se establece la abominación desoladora. Al final de este período de tiempo, los siervos vivientes de Dios, que han llegado hasta aquí, serán bendecidos de una manera muy especial.

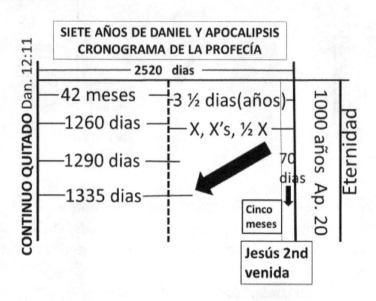

Los 2.300 días van desde el comienzo de la tribulación de siete años hasta el momento en que comienzan los cinco meses de Apocalipsis 9: 5,10. Ese es el tiempo total de prueba para los siervos de Dios.

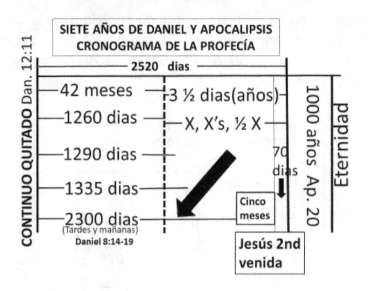

Finalmente, pondré los 1260 días en nuestra línea de tiempo cuando el poder de los hijos de Dios será completamente destrozado y "todas estas cosas serán cumplidas" como nos dice Daniel 12: 7:

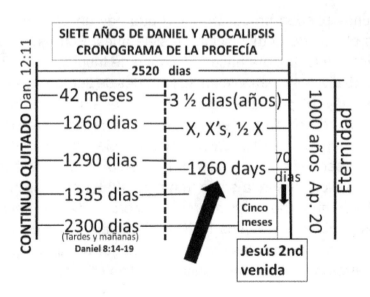

A continuación se muestra el gráfico completo de la línea de tiempo de siete años que muestra la posición bíblica correcta de todos los períodos proféticos del tiempo del fin ubicados en Daniel y Apocalipsis.

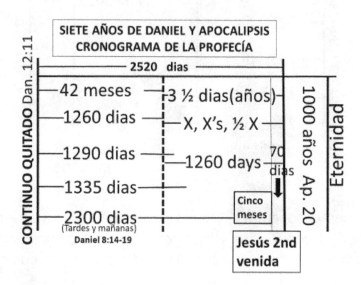

Algunos pueden preguntarse por qué hay un período de 70 días al final de la tribulación de siete años. Esa es una muy buena pregunta para hacer. El tiempo de tribulación de 2.520 días se divide igualmente en 36 períodos de tiempo de setenta días. Hay 18 períodos de 70 días en el ala izquierda y 18 períodos de 70 días en el ala derecha. Este autor cree que el último período de 70 días tiene algunos roles muy importantes que desempeñar. (1) Marca el momento en que se abre el sexto sello y suena la sexta trompeta. (2) Es el cumplimiento de las palabras de Jesús acerca de "acortar el tiempo por amor a los elegidos" en Marcos 13:20. (3) También revela los últimos setenta días cuando las siete últimas plagas de Apocalipsis 16 se derraman sobre la humanidad perdida.

Haga los cálculos: sume los días: 2,300 + 150 (5 meses) + 70 = 2520 días (7 años).

Vea el video de Youtube: **All the Last Day Appointed Bible Times** por Earl Schrock

¡PERO ESO NO ES TODO!

Esta misma gráfica de línea de tiempo se usa con el libro de Apocalipsis para establecer el tiempo sugerido para los siete sellos, siete trompetas, siete truenos, siete ángeles, siete ayes y siete lamentos. Todos estos sietes tienen lugar simultáneamente, al mismo tiempo y en la misma ubicación en la línea de tiempo, durante la próxima tribulación de 7 años de la siguiente manera:

Línea de tiempo de siete años que revela el momento para la apertura de los siete sellos, el sonido de las siete trompetas, el aplauso de los siete truenos, el grito de los siete ángeles, el momento de los siete ayes y la colocación de los siete lamentos, que se llevan a cabo simultáneamente.

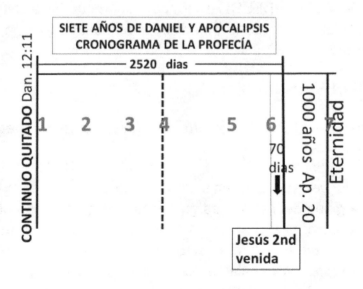

Cuando se junta con todos los períodos proféticos de Daniel y Apocalipsis, aparece:

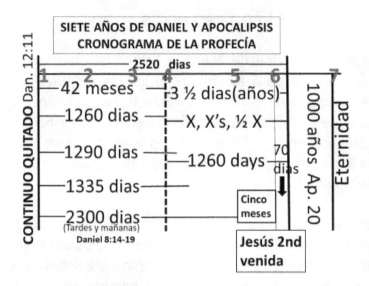

PREGUNTA: ¿Se menciona lo PERPETUO o CONTINUO y la ABOMINACIÓN DESOLADORA en algún otro lugar del libro de Daniel, aparte de lo que discutimos hasta ahora en este capítulo?

RESPUESTA: SI.

Note Daniel 11: 20-45: (con errores de interpretación corregidos y versículos numerados).

20 Entonces sucederá en su silla uno que hará pasar exactor por la gloria del reino; mas en pocos días será quebrantado, no en enojo, ni en batalla. 21 Y sucederá en su lugar **un vil**, al cual no darán la honra del reino: vendrá empero con paz, y tomará el reino con halagos. 22 Y con los brazos de <u>inundación</u> serán inundados delante de él, y serán quebrantados; y aun también el <u>príncipe del pacto</u>. 23 Y después de los conciertos con él, él hará engaño, y subirá, y saldrá vencedor con poca

gente. 24 Estando la provincia en paz y en abundancia, entrará y hará lo que no hicieron sus padres, ni los padres de sus padres; presa, y despojos, y riquezas repartirá á sus soldados; y contra las fortalezas formará sus designios: y esto por tiempo. 25 Y despertará sus fuerzas y su corazón contra el rey del mediodía con grande ejército: y el rey del mediodía se moverá á la guerra con grande y muy fuerte ejército; mas no prevalecerá, porque le harán traición. 26 Aun los que comerán su pan, le quebrantarán; y su ejército será destruído, y caerán muchos muertos. 27 Y el corazón de estos dos reyes será para hacer mal, y en una misma mesa tratarán mentira: mas no servirá de nada, porque **el plazo aun no es llegado**. 28 Y volveráse á su tierra con grande riqueza, y su corazón será contra **el pacto santo**: hará pues, y volveráse á su tierra. 29 **Al tiempo señalado** tornará al mediodía; mas no será la postrera venida como la primera. 30 Porque vendrán contra él naves de Chîttim, y él se contristará, y se volverá, y enojaráse contra **el pacto santo**, y hará: volveráse pues, y pensará en los que habrán desamparado **el santo pacto**. 31 Y serán puestos brazos de su parte; y contaminarán el santuario de fortaleza, y quitarán el **continuo**, y pondrán **la abominación espantosa**. 32 Y con lisonjas hará pecar á los violadores **del pacto**: mas el pueblo que conoce á su Dios, se esforzará, y hará. 33 Y los sabios del pueblo darán sabiduría á muchos: y caerán á cuchillo y á fuego, en cautividad y despojo, por días. 34 Y en su caer serán ayudados de pequeño socorro: y muchos se juntarán á ellos con lisonjas. 35 Y algunos de los sabios caerán para ser purgados, y limpiados, y emblanquecidos, hasta **el tiempo determinado**: porque aun para esto **hay plazo**. 36 Y el rey hará á su voluntad; y se ensoberbecerá, y se engrandecerá sobre todo dios: y contra el Dios de los dioses hablará maravillas, y será prosperado, hasta que sea consumada la ira: porque hecha está determinación. 37 Y del Dios de sus padres no se cuidará, ni del amor de las mujeres: ni se cuidará de dios alguno, porque sobre todo se engrandecerá. 38 Mas honrará en su lugar al dios Mauzim, dios que sus padres no conocieron: honrarálo con oro, y plata, y piedras preciosas, y con cosas de gran precio. 39 Y con el dios ajeno que conocerá, hará á los baluartes de Mauzim crecer en gloria: y harálos enseñorear sobre muchos, y por interés repartirá la tierra. 40 Empero al cabo del tiempo el rey del mediodía se acorneará con él; y el rey del norte levantará contra él como tempestad, con carros y gente de á caballo, y muchos navíos; y entrará por las tierras, é inundará, y pasará. 41 Y vendrá á **la tierra deseable**, y muchas provincias caerán; mas éstas escaparán de su mano: Edom, y Moab, y lo primero de los hijos de Ammón. 42 Asimismo extenderá su mano á las otras tierras, y no escapará el país de Egipto. 43 Y se apoderará de los tesoros de oro y plata, y de todas las cosas preciosas de Egipto, de Libia, y Etiopía por donde pasará. 44 Mas nuevas de oriente y del norte lo espantarán; y saldrá **con grande ira** para destruir y matar muchos. 45 Y plantará la tiendas de su palacio entre los mares, en el monte deseable del santuario; y vendrá hasta su fin, y no tendrá quien le ayude.

Debido a que ahora sabemos que EL LLEVAR EL CONTINUO y el establecimiento de la ABOMINACIÓN DE LA DESOLACIÓN es parte del próximo período de tribulación de siete años, podemos trazar un mejor mapa de los eventos del capítulo once de Daniel.

Hasta este punto, era imposible relacionarse con el capítulo 11 de Daniel debido a la escasa y dispersa información que proporciona. Pero el versículo 21 nos presenta el mismo poder que se encuentra en el resto del libro de Daniel, el Poder del Cuerno Pequeño, al que Daniel 11:21 llama "una persona vil".

ENTENDIENDO EL PACTO

Otro término que ha surgido al releer el capítulo once de Daniel es la palabra PACTO. En el capítulo once de Daniel se le llama el PACTO SANTO en los versículos 28 y 30. En este librito de estudio bíblico vimos por primera vez la palabra "pacto" en Daniel 9:4 y 27:

"Y oré á Jehová mi Dios, y confesé, y dije: Ahora Señor, Dios grande, digno de ser temido, que guardas **el pacto** y la misericordia con los que te aman y guardan **tus mandamientos**."

"Y en otra semana confirmará **el pacto** á muchos, y á la mitad de la semana hará cesar el sacrificio y la ofrenda: después con la muchedumbre de las **abominaciones será el desolar**, y esto hasta una entera consumación; y derramaráse la ya determinada sobre el pueblo asolado."

La palabra "pacto" aparece cinco veces en Daniel 11: 22-32:

"Y con los brazos de inundación serán inundados delante de él, y serán quebrantados; y aun también el príncipe **del pacto**. 23 Y después de los conciertos con él, él hará engaño, y subirá, y saldrá vencedor con poca gente. 24 Estando la provincia en paz y en abundancia, entrará y hará lo que no hicieron sus padres, ni los padres de sus padres; presa, y despojos, y riquezas repartirá á sus soldados; y contra las fortalezas formará sus designios: y esto por tiempo. 25 Y despertará sus fuerzas y su corazón contra el rey del mediodía con grande ejército: y el rey del mediodía se moverá á la guerra con grande y muy fuerte ejército; mas no prevalecerá, porque le harán traición. 26 Aun los que comerán su pan, le quebrantarán; y su ejército será destruído, y caerán muchos muertos. 27 Y el corazón de estos dos reyes será para hacer mal, y en una misma mesa tratarán mentira: mas no servirá de nada, porque el plazo aun no es llegado. 28 Y volveráse á su tierra con grande riqueza, y su corazón será contra **el pacto santo**: hará pues, y volveráse á su tierra. 29 Al tiempo señalado tornará al mediodía; mas no será la postrera venida como la primera. 30 Porque vendrán contra él naves de Chîttim, y él se contristará, y se volverá, y enojaráse contra **el pacto santo**, y hará: volveráse pues, y pensará en los que habrán desamparado **el santo pacto**. 31 Y serán puestos brazos de su parte; y contaminarán el santuario de fortaleza, y quitarán el continuo sacrificio, y pondrán la abominación espantosa. 32 Y con lisonjas hará pecar á los violadores **del pacto**: mas el pueblo que conoce á su Dios, se esforzará, y hará."

De la información que tenemos arriba, el Poder del Cuerno Pequeño del libro de Daniel no solo está en contra del "PACTO SANTO" sino que el Poder del Cuerno Pequeño también está en contra del "PRÍNCIPE DEL PACTO", como se revela en el versículo 22.

PREGUNTAS:

1. **¿Qué es el PACTO o PACTO SANTO? Y**
2. **¿Quién es el PRÍNCIPE DEL PACTO?**

Definición de la palabra pacto: Un pacto generalmente es una promesa, acuerdo o compromiso entre dos o más partes.

3. **¿Qué dice la Biblia sobre la palabra PACTO?**

Hay varios pactos mencionados en la Biblia. La mayoría de los pactos son entre Dios y un individuo y sus descendientes. Están los pactos entre Dios y Abraham, Dios e Isaac, Dios y Jacob, Dios y Moisés, etc.

Pero el primer pacto o promesa en la Biblia se hizo en el Jardín del Edén entre Dios y Satanás. Dios dijo en Génesis 3:14,15:

"Y Jehová Dios dijo á la serpiente: Por cuanto esto hiciste, maldita serás entre todas las bestias y entre todos los animales del campo; sobre tu pecho andarás, y polvo comerás todos los días de tu vida: Y enemistad pondré entre ti y la mujer, y entre tu simiente y la simiente suya; ésta te herirá en la cabeza, y tú le herirás en el calcañar."

La serpiente es Satanás. Apocalipsis 12:9 y 20:2 dicen:

"Y fué lanzado fuera aquel gran dragón, la serpiente antigua, que se llama Diablo y Satanás, el cual engaña á todo el mundo; fué arrojado en tierra, y sus ángeles fueron arrojados con él."

"Y prendió al dragón, aquella serpiente antigua, que es el Diablo y Satanás, y le ató por mil años."

La "simiente" es Jesucristo nuestro Salvador. Gálatas 3:16 dice:

"A Abraham fueron hechas las promesas, y á su simiente. No dice: Y á las simientes, como de muchos; sino como de uno: Y á tu simiente, la cual es Cristo.."

Jesucristo, nuestro Señor y Salvador, vino a esta tierra para derrotar a Satanás y rescatar a la humanidad perdida. Él vivió la vida perfecta que no podemos vivir, murió nuestra muerte eterna en la cruz del Calvario, luego resucitó; derrotando completamente a "esa serpiente antigua, llamada Diablo", para que nosotros, Su reino, pudiéramos vivir para siempre en la paz de una eternidad sin pecado. Jesús aplastó la cabeza de la serpiente, tal como prometió o hizo pacto.

La mujer es la iglesia es el reino de Dios de Cristo. Efesios 5:22-33 dice:

"Las casadas estén sujetas á sus propios maridos, como al Señor. Porque el marido es cabeza de la mujer, así como Cristo es cabeza de la iglesia; y él es el que da la salud al cuerpo. Así que, como la iglesia está sujeta á Cristo, así también las casadas lo estén á sus maridos en todo. Maridos, amad á vuestras mujeres, así como Cristo amó á la iglesia, y se entregó á sí mismo por ella, Para santificarla limpiándola en el lavacro del agua por la palabra, Para presentársela gloriosa para sí, una iglesia que no tuviese mancha ni arruga, ni cosa semejante; sino que fuese santa y sin mancha. Así también los maridos deben amar á sus mujeres como á sus mismos cuerpos. El que ama á su mujer, á sí mismo se ama. Porque ninguno aborreció jamás á su propia carne, antes la sustenta y regala, como también Cristo á la iglesia; Porque somos miembros de su cuerpo, de su carne y de sus huesos. Por esto dejará el hombre á su padre y á su madre, y se allegará á su mujer, y serán dos en una carne. Este misterio grande es: mas yo digo esto con respecto á Cristo y á la iglesia. Cada uno empero de vosotros de por sí, ame también á su mujer como á sí mismo; y la mujer reverencie á su marido."

También está el pacto que Dios hizo con toda la humanidad. Dios dijo: "Yo seré su Dios si ustedes son mi pueblo". Note Levítico 26: 1-13:

"NO haréis para vosotros ídolos, ni escultura, ni os levantaréis estatua, ni pondréis en vuestra tierra piedra pintada para inclinaros á ella: porque yo soy Jehová vuestro Dios. Guardad mis sábados, y tened en reverencia mi santuario: Yo Jehová. Si anduviereis en mis decretos, y guardareis mis mandamientos, y los pusiereis por obra; Yo daré vuestra lluvia en su tiempo, cy la tierra rendirá sus producciones, y el árbol del campo dará su fruto; Y la trilla os alcanzará á la vendimia, y la vendimia alcanzará á la sementera, y comeréis vuestro pan en hartura y habitaréis seguros en vuestra tierra: Y yo daré paz en la tierra, y dormiréis, y no habrá quien os espante: y haré quitar las malas bestias de vuestra tierra, y no pasará por vuestro país la espada: Y perseguiréis á vuestros enemigos, y caerán á cuchillo delante de vosotros: Y cinco de vosotros perseguirán á ciento, y ciento de vosotros perseguirán á diez mil, y vuestros enemigos caerán á cuchillo delante de vosotros. Porque yo me volveré á vosotros, y os haré crecer, y os multiplicaré, y afirmaré **mi pacto** con vosotros: Y comeréis lo añejo de mucho tiempo, y sacareis fuera lo añejo á causa de lo nuevo: Y pondré mi morada en medio de vosotros, y mi alma no os abominará: Y andaré entre vosotros, y yo seré vuestro Dios, y vosotros seréis mi pueblo. Yo Jehová vuestro Dios, que os saqué de la tierra de Egipto, para que no fueseis sus siervos; y rompí las coyundas de vuestro yugo, y os he hecho andar el rostro alto."

Note lo siguiente:

"Y él os anunció **su pacto**, el cual os mandó poner por obra, **las diez palabras**; y escribiólas en dos tablas de piedra." Deuteronomio 4:13

"Y él estuvo allí con Jehová cuarenta días y cuarenta noches: no comió pan, ni bebió agua; y escribió en tablas las palabras de **la alianza, las diez palabras**. Éxodo 34:28

"TENIA empero también **el primer pacto** reglamentos del culto, y santuario mundano. Porque el tabernáculo fué hecho: el primero, en que estaban las lámparas, y la mesa, y los panes de la proposición; lo que llaman el Santuario. Tras el segundo velo estaba el tabernáculo, que llaman el Lugar Santísimo; El cual tenía un incensario de oro, y el arca **del pacto** cubierta de todas partes alrededor de oro; en la que estaba una urna de oro que contenía el maná, y la vara de Aarón que reverdeció, **y las tablas del pacto**; Y sobre ella los querubines de gloria que cubrían el propiciatorio; de las cuales cosas no se puede ahora hablar en particular. Hebreos 9:1-5

Note también que la caja llamada Arca, que hizo Moisés (Éxodo 25: 10-22), se llama **Arca de la Alianza**. También se le llama el Arca del Testimonio (Éxodo 26:33).

El libro de la ley, la Torá, que Moisés escribió con sus propios dedos se colocó en el exterior del **Arca de la Alianza**:

"Y como acabó Moisés de escribir las palabras de esta ley en un libro hasta concluirse, Mandó Moisés á los Levitas que llevaban el arca del pacto de Jehová, diciendo: Tomad este libro de la ley, y ponedlo al lado del arca del pacto de Jehová vuestro Dios, y esté allí por testigo contra ti." Deuteronomio 31:24-26.

Pero la ley **del Pacto** de los **Diez Mandamientos**, escrita por el dedo de Dios, fue puesta dentro del Arca que está cubierta por el Propiciatorio, para la Gloria Shekinah de Dios mismo.

"En el arca ninguna cosa había más de las dos tablas de piedra que había allí puesto Moisés en Horeb, donde Jehová hizo la alianza con los hijos de Israel, cuando salieron de la tierra de Egipto. 1 Reyes 8:9.

El Arca de la Alianza se colocó en el centro del Santuario o Tienda de Reunión, en el Lugar Santísimo haciendo de los Diez Mandamientos el centro, eclipsado por la presencia misma de Dios con la Gloria Shekinah del Propiciatorio (Éxodo 26:33, 34).

El pacto, al que se hace referencia en el libro de Daniel, son los **DIEZ MANDAMIENTOS**.

4. ¿Quién es el PRÍNCIPE DEL PACTO?

En nuestro estudio del capítulo ocho de Daniel, descubrimos que Jesús es el Príncipe de los príncipes, como se menciona en Daniel 8:25. Jesús es el Hijo de Dios el Padre (1 Juan 5:20). Dios le dio a la humanidad los Diez Mandamientos, que Él mismo escribió en dos tablas de piedra con Su propio dedo.

Así, Jesús no es solo nuestro "Príncipe y Salvador", como nos dice Hechos 5:31, sino que Jesucristo es también el PRÍNCIPE DEL PACTO.

Como discutimos en nuestra consideración de Daniel ocho, el Poder del Cuerno Pequeño desafiará a Jesús, el Príncipe de paz, pero no tendrá éxito y será derrotado.

DEFINIENDO LO PERPETUO O CONTINUO

Por supuesto, la siguiente pregunta que debemos considerar es:

PREGUNTA: ¿QUÉ ES LO PERPETUO O CONTINUO QUE SERÁ LLEVADO EN EL FUTURO POR EL PEQUEÑO PODER DEL CUERNO?

Como ocurre con todos los períodos de tiempo en la Biblia, no tenemos el privilegio o el derecho de colocar estos períodos de tiempo en cualquier lugar que queramos en la historia de la humanidad. Cada período de tiempo debe colocarse en los puntos de inicio y finalización correctos dictados por las Escrituras. En este caso, la profecía del tiempo futuro de 1.290 días debe comenzar cuando se abandona el PERPETUO o CONTINUO. Daniel 12:11 dice:

> "Y desde el tiempo que fuere quitado el continuo sacrificio hasta la abominación espantosa, habrá mil doscientos y noventa días."

En otras palabras: Desde el momento en que se quita el continuo HASTA que se establece la abominación desoladora, habrá 1.290 días, o se podría decir, hay 1.290 días entre el momento en que se quita el continuo HASTA que se establece la abominación desoladora. hasta. De cualquier forma que se mire, el período de 1.290 días comienza cuando se quita el

CONTINUO y termina cuando se establece o "establece" la abominación desoladora.

5. ¿Qué es el perpetuo y qué es la abominación desoladora?

Recuerde: Sola Scriptura; la Biblia solamente. La Biblia debe interpretarse a sí misma 2 Pedro 1:20, 21 dice:

> "Entendiendo primero esto, que ninguna profecía de la Escritura es de particular interpretación; Porque la profecía no fué en los tiempos pasados traída por voluntad humana, sino los santos hombres de Dios hablaron siendo inspirados del Espíritu Santo."

Recopilemos algunas pistas en nuestro intento de identificar el PERPETUO o CONTINUO Bíblico:

1. Es algo que se puede quitar, quitar y abandonar.
2. Es algo que se puede reemplazar.
3. Será reemplazada por la abominación desoladora.
4. Es algo que afectará al pueblo de Dios ya que hay una bendición especial para los que permanecen fieles desde los 1.290 días hasta los 1.335 días.
5. Está aprobado por Dios mientras que la abominación desoladora no está aprobada.
6. Está relacionado con el pacto, que son los Diez Mandamientos.

PREGUNTA: ¿Qué parte del Sagrado Pacto de los Diez Mandamientos puede ser desafiado, eliminado, abandonado y reemplazado?

RESPUESTA: Solo uno de los Diez Mandamientos puede ser "quitado" y reemplazado por otra cosa. Ese es el séptimo día sábado, el cuarto mandamiento, que bíblicamente es desde la puesta del sol del viernes por la noche hasta la puesta del sol del sábado por la noche (Génesis 1:1 a 2:4)

PREGUNTA: ¿Existe un texto en la Biblia que respalde el sábado del séptimo día como el perpetuo o CONTINUO de Daniel 12:11?

RESPUESTA: Sí. Note Éxodo 31:12-17:

"Habló además Jehová á Moisés, diciendo: Y tú hablarás á los hijos de Israel, diciendo: Con todo eso vosotros guardaréis mis sábados: porque es señal entre mí y vosotros por vuestras edades, para que sepáis que yo soy Jehová que os santifico. Así que guardaréis el sábado, porque santo es á vosotros: el que lo profanare, de cierto morirá; porque cualquiera que hiciere obra alguna en él, aquella alma será cortada de en medio de sus pueblos. Seis días se hará obra, mas el día séptimo es sábado de reposo consagrado á Jehová; cualquiera que hiciere obra el día del sábado, morirá ciertamente. Guardarán, pues, **el sábado** los hijos de Israel: celebrándolo por sus edades por **pacto perpetuo**: Señal es para siempre entre mí y los hijos de Israel; porque en seis días hizo Jehová los cielos y la tierra, y en el séptimo día cesó, y reposó."

El sábado CONTINUO o PERPETUO será "quitado" en un futuro próximo.

Es muy importante darse cuenta de lo que es el CONTINUO, porque todos los períodos proféticos de Daniel y Apocalipsis comienzan cuando el sábado se abandona por la fuerza. Esto no debería sorprendernos de que el sábado será desafiado y abandonado en un futuro cercano. Mire todo el mundo religioso alrededor de este globo. Incluso ahora, el día de reposo del séptimo día no es respetado por la mayoría de las organizaciones religiosas. De hecho, muchos de ellos niegan descaradamente el sábado con las siguientes falsas excusas que no pueden ser fundamentadas por las Escrituras.

1. Jesús cambió el sábado por el domingo.
2. Jesús abolió el sábado en la cruz.
3. Pablo cambió el sábado por el domingo.
4. Los apóstoles cambiaron el sábado por el domingo.
5. El sábado del séptimo día fue abandonado y reemplazado por el primer día de la semana, el domingo, en honor a la resurrección.
6. Jesús es el sábado.

Todas estas ridículas excusas, fabricadas por el hombre, se utilizan para negar que se honra el séptimo día del pacto de los Diez Mandamientos, el sábado. Note Mateo 15:9:

"Mas en vano me honran, Enseñando doctrinas y mandamientos de hombres."

PREGUNTA: ¿Cuál es el CONTINUO o PERPETUO de Daniel 12:11 que será "quitado" que marca el comienzo de los períodos de tiempo en Daniel y Apocalipsis?

RESPUESTA: El cuarto mandamiento del pacto de los Diez Mandamientos, el sábado del séptimo día, es el CONTINUO de Daniel 12:11 que será prohibido en el futuro.

PREGUNTA: ¿Qué es la ABOMINACIÓN DE LA DESOLACIÓN que se "instalará" en su lugar?

IDENTIFICAR LA ABOMINACIÓN DE LA DESOLACIÓN

¿Qué es una "abominación desoladora" o una "abominación desoladora"?

Una "abominación" es aquello que es detestable e inaceptable por nuestro Dios creador.

Una "desolación" es un vacío, vacío, destrucción total, sin vida, sin muerte.

Una "abominación que causa desolación" es un acto detestable contra Dios que hace que Él reaccione de tal manera que provoque la destrucción completa. Ejemplos bíblicos de "abominación desoladora" o aquellos eventos que provocaron la ira de Dios son:

1. La "abominación" fue el pecado desenfrenado antes del diluvio en los días de Noé. La "desolación" fue la destrucción de todos los vivos a causa del pecado: Génesis 6-9.
2. Destrucción de la pecadora Sodoma y Gomorra en los días de Abraham: Génesis 18,19.
3. La destrucción de las diez tribus rebeldes del norte de Israel: 2 Reyes 17,18.
4. El cautiverio de las dos tribus del sur infieles a través de Nabucodonosor: Daniel 1.
5. La próxima tribulación de siete años que revela la ira de Dios contra aquellos que rehúsan confiar en Él y obedecerle en el tiempo del fin: Mateo 24:21.

EJEMPLOS BÍBLICOS DE LA PALABRA ABOMINACIÓN:

"Porque el perverso es abominado de Jehová: Mas su secreto es con los rectos." Proverbios 3:32

"El que aparta su oído para no oir la ley, Su oración también es abominable."

Proverbios 28:9

"EL peso falso abominación es á Jehová: Mas la pesa cabal le agrada." Proverbios 11:1

"Prevaricó Judá, y en Israel y en Jerusalem ha sido cometida abominación; porque Judá ha profanado la santidad de Jehová que amó, y casádose con hija de dios extraño." Malaquías 2:11

EJEMPLOS BÍBLICOS DE LA PALABRA DESOLACIÓN:

"Estas dos cosas te han acaecido; ¿quién se dolerá de ti? asolamiento y quebrantamiento, hambre y espada. ¿Quién te consolará?" Isaías 51:19.

"Tus santas ciudades están desiertas, Sión es un desierto, Jerusalem una soledad. 11 La casa de nuestro santuario y de nuestra gloria, en la cual te alabaron nuestros padres, fué consumida al fuego; y todas nuestras cosas preciosas han sido destruídas."

Isaías 64:10, 11.

Establecer una "abominación desoladora" es establecer algo que va en contra de la voluntad de Dios, provocando sus acciones de ira e ira destructivas contra la humanidad.

Es importante notar el término "establecer" ya que nos remite al capítulo tres de Daniel cuando el rey Nabucodonosor "instaló" la imagen de oro que promovía la ADORACIÓN FORZADA.

PREGUNTA: ¿Cuál es la ABOMINACIÓN DE LA DESOLACIÓN que se "establecerá" en lugar del sábado del séptimo día?

RESPUESTA: El tiempo del fin "ABOMINACIÓN QUE CAUSA DESOLACIÓN" es el establecimiento de un falso día de adoración que será exigido a toda la humanidad, para reemplazar el séptimo día sábado. Lo más probable es que ese falso día de adoración sea el primer día de la semana, el domingo, ya que ya es popular en todo el mundo.

Daniel 12:13:

"Y tú irás al fin, y reposarás, y te levantarás en tu suerte al fin de los días."

Cuando Daniel escuchó estos períodos de tiempo tremendamente largos, anotó en Daniel 12:7,11,12; el Señor debió haber notado la decepción en su expresión facial. Daniel sabía que los setenta años de cautiverio habían pasado y ahora estaba ansioso por que sus compatriotas regresaran a su tierra natal. Para él, 1.290 días y 1.335 días adicionales deben haber sido abrumadores. Pero el Señor le dijo que siguiera adelante con su propia vida. Le dijo a Daniel que los períodos de tiempo son para el fin de la historia del mundo. Dios animó a Daniel diciéndole "al final de los días", después de los 1000 años, recibirá la vida eterna.

Esta información debería ayudarnos a comprender mejor la información que se encuentra en Daniel 12:1-4:

"Y EN aquel tiempo se levantará Miguel, el gran príncipe que está por los hijos de tu pueblo; y será tiempo de angustia, cual nunca fué después que hubo gente hasta entonces: mas en aquel tiempo será libertado tu pueblo, todos los que se hallaren escritos en el libro. Y muchos de los que duermen en el polvo de la tierra serán despertados, unos para vida eterna, y otros para vergüenza y confusión perpetua. Y los entendidos resplandecerán como el resplandor del firmamento; y los que enseñan á justicia la multitud, como las estrellas á perpetua eternidad. Tú empero Daniel, cierra las palabras y sella el libro hasta el tiempo del fin: pasarán muchos, y multiplicaráse la ciencia."

A Daniel se le animó a seguir con su vida diaria y no preocuparse por esta visión porque con el tiempo, en **el último día**, resucitará de entre los muertos, junto con todos los demás santos, para pasar la eternidad con Dios. Paul creía lo mismo. Escribe en 2 Timoteo 4: 8:

"Por lo demás, me está guardada la corona de justicia, la cual me dará el Señor, juez justo, en aquel día; y no sólo á mí, sino también á **todos** los que aman su venida."

PREGUNTA: ¿Cuándo es el último día? O ¿Cuándo es el día en que Daniel y Pablo, con todos los santos, reciben la vida eterna?

Marta, la hermana de Lázaro, sabía sobre el último día y la resurrección de los muertos cuando recibirían un cuerpo inmortal eterno glorificado: Fíjense en Juan 11:23, 24:

"Dícele Jesús: Resucitará tu hermano. 24 Marta le dice: Yo sé que resucitará en la resurrección en el **día postrero**."

En Juan 6:38-40 Jesús dijo:

"Porque he descendido del cielo, no para hacer mi voluntad, mas la voluntad del que me envió. Y esta es la voluntad del que me envió, del Padre: Que todo lo que me diere, no pierda de ello, sino que lo resucite en el **día postrero**. Y esta es la voluntad del que me ha enviado: Que todo aquel que ve al Hijo, y cree en él, tenga vida eterna: y yo le resucitaré en el **día postrero**."

El último día, el día en que se recompensa la vida eterna y la muerte eterna, será el "último día" después de los 1000 años de Apocalipsis 20, cuando el pecado sea destruido y Dios cree "un cielo nuevo y una tierra nueva".

Vea el video de YouTube **DANIEL CAPÍTULO DOCE EN ESPAÑOL** por Earl Schrock

DANIEL CAPÍTULO DOCE (RVR)

1 Y EN aquel tiempo se levantará Miguel, el gran príncipe que está por los hijos de tu pueblo; y será tiempo de angustia, cual nunca fué después que hubo gente hasta entonces: mas en aquel tiempo será libertado tu pueblo, todos los que se hallaren escritos en el libro. 2 Y muchos de los que duermen en el polvo de la tierra serán despertados, unos para vida eterna, y

otros para vergüenza y confusión perpetua. 3 Y los entendidos resplandecerán como el resplandor del firmamento; y los que enseñan á justicia la multitud, como las estrellas á perpetua eternidad. 4 Tú empero Daniel, cierra las palabras y sella el libro hasta el tiempo del fin: pasarán muchos, y multiplicaráse la ciencia. 5 Y yo, Daniel, miré, y he aquí otros dos que estaban, el uno de esta parte á la orilla del río, y el otro de la otra parte á la orilla del río. 6 Y dijo uno al varón vestido de lienzos, que estaba sobre las aguas del río: ¿Cuándo será el fin de estas maravillas? 7 Y oía al varón vestido de lienzos, que estaba sobre las aguas del río, el cual alzó su diestra y su siniestra al cielo, y juró por el Viviente en los siglos, que será por tiempo, tiempos, y la mitad. Y cuando se acabare el esparcimiento del escuadrón del pueblo santo, todas estas cosas serán cumplidas. 8 Y yo oí, mas no entendí. Y dije: Señor mío, ¿qué será el cumplimiento de estas cosas? 9 Y dijo: Anda, Daniel, que estas palabras están cerradas y selladas hasta el tiempo del cumplimiento. 10 Muchos serán limpios, y emblanquecidos, y purificados; mas los impíos obrarán impíamente, y ninguno de los impíos entenderá, pero entenderán los entendidos. 11 Y desde el tiempo que fuere quitado el continuo sacrificio hasta la abominación espantosa, habrá mil doscientos y noventa días. 12 Bienaventurado el que esperare, y llegare hasta mil trescientos treinta y cinco días. 13 Y tú irás al fin, y reposarás, y te levantarás en tu suerte al fin de los días.

CAPÍTULO TRECE

EL VINAGRE EN LA CRUZ DEL CALVARIO

Muchos de nosotros hemos leído o nos han enseñado que a Jesús le ofrecieron vinagre en dos ocasiones distintas mientras lo crucificaban. Numerosos estudiosos de la Biblia han escrito sobre el vinagre en la cruz del Calvario y han presentado sus diversas opiniones personales. La primera vez que se le ofreció la bebida amarga fue a la tercera hora (9 a.m.). La segunda vez le fue ofrecido a la novena hora (3 p.m.), seis horas después. Rechazó (Mateo 27:34) la bebida amarga a la hora tercera, pero a la hora novena, realmente la pidió cuando dijo: "Tengo sed" (Juan 19:28). Cuando se le dio, lo bebió (Mateo 27:48).

El consenso general de los numerosos eruditos bíblicos es que el vinagre estaba en el lugar de la crucifixión para ser ofrecido a los crucificados para embotar sus sentidos y hacer la crucifixión más tolerable.

Algunos expositores de la Biblia concluyen que Jesús rechazó el vinagre la primera vez para poder experimentar el sufrimiento y soportar la cruz sin ninguna ayuda entumecida. En la segunda ocasión, enseñan que pidió el vinagre porque tenía sed y quería aliviar el dolor. Estas conclusiones son meras opiniones y ninguna de las dos está respaldada por las Escrituras.

¿POR QUÉ FUE EL VINAGRE EN LA CRUZ?

Un par de preguntas para considerar son: (1) ¿Por qué estaba el vinagre en la cruz en primer lugar? y (2) ¿Estaba el vinagre allí para mostrar compasión a los empalados en el madero (Hechos 10:39)?

Primero debemos reconocer que fueron los soldados (Mateo 27: 27-36) los que le ofrecieron el vinagre a Jesús (Lucas 23:36) al comienzo de su crucifixión y no uno de sus amigos. Jesús estaba siendo custodiado por cuatro soldados romanos (Juan 19:23). No solo estaban allí para crucificar a Jesús, sino que también estaban allí para protegerlo de otros que pudieran interferir con su deber. El vinagre no podría haber sido ofrecido por ningún transeúnte ya que no se les habría permitido acercarse lo suficiente a la víctima para hacer ese gesto humano. Solo los soldados romanos tenían la capacidad de darle a Jesús la bebida fuerte.

La oferta de vinagre no era para mostrar compasión a los que colgaban de la cruz. Los romanos habían ideado la crucifixión como un método terrible de ejecución, haciéndola lo más humillante y dolorosa posible. La humillación vendría cuando el criminal sería desnudado (Mateo 27:35, Juan 19:23) para que todos lo vieran, y sus crímenes serían atados en la cruz (Juan 19:19-22) para que todos los leyeran. El dolor insoportable sería el resultado natural de primero ser azotado (Marcos 15:15) y luego colgado en la cruz con clavos que perforan las manos y los pies (Salmo 22:16, Lucas 24:40). Los romanos odiaban a los judíos, por lo que mostrar compasión al ofrecer asistencia medicinal al crucificado sería incongruente y contraproducente.

El vinagre estaba ubicado en el Gólgota (Marcos 15:22) porque los soldados romanos estaban allí. El vinagre era una parte básica de la dieta de un soldado. La bebida amarga barata (Mateo 27:34; Marcos 15:23) no se ofreció en una muestra de compasión; Lo más probable es que se ofreciera como una burla (Lucas 23:36).

Forzar vinagre en el rostro roto e hinchado de Jesús habría aumentado Su dolor cuando el líquido ardiente entró en contacto con su rostro magullado y sangrante y sus labios partidos. Ofrecerlo como un copero ofrece vino a un rey (Génesis 40:21; 2 Crónicas 9: 4) se sumaría a la burla de los soldados romanos, tal como lo llamaban "el rey de los judíos" y se burlaban de Él para "salvar a ti mismo"(Lucas 23:37). Entonces, ¿por qué Jesús rechazó el vinagre cuando se lo ofreció por primera vez y lo bebió cuando se le dio la segunda vez?

Para darnos cuenta de por qué Jesús primero se negó y luego pidió el vinagre, debemos comprender (1) el mensaje del evangelio que Jesús predicó mientras estuvo en esta tierra y (2) debemos comprender la enseñanza bíblica de un voto nazareo.

EL REINO DE DIOS ESTÁ A LA MANO (CERCA).

¿Cuál fue el mensaje que Jesús proclamó mientras iba de pueblo en pueblo con sus discípulos? Note Marcos 1:14,15 "Mas después que Juan fué encarcelado, Jesús vino á Galilea predicando el evangelio del reino de Dios, Y diciendo: El tiempo es cumplido, y el reino de Dios está cerca: arrepentíos, y creed al evangelio." También en Lucas 8:1, "Y ACONTECIO después, que él caminaba por todas las ciudades y aldeas, predicando y anunciando el evangelio del reino de Dios."

La cercanía del reino de Dios fue también el mensaje de Juan antes de bautizar a Jesús. *"Y EN aquellos días vino Juan el Bautista predicando en el desierto de Judea, 2 Y diciendo:*

Arrepentíos, que el reino de los cielos se ha acercado." (Mateo 3:1,2). La promesa de que el reino de Dios está "cerca" o "a la mano" significa que pronto estaría disponible para toda la humanidad en ese momento, en sus días, no retrasado 2000 años después, en nuestros días.

El reino de Dios no es un lugar; es una relación. Una relación entre lo creado (la humanidad) y su Creador (Juan 1: 1-5). El reino de los cielos es una relación establecida o construida por Jesús para toda la humanidad mediante Su vida, muerte y resurrección. El reino de los cielos está dentro de ti (Lucas 17:21). Es el reino "construido sin manos" (Marcos 14:58) como se demuestra en el capítulo dos de Daniel.

EL REINO DE DIOS Y VINAGRE

¿Qué tiene que ver el reino de Dios con que Jesús bebiera el vinagre justo antes de morir en la cruz?

La pregunta que muchas personas se hacen es: "¿Cuándo comenzó el reino de Dios, que Jesús preparó" sin manos "desde la" fundación del mundo? "En otras palabras, ¿cuándo se hizo disponible el reino de los cielos para toda la humanidad?

Respuesta: En la cruz.

Jesús hizo una declaración controvertida cuando dijo a sus discípulos: "Y os digo en verdad, que hay algunos de los que están aquí, que no gustarán la muerte, hasta que vean el reino de Dios." (Lucas 9:27). Compare eso con Marcos 9:1, "TAMBIÉN les dijo: De cierto os digo que hay algunos de los que están aquí, que no gustarán la muerte hasta que hayan visto el reino de Dios que viene con potencia." Ese poder llegó cincuenta días después en el aposento alto (Hechos 2:1-4).

Hay dos explicaciones o entendimientos para el Reino de Dios. Las dos explicaciones caen bajo las categorías de (1) reino de gracia y (2) reino de gloria. El Reino de Dios de "GRACIA" (Hebreos 12:28) fue establecido en la cruz. El Reino eterno de Dios de "GLORIA" (2 Timoteo 4:18) se establecerá en el tiempo del fin (Mateo 16:27; 25: 31-46) cuando el pecado sea destruido para siempre y Dios cree "un cielo nuevo y una tierra nueva" (Apocalipsis 21:1) "en los cuales mora la justicia." (2 Pedro 3:11-13).

Hay muchos a quienes se les ha enseñado que el reino de gracia de Dios no se creará hasta que Jesús venga por segunda vez. Por esa razón, estas personas tienen la impresión de que Jesús les mintió a sus discípulos acerca de que algunos de ellos estaban vivos para ver establecido el reino de Dios (Marcos 9: 1). No es que Jesús haya pecado al mentir que ellos tienen este malentendido; es que no se dan cuenta de la naturaleza del Reino de Dios. Recuerde que el Reino de Dios no es un lugar; es una relación. Una relación entre lo creado y el Creador que Jesús estableció con Su vida, muerte y resurrección para ti y para mí. El reino de Dios de gracia está disponible aquí y ahora para todos los que deseen tener una relación eterna y entrañable con Jesús como su rey con el Espíritu Santo que vive en su interior (2 Corintios 1:22).

Jesús estableció el reino de la gracia mientras colgaba de la cruz y el poder de ese reino se demostró cincuenta días después en el aposento alto (Hechos 2: 1-4) tal como lo prometió (Lucas 9:27). El único requisito para entrar en este reino gracia actual es tener el "vestido de boda" (Mateo 22:1-14), que representa Su justicia, que solo está disponible al aceptar a Jesús como nuestro salvador personal que vivió y murió en nuestro lugar.

¿Cómo sabemos que Jesús estableció el Reino de Dios mientras moría en la cruz? Para responder a esta pregunta, debemos entender el voto bíblico de un nazareo. En la Biblia, solo tenemos otros tres ejemplos de personas apartadas bajo el juramento nazareo. Ellos son: (1) Sansón en Jueces 13: 5-7, y (2) Samuel en 1 Samuel 1:11, y (3) Juan el Bautista en Lucas 1:11-17.

Considere Números 6:1-8:

"Y HABLO Jehová á Moisés, diciendo: Habla á los hijos de Israel, y diles: El hombre, ó la mujer, cuando se apartare haciendo voto de Nazareo, para dedicarse á Jehová, Se abstendrá de vino y de sidra; vinagre de vino, ni vinagre de sidra no beberá, ni beberá algún licor de uvas, ni tampoco comerá uvas frescas ni secas. Todo el tiempo de su nazareato, de todo lo que se hace de vid de vino, desde los granillos hasta el hollejo, no comerá. Todo el tiempo del voto de su nazareato no pasará navaja sobre su cabeza, hasta que sean cumplidos los días de su apartamiento á Jehová: santo será; dejará crecer las guedejas del cabello de su cabeza. Todo el tiempo que se apartaré á Jehová, no entrará á persona muerta. Por su padre, ni por su madre, por su hermano, ni por su hermana, no se contaminará con ellos cuando murieren; porque consagración de su Dios tiene sobre su cabeza. Todo el tiempo de su nazareato, será santo á Jehová."

El que está bajo la promesa de un nazareo debe cumplir con tres requisitos. No pueden (1) beber ni comer ningún producto de la uva o de la vid, incluido el vinagre. (2) No pueden cortarse el pelo ni afeitarse la cabeza. Y (3) no pueden entrar en contacto con un cadáver.

El que está bajo la promesa de un nazareo debe cumplir con tres requisitos. No pueden (1) beber ni comer ningún producto de la uva o de la vid, incluido el vinagre. (2) No pueden cortarse el pelo ni afeitarse la cabeza. Y (3) no pueden entrar en contacto con un cadáver.

JESÚS Y SU VOTO NAZARITA

En la fiesta de la Pascua con sus discípulos, antes de la crucifixión, Jesús se puso bajo el voto de un nazareo. "Después de tomar la copa, dio gracias y dijo: "Y tomando el vaso, habiendo dado gracias, dijo: Tomad esto, y partidlo entre vosotros; Porque os digo, que no beberé más del fruto de la vid, hasta que el reino de Dios venga." Lucas 22:17,18. Considere también Mateo 26:26-29:

> "Y comiendo ellos, tomó Jesús el pan, y bendijo, y lo partió, y dió á sus discípulos, y dijo: Tomad, comed. esto es mi cuerpo. Y tomando el vaso, y hechas gracias, les dió, diciendo: Bebed de él todos; Porque esto es mi sangre del nuevo pacto, la cual es derramada por muchos para remisión de los pecados. Y os digo, que desde ahora no beberé más de este fruto de la vid, hasta aquel día, cuando lo tengo de beber nuevo con vosotros en el reino de mi Padre."

Jesús les dijo previamente en Lucas 22 versículos 15 y 16, "Y les dijo: En gran manera he deseado comer con vosotros esta pascua antes que padezca; Porque os digo que no comeré más de ella, hasta que se cumpla en el reino de Dios." El versículo 19 continúa, "Y tomando el pan, habiendo dado gracias, partió, y les dió, diciendo: Esto es mi cuerpo, que por vosotros es dado: haced esto en memoria de mí." Jesús no solo dijo que no participaría de ninguna uva o producto de la vid, sino que también añadió al voto diciendo que no comería pan "hasta que el reino de Dios venga." (Lucas 22:18).

JESÚS GUARDÓ EL VOTO DE NAZARITA

Jesús comenzó su juramento de nazareo en la última cena mientras estaba en el aposento alto con sus discípulos (Lucas 22: 11,12), antes de que fueran al huerto de Getsemaní (Mateo 26:36), y antes de que fuera hecho prisionero por "*los príncipes de los sacerdotes, y de los ancianos*" (Mateo 26:47-50). Jesús terminó su voto nazareo mientras moría en la cruz.

Desde el momento en que Jesús salió del aposento alto con sus discípulos, hasta la cruz, Jesús (1) no comió ni bebió ningún producto de la vid, (2) no se cortó el cabello y (3) no vino a la presencia. de un cadáver como se exige en el capítulo seis de Números; (4) ni comió pan, como prometió más específicamente.

La primera oferta de vinagre fue presentada a Jesús al comienzo de la crucifixión a la tercera hora o a las nueve de la mañana (Mateo 27:1,33,34), pero Jesús rechazó el vinagre. Jesús sabía que no era el momento de establecer el reino, así que cuando el vinagre tocó Sus labios, lo rechazó. Para cuando llegó la segunda oferta de vinagre, a la hora novena oa las tres de la tarde (Mateo 27: 46-48), Jesús terminó o completó Su voto nazareo bebiendo el vinagre, un producto de la vid. Sabía que todo se había cumplido como estaba profetizado en las Escrituras y había llegado el momento de que Él cumpliera las Escrituras (Juan 19:28), estableciera el Reino de Dios y muriera (Juan 19:30).

Jesús es el cordero pascual del sacrificio (1 Corintios 5:7). Él es "*el Cordero de Dios, que quita el pecado del mundo.*" (Juan 1:29). El día en que Jesús fue crucificado fue el día de la Pascua judía (Marcos 14:12-17). Jesús no pudo beber la primera oferta de vinagre y morir a la tercera hora (Marcos 15:25); Jesús tuvo que morir a la hora novena, que es el tiempo establecido en el que históricamente se sacrificó el cordero pascual (Éxodo 12:6). Tuvo que morir en el momento específico en que bebió el vinagre, a la hora novena (Marcos 15:34), para cumplir con las Escrituras (Salmo 69:21), honrar el voto nazareo y revelar el comienzo del reino de Dios. que está disponible para ti y para mí aquí y ahora.

Piense en Jesús en la cruz mientras lee el Salmo 69:17-21:

"Y no escondas tu rostro de tu siervo; Porque estoy angustiado; apresúrate, óyeme. Acércate á mi alma, redímela: Líbrame á causa de mis enemigos. Tú sabes mi afrenta, y mi confusión, y mi oprobio: Delante de ti están todos mis enemigos. La afrenta ha quebrantado mi corazón, y estoy acongojado: Y esperé quien se compadeciese de mí, y no lo hubo: Y consoladores, y ninguno hallé. Pusiéronme además hiel por comida, Y en mi sed me dieron á beber vinagre."

Jesús mantuvo su voto de nazareo al no beber el vinagre en la primera oferta. Completó Su juramento nazareo bebiéndolo la segunda vez que fue entregado a Sus labios. También demostró más y más específicamente que el reino de Dios había llegado al comer pan después de Su resurrección. La escritura informa que en el día de su resurrección, Jesús "partió el pan" con dos de sus discípulos (Lucas 24:13,30) en el camino a Emaús. Jesús también "comió y bebió con" los discípulos "después que resucitó de entre los muertos" (Hechos 10:41). Para comprender mejor Su voto nazareo, tenga todo esto en cuenta al leer todo el Salmo 22 y Lucas 23.

La Biblia que menciona las dos ofertas de vinagre en la cruz no es por accidente o casualidad. Estos dos incidentes están incluidos específicamente en los evangelios por la voluntad de Dios para nuestro crecimiento y entendimiento (2 Timoteo 3:16,17). Los escritores de los evangelios que registran este evento fueron inspirados por el Espíritu Santo (2 Pedro 1:19-21) para incluir los incidentes del vinagre por dos razones específicas.

Creo que una de las razones por las que el vinagre en la cruz se incluyó en la Santa Biblia es para que podamos confirmar cuándo el reino de Dios estuvo disponible para toda la humanidad y cómo llegó a existir a través del sacrificio de Jesús mismo (Génesis 22:8), " *el Cordero de Dios, que quita el pecado del mundo"* Juan 1:29.

La segunda razón por la que el vinagre en la cruz fue incluido en la historia de la salvación es porque fue un cumplimiento de la profecía y la ley mosaica. En la ley de sacrificio ceremonial mosaica, dos corderos, de un año, debían ser sacrificados todos los días sin interrupción. Note el siguiente texto importante de Números 28:1-8:

"Y HABLO Jehová á Moisés, diciendo: Manda á los hijos de Israel, y diles: Mi ofrenda, mi pan con mis ofrendas encendidas en olor á mí agradable, guardaréis, ofreciéndomelo á su tiempo. Y les dirás: Esta es la ofrenda encendida que ofreceréis á Jehová: dos corderos sin tacha de un año, cada un día, será el holocausto continuo. El un cordero ofrecerás por la mañana, y el otro cordero ofrecerás entre las dos tardes: Y la décima de un epha de flor de harina, amasada con una cuarta de un hin de aceite molido, en presente. Es holocausto continuo, que fué hecho en el monte de Sinaí en olor de suavidad, ofrenda encendida á Jehová. Y su libación, la cuarta de un hin con cada cordero: derramarás libación de superior (**fermentado**) vino á Jehová en el santuario. Y ofrecerás el segundo cordero entre las dos tardes: conforme á la ofrenda de la mañana, y conforme á su libación ofrecerás, ofrenda encendida en olor de suavidad á Jehová."

(El "shekhar" 7941 de Strong es una bebida fuerte, fermentada o de **vinagre** que se ofrece **sólo** con el sacrificio continuo o perpetuo de **la mañana** y de **la tarde**.)

En el sistema de la ley de sacrificios ceremoniales mosaicos, la **ÚNICA** ofrenda de sacrificio hecha al Señor con bebida **fermentada** o **vinagre** era la ofrenda diaria de alimentos, que se hacía dos veces al día, una por la **mañana** y otra por la **noche**. Jesús cumplió esta ley ceremonial cuando le ofrecieron vinagre por la mañana y vinagre por la tarde. Debido a Su voto nazareo, no pudo beber el vinagre hasta poco antes de Su muerte, en el sacrificio vespertino para traer el reino de Dios.

EL REINO DE LOS CIELOS, REINO DE DIOS

El Reino de Dios (reino de los cielos) existe aquí y ahora mismo para que Su pueblo alrededor de este mundo tenga un lugar de unificación bajo un Rey (Ezequiel 37:18-28). No en un edificio o en una sola congregación, sino en una relación unificadora con Jesús (Juan 11:52). A este gran grupo de devotos adoradores de Dios ubicados en todos los países del mundo, llamo "La Iglesia Invisible". Dios los llama "El Reino de los Cielos". La Iglesia Invisible no tiene muros, no recolecta ofrendas y no realiza reuniones regulares donde todos los miembros se reúnen colectivamente. La "Iglesia Invisible" o el reino de Dios, es el pueblo mundial de Dios, la Nueva Jerusalén, el Monte

Sión, unidos en un solo nombre. Ese único nombre es Jesús (Hechos 4:12). El deseo de Dios es tener "un rebaño con un solo pastor".

Note las palabras de Jesús que se encuentran en Juan 10:11-18:

> "Yo soy el buen pastor: el buen pastor su vida da por las ovejas. Mas el asalariado, y que no es el pastor, de quien no son propias las ovejas, ve al lobo que viene, y deja las ovejas, y huye, y el lobo las arrebata, y esparce las ovejas. Así que, el asalariado, huye, porque es asalariado, y no tiene cuidado de las ovejas. Yo soy el buen pastor; y conozco mis ovejas, y las mías me conocen. Como el Padre me conoce, y yo conozco al Padre; y pongo mi vida por las ovejas. También tengo otras ovejas que no son de este redil; aquéllas también me conviene traer, y oirán mi voz; **y habrá un rebaño, y un pastor**. Por eso me ama el Padre, porque yo pongo mi vida, para volverla á tomar. Nadie me la quita, mas yo la pongo de mí mismo. Tengo poder para ponerla, y tengo poder para volverla á tomar. Este mandamiento recibí de mi Padre."

El reino de Dios existe para que Su pueblo alrededor de este mundo pueda alabar al Rey del universo en pura reverencia y obediencia de la manera que Él exige ser adorado en Su Palabra. Por esta razón, el capítulo dos de Daniel revela a la Iglesia Invisible o reino de Dios como una piedra "cortada de un monte sin manos" (Daniel 2:34,45) que comienza pequeña, en la cruz, y crece para envolver todo este planeta. (Daniel 2:35). **

A medida que lee la Biblia, la Palabra de Dios, busque diariamente por sí mismo para descubrir la verdadera adoración que Dios exige. *"Escogeos hoy á quién sirváis…. que yo y mi casa serviremos á Jehová"* (Josué 24:15).

Si aún no lo ha hecho, ¿no le dará su corazón, mente y alma a Dios y entrará en Su reino de gracia aquí y ahora? Él preparó este reino para ti desde la fundación del mundo y lo aseguró con Su muerte en la cruel cruz. Entrar en el reino de la gracia te preparará para entrar en Su futuro eterno reino de gloria.

** Aprenda más sobre el reino de Dios leyendo el libro electrónico, "The Kingdom of Heaven and the Kingdom of God" de Earl B. Schrock, que se encuentra en Xlibris, com, Amazon, Barnes and Noble, etc.

CAPÍTULO CATORCE

COMPRENDER LA MECÁNICA BÍBLICA DE: BUCLES DE PROFECÍA, DIVISIONES NATURALES Y BUCLES DE TIEMPO.

Comprensión de la mecánica bíblica; La estructura de la escritura de la Biblia, ya sea en toda la Biblia, en un libro completo, en un capítulo completo o en los versículos mismos, ayuda a los estudiantes de la Biblia a dividir correctamente la Palabra de Dios.

(2 Timoteo 2:15) para que se pueda determinar el significado correcto.

UN BUCLE DE PROFECÍA o Bible Loop, es un estilo de escritura bíblica en el que los versículos siguen un ciclo de pensamiento completo para agregar información a los versículos anteriores. (Prefiero usar el término BUCLE DE PROFECÍA, ya que es de vital importancia para comprender la profecía bíblica).

EN el capítulo dos de Daniel encuentro dieciocho (18) BUCLE DE PROFECÍA; son los siguientes:

El versículo 12 retrocede para agregar información sobre el versículo 5
El versículo 16 retrocede para agregar información sobre el versículo 2

El versículo 19 retrocede para agregar información sobre el versículo 2
El versículo 24 retrocede para agregar información sobre el versículo 16
El versículo 26 retrocede para agregar información sobre el versículo 5
El versículo 27, 28 retrocede para agregar información sobre el versículo 10.
El versículo 31 retrocede para agregar información sobre el versículo 2
El versículo 37,38 retrocede para agregar información sobre el versículo 32a.
El versículo 39 retrocede para agregar información sobre el versículo 32b.
El versículo 40 retrocede para agregar información sobre el versículo 33
El versículo 40b retrocede para agregar información sobre el versículo 35
El versículo 41-44 retrocede para agregar información sobre el versículo 33.
El versículo 44 retrocede para agregar información sobre el versículo 42
El versículo 45 retrocede para agregar información sobre el versículo 34
El versículo 45 retrocede para agregar información sobre el versículo 40b.
El versículo 46 retrocede para agregar información sobre el versículo 6
El versículo 47 retrocede para agregar información sobre el versículo 28
El versículo 48 retrocede para agregar información sobre el versículo 6

LAS DIVISIONES NATURALES tienen lugar dentro de un capítulo de la Biblia cuando hay un se introduce un cambio de conversación o un nuevo tema. Un BOSQUEJO cuidadoso de un capítulo de la Biblia revela las DIVISIONES NATURALES.

En mi opinión, el capítulo dos de Daniel tiene 8 divisiones naturales. Las divisiones naturales son:

1. versículos 1-12
2. versículos 13-16
3. versículos 17-23
4. versículos 24-27
5. versículos 28-30
6. versículos 31-35
7. versículos 36-45
8. versículos 46-49

LOS BUCLES DE TIEMPO ocurren en las Escrituras cuando los versículos, capítulos o capítulos tienen un comienzo ininterrumpido y un punto final en el tiempo y luego regresan a otro punto de comienzo. En este caso del capítulo dos de Daniel, hay tres ciclos de tiempo como se muestra a continuación.

Los versículos que componen el capítulo dos de Daniel son del 1 al 49. Hay tres ciclos de tiempo distintos en el capítulo dos de Daniel. Se colocan en tres ciclos de tiempo debido al lugar donde estos versículos caen en una línea de tiempo histórica:

Los tres ciclos de tiempo son:

1. versículos 1-35;
2. versículos 36 al 45
3. versículos 46 al 49.

El **primer** ciclo de tiempo de los versículos 1 al 35 va desde el día de Daniel hasta el final de la tribulación de siete años. Luego, el siguiente versículo, el versículo 36, se remonta al día de Daniel.

Este **segundo** ciclo de tiempo de los versículos 36 al 45 va desde el día de Daniel hasta el final de la tribulación de siete años. Luego, el siguiente versículo, el versículo 46, se remonta al día de Daniel.

Este **tercer** ciclo de los versículos 46 al 49 permanece en el día de Daniel en la tabla.

TABLA HISTÓRICA DE BUCLES DE TIEMPO PARA DANIEL CAPÍTULO DOS

Babilonia	Medo-Persia	Grecia	Roma	Am. Bible Soc.	Tiempo de problemas	
605 AC	**538 AC**	**330 AC**	**168 AC**	**1800 DC**	**7** AÑOS TRIBULACIÓN	
Vs1-32			33a	33b	34	35
Vs 36-38	39a	39b	40	41	42-44	45
Versos 46-49						

Es posible que tenga una diferencia de opinión sobre el número y la ubicación de los bucles de profecía, las divisiones naturales y los bucles de tiempo en el capítulo dos de Daniel y eso está bastante bien.

LA PÁGINA SIGUIENTE CONTIENE TODOS LOS BUCLES DE TIEMPO DE LA PROFECÍA PARA EL LIBRO DANIEL

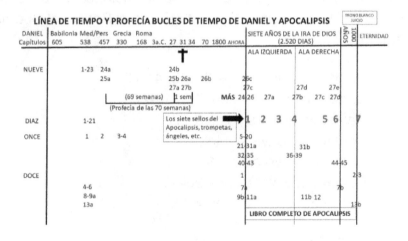

LÍNEA DE TIEMPO Y PROFECÍA BUCLES DE TIEMPO DE DANIEL Y APOCALIPSIS — TRONO BLANCO JUICIO

DANIEL Capítulos	Babilonia 605	Med/Pers 538	457	Grecia 330	Roma 168	3a.C.	27 31 34	70 1800 AHORA	SIETE AÑOS DE LA IRA DE DIOS (2.520 DIAS)	1000 AÑOS	ETERNIDAD

ALA IZQUIERDA | ALA DERECHA

UNO — 1-20 / 21
DOS — 1-32 ... 33a ... 33b 34 ... 35
36-38 / 39a / 39b / 40 ... 41 42-44 ... 45
46-49
TRES — 1-30
CUATRO — 1-37 ... LIBRO COMPLETO DE APOCALIPSIS
CINCO — 1-31
SIES — 1-28 ... Los siete sellos del Apocalipsis, trompetas, ángeles, etc. → 1 2 3 4 5 6 7
SIETE — 1-3
4 5 6 7 ... 8 ... 9,10 11
12 ... 13 14
15,16 ... 17 ... 18
19,20a ... 20b 21 ... 22
23 ... 24 ... 25 ... 26 27
28
OCHO — 1-3 4 5-8 ... 9-12
13 ... 14
15-17a ... 17b
18 ... 19
20 21 22 ... 23-26
27

LÍNEA DE TIEMPO Y PROFECÍA BUCLES DE TIEMPO DE DANIEL Y APOCALIPSIS — TRONO BLANCO JUICIO

DANIEL Capítulos	Babilonia 605	Med/Pers 538	457	Grecia 330	Roma 168	3a.C.	27 31 34	70 1800 AHORA	SIETE AÑOS DE LA IRA DE DIOS (2.520 DIAS)	1000 AÑOS	ETERNIDAD

ALA IZQUIERDA | ALA DERECHA

✝

NUEVE — 1-23 24a ... 24b
25a ... 25b 26a 26b ... 26c
27a 27b ... 27c ... 27d 27e
(69 semanas) 1 sem | MÁS 24 26 27a 27b 27c 27d
(Profecía de las 70 semanas)
DIAZ — 1-21 ... Los siete sellos del Apocalipsis, trompetas, ángeles, etc. → 1 2 3 4 5 6 7
ONCE — 1 2 3-4 ... 5-20
21 31a ... 31b
32 35 ... 36-39
40 43 ... 44 45
DOCE — 1 ... 2 3
4-6 ... 7 ... 7b
8-9a ... 9b 11a ... 11b 12
13a ... 13b
LIBRO COMPLETO DE APOCALIPSIS

CAPÍTULO QUINCE

EL PODER DEL PEQUEÑO CUERNO

PREGUNTA: ¿Qué dice la Biblia sobre el PODER DEL PEQUEÑO CUERNO?

RESPUESTA: Las siguientes son las ubicaciones de todos los textos en el libro de Daniel que se refieren al Poder del Cuerno Pequeño.

1. Daniel dos: versículos 33-35, 41-45
2. Daniel siete: versículos 7, 8; 19-27
3. Daniel ocho: versículos 8-27
4. Daniel nueve: versículo 27
5. Daniel diez: versículo 14
6. Daniel once: versículos 20-45
7. Daniel doce: versículos 4-13

Daniel 2:33-35, 41-45

33 Sus piernas de hierro; sus pies, en parte de hierro, y en parte de barro cocido. 34 Estabas mirando, hasta que una piedra fué cortada, no con mano, la cual hirió á la imagen en sus pies de hierro y de barro cocido, y los desmenuzó. 35 Entonces fué también desmenuzado el hierro, el barro cocido, el metal, la plata y el oro, y se tornaron como tamo de las eras del verano: y levantólos el viento, y nunca más se les halló

lugar. Mas la piedra que hirió á la imagen, fué hecha un gran monte, que hinchió toda la tierra

41 Y lo que viste de los pies y los dedos, en parte de barro cocido de alfarero, y en parte de hierro, el reino será dividido; mas habrá en él algo de fortaleza de hierro, según que viste el hierro mezclado con el tiesto de barro. 42 Y por ser los dedos de los pies en parte de hierro, y en parte de barro cocido, en parte será el reino fuerte, y en parte será frágil. 43 Cuanto á aquello que viste, el hierro mezclado con tiesto de barro, mezcláranse con simiente humana, mas no se pegarán el uno con el otro, como el hierro no se mistura con el tiesto. 44 Y en los días de estos reyes, levantará el Dios del cielo un reino que nunca jamás se corromperá: y no será dejado á otro pueblo este reino; el cual desmenuzará y consumirá todos estos reinos, y él permanecerá para siempre. 45 De la manera que viste que del monte fué cortada una piedra, no con manos, la cual desmenuzó al hierro, al metal, al tiesto, á la plata, y al oro; el gran Dios ha mostrado al rey lo que ha de acontecer en lo por venir: y el sueño es verdadero, y fiel su declaración.

Daniel 7:7,8; 19-27

7 Después de esto miraba yo en las visiones de la noche, y he aquí la cuarta bestia, espantosa y terrible, y en grande manera fuerte; la cual tenía unos dientes grandes de hierro: devoraba y desmenuzaba, y las sobras hollaba con sus pies: y era muy diferente de todas las bestias que habían sido antes de ella, y tenía diez cuernos. 8 Estando yo contemplando los cuernos, he aquí que otro cuerno pequeño subía entre ellos, y delante de él fueron arrancados tres cuernos de los primeros; y he aquí, en este cuerno había ojos como ojos de hombre, y una boca que hablaba grandezas.

19 Entonces tuve deseo de saber la verdad acerca de la cuarta bestia, que tan diferente era de todas las otras, espantosa en gran manera, que tenía dientes de hierro, y sus uñas de metal, que devoraba y desmenuzaba, y las sobras hollaba con sus pies: 20 Asimismo acerca de los diez cuernos que tenía en su cabeza, y del otro que había subido, de delante del cual habían caído tres: y este mismo cuerno tenía ojos, y boca que hablaba grandezas, y su parecer mayor que el de sus compañeros. 21 Y veía yo que este cuerno hacía guerra contra los santos, y los vencía, 22 Hasta tanto que vino el Anciano de grande edad, y se dió el juicio á los santos del Altísimo; y vino el tiempo, y los santos poseyeron el reino. 23 Dijo así: La cuarta bestia será un cuarto reino en la tierra, el cual será más grande que todos los otros reinos, y á toda la tierra devorará, y la hollará, y la despedazará. 24 Y los diez cuernos significan que de aquel reino se levantarán diez reyes; y tras ellos se levantará otro, el cual será mayor que los primeros, y á tres reyes derribará. 25 Y hablará palabras contra el Altísimo, y á los santos del Altísimo quebrantará, y pensará en mudar los tiempos y la ley: y entregados serán en su mano hasta tiempo, y tiempos, y el medio de un tiempo. 26 Empero se sentará el juez, y quitaránle su señorío, para que sea destruído y arruinado hasta el extremo; 27 Y que el reino, y el señorío, y la majestad de los reinos debajo de todo el cielo, sea dado al pueblo de los santos del Altísimo; cuyo reino es reino eterno, y todos los señoríos le servirán y obedecerán.

Daniel 8:8-27:

8 Y engrandecióse en gran manera el macho de cabrío; y estando en su mayor fuerza, aquel gran cuerno fué quebrado, y en su lugar subieron otros cuatro maravillosos hacia los cuatro vientos del cielo. 9 Y del uno de ellos salió un cuerno pequeño, el cual creció mucho al mediodía, y al oriente, y

hacia la tierra deseable. 10 Y engrandecióse hasta el ejército del cielo; y parte del ejército y de las estrellas echó por tierra, y las holló. 11 Aun contra el príncipe de la fortaleza se engrandeció, y por él fué quitado el continuo sacrificio, y el lugar de su santuario fué echado por tierra. 12 Y el ejército fué le entregado á causa de la prevaricación sobre el continuo sacrificio: y echó por tierra la verdad, é hizo cuanto quiso, y sucedióle prósperamente. 13 Y oí un santo que hablaba; y otro de los santos dijo á aquél que hablaba: ¿Hasta cuándo durará la visión del continuo sacrificio, y la prevaricación asoladora que pone el santuario y el ejército para ser hollados? 14 Y él me dijo: Hasta dos mil y trescientos días de tarde y mañana; y el santuario será purificado. 15 Y acaeció que estando yo Daniel considerando la visión, y buscando su inteligencia, he aquí, como una semejanza de hombre se puso delante de mí. 16 Y oí una voz de hombre entre las riberas de Ulai, que gritó y dijo: Gabriel, enseña la visión á éste. 17 Vino luego cerca de donde yo estaba; y con su venida me asombré, y caí sobre mi rostro. Empero él me dijo: Entiende, hijo del hombre, porque al tiempo se cumplirá la visión. 18 Y estando él hablando conmigo, caí dormido en tierra sobre mi rostro: y él me tocó, é hízome estar en pie. 19 Y dijo: He aquí yo te enseñaré lo ha de venir en el fin de la ira: porque al tiempo se cumplirá: 20 Aquel carnero que viste, que tenía cuernos, son los reyes de Media y de Persia. 21 Y el macho cabrío es el rey de Javán: y el cuerno grande que tenía entre sus ojos es el rey primero. 22 Y que fué quebrado y sucedieron cuatro en su lugar, significa que cuatro reinos sucederán de la nación, mas no en la fortaleza de él. 23 Y al cabo del imperio de éstos, cuando se cumplirán los prevaricadores, levantaráse un rey altivo de rostro, y entendido en dudas. 24 Y su poder se fortalecerá, mas no con fuerza suya, y destruirá maravillosamente, y prosperará; y hará arbitrariamente, y destruirá fuertes y al pueblo de los santos. 25 Y con su sagacidad hará prosperar el engaño en su mano; y en su corazón se engrandecerá, y con paz destruirá á muchos: y contra el príncipe de los príncipes se levantará; mas sin mano será quebrantado. 26 Y la visión de la tarde y la mañana que está dicha, es verdadera: y tú guarda la visión, porque es para muchos días. 27 Y yo Daniel fuí quebrantado, y estuve enfermo algunos días: y cuando convalecí, hice el negocio del rey; mas estaba espantado acerca de la visión, y no había quien la entendiese.

Daniel 9:27:

27 Y en otra semana confirmará el pacto á muchos, y á la mitad de la semana hará cesar el sacrificio y la ofrenda: después con la muchedumbre de las abominaciones será el desolar, y esto hasta una entera consumación; y derramaráse la ya determinada sobre el pueblo asolado.

Daniel 10:14:

14 Soy pues venido para hacerte saber lo que ha de venir á tu pueblo en los postreros días; porque la visión es aún para días;

Daniel 11:14-19

(La actividad anterior al cuerno pequeño se encuentra en los versículos 14-19, como se muestra a continuación).

14 Y en aquellos tiempos se levantarán muchos contra el rey del mediodía; é hijos de disipadores de tu pueblo se levantarán para confirmar la profecía, y caerán. 15 Vendrá pues el rey del norte, y fundará baluartes, y tomará la ciudad fuerte; y los brazos del mediodía no podrán permanecer, ni su pueblo escogido, ni habrá fortaleza que pueda resistir. 16 Y el que vendrá contra él, hará á su voluntad, ni habrá quien se le pueda parar delante; y estará en la tierra deseable, la cual será

consumida en su poder. 17 Pondrá luego su rostro para venir con el poder de todo su reino; y hará con aquél cosas rectas, y daréle una hija de mujeres para trastornarla: mas no estará ni será por él. 18 Volverá después su rostro á las islas, y tomará muchas; mas un príncipe le hará parar su afrenta, y aun tornará sobre él su oprobio. 19 Luego volverá su rostro á las fortalezas de su tierra: mas tropezará y caerá, y no parecerá más.

Daniel 11:20-45:

20 Entonces sucederá en su silla uno que hará pasar exactor por la gloria del reino; mas en pocos días será quebrantado, no en enojo, ni en batalla. 21 Y sucederá en su lugar un vil, al cual no darán la honra del reino: vendrá empero con paz, y tomará el reino con halagos. 22 Y con los brazos de inundación serán inundados delante de él, y serán quebrantados; y aun también el príncipe del pacto. 23 Y después de los conciertos con él, él hará engaño, y subirá, y saldrá vencedor con poca gente. 24 Estando la provincia en paz y en abundancia, entrará y hará lo que no hicieron sus padres, ni los padres de sus padres; presa, y despojos, y riquezas repartirá á sus soldados; y contra las fortalezas formará sus designios: y esto por tiempo. 25 Y despertará sus fuerzas y su corazón contra el rey del mediodía con grande ejército: y el rey del mediodía se moverá á la guerra con grande y muy fuerte ejército; mas no prevalecerá, porque le harán traición. 26 Aun los que comerán su pan, le quebrantarán; y su ejército será destruído, y caerán muchos muertos. 27 Y el corazón de estos dos reyes será para hacer mal, y en una misma mesa tratarán mentira: mas no servirá de nada, porque el plazo aun no es llegado. 28 Y volveráse á su tierra con grande riqueza, y su corazón será contra el pacto santo: hará pues, y volveráse á su tierra. 29 Al tiempo señalado tornará al mediodía; mas no será la postrera venida como la primera. 30 Porque vendrán contra él naves de Chîttim,

y él se contristará, y se volverá, y enojaráse contra el pacto santo, y hará: volveráse pues, y pensará en los que habrán desamparado el santo pacto. 31 Y serán puestos brazos de su parte; y contaminarán el santuario de fortaleza, y quitarán el continuo sacrificio, y pondrán la abominación espantosa. 32 Y con lisonjas hará pecar á los violadores del pacto: mas el pueblo que conoce á su Dios, se esforzará, y hará. 33 Y los sabios del pueblo darán sabiduría á muchos: y caerán á cuchillo y á fuego, en cautividad y despojo, por días. 34 Y en su caer serán ayudados de pequeño socorro: y muchos se juntarán á ellos con lisonjas. 35 Y algunos de los sabios caerán para ser purgados, y limpiados, y emblanquecidos, hasta el tiempo determinado: porque aun para esto hay plazo. 36 Y el rey hará á su voluntad; y se ensoberbecerá, y se engrandecerá sobre todo dios: y contra el Dios de los dioses hablará maravillas, y será prosperado, hasta que sea consumada la ira: porque hecha está determinación. 37 Y del Dios de sus padres no se cuidará, ni del amor de las mujeres: ni se cuidará de dios alguno, porque sobre todo se engrandecerá. 38 Mas honrará en su lugar al dios Mauzim, dios que sus padres no conocieron: honrarálo con oro, y plata, y piedras preciosas, y con cosas de gran precio. 39 Y con el dios ajeno que conocerá, hará á los baluartes de Mauzim crecer en gloria: y harálos enseñorear sobre muchos, y por interés repartirá la tierra. 40 Empero al cabo del tiempo el rey del mediodía se acorneará con él; y el rey del norte levantará contra él como tempestad, con carros y gente de á caballo, y muchos navíos; y entrará por las tierras, é inundará, y pasará. 41 Y vendrá á la tierra deseable, y muchas provincias caerán; mas éstas escaparán de su mano: Edom, y Moab, y lo primero de los hijos de Ammón. 42 Asimismo extenderá su mano á las otras tierras, y no escapará el país de Egipto. 43 Y se apoderará de los tesoros de oro y plata, y de todas las cosas preciosas de Egipto, de Libia, y Etiopía por donde pasará. 44 Mas nuevas de oriente y del norte lo espantarán; y saldrá con grande ira para destruir y matar muchos. 45 Y plantará la tiendas de su palacio entre los mares, en el monte deseable del santuario; y vendrá hasta su fin, y no tendrá quien le ayude.

Daniel 12:4-13:

4 Tú empero Daniel, cierra las palabras y sella el libro hasta el tiempo del fin: pasarán muchos, y multiplicaráse la ciencia. 5 Y yo, Daniel, miré, y he aquí otros dos que estaban, el uno de esta parte á la orilla del río, y el otro de la otra parte á la orilla del río. 6 Y dijo uno al varón vestido de lienzos, que estaba sobre las aguas del río: ¿Cuándo será el fin de estas maravillas? 7 Y oía al varón vestido de lienzos, que estaba sobre las aguas del río, el cual alzó su diestra y su siniestra al cielo, y juró por el Viviente en los siglos, que será por tiempo, tiempos, y la mitad. Y cuando se acabare el esparcimiento del escuadrón del pueblo santo, todas estas cosas serán cumplidas. 8 Y yo oí, mas no entendí. Y dije: Señor mío, ¿qué será el cumplimiento de estas cosas? 9 Y dijo: Anda, Daniel, que estas palabras están cerradas y selladas hasta el tiempo del cumplimiento. 10 Muchos serán limpios, y emblanquecidos, y purificados; mas los impíos obrarán impíamente, y ninguno de los impíos entenderá, pero entenderán los entendidos. 11 Y desde el tiempo que fuere quitado el continuo sacrificio hasta la abominación espantosa, habrá mil doscientos y noventa días. 12 Bienaventurado el que esperare, y llegare hasta mil trescientos treinta y cinco días. 13 Y tú irás al fin, y reposarás, y te levantarás en tu suerte al fin de los días.

TEXTOS DE APOCALIPSIS SOBRE EL PEQUEÑO PODER DEL CUERNO

Apocalipsis 12:3,4:

3 Y fué vista otra señal en el cielo: y he aquí un grande dragón bermejo, que tenía siete cabezas y diez cuernos, y en sus cabezas siete diademas. 4 Y su cola arrastraba la tercera parte de las estrellas del cielo, y las echó en tierra. Y el dragón se paró delante de la mujer que estaba para parir, á fin de devorar á su hijo cuando hubiese parido.

Apocalipsis 13:

1 Y YO me paré sobre la arena del mar, y vi una bestia subir del mar, que tenía siete cabezas y diez cuernos; y sobre sus cuernos diez diademas; y sobre las cabezas de ella nombre de blasfemia. 2 Y la bestia que vi, era semejante á un leopardo, y sus pies como de oso, y su boca como boca de león. Y el dragón le dió su poder, y su trono, y grande potestad. 3 Y vi una de sus cabezas como herida de muerte, y la llaga de su muerte fué curada: y se maravilló toda la tierra en pos de la bestia. 4 Y adoraron al dragón que había dado la potestad á la bestia, y adoraron á la bestia, diciendo: ¿Quién es semejante á la bestia, y quién podrá lidiar con ella? 5 Y le fué dada boca que hablaba grandes cosas y blasfemias: y le fué dada potencia de obrar cuarenta y dos meses. 6 Y abrió su boca en blasfemias contra Dios, para blasfemar su nombre, y su tabernáculo, y á los que moran en el cielo. 7 Y le fué dado hacer guerra contra los santos, y vencerlos. También le fué dada potencia sobre toda tribu y pueblo y lengua y gente. 8 Y todos los que moran en la tierra le adoraron, cuyos nombres no están escritos en el libro de la vida del Cordero, el cual fué muerto desde el principio del mundo. 9 Si alguno tiene oído, oiga. 10 El que lleva en cautividad, va en cautividad: el que á cuchillo matare, es necesario que á cuchillo sea muerto. Aquí está la paciencia y la fe de los santos. 11 Después vi otra bestia que subía de

la tierra; y tenía dos cuernos semejantes á los de un cordero, mas hablaba como un dragón. 12 Y ejerce todo el poder de la primera bestia en presencia de ella; y hace á la tierra y á los moradores de ella adorar la primera bestia, cuya llaga de muerte fué curada. 13 Y hace grandes señales, de tal manera que aun hace descender fuego del cielo á la tierra delante de los hombres. 14 Y engaña á los moradores de la tierra por las señales que le ha sido dado hacer en presencia de la bestia, mandando á los moradores de la tierra que hagan la imagen de la bestia que tiene la herida de cuchillo, y vivió. 15 Y le fué dado que diese espíritu á la imagen de la bestia, para que la imagen de la bestia hable; y hará que cualesquiera que no adoraren la imagen de la bestia sean muertos. 16 Y hacía que á todos, á los pequeños y grandes, ricos y pobres, libres y siervos, se pusiese una marca en su mano derecha, ó en sus frentes: 17 Y que ninguno pudiese comprar ó vender, sino el que tuviera la señal, ó el nombre de la bestia, ó el número de su nombre. 18 Aquí hay sabiduría. El que tiene entendimiento, cuente el número de la bestia; porque es el número de hombre: y el número de ella, seiscientos sesenta y seis.

Apocalipsis 17:

1 Y VINO uno de los siete ángeles que tenían las siete copas, y habló conmigo, diciéndome: Ven acá, y te mostraré la condenación de la grande ramera, la cual está sentada sobre muchas aguas: 2 Con la cual han fornicado los reyes de la tierra, y los que moran en la tierra se han embriagado con el vino de su fornicación. 3 Y me llevó en Espíritu al desierto; y vi una mujer sentada sobre una bestia bermeja llena de nombres de blasfemia y que tenía siete cabezas y diez cuernos. 4 Y la mujer estaba vestida de púrpura y de escarlata, y dorada con oro, y adornada de piedras preciosas y de perlas, teniendo un cáliz de oro en su mano lleno de abominaciones y de

la suciedad de su fornicación; 5 Y en su frente un nombre escrito: MISTERIO, BABILONIA LA GRANDE, LA MADRE DE LAS FORNICACIONES Y DE LAS ABOMINACIONES DE LA TIERRA. 6 Y vi la mujer embriagada de la sangre de los santos, y de la sangre de los mártires de Jesús: y cuando la vi, quedé maravillado de grande admiración. 7 Y el ángel me dijo: ¿Por qué te maravillas? Yo te diré el misterio de la mujer, y de la bestia que la trae, la cual tiene siete cabezas y diez cuernos. 8 La bestia que has visto, fué, y no es; y ha de subir del abismo, y ha de ir á perdición: y los moradores de la tierra, cuyos nombres no están escritos en el libro de la vida desde la fundación del mundo, se maravillarán viendo la bestia que era y no es, aunque es. 9 Y aquí hay mente que tiene sabiduría. Las siete cabezas son siete montes, sobre los cuales se asienta la mujer. 10 Y son siete reyes. Los cinco son caídos; el uno es, el otro aun no es venido; y cuando viniere, es necesario que dure breve tiempo. 11 Y la bestia que era, y no es, es también el octavo, y es de los siete, y va á perdición. 12 Y los diez cuernos que has visto, son diez reyes, que aun no han recibido reino; mas tomarán potencia por una hora como reyes con la bestia. 13 Estos tienen un consejo, y darán su potencia y autoridad á la bestia. 14 Ellos pelearán contra el Cordero, y el Cordero los vencerá, porque es el Señor de los señores, y el Rey de los reyes: y los que están con él son llamados, y elegidos, y fieles. 15 Y él me dice: Las aguas que has visto donde la ramera se sienta, son pueblos y muchedumbres y naciones y lenguas. 16 Y los diez cuernos que viste en la bestia, éstos aborrecerán á la ramera, y la harán desolada y desnuda: y comerán sus carnes, y la quemarán con fuego: 17 Porque Dios ha puesto en sus corazones ejecutar lo que le plugo, y el ponerse de acuerdo, y dar su reino á la bestia, hasta que sean cumplidas las palabras de Dios. 18 Y la mujer que has visto, es la grande ciudad que tiene reino sobre los reyes de la tierra.

PREGUNTA: ¿QUIÉN O QUÉ ES "EL PEQUEÑO PODER DEL CUERNO"?

RESPUESTA: EN ESTE MOMENTO, NO LO SÉ CON SEGURIDAD.

Hay mucha especulación sobre la identidad del futuro Little Horn Power. Pero eso es especulación, ya que hay mucha información para continuar, como se reveló anteriormente, pero muy poca información que se congele para armar el rompecabezas de manera adecuada para identificar realmente el Little Horn Power del tiempo final. Dado que Little Horn Power es un evento futuro, es posible que no sepamos todas las respuestas a la identidad de este poder hasta que llegue. Pero aquellos que estén familiarizados con los libros proféticos de Daniel y Apocalipsis podrán identificarlo correctamente en el momento adecuado, cuando aparezca.

CAPITULO DIEZISEIS

¿Cuáles son algunas de las lecciones de profecía más importantes que se pueden aprender de cada uno de los doce capítulos de Daniel?

CAPÍTULO UNO: El libro de Daniel expone la dilución y contaminación de la adoración verdadera al mezclar lo sagrado con lo profano, como se revela en Daniel 1: 2. Nabucodonosor comenzó la dilución de la adoración verdadera cuando mezcló los elementos de adoración del templo de Dios en Jerusalén con los elementos de adoración de ídolos en su propio templo. También cambió los nombres hebreos por nombres paganos, promovió una dieta pagana y ofreció una educación pagana. Nuestro trabajo hoy es mantener la adoración de Dios tan pura como el oro como se revela en las Escrituras, evitando la fusión de las tradiciones, la cultura y las ideas del hombre. Debemos entender la adoración que Dios demanda, como se revela en la Santa Biblia, y adorarlo lo mejor que podamos, en todo lo que hacemos, a medida que somos guiados y guiados por el Espíritu Santo que mora en nosotros.

CAPÍTULO DOS: El sueño del rey Nabucodonosor no solo revela la evolución de la historia sobre el pueblo de Dios desde los días de Daniel hasta el fin del mundo, sino que también revela la fuente de la adoración pagana que se infiltró en la verdadera adoración de Dios provocando la confusión y la variedad de características de adoración en todo el mundo.

el mundo de hoy, especialmente en la cristiandad. Su sueño también revela que la piedra que golpea la imagen es el Reino de Dios, iluminándonos dónde se originó y su historia. Este capítulo también nos ayuda a comprender que el término "tierra", en la profecía bíblica, no se aplica a todo este globo o planeta. En la profecía bíblica, el término "tierra" se aplica al pueblo de Dios. Esa es la "tierra" que gobernaron los cuatro imperios de Babilonia, Medo-Persia, Grecia y Roma. Ninguno de ellos gobernó jamás el planeta entero. Las tres divisiones en la profecía bíblica que se refieren al pueblo de Dios son: cielo, tierra y mar. La "gente del cielo" sirve a Dios al 100%. La "gente de la tierra" le sirve parcialmente y la "gente del mar" se niega a servirle (Ver Apocalipsis 5: 3; 7: 3; 12:12; Éxodo 20: 4, etc.). El sueño del rey Nabucodonosor nos lleva desde los días de Daniel hasta el final de la tribulación de siete años.

La piedra que golpea la estatua es cortada de una montaña sin manos (versículo 34) y luego crece hasta convertirse en una gran montaña y llena toda la "tierra" (versículo 35). PREGUNTA: ¿Cuál es la montaña de la que se cortó la piedra? RESPUESTA: La piedra está tallada en la montaña que es el monte Sion (Daniel 9: 16,20), el pueblo santo de Dios, los israelitas. Jesús es la "principal piedra del ángulo". La piedra de Daniel dos representa el Reino de Dios que Jesús estableció con su muerte en la cruz, después de beber el vinagre. (Lea el capítulo "El vinagre en la cruz del Calvario" en la página 450). El Mesías solo podía salir de una tribu de Israel (Juan 4:22), como Dios le prometió a Abraham en Génesis 22:18 y fue cortado un pedazo de esa montaña para comenzar el Reino de Dios. Desde la cruz del Calvario, el mensaje de un Salvador misericordioso ha crecido desde un pequeño grupo de personas hasta ahora, que incluye a todo el planeta. Todos los que han aceptado a Jesús como su Salvador desde la cruz han heredado (Gálatas 3:29) y morado en el reino de Dios (Colosenses 1: 9-14).

CAPÍTULO TRES: Este capítulo es importante porque prepara a los que viven en los últimos días para ser fieles a Dios, incluso frente a la muerte, cuando llega el momento de la persecución. Dios dijo: "Nunca te dejaré ni te desampararé" en Hebreos 13: 5. Este capítulo también responde a la pregunta que surgió en las mentes de los estudiantes de la Biblia con respecto a Apocalipsis 13:18 acerca de la identidad de un hombre, en la Biblia, cuyo "número es 666". El "número de un hombre" apunta al rey Nabucodonosor que representa la ADORACIÓN FORZADA de la que nos advierte Apocalipsis. Puso una estatua, en el llano de Dura en el año 600 AC, que tenía 60 codos de alto y 6 codos de ancho (Versículo uno). También vea Esdras 2:13. De los cautivos del rey Nabucodonosor, uno se llama Adonikam y tuvo 666 antepasados que regresaron a Jerusalén. En el futuro se "establecerá" una "abominación desoladora" y el pueblo de Dios se verá obligado a adorarla frente a la muerte, tal como lo experimentaron los 3 hebreos.

CAPÍTULO CUATRO: Este sueño nuevamente confirma que en la profecía bíblica la "tierra" es el pueblo de Dios o el área de tierra que ocupan, que era Mesopotamia y las naciones circundantes (Salmo 80: 8-11) en la era de Daniel. Pero no solo eso. De este sueño llegamos a una comprensión de lo que es un "tiempo" en la profecía bíblica. El rey debía ser sacado al campo "siete veces". Una vez en la profecía bíblica es un año, el tiempo que le toma a la tierra dar la vuelta al sol en una revolución. Más adelante en Daniel y en Apocalipsis se menciona "un tiempo, tiempos y medio tiempo". Eso se calcula en tres años y medio o 1.260 días, dándose cuenta de que un año profético es de 360 días como lo determinaron originalmente los babilonios con el número 6 como denominador común. De ellos tenemos 60 segundos en un minuto, 60 minutos en una hora, 24 horas en un día, 12 meses en un año con 30 días por mes y 360 días en un año. También tenemos 360 grados en círculo, gracias a los babilonios.

CAPÍTULO CINCO: Este capítulo nos presenta a Belsasar, el beligerante rey de Babilonia, sirviendo como rey junto con su padre. El suyo es otro ejemplo de la insensibilidad babilónica al mezclar los elementos de adoración pura del Dios verdadero con la adoración falsa de ídolos de madera, hierro, bronce, plata y oro. También revela que beber hasta el exceso de emborracharse puede hacer que una persona haga y diga cosas de las que pronto se arrepentirá.

CAPÍTULO SEIS: El capítulo seis de Daniel es una historia bíblica bien conocida por personas de todas las edades acerca de Daniel y el foso del León. La integridad de Daniel lo precedió y su reputación de honestidad fue muy respetada por quienes lo dominaban y odiada por los deshonestos que servían a sus órdenes. En esta historia se nos recuerda que debemos ser honestos en todas las cosas y ser fieles a Dios en nuestra adoración y confiar en Él en todas las condiciones y amenazas, incluso ante la amenaza de nuestras vidas.

CAPÍTULO SIETE: Las cuatro bestias que Daniel atestigua que suben del mar representan a Babilonia, Medo-Persia, Grecia y Roma. Es muy importante que entendamos esta profecía con respecto al simbolismo de la bestia combinada de Apocalipsis 13, así como otras interpretaciones importantes de la profecía en el libro de Apocalipsis. En este capítulo, el "mar" representa al pueblo hebreo rebelde que le había dado la espalda a Dios. Los cuatro vientos representan contienda, agitación y conflicto. Este sueño nos lleva desde el día de Daniel hasta el final de los 1000 años de Apocalipsis 20, que incluye el juicio celestial mencionado en los versículos 13,14,26,27 que tiene lugar durante esos 1000 años. También se nos presenta el Poder del Cuerno Pequeño, en el versículo 8, que jugará un papel importante en "el tiempo señalado del fin". En este capítulo tenemos la primera mención de "el tiempo, tiempos y medio tiempo" en el versículo 25 que resulta ser tres años y medio o 1.260 días literales.

CAPÍTULO OCHO: Este capítulo es importante porque confirma que los dos imperios que seguirán después del Imperio babilónico es el de los medopersas y el de los griegos. Al final del imperio griego, las ideas de adoración pagana de las tres naciones gobernantes se esparcirán por todo el mundo entonces conocido en todas las direcciones de la brújula a medida que se difunda el pueblo de Dios. También se proporciona mucha más información sobre el Poder del Cuerno Pequeño y su catastrófica influencia sobre el pueblo de Dios de los últimos días. En el versículo 13 se introduce el término CONTINUO o PERPETUO junto con la fase "la abominación o la transgresión desoladora". Este versículo en particular habla de que el "santo" y el "ejército" son derrotados o pisoteados. Daniel 8: 9-26 trata principalmente con el tiempo señalado del fin, que aún es futuro (versículos 16,19,23,26). El versículo 14 es importante porque proporciona la cantidad de tiempo en el que se abusará del "santo" y del "anfitrión". Afirma que se abusará de lo santo durante un poco más de 6 años, pero que se reconciliará o reivindicará al final de "las 2.300 tardes y mañanas", que son 2.300 días literales de 24 horas. En este capítulo nos damos cuenta de que un cuerno puede representar un reino pero también representa poder. Un solo cuerno enorme es más poderoso que dos cuernos separados. En el "tiempo señalado del fin", Little Horn Power se aliará con tres de los 10 cuernos y la combinación de cuatro cuernos unidos frente a 7 cuernos independientes lo convertirá en el matón más fuerte del bloque.

CAPÍTULO NUEVE: En este capítulo Daniel está recordando las profecías que tenía en Daniel 7 y 8, buscando comprenderlas. Los había escrito, pero no los entendía, sobre todo teniendo en cuenta que los setenta años de cautiverio estaban casi cumplidos. De Daniel 9: 3-23 Daniel está en oración con un ejemplo de una de las mejores oraciones de la Biblia. Cuando se acerca al final de su petición, el ángel Gabriel lo visita para responder a sus preguntas. En Daniel 9: 24-27 el ángel le da a Daniel más información para agregar a la que tenía anteriormente. La Biblia no dice si Daniel entendió esta información adicional o no y es muy poco probable que alguien más lo hiciera hasta esta generación actual. Esta profecía de 70 semanas tiene 490 años y comenzó en el 457 a. C., casi 80 años después de que Daniel tuvo la visión. Aquellos que estaban familiarizados con Daniel probablemente estaban muertos cuando llegó el año 457 a. C. y los únicos que lo encontraron fueron los que realmente leyeron sus cartas. El libro de Daniel no estuvo disponible en inglés hasta 1535 y para el público en general hasta 1816 cuando se formó la American Bible Society con el objetivo de poner la Biblia en todos los hogares del mundo entero. La primera persona en promover un entendimiento entre el público sobre la profecía de Daniel 9: 24-27 fue un predicador bautista llamado William Miller (1782-1849) en 1823. La profecía de las setenta semanas señala el año en que Jesús fue bautizado y crucificado también. como el año en que moriría Esteban, el primer mártir cristiano. La profecía de las setenta semanas va del 457 a. C. al 34 d. C. La profecía es en realidad más ventajosa para esta generación que cualquier otra porque el mensaje nos suena alto y claro, tenemos acceso a él y lo entendemos, y se aplica directamente a nosotros. La profecía de las 70 semanas no solo estaba dirigida a los hijos de Israel, sino que también nos corresponde a nosotros preparar nuestras vidas de acuerdo con la voluntad de Dios, antes de la segunda venida de Jesús. Nos dice, en dos ocasiones distintas, que una tribulación de siete años del pueblo de Dios es real y que vendrá en un futuro cercano. Esa tribulación de siete años tiene una duración de 2.520 días. 70 X 7 = 490. 490 X 360 = 176,400. 176,400 dividido por 70 = 2,520. 2,520 dividido por 360 = 7 años.

CAPÍTULO DIEZ: El capítulo diez de Daniel es la introducción a las visiones de Daniel 11 y 12. El mensajero en la conversación le recuerda a Daniel en el versículo 14 que la información que está a punto de recibir se refiere a los "últimos días", que es un camino en el futuro para Daniel., pero no muy lejos en el futuro para nosotros. En el versículo 20, el mensajero le dice a Daniel que en su futuro los persas derrotarán a los babilonios y gobernarán al pueblo de Dios. También refuerza el punto de que la nación de Grecia superará a los persas en una fecha posterior, lo que concuerda con el sueño del rey Nabucodonosor en el capítulo dos.

CAPÍTULO ONCE: Los versículos 1-4 no son difíciles de entender. El mensajero le recuerda a Daniel que los persas reinarán sobre los cautivos hebreos y que los griegos derrotarán a los persas en el futuro. Como se mencionó en el capítulo 7 de Daniel, el imperio griego, junto con sus enseñanzas paganas, circulará en las cuatro direcciones de la brújula. En los versículos 5-42 la información está fragmentada, dispersa y es difícil de entender o interpretar, sin entender el capítulo doce de Daniel.

CAPÍTULO DOCE: Al final de Daniel 11:42, las condiciones en todo el mundo son drásticas y la gente del tiempo del fin de Dios está a punto de ser completamente probada. En ese momento, los siervos de Dios de los últimos días estarán en confusión y, como dice Daniel 12:1, "habrá un tiempo de angustia como nunca lo fue". Miguel, el nombre de Jesús en el cielo, defenderá a sus elegidos y librará a su pueblo proveyendo para sus necesidades y defensa. Los versículos dos y tres nos llevan más lejos en el futuro hasta el final de los 1000 años de Apocalipsis 20 en el momento llamado "el último día" o "fin de los días" como se indica en el versículo 13. El versículo 7 nos permite saber que durante los 1260 días de los próximos 2520 días, "el pueblo santo" será "completamente destrozado". En el versículo 9 se le recuerda a Daniel que esta visión no es para su día sino para "el tiempo del fin" cuando la visión será entendida. El versículo 10 revela los resultados del tiempo de angustia y los siguientes siete años de tribulación, en el que los siervos obedientes de Dios y los seguidores rebeldes de Dios serán claramente separados y definidos.

El capítulo doce versículo once (12:11) es probablemente el versículo más importante de la Biblia cuando se trata de colocar los períodos de tiempo, mencionados en los libros de Daniel y Apocalipsis, en una línea de tiempo. El profético "tiempo, tiempos y medio tiempo", los 1260, 1290, 1335, 2300, 3 1/2 días y los 42 meses del tiempo del fin serán establecidos cuando "el continuo sea quitado".

Los 4 eventos íntimamente ligados a todos estos períodos de tiempo proféticos anteriores son:

1. El pacto o pacto santo: que son los Diez Mandamientos de Éxodo 20: 1-17, que el Poder del Cuerno Pequeño desprecia.
2. El continuo: que es el séptimo día Sábado del cuarto mandamiento (Éxodo 20: 8-11) que el Poder del Cuerno

Pequeño eliminará y reemplazará con otro falso día de adoración.

3. **La abominación desoladora.** El falso día de adoración que el Poder del Cuerno Pequeño establecerá en lugar del sábado del séptimo día y obligará a la gente a inclinarse ante él.

4. El Poder del Cuerno Pequeño está conectado a todos estos períodos de tiempo porque todos se cumplen durante la próxima tribulación de siete años.

Ningún versículo individual de la Biblia es independiente del capítulo en el que se encuentra. Se debe realizar todo el capítulo para comprender y ubicar correctamente los períodos de tiempo.

El cuadro a continuación demuestra todos los períodos de tiempo bíblicos proféticos asociados con la próxima tribulación de siete años junto con la posición única de los siete sellos, trompetas, ángeles, truenos, ayes y lamentos que tienen lugar simultáneamente.

TODOS LOS PERÍODOS DE TIEMPO PROFÉTICO BÍBLICO DEL TIEMPO FINAL

TIEMPO	DANIEL	REVELACIÓN
Tiempo, tiempos, medio tiempo 7:25 & 12:7 (1.260 dias)		12:14
2.300 dias	8:14	
1.290 dias	12:11	
1,335 dias	12:12	
1,260 dias		11:3 & 12:6
42 meses (1.260 dias)		11:2 & 13:5
5 meses (150 dias)		9:5,10
3 ½ dias (1.260 dias)		11:9,11

DANIEL Y REVELACIÓN CRONOGRAMA DE TRIBULACIÓN DE SIETE AÑOS

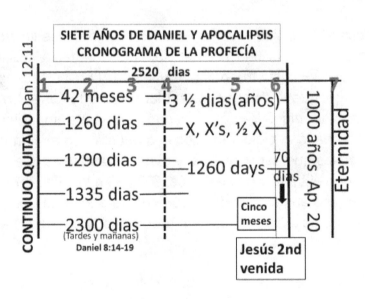

APOCALIPSIS 10 (RVR)

1 Y VI otro ángel fuerte descender del cielo, cercado de una nube, y el arco celeste sobre su cabeza; y su rostro era como el sol, y sus pies como columnas de fuego. 2 Y tenía en su mano un librito abierto: y puso su pie derecho sobre el mar, y el izquierdo sobre la tierra; 3 Y clamó con grande voz, como cuando un león ruge: y cuando hubo clamado, siete truenos hablaron sus voces.

4 Y cuando los siete truenos hubieron hablado sus voces, yo iba á escribir, y oí una voz del cielo que me decía: Sella las cosas que los siete truenos han hablado, y no las escribas. 5 Y el ángel que vi estar sobre el mar y sobre la tierra, levantó su mano al cielo, 6 Y juró por el que vive para siempre jamás, que ha criado el cielo y las cosas que están en él, y la tierra y las cosas que están en ella, y el mar y las cosas que están en él, que el tiempo no será más. 7 Pero en los días de la voz del séptimo ángel, cuando él comenzare á tocar la trompeta, el misterio de Dios será consumado, como él lo anunció á sus siervos los profetas.

8 Y la voz que oí del cielo hablaba otra vez conmigo, y decía: Ve, y toma el librito abierto de la mano del ángel que está sobre el mar y sobre la tierra. 9 Y fuí al ángel, diciéndole que me diese el librito, y él me dijo: Toma, y trágalo; y él te hará amargar tu vientre, pero en tu boca será dulce como la miel. 10 Y tomé el librito de la mano del ángel, y lo devoré; y era

dulce en mi boca como la miel; y cuando lo hube devorado, fué amargo mi vientre. 11 Y él me dice: Necesario es que otra vez profetices á muchos pueblos y gentes y lenguas y reyes.

(QUE LOS ÚLTIMOS ELIGEN SIERVOS DE DIOS ENTIENDE EL MENSAJE ANTERIOR)

CPSIA information can be obtained
at www.ICGtesting.com
Printed in the USA
JSHW050840221221
21452JS00001B/2